Global Development Finance

1997

Global Development Finance

1997

VOLUME 1

ANALYSIS
AND SUMMARY
TABLES

The World Bank
Washington, D.C.

ISBN 0-8213-3788-2 (vol. 1)
ISBN 0-8213-3789-0 (two-volume set)

ISSN 1020-5454

Contents

Tables

Figures

Boxes

Preface

Global Development Finance was formerly published as *World Debt Tables*. The new name reflects the report's expanded scope and greater coverage of private financial flows.

Global Development Finance consists of two volumes. Volume 1 contains analysis and commentary on recent developments in international finance for developing countries, together with summary statistical tables for selected regional and analytical groups comprising 150 developing countries.

Volume 2 contains statistical tables on the external debt of the 136 countries that report public and publicly guaranteed debt under the Debtor Reporting System (DRS). New to Volume 2 are summary debt statistics and resource flow tables for selected variables. The Republic of Korea is now classified as a high-income country. Reported for the first time are the IBRD and IMF obligations and short-term debt of Bosnia and Herzegovina.

For the convenience of readers, charts on pages xi to xiii summarize graphically the relation between the debt stock and its components; the computation of net flows, aggregate net resource flows, and aggregate net transfers; and the relation between net resource flows and the balance of payments. Exact definitions of these and other terms used in *Global Development Finance* are found in the Sources and Definitions section.

The economic aggregates presented in the tables are prepared for the convenience of users; their inclusion is not an endorsement of their value for economic analysis. Although debt indicators can give useful information about developments in debt-servicing capacity, conclusions drawn from them will not be valid unless accompanied by careful economic evaluation. The macroeconomic information provided is from standard sources, but many series, especially for African countries, are incomplete; thus it may be convenient or necessary to substitute other data series for those used here.

This report was prepared by a team led by Ronald Johannes and comprising Andrea Anayiotos, Gholam Azarbayejani, Aysel Basci, Swati Ghosh, Leonardo Hernandez, Kwang Jun, Himmat Kalsi, Carmini Michelitsch, Antonio Parra, Malvina Pollock, Robert Powell, Geeta Sethi, Sergei Shatalov, William Shaw, Margrete Stevens, Manuel Trucco, and Juan Carlos Villanova. The team was assisted by Sheilah King-Watson, Elena Mekhova, Margarita Ortiz, and Rose Vo. Meta de Coquereaumont and Paul Holtz were the principal editors. The volume was laid out by Mark Bock and Glenn McGrath. The work was carried out under the general direction of Masood Ahmed, Amar Bhattacharya, Frederick Kilby, and Sarwar Lateef. This report was initiated under the guidance of Michael Bruno, Senior Vice President, Development Economics and Chief Economist of the World Bank, 1993–96, and is dedicated to his memory.

Acronyms and abbreviations

BIS	Bank for International Settlements
CFA	Communauté financière africaine (franc zone)
CRS	Creditor Reporting System (of the OECD)
DAC	Development Assistance Committee (of the OECD)
DDSR	Debt and debt service reduction
DRE	Debt reduction equivalent
DRS	Debtor Reporting System (of the World Bank)
EDT	Total external debt, including short-term and use of IMF credit
FDI	Foreign direct investment
GATS	General Agreement on Trade in Services
GDP	Gross domestic product
GNP	Gross national product
IBRD	International Bank for Reconstruction and Development/World Bank
IDA	International Development Association (of the World Bank)
IFC	International Finance Corporation (of the World Bank)
IMF	International Monetary Fund
INT	Total interest payments on long-term and short-term debt, including IMF charges
HIPC	Heavily indebted poor countries
LDOD	Total long-term debt outstanding and disbursed
LIBOR	London interbank offered rate
LILIC	Less indebted low-income country
LIMIC	Less indebted middle-income country
Mercosur	Southern Cone Common Market (Argentina, Brazil, Paraguay, Uruguay)
MGS	Imports of goods and services
MILIC	Moderately indebted low-income country
MIMIC	Moderately indebted middle-income country
MYRA	Multiyear rescheduling agreement
NGO	Nongovernmental organization
ODA	Official development assistance
OECD	Organization for Economic Cooperation and Development
PV	Present value
RES	International reserves
RXD	Revised External Debt (Reporting System of the World Bank)
SDR	Special drawing right (of the IMF)
SILIC	Severely indebted low-income country
SILMIC	Severely indebted lower-middle-income country
SIMIC	Severely indebted middle-income country
TDS	Total debt service on long-term debt and short-term (interest only), including IMF credits
TRIMs	Trade-Related Investment Measures
TRIPs	Trade-Related Aspects of Intellectual Property Rights
XGS	Exports of goods and services

Dollars are current U.S. dollars unless otherwise specified.

Debt stock and its components

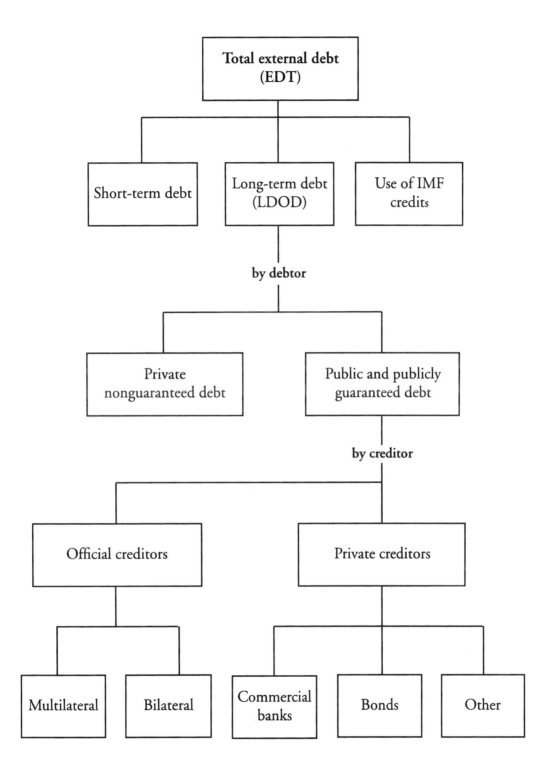

xii

Aggregate net resource flows and net transfers (long-term) to developing countries

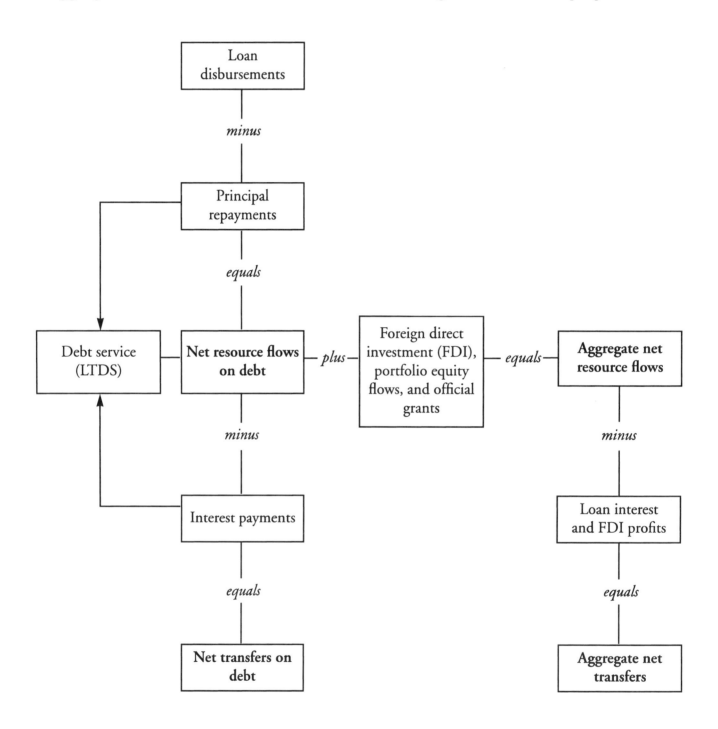

Note: Includes only loans with an original maturity of more than one year (long-term loans). Excludes IMF transactions.

Aggregate net resource flows (long-term) and the balance of payments

	Credits	*Debits*
Current account	• Exports of goods and services • Income received • Current transfers Including workers' remittances and private grants	• Imports of goods and services • Income paid • Current transfers
	• Official unrequited transfers (by foreign governments)	• Official unrequited transfers (by national government)
Capital and financial account	• Official unrequited transfers (by foreign governments) • Foreign direct investment (by nonresidents) (disinvestment shown as negative) • Portfolio investment (by nonresidents) (amortizations shown as negative) • Other long-term capital inflows (by nonresidents) (amortizations shown as negative)	• Official unrequited transfers (by national government) • Foreign direct investment (by residents) (disinvestment shown as negative) • Portfolio investment (abroad by residents) (amortizations shown as negative) • Other long-term capital outflow (by residents) (amortizations shown as negative)
	• Short-term capital inflow	• Short-term capital outflow
Reserve account	Net changes in reserves	

☐ Aggregate net resource flows

▨ Net resource flows on debt (long-term)

 Part I

External finance
for developing countries

 Overview

The divergence between the growth in private capital flows and the stagnation in official flows to developing countries that has characterized the 1990s continued in 1996. Net long-term external capital flows to developing countries rose to an estimated $285 billion in 1996, up $47 billion, or 20 percent, from 1995 (table 1). Private capital flows jumped $60 billion from 1995, while official-source financing shrank by $12 billion.[1] Grants and other official concessional finance—the bulk of aid flows—fell an estimated $1 billion, dropping close to the level in 1990 in nominal terms, an even more substantial fall in real terms.

All developing regions experienced an increase in net flows in 1996. Latin America saw just a small increase of $2 billion, but that followed a large increase in 1995, when official lending jumped and access to private markets improved toward the end of the year. East Asia's $20 billion rise in net flows reflected increases in bank lending and bond issuance to the region and an increase in foreign direct investment to China, partially offset by a decline in bilateral (government to government) nonconcessional loans to some upper-middle-income countries. Europe and Central Asia—a heterogeneous set of countries—experienced an increase of $5 billion, thanks largely to portfolio equity investments in stock markets (notably in the Czech Republic, Poland, and Russia). South Asia's increase of $9 billion was due in part to investment in the Indian stock market and in part to a recovery in net disbursements following India's exceptional repayment of aid loans the preceding year. The $8 billion increase to the Middle East and North Africa reflected a significant upturn in commercial bank lending (to Algeria, Iran, Lebanon, and Tunisia) and foreign direct investment (and again an exceptional repayment in 1995). Finally, Sub-Saharan Africa's $3 billion increase came mostly from increased bank lending (notably to South Africa) and a small rise in foreign direct investment.

Table 1 Aggregate net long-term resource flows to developing countries, 1990–96
(billions of U.S. dollars)

Type of flow	1990	1991	1992	1993	1994	1995	1996[a]
Aggregate net resource flows	100.6	122.5	146.0	212.0	207.0	237.2	284.6
Official development finance	56.3	65.6	55.4	55.0	45.7	53.0	40.8
Grants	29.2	37.3	31.6	29.3	32.4	32.6	31.3
Loans	27.1	28.3	23.9	25.7	13.2	20.4	9.5
Bilateral	11.6	13.3	11.3	10.3	2.9	9.4	–5.6
Multilateral	15.5	15.0	12.5	15.4	10.3	11.1	15.0
Total private flows	44.4	56.9	90.6	157.1	161.3	184.2	243.8
Debt flows	16.6	16.2	35.9	44.9	44.9	56.6	88.6
Commercial banks	3.0	2.8	12.5	–0.3	11.0	26.5	34.2
Bonds	2.3	10.1	9.9	35.9	29.3	28.5	46.1
Others	11.3	3.3	13.5	9.2	4.6	1.7	8.3
Foreign direct investment	24.5	33.5	43.6	67.2	83.7	95.5	109.5
Portfolio equity flows	3.2	7.2	11.0	45.0	32.7	32.1	45.7

Note: Developing countries are defined as low- and middle-income countries with 1995 per capita incomes of less than $765 (low) and $9,385 (middle).
a. Preliminary.
Source: World Bank Debtor Reporting System.

Improving access to private flows— and managing them well

While all regions experienced an increase in net flows, there are enormous differences among countries, especially between those that enjoy access to private capital markets and those that do not. This second group must rely primarily on official-source flows to supplement domestic savings. And while bond and equity markets are flourishing, official-source flows have been shrinking.

Bond and equity markets have proved robust in the aftermath of the Mexican peso crisis, while investors have grown somewhat more mature and discriminating in their assessment of risk. Commercial banks are increasingly financing large-scale infrastructure projects (mostly power). And foreign direct investment, which can bring new technology and access to export markets, faces reduced regulatory barriers.

Aid, meanwhile, has fallen prey to cutbacks. Furthermore, a significant share of official assistance is now devoted to purposes other than long-term economic development. Some of the world's poorest countries suffer from debt overhangs, and even after debt forgiveness will require substantial official support to supplement their own development efforts.

But even countries that are receiving strong private inflows face the problem of managing those flows. Countries receiving large private capital inflows are paying closer attention to macroeconomic management and strengthening their banking systems. One issue is whether security of access—the ability of a borrower to issue new financial instruments on a regular basis—will be better in the future. Another is how to channel the flows to productive uses, for example, how to ensure an efficient, undistorted allocation of credit to infrastructure projects. More flows do not always mean better use of them, and the recent surge in private capital has underscored the need to reform financial sectors. A third issue is how to attract long-term equity funds.[2]

This report reaches several key conclusions:

• Private capital flows to developing countries have continued their strong growth. Private sources now account for more than four-fifths of total flows. The two biggest low-income countries, China and India, have experienced substantial inflows, but virtually all the remaining increase has gone to middle-income countries.

• Private capital markets have matured somewhat, with a broader range of investors, deeper international and domestic securities markets, greater participation of private sector borrowers, and improved creditworthiness and macroeconomic management in developing countries—a change to which the markets themselves have added impetus. The outcome is improved security of access to international markets for countries that continue to follow sound policies.

• Capital market finance for infrastructure projects, especially through commercial bank lending, is an important component of international flows, amounting to nearly $22 billion a year (gross) over the past three years. Further growth is likely. The use of guarantees is expanding as well. Guarantees can enhance the credibility of policies, but only if accompanied by genuine liberalization of domestic price and regulatory rules. Infrastructure that is hard to finance privately—such as rural roads in the poorest countries—will need continuing support from bilateral and multilateral agencies.

• Foreign direct investment has continued to grow and to reach a broader range of countries. Like trade, it is an important channel of global integration and technology transfer. Many developing countries are making earlier trade and investment reforms more credible by adopting investment regimes of open admission, most-favored nation treatment, and nondiscrimination between domestic and foreign investors.

• In the 1990s aid's traditional role of financing long-term development and faster poverty reduction has to some extent given way to funding emergency relief and peacekeeping activities (some 12 percent of aid flows) and supporting the reforms of the transition economies of Eastern Europe and the former Soviet Union. That traditional role has borne the brunt of recent cutbacks and remains vulnerable to further declines. Limited resources for aid need to be enhanced by better donor coordination and a stronger focus on the poorest countries.

• The heavily indebted poor countries (HIPCs) Debt Initiative is now being implemented, and work is under way on some half-dozen countries.

While a necessary step, the initiative will not be enough to reinvigorate private sector investment unless accompanied by strong reform efforts. For that reason, continued official support of adjustment programs is an indispensable accompaniment to debt relief.

Private capital flows are up strongly again

Private net capital flows to developing countries grew strongly in 1996, reaching an estimated $244 billion, a fivefold rise since 1990 (table 2). Private flows now account for 86 percent of total aggregate net long-term flows (82 percent if 1995 and 1996 are averaged to spread out the impact of the exceptional financings for Mexico).

All categories of private flows rose between 1995 and 1996. Bond issuance, portfolio equity investment, foreign direct investment, and, to a lesser extent, commercial bank lending and bank lending guaranteed by export credit agencies (shown under other private flows) were all up strongly.

Portfolio investment contributed $31 billion to the rise in net flows. The big increases came from bond issuance and from equity investment in local stock markets. Bond issuance was up $17 billion to $46 billion, while portfolio equity investment was up $14 billion to $46 billion, $11 billion of it in direct portfolio investment and $3 billion in international issues.[3]

Bond issuance was especially strong from Latin America, East Asia, and Europe and Central Asia. In Latin America increasing investor confidence permitted larger volumes of borrowing at improved terms. Mexican borrowers issued nearly $18 billion in bonds, much of it representing

Mexican government refinancing of U.S. Treasury loans extended in 1995 and of Brady bonds issued in 1989. Thus gross bond issuance for the year included a once-for-all hump. The surge of issues extended throughout Latin America, with Argentina, Brazil, Chile, Colombia, and Venezuela borrowing large amounts, and Uruguay also tapping the market.

East Asian countries were again major borrowers, with the Philippines enjoying better access that enabled it to more than double its borrowing amounts; part of these issues represented a refinancing of Brady bonds. Indonesian borrowers were also active, both public and private sector, and borrowings for the year increased more than $1 billion, as they did for China and Thailand.

Investor sentiment toward the countries of Europe and Central Asia improved greatly in 1995–96. The Czech Republic, Estonia, Hungary, Lithuania, Poland, Romania, Slovenia, and Turkey all borrowed significant amounts, and toward the end of the year Russia floated a $1 billion eurobond, marking its return to international capital markets as a sovereign borrower. While other countries did not borrow in quite the same amounts, some did borrow substantially—Ghana and South Africa, India and Pakistan, and Lebanon, Morocco, and Tunisia.

Portfolio equity investment (investment in stocks traded internationally or locally) moved ahead strongly in 1996, following the pause induced by the Mexican peso devaluation and the rise in short-term U.S. dollar interest rates in 1994 (figure 1). In international markets the volume of new equity issues exceeded that of 1995,

Table 2 Aggregate net private capital flows to developing countries, 1990–96
(billions of U.S. dollars)

Type of flow	1990	1991	1992	1993	1994	1995	1996[a]
Total private flows	44.4	56.9	90.6	157.1	161.3	184.2	243.8
Portfolio flows	5.5	17.3	20.9	80.9	62.0	60.6	91.8
Bonds	2.3	10.1	9.9	35.9	29.3	28.5	46.1
Equity	3.2	7.2	11.0	45.0	32.7	32.1	45.7
Foreign direct investment	24.5	33.5	43.6	67.2	83.7	95.5	109.5
Commercial banks	3.0	2.8	12.5	−0.3	11.0	26.5	34.2
Others	11.3	3.3	13.5	9.2	4.6	1.7	8.3
Memo items							
Aggregate net resource flows	100.6	122.5	146.0	212.0	207.0	237.2	284.6
Private flows' share (percent)	44.1	46.4	62.1	74.1	77.9	77.7	85.7

a. Preliminary.
Source: World Bank Debtor Reporting System.

Figure 1 Financing flowing through portfolio investments to developing countries surged ahead in 1996

Billions of U.S. dollars

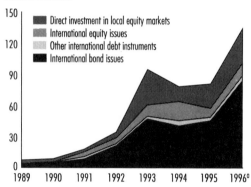

a. Preliminary.

Note: Funds raised on international capital markets on a gross basis, except for direct investment in equity markets, which is on a net basis.

Source: World Bank Debtor Reporting System.

but remained well below the peak of 1994. Chinese corporations continued to be active in capital markets, along with companies in a wide range of other countries, including India (returning after a lull in 1995), Malaysia and Thailand, Argentina, Chile, and Mexico, Ghana and South Africa, and Croatia, the Czech Republic, Hungary, and Russia. An estimated $34 billion in external flows went directly to domestic stock markets through pension funds, mutual funds, hedge funds, and other investment vehicles. While the quality of data in this area makes analysis difficult, it seems clear that the big increases went to Latin America and Eastern Europe (and, to a lesser degree, to India). Recipients of substantial inflows included Brazil, Mexico, and Peru, as well as the Czech Republic, Poland, and Russia.

Borrowing through commercial bank loans also rose in 1996, up $8 billion from 1995. One noteworthy aspect of this borrowing was the prominence of private sector borrowers, who accounted for some 60 percent of all new loans (in both 1995 and 1996). Especially large volumes of borrowing by the private (or corporatized) sector were undertaken in Chile, China, Indonesia, Malaysia, Mexico, South Africa, Thailand, and Turkey. A second aspect of the growth in commercial bank lending is that roughly half of new lending is project lending, of which the major part goes to support infrastructure.

The overall level of foreign direct investment moved strongly ahead in 1996, up $14 billion at $110 billion. Foreign direct investment continued to grow fast in China, but there were significant drops in two countries that are large recipients: Chile and Hungary. Countries that are estimated to have experienced substantial increases in inflows of foreign direct investment in 1996 include Argentina and Mexico.

Private net flows recorded increases in all instruments in 1996 and in all regions of the developing world, though the increases were much greater for some regions than for others (table 3). Europe and Central Asia experienced only a marginal increase, but that followed a jump in 1995, partly reflecting the one-time impact of privatizations in Hungary.

The distribution of these increases was far from even by income group, however. Of the $60 billion increase in 1996, $14 billion went to low-income countries. Low-income countries—excluding China and India, which enjoy good market access—received an increase of $2 billion and a total of just $7 billion in private flows in 1996. These countries are shut out of the bond markets by creditworthiness considerations, and only a handful—for example, Ghana and Pakistan—can hope to access medium- to long-term commercial bank lending. In the past three years private capital has been spread more widely among middle-income countries, as indicated by the decline in the share of the top twelve countries from 87 percent in 1992 to 73 percent in 1996.

A similar picture emerges for net private flows as a share of recipient GNP (using 1995 numbers). Middle-income countries received an average of 3.2 percent of GNP in private flows. Low-income countries received 4.2 percent of GNP, but without China and India that share falls sharply to 1.5 percent, reflecting the large flows to China. By region, the Middle East and North Africa stands out for attracting a low share of 0.7 percent, and South Asia is not much higher at 1.1 percent.

Among middle-income countries that were the largest recipients by dollar amounts, Malaysia had the largest share as a percentage of GNP at 14.8 percent, followed by Indonesia at 6.2 percent, Mexico at 4.3 percent, Argentina at 3.6 percent, and Brazil at 2.9 percent (all 1995 ratios). Among

Table 3 Net private capital flows to developing countries by country group, 1990–96

(billions of U.S. dollars)

Country group or country	1990	1991	1992	1993	1994	1995	1996[a]
All developing countries	44.4	56.9	90.6	157.1	161.3	184.2	243.8
Sub-Saharan Africa	0.3	0.8	−0.3	−0.5	5.2	9.1	11.8
East Asia and the Pacific	19.3	20.8	36.9	62.4	71.0	84.1	108.7
South Asia	2.2	1.9	2.9	6.0	8.5	5.2	10.7
Europe and Central Asia	9.5	7.9	21.8	25.6	17.2	30.1	31.2
Latin America and the Caribbean	12.5	22.9	28.7	59.8	53.6	54.3	74.3
Middle East and North Africa	0.6	2.2	0.5	3.9	5.8	1.4	6.9
Income group							
Low-income countries	11.4	12.1	25.4	50.0	57.1	53.4	67.1
Middle-income countries	32.0	44.0	64.8	107.1	104.2	130.7	176.7
Top country destinations[b]							
China	8.1	7.5	21.3	39.6	44.4	44.3	52.0
Mexico	8.2	12.0	9.2	21.2	20.7	13.1	28.1
Brazil	0.5	3.6	9.8	16.1	12.2	19.1	14.7
Malaysia	1.8	4.2	6.0	11.3	8.9	11.9	16.0
Indonesia	3.2	3.4	4.6	1.1	7.7	11.6	17.9
Thailand	4.5	5.0	4.3	6.8	4.8	9.1	13.3
Argentina	−0.2	2.9	4.2	13.8	7.6	7.2	11.3
India	1.9	1.6	1.7	4.6	6.4	3.6	8.0
Russia	5.6	0.2	10.8	3.1	0.3	1.1	3.6
Turkey	1.7	1.1	4.5	7.6	1.6	2.0	4.7
Chile	2.1	1.2	1.6	2.2	4.3	4.2	4.6
Hungary	−0.3	1.0	1.2	4.7	2.8	7.8	2.5
Percentage share of top twelve countries	83.6	76.8	87.4	84.1	75.4	73.3	72.5

Note: Private flows include commercial bank lending guaranteed by export credit agencies.

a. Preliminary.

b. Country ranking is based on cumulative 1990–95 private capital flows received. Private flows include commercial bank loans guaranteed by export credit agencies.

Source: World Bank Debtor Reporting System and staff estimates.

low-income countries Angola had the largest share at 12.5 percent of GNP, followed by Ghana at 8.5 percent, China at 6.8 percent, Pakistan at 2.4 percent, and India at 1.1 percent.

Official flows continue to shrink

A different world is revealed by the numbers for official flows, based on preliminary estimates for 1996 and actual data for 1995 (table 4). The story is one of a decline in concessional flows in both nominal and real terms in 1996—back to the level of 1990 in nominal terms—and of a modest increase in multilateral nonconcessional lending. Bilateral nonconcessional lending, adjusted for the Mexican repayment to the U.S. Treasury, changed little.

The net inflow of official concessional finance, which includes official development assistance and other official aid to low- and middle-income countries, is down an estimated $0.8 billion, with the decline coming from a $1.3 billion fall in grants. Nor is the outlook for concessional flows any bet-

ter, judging from lower donor commitments for concessional finance.

The cuts in long-term development assistance in recent years are more severe than the totals for official concessional flows would suggest. There has been a marked shift in official concessional flows in the 1990s to funding refugee relief and other emergency aid, including peacekeeping efforts, in Haiti, Rwanda, the former Yugoslav republics, and elsewhere. The Organization for Economic Cooperation and Development (OECD) estimates that about 12 percent of all official development assistance (including technical cooperation grants) is now devoted to emergency aid, compared with less than 2 percent in 1990.

The distribution of this concessional finance by region continues to show a substantial concentration in Sub-Saharan Africa (figure 2). The most significant shift in recent years has been the rapid rise in the share of Europe and Central Asia from virtually nothing in 1990 to an estimated 20 percent in 1996, and the decline in concessional flows to the middle-income countries of East Asia.

Table 4 Official net flows of development finance, 1990–96

(billions of U.S. dollars)

Category	1990	1991	1992	1993	1994	1995	1996[a]
Official development finance	56.3	65.6	55.4	55.0	45.7	53.0	40.8
Concessional finance	43.9	53.3	46.1	43.4	46.7	45.2	44.4
Grants	29.2	37.3	31.6	29.3	32.4	32.6	31.3
Loans	14.8	15.9	14.6	14.2	14.3	12.6	13.1
Bilateral	8.7	9.2	7.4	7.3	6.0	4.8	4.8
Multilateral	6.1	6.7	7.2	6.9	8.3	7.8	8.3
Nonconcessional finance	12.3	12.4	9.3	11.5	–1.1	7.8	–3.6
Bilateral	2.9	4.1	3.9	3.1	–3.1	4.6	–10.4
Multilateral	9.4	8.3	5.4	8.4	2.0	3.2	6.8
Memo items							
Use of IMF credit	0.1	3.2	1.2	1.6	1.6	16.8	0.6
Technical cooperation grants	14.2	15.7	17.9	18.5	17.4	20.7	20.0

Note: Official concessional finance comprises inflows of official development assistance (excluding technical cooperation grants) and official aid to Eastern Europe and the former Soviet Union. Memo items are not included in preceding aggregates.
a. Preliminary.
Source: World Bank Debtor Reporting System.

Figure 2 Official concessional finance remains concentrated in Sub-Saharan Africa . . .

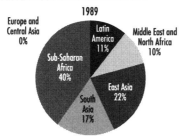

1989

. . . though Europe and Central Asia's share has grown enormously

1996

Note: Includes official development assistance and official aid to middle- and low-income countries; excludes offical development assistance to high-income countries.
Source: OECD Development Assistance Committee and World Bank Debtor Reporting System.

Multilateral nonconcessional lending increased significantly, largely because of lending to Latin America by the Inter-American Development Bank and to Europe by the European Investment Bank. While overall bilateral nonconcessional lending is down because of the Mexican repayment (ahead of time), there was a substantial increase in lending to Russia, particularly by France and Germany.

A transformation of debt restructuring, and the HIPC Debt Initiative

The transformation of debt restructuring operations since the inception of the Brady Plan in 1989 was illustrated by market-based swaps and the debt buybacks of Mexico and the Philippines. Both countries replaced collateralized Brady bonds with uncollateralized instruments, effectively retiring the old bonds at a discount to par and exchanging them for higher-yielding instruments. In two operations Mexico retired $3.6 billion in Brady bonds through a $1.75 billion thirty-year bond swap and a debt buyback funded by a $1.0 billion twenty-year bond issue. The Philippines swapped some $0.8 billion for a $0.7 billion uncollateralized twenty-year bond.

Panama completed a debt reduction operation that restructured $3.9 billion in debt, including $2.0 billion of past-due interest. Peru completed an operation that restructured $8.0 billion in debt, including $3.8 billion of past-due interest. Ethiopia, Mauritania, and Senegal bought back significant portions of their commercial bank debt at large discounts to par, funded under the Debt Reduction Facility of the International Development ment Association.

Over the past year, official debt restructuring has been active within the Paris Club of official creditors and elsewhere (details of all operations are given in appendix 3). Among middle-income countries, Russia received the largest-ever rescheduling by the Paris Club, covering $40 billion in debt, to be repaid over twenty-five years with a rising repayment profile. A considerable number of low-income countries received debt relief under Naples terms (which provide for two-thirds reduction in present value terms of certain categories of official debt), including debt stock reduction operations for Benin, Burkina Faso, Guyana, and Mali.

During the past year agreement was reached on a framework for resolving the debt problems of the heavily indebted poor countries (HIPCs), and the HIPC Debt Initiative moved into the implementation phase. The World Bank established a HIPC Trust Fund and set aside $500 million to cover its initial contribution. The International Monetary Fund has committed itself to participating in the initiative through special Enhanced Structural Adjustment Facility operations. The Paris Club

has agreed to go beyond Naples terms to provide debt reduction of up to 80 percent on a case-by-case basis.

Notes

1. Official flows would show a $5 billion rise, accounted for entirely by nonconcessional loans, if nonconcessional flows were adjusted to exclude Mexico's exceptional borrowings in 1995 and repayments in 1996.
2. Issues of macroeconomic management and dealing with portfolio equity flows are examined in a forthcoming World Bank study, *The Road to Financial Integration,* New York: Oxford University Press.
3. The data on portfolio equity flows are subject to considerable uncertainty. In this year's edition of *Global Development Finance*, we are publishing, for the first time, detailed data for 1995 based on the sources described in appendix 5.

CHAPTER 1

Advances in global markets

Capital flows to developing countries have proved resilient in the aftermath of the Mexican peso crisis. Flows of capital have increased and international markets have become broader, deeper, and more careful in their assessments of country creditworthiness. At the same time, efforts have been made to prevent future crises and to minimize their effects: the International Monetary Fund (IMF) has doubled its emergency financing resources and set standards for more timely and reliable economic and financial data.

Developing countries have played a part in these advances by improving policies, diversifying inflows (in particular, lengthening the maturity of borrowings), strengthening banking systems, and forging agreements among central banks. For many countries reform efforts have been rewarded by new or upgraded credit ratings. And developing country capital markets have continued to deepen, although structural weaknesses remain. Continued reform of financial sectors is important to ensure the efficient use of capital and to mobilize domestic savings.

Private markets and their participants (investors and borrowers) have matured in both the range and the depth of financial instruments and investor funds. But the advance has been modest, and it would be premature to conclude that all investors (institutional and retail) are carefully assessing risks or that all borrowing countries are free from macroeconomic uncertainty. Concerns about private markets include volatility (fluctuations in net flows, often associated with the buying or selling of existing financial instruments) and security of access (the ability of borrowers to regularly issue new financial instruments).

Volatility seems to be an inescapable fact of financial markets in the short run. Developing countries are, and will continue to be, more sus-ceptible to both domestic shocks and factors in the international environment, such as global interest rates. However, because sharp changes in the international environment are now less likely, flows to developing countries in the aggregate will be less prone to volatility. At the individual country level though, the international environment could interact with domestic conditions to give rise to considerable volatility. Such swings are not necessarily bad, and may even be desirable, for example, in accommodating shifts in the current account over a few years in response to an external terms of trade shock.

Security of access is not fully ensured. The ability of private markets and official efforts to avert or mitigate crises remains uncertain. A few developing countries could experience difficulty in borrowing if, for example, international interest rates rose sharply. Thus a central question remains: how secure will access to the international capital markets prove to be in the face of future economic shocks?

This chapter argues that:
Aggregate capital flows to developing countries are rising but will fluctuate from year to year. Countries with sound policies will have secure access to international markets. Conversely, markets will respond swiftly to policy shortfalls, and some countries may lose access. Countries receiving private capital flows can expect to experience short-run volatility.

There are three reasons for cautious optimism on the sustainability of capital flows to developing countries:

• Foreign investors and domestic borrowers are maturing. Developing countries now attract a broad range of foreign investors with long-term investment horizons—including multinational corporations, banks, bondholders, pension funds, and mutual funds—and these investors appear to be scrutinizing country creditworthiness more carefully. The private sector is setting the pace on the borrowing side also, and governments are improving their credit ratings and building up reserves.

• International and domestic capital markets for developing countries are also maturing. Regulatory changes that have facilitated the issuance of foreign bonds, private placements, and American depository receipts (ADRs), in which developing countries figure prominently, reflect the increasing sophistication of international markets. Rising market capitalization and better regulations and financial infrastructure also have deepened local securities markets, though there is still a long way to go in eradicating structural weaknesses.

• Stronger official measures are in place for dealing with crises, notably the IMF's doubling of its emergency resources to SDR 34 billion (about $48 billion) and possible regional cooperation among East Asian central banks.

These longer-term issues are discussed in greater depth in a forthcoming World Bank study on private capital flows.[1]

Modest maturing of foreign investors and domestic borrowers

Foreign investors and domestic borrowers have matured during the 1990s. In the past two years the shock to capital markets of Mexico's December 1994 peso crisis has been absorbed, and a broad base of foreign investors has emerged. Moreover, investors have become more discriminating in the terms they offer borrowers, presumably lessening the likelihood of contagion should a crisis occur. And because developing countries have redoubled their reform efforts and their market creditworthiness has improved, they have been able to access a wider and more sophisticated range of capital market instruments. In most cases new borrowers come from the private sector.

Over time the discrimination among developing countries by investors can lead to reappraisals of country creditworthiness—as reflected, for example, by secondary market spreads on Brady bonds (figure 1.1). At the time of the Mexican peso devaluation, spreads on Brady bonds (relative to U.S. Treasury bonds) rose sharply. Subsequently, a clear correlation emerged between spreads and

investor perceptions of risk. Compared with Poland and the Philippines, spreads for Argentina, Brazil, and Mexico widened substantially after the December 1994 crisis and have since come down only gradually.

Furthermore, the cost and maturity of new borrowing vary widely between highly rated and less highly rated countries. For instance, the average spread on new bond issues in 1996 was 511 basis points for Argentina and 498 basis points for Mexico, while it was 126 basis points for Chile and 83 basis points for Thailand, and the second two countries borrowed at longer maturities.

The investor base also has grown in recent years. In the 1970s commercial banks dominated international markets. Today a diverse group of multinational corporations engages in foreign direct investment, which accounted for more than two-fifths of private flows to developing countries in 1996. The structural forces driving foreign direct investment—increased global competitiveness, liberalized trade, reduced communications and transport costs, and policy reforms in recipient countries—are likely to continue. Pension funds also have become a major force in the securities markets, with U.S. funds investing 1.5–2.0 percent of their assets—$50–70 billion—in emerging markets in 1995, up from a fraction of a percent in 1990. Mutual funds also have 1.5–2.0 percent of their holdings invested in emerging markets. Commercial banks have experienced a resurgence of lending to developing countries,

Figure 1.1 Stripped spreads on Brady bonds reflect investor perceptions of country creditworthiness

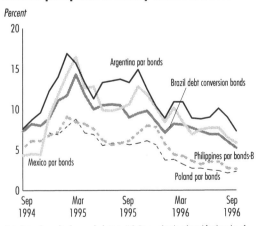

Note: Stripped spread is the spread relative to U.S. Treasury bonds, adjusted for the value of special features such as collateral.
Source: JP Morgan.

about half of it in the form of project finance (discussed in chapter 2), as distinct from general balance of payments support to sovereign borrowers. This new diversity of commercial bank lending tends to enhance the stability of net flows. Thus the broader investor base has helped flows to become less susceptible to abrupt reversal.

Borrowers also have grown more diverse, and many countries have relaxed capital account restrictions on the private sector. Indeed, the most striking feature of capital flows to developing countries in recent years was that private borrowers outstripped public borrowers during 1993–96 and now account for two-thirds of net flows (table 1.1).

During 1993–96 public sector flows (comprising grants, official creditors, and private creditors) remained fairly constant. Net flows to private recipients soared, however, by about $69 billion. About $42 billion of the jump is accounted for by foreign direct investment.[2] Most of the rest is accounted for by commercial bank loans, with bond issuance also rising.

More does not necessarily mean better in regard to external capital flows. Such inflows, in the context of distorted domestic market conditions, can give rise to excessive bank lending, inefficient allocation of resources, and future balance of payments crises. That said, the forces underlying the surge in private capital flows and developing country responses to the surge give grounds for supposing that it is broadly and soundly based, for at least three reasons.

First, the extensive macroeconomic stabilization and structural reform programs adopted by developing countries in the 1980s and early 1990s have started to bear fruit, as evidenced by the recent assessments of capital market rating agencies (table 1.2). Many developing countries have recently had their ratings upgraded, and many have been awarded ratings for the first time. Few countries have seen their ratings downgraded. In December 1996 fifteen developing countries were considered investment grade, and another seventeen had ratings below investment grade. Since 1994 spreads have generally narrowed for private sector issues and have been unchanged or slightly wider for public sector issues (see table A5.4, appendix 5).

Second, in a broader sense the maturing of borrower countries has been reflected in their generally prudent policy responses to the recent surge in private inflows and to the volatility following the Mexican peso crisis. As a result many of the major recipient countries have built up larger cushions of foreign exchange reserves. According to preliminary estimates, about one-quarter of net inflows to developing countries in 1994–96—totaling $831 billion, including $102 billion in short-term flows—went to build up reserves. Much of this buildup has been in U.S. dollars. Countries experiencing strong increases in their reserve positions, especially since the second half of 1995, include Argentina, Brazil, the Czech Republic, Hungary, Indonesia, Thailand, and Turkey. China's foreign exchange reserves rose above $100 billion during 1996, higher in absolute terms than Germany's foreign reserves, and equivalent to about nine months of imports.

Third, in the 1990s net flows to developing countries have been driven by structural factors such as increasing financial integration, as shown by portfolio diversification (especially by mutual and pension funds). Portfolio diversification is a long-

Table 1.1 Aggregate net long-term resource flows to developing countries by public and private recipients, 1990–96

(billions of U.S. dollars)

Category	1990	1991	1992	1993	1994	1995	1996[a]
Aggregate net resource flows	100.6	122.5	146.2	212.0	207.0	237.2	284.6
Public sector recipients	62.8	73.3	71.6	80.9	66.7	76.1	84.8
Private sector recipients	37.8	49.2	74.6	131.2	140.3	161.2	199.7
Foreign direct investment	24.5	33.5	43.6	67.2	83.7	95.5	109.5
Portfolio equity flows	3.2	7.2	11.0	45.0	32.7	32.1	45.7
Private nonguaranteed debt	10.1	8.5	19.7	18.9	23.9	33.6	44.5
Bonds	0.3	1.6	7.4	17.9	14.8	10.6	20.8

a. Preliminary.
Source: World Bank Debtor Reporting System.

14

Table 1.2 Changes in country creditworthiness, September 1994–December 1996

Grade and country	Upgraded	New assignment	Reconfirmed	Downgraded	Moody's	Standard & Poor's
Investment grade						
Chile	••				Baa1	A–/AA (S)
China			•		A3	BBB (P)
Colombia	•	•			Baa3	BBB–/A+ (P)
Cyprus		•			A2	AA–/AA+ (S)
Czech Republic	••				Baa1	A (S)
India	••				Baa3	BB+/BBB+ (P)
Indonesia	•	•			Baa3	BBB/A+ (S)
Korea, Republic of	•				A1	AA– (S)
Malaysia	••				A1	A+/AA+ (P)
Poland	•	••			Baa3	BBB–/A– (S)
Slovak Republic	••	•			Baa3	BBB–/A (S)
Slovenia		••			A3	A/AA (S)
South Africa	•	•			Baa3	BB+/BBBı (P)
Thailand	•				A2	A/AA (S)
Tunisia		•			Baa3	—
Below investment grade						
Argentina			••		B1	BB–/BBB– (S)
Barbados		•			Ba2	—
Brazil	•••	•		•	B1	B+/BB (P)
Egypt		•			Ba2	—
Hungary	•	•		•	Ba1	BBB–/A– (S)
Jordan		•			Ba3	BB–/BBB– (S)
Kazakstan		••			Ba3	BB– (S)
Mexico				•	Ba2	BB/BBB+ (S)
Pakistan		••		•	B2	B+ (S)
Paraguay		•			—	BB–/BBB– (S)
Philippines	•	•	•		Ba2	BB/BBB+ (P)
Romania		••			Ba3	BB–/BBB– (S)
Russian Federation		••			Ba2	BB– (S)
Trinidad and Tobago	•				Ba1	BB+/BBB+ (P)
Turkey	•		•	•	Ba3	B (S)
Uruguay					Ba1	BB+/BBB (S)
Venezuela			•	•	Ba2	B (S)

— Not available.
S = stable outlook.
P = positive outlook.
Note: Developments reflect changes in credit ratings by Moody's and Standard & Poor's. More than one symbol implies either more than one change or a change by both the credit rating agencies. Changes are for both foreign currency debt and local currency debt.
a. When two ratings are given by one agency, the first applies to foreign currency debt and the second to domestic currency debt.
Source: Moody's and Standard & Poor's.

term adjustment that takes years to work through, with some source countries (the United Kingdom, the Netherlands) holding larger shares of foreign assets in total assets than others. However, the overall share held in emerging markets remains small. Increasing integration is a two-way street. Thus gross outflows for some developing countries are significant—Brazil and China, for example, are engaged in outward foreign direct investment.

Modest maturing of international and domestic markets

Over the past two years international capital markets—especially for depository receipts, bonds, and bank loans—have shown a capacity to embrace new borrowers and to devise flexible ways to accommodate old ones. As a result developing country borrowers have been able to broaden the range of markets that they can access. Not that domestic markets in developing countries have stood still: local currency markets have experienced fast growth, and liquidity and regulatory and financial infrastructure have been improving.

International equity issues by developing countries rose from almost nothing in 1990 to $18 billion in 1994 (figure 1.2). Although the market suffered a setback in 1994–95, volume rebounded in 1996. A large volume of privately placed shares has been notable among offerings in 1993–96. They reflect the increasing depth of the depository receipt market, which offers access to equity markets to small companies that are unwilling or unable to pay the higher transactions costs of a fully listed offering. In 1995 four of the twelve top-traded American depository receipts in New York were from developing country issuers, reflecting also the interest in telecommunications stocks (figure 1.3).

The increasing depth of the bond markets has been evident from the high rate of issuance since the second half of 1995, a rate exceeding that of 1994. Some of the biggest borrowers have come from Latin America, underscoring the rapid renewal of that region's market access; the relatively modest issues by East Asian borrowers owe more to lack of demand than to market constraints. Argentina, Mexico, and Russia each made single bond issues of $1 billion.

Broader geographic range in bond issues also emerged, with borrowings in Deutsche marks and Dutch guilders by Argentina, Italian lire by

Argentina and Brazil, and British pounds by Brazil and South Africa. Access to the domestic yen market for foreign (Samurai) bonds was eased in 1996 through a regulatory change permitting access to borrowers with credit ratings below investment grade (that is, below BBB/Baa2). Issues were made by Brazil, Mexico, the Philippines, and Romania.

Sovereign issuers were also able to extend their maturities, with China issuing a 100-year tranche and Colombia a 20-year U.S. dollar Yankee bond, and to widen the variety of instruments, with Pakistan issuing its first floating rate note. Stronger economic performance and improved creditworthiness enabled several newcomers and small countries to tap the markets. Slovakia, Slovenia, and South Africa now enjoy investment-grade ratings, and Jordan and Romania have below-investment-grade ratings.

Private companies and public corporations also have been able to issue bonds in larger amounts and for longer maturities—for example, the DM 1 billion 5-year issue by Companhia Energetica de São Paulo, an electric utility, and the $150 million 100-year issue by another electric utility, Malaysia's Tenaga Nasional Berhad. An Indian company, Reliance Industries, issued 20- and 30-year tranches in the domestic U.S. dollar market, and a Philippine company, Metro Pacific Capital, issued convertible infrastructure-linked U.S. dollar debt.

Developing country securities markets also have deepened, notwithstanding the turbulence

Figure 1.2 International equity issues by developing countries are recovering

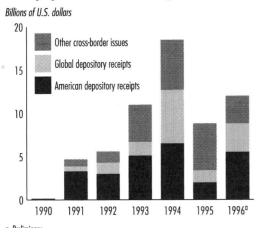

a. Preliminary.
Source: Euromoney Bondware and World Bank staff estimates.

Figure 1.3 Four of the twelve top-traded depository receipts in 1995 came from developing countries

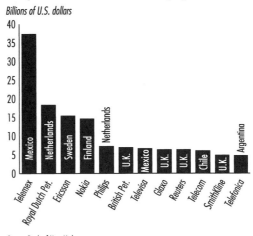

Source: Bank of New York.

of early 1995. By July 1996 emerging stock markets accounted for about 10 percent—$1.5 trillion—of global equity capitalization (figure 1.4). Turnover in domestic stock markets, another measure of depth, also has risen substantially over the past decade (table 1.3). Although market activity declined in 1995, it largely recovered in 1996.

Developing countries have opened up their stock markets since portfolio equity flows began surging in 1989, progressing from the early days of quantitative restrictions in the form of approved closed-end mutual funds. While a variety of restrictions remain, the markets are quite open to foreign investors in some respects. Foreign investment ceilings are generally nonbinding at 100 percent of common stock (India and the Republic of Korea are significant exceptions), withholding taxes are usually below 25 percent (Chile is an exception), and repatriation of income and capital is unrestricted.

Growth in money market instruments, driven by government need for financing in domestic currency and investor demand for diversification into liquid instruments, has been an important development in local currency markets. Ten developing countries—Argentina, the Czech Republic, Indonesia, Malaysia, Mexico, the Philippines, Poland, South Africa, Thailand, and Turkey—have money markets that are open to foreign investment and have attracted significant investor interest. The main instruments traded are treasury bills, commercial bank deposits, and foreign exchange forward contracts. In addition, other local currency markets—such as those in Brazil and Russia—have experienced inflows. The opening of these markets to foreign investors has

Figure 1.4 Emerging stock markets account for a significant share of global capitalizations

World market capitalization

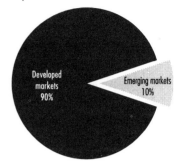

Emerging market capitalization

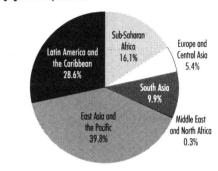

Selected emerging market capitalizations

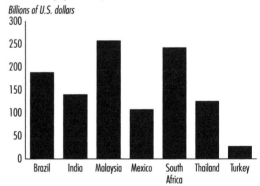

Source: International Finance Corporation Emerging Markets Database and Morgan Stanley.

Table 1.3 Traded value in selected developing country stock markets, 1986–96
(millions of U.S. dollars)

Country	1986	1987	1988	1989	1990	1991	1992	1993	1994	1995	1996 [a]
Brazil	28.9	9.6	18.0	16.8	5.6	13.4	20.5	57.4	109.5	79.2	96.7
Czech Rep.	—	—	—	—	—	—	—	—	1.3	3.6	10.0
Hungary	—	—	—	—	—	0.1	0.0	0.1	0.3	0.4	1.3
India	10.8	6.7	12.2	17.4	21.9	24.3	20.6	21.9	27.3	13.7	24.7
Korea, Rep. of	10.9	24.9	79.2	121.3	75.9	85.5	116.1	211.7	286.1	185.2	196.8
Mexico	3.8	15.6	5.7	6.2	12.2	31.7	44.6	62.5	83.0	34.4	52.9
Philippines	0.6	1.5	0.9	2.4	1.2	1.5	3.1	6.8	13.9	14.7	25.2
Poland	—	—	—	—	—	0.0	0.2	2.2	5.1	2.8	6.0

— Not available.

a. Data are annualized based on information through September 1996.

Source: International Finance Corporation Emerging Markets Database.

been driven by fiscal pressure to reduce the cost of domestic borrowing. These inflows totaled several billion U.S. dollars in 1996, and they are growing.

In 1996 several developing countries introduced regulatory changes to liberalize their stock markets. South Africa's Johannesburg Stock Exchange, which now operates an automated trading facility, adopted deregulation that introduced negotiated commissions, permits dual capacity between brokers and market makers, and allows limited liability corporate membership. Thailand's stock exchange strengthened information requirements and has permitted the establishment of a trust fund to give foreign investors greater latitude in buying company shares than the current 49 percent ceiling. And Indonesia's stock market regulatory authority, Bapepam, raised the ceiling on aggregate foreign ownership from 49 percent to 89 percent for listed companies and to 100 percent for mutual funds.

With the exception of Brazil's Bolsa de Mercadorias e de Futuros, the fifth-largest futures exchange in the world (with annual trading volume of about $1.5 trillion), developing country derivatives markets remain much smaller than their industrial country counterparts. Derivatives markets add greatly to the liquidity of the underlying market. For many developing countries, however, development of a derivatives market is a lower priority than ensuring an adequately capitalized and properly regulated banking system and deepening of money markets.

Finally, the long-term picture for developing country financial markets is being strengthened by pension fund reform. Chile's reforms of the early 1980s are a notable example: the move from an unfunded defined benefit plan to a funded defined contribution plan, the privatization of pension fund administration, and the separation of the social safety net from mandated savings. Although the primary motivation for such reform has been to ensure that pension funds become solvent, a secondary purpose has been to deepen securities markets (although these efforts remain at an early stage). Countries with backgrounds as diverse as Argentina, Colombia, Croatia, Latvia, Mexico, and Peru have adopted pension fund reform, and Costa Rica and Poland, among others, are contemplating it.

Stronger official measures for dealing with crises

In 1995–96 the IMF formalized the procedures used in the Mexico crisis as a mechanism for emergency financial support to other countries experiencing crises. In addition, it established guidelines to support currency stabilization funds and expanded the scope of emergency financing to include postconflict situations. The readiness of recipient governments to adopt strong adjustment measures early on remains a central element of emergency financing. Support for currency stabilization funds is intended to increase confidence in an exchange rate peg or preannounced crawl in the context of strong anti-inflationary policies. And emergency assistance in postconflict countries is intended for urgent balance of payments support in the context of coordinated international assistance efforts.

The IMF's resources for responding to potential crises come from borrowing arrangements with governments, central banks, and the Bank for International Settlements (BIS). Its General Arrangements to Borrow are lines of credit, currently totaling SDR 17 billion, from eleven industrial countries or their central banks. In January 1997 the IMF board adopted a decision on New Arrangements to Borrow, following agreement by the twenty-five potential participants. They were drawn from OECD countries, the Hong Kong Monetary Authority, Kuwait, Malaysia, Saudi Arabia, Singapore, and Thailand. The New Arrangements to Borrow will make available resources of up to SDR 34 billion (about $48 billion) and will be the facility of first and principal recourse, ahead of the General Arrangements to Borrow. The maximum combined amount available under the two facilities will also be SDR 34 billion.

In the aftermath of the Mexican crisis, central banks in a number of East Asian countries have taken steps to forestall potentially destabilizing liquidity crises in the future. Lines of credit have been agreed in the form of repurchase transactions denominated in U.S. dollars, and discussions are under way on more permanent forms of regional monetary cooperation, such as institutional arrangements similar to those of the BIS. The large foreign exchange reserves held by these countries

---

Box 1.1 The IMF's special data dissemination standard

In April 1996 the International Monetary Fund (IMF) adopted the special data dissemination standard aimed at member countries that have or seek access to international capital markets. The goal of this standard, participation in which is voluntary, is to guide and encourage members to publish timely economic data for market participants to use to evaluate a country's policies and prospects. The standard has four dimensions:

• *Coverage, periodicity, and timeliness.* The standard focuses on data that reflect economic performance and policies in four sectors: real (data on national accounts), fiscal (data on government operations), financial (analytical accounts of the banking system), and external (balance of payments accounts). Periodicity and timeliness standards are prescribed. In the real sector, for example, data on national accounts and the labor market are to be disseminated quarterly and data on production and price indices are to come out monthly. In the fiscal sector, information on government operations should be disseminated annually. In the financial sector the accounts of the banking sector should come out monthly, interest rates and stock market prices daily, and balance of payment data quarterly. The standard specifies the minimum coverage required, but countries are encouraged to disseminate other relevant data that make economic performance more transparent.

• *Public access.* Ready and equal access to data by the public, including market participants, is essential. To support such access, the standard recommends advance dissemination of release calendars and simultaneous release of data to all interested parties.

• *Integrity.* To help users assess the integrity of data, the standard advises governments to provide certain assurances, including dissemination of the terms and conditions under which data are produced (with respect to the confidentiality of individually identifiable information, for example), identification of internal government access to data before release, identification of ministerial commentary on data, and information about revision and advance notice of major changes in methodology.

• *Quality.* To help users assess quality, the standard prescribes dissemination of documentation, methodology, and sources used in preparing statistics, dissemination of component details, and reconciliation with related data and statistical frameworks.

---

make such self-insurance a potentially important buffer against volatility.

Finally, efforts have been made to strengthen the public availability of timely economic and financial data on borrowing countries. Some countries have started to provide the financial markets with better information, for example, on foreign exchange reserves. The IMF has drawn up standards for the dissemination of data, including coverage, periodicity, timeliness, public access, integrity, and quality (box 1.1). While some countries must first develop the technical capacity to produce the data (and others will disagree that certain data are appropriate to their economies), the standards will serve as a useful benchmark for international comparisons.

Notes

1. World Bank, *The Road to Financial Integration,* New York: Oxford University Press, forthcoming.

2. This figure might be overstated because some foreign direct investment—especially in transition economies—has taken the form of joint ventures with state-owned enterprises.

CHAPTER 2

Project finance for infrastructure

Developing countries increasingly are financing their infrastructure through international capital markets, a trend reflected in the growth of their commercial bank borrowing and their increased use of bond and equity markets. Finance for infrastructure projects typically comes in a package bundling commercial bank loans, export credit guarantees, equity, debt, and contingent liabilities of the host government ranging from "full faith and credit guarantees" to "comfort letters." Power generation, telecommunications, and transport have attracted the most project finance.

International capital markets contribute a substantial amount to infrastructure project finance—about $22 billion a year—but still far less than is required to provide adequate levels of infrastructure services. Ultimately, most of the funds needed must be generated domestically, in particular through appropriate consumer pricing, but external finance can play an important complementary role. Most external finance has gone to private borrowers, though private provision of infrastructure remains a fraction of the total in developing countries, probably less than 10 percent in East Asia and a somewhat larger share in Latin America.

How broadly based is the recent growth of infrastructure finance, and what are the prospects for future growth? And what steps can be or are being taken to remove constraints on infrastructure project finance? This chapter argues that:

The fast growth of the market for infrastructure finance in the 1990s is likely to continue and to broaden because of the desire of governments to deliver efficient, high-grade services and the potential for increased developing country access to international capital markets. Private sector borrowers will lead the way, supported by guarantees that should encourage—not substitute for—getting the prices and the regulatory rules right.

Underlying this argument are the following key points:
• Capital market finance for infrastructure has grown rapidly in the 1990s, increasing some eightfold to about $22 billion in 1995. But the growth has been uneven, varying across regions, countries, and sectors. Among infrastructure sectors, power generation and telecommunications have led in attracting financing, while power transmission, power distribution, and water supply have lagged.
• The private sector has outpaced the public sector in borrowing, although with the help of substantial public guarantees. Lenders have often been covered by guarantees from export credit agencies.
• Guarantees from host governments, export credit agencies, and multilateral institutions can mitigate the present and future policy uncertainties and the commercial and foreign exchange risks inherent in large-scale infrastructure financing. But care must be taken to ensure that guarantees do not merely substitute for the removal of market distortions.

Infrastructure finance growing rapidly in the 1990s

It is difficult to describe the growth in private finance for infrastructure without first discussing the data definitions. Figures on private finance for developing country infrastructure vary widely, in part because of a lack of agreed definitions and in part because some data refer to expected transactions and some to realized ones. Some estimates amount to multiples of the figures used here.

The discussion here is confined to external finance provided through international capital markets, the main source of private finance for infrastructure in developing countries. Thus it includes not only project finance as conventionally understood in commercial banking—limited recourse financing of specific projects—but also project finance through capital markets. And it includes investments not only by special-purpose companies but also by public bodies and private corporations whose business is infrastructure.

To understand what underlies different estimates of external finance for infrastructure, it is useful to divide projects into three categories: a "wish list" of transactions, which includes any transactions on which governments and sponsors or other potential investors have had conversations or made plans; commitments, which are transactions on which the interested parties have given undertakings (for example, signed a memorandum of understanding); and closed deals, which are transactions that have been signed and financially closed. A wish list may serve as the basis for some of the high estimates of private infrastructure finance. But many transactions that reach the commitment stage, or even the stage of signing, languish for years and are eventually abandoned. For that reason the figures in this chapter reflect only closed deals.

Even for closed deals there is a gray area on what constitutes infrastructure project finance. As conventionally understood by commercial bankers, it refers to loans for infrastructure based on limited recourse to the project's cash flow (box 2.1). But in recent years a large volume of external finance has been raised through bond issues and equity flotations (which can be made on a limited recourse basis). This has included financing for privatizations, such as Malaysia's partial privatization of telecommunications and electricity assets and Chile's privatization of its telecommunications and energy sectors. (In one month in 1995 Telekom Malaysia raised $500 million through ten- and thirty-year bonds). Since the purpose of this chapter is to provide a comprehensive economic picture of capital market finance for infrastructure, the data cover all three instruments—loans, bonds, and equity—that have supported infrastructure. They exclude foreign direct investment (discussed at length in chapter 3), however, because comparable sectoral disaggregations are not available.

On the basis of that definition private external finance to developing countries in support of infrastructure has grown strongly throughout the 1990s (table 2.1). While syndicated loans account for the bulk of the external finance, bond and equity issues combined were not far short of loans in 1995 and exceeded them in 1991–94.

Box 2.1 Measuring the flow of infrastructure finance

The data in this chapter on private financing for infrastructure development cover closed and signed transactions—international loan syndications and bond and equity issues—reported by capital market sources. The estimates of private finance through syndicated lending are compiled on the basis of information from capital market sources and are usually higher than estimates from commercial bank sources, which refer only to bank loans for limited recourse project finance. Limited recourse finance is capital raised for a particular project by the project company, the repayment of which is based on the future cash flow generated by the project, with the assets of the project company serving as additional security (in most cases a separate company is created by the project sponsors to undertake the project). Under this arrangement the creditors do not have recourse to the project sponsors for full repayment of loans, although the sponsors often arrange for guarantees from third parties and also assume certain risks themselves.

The broader definition of private finance used here measures the capital raised through international markets for financing infrastructure through bank loans, bonds, and equity offerings. Common forms of private financing are build-operate-transfer (BOT), build-own-operate-transfer (BOOT), and build-own-operate (BOO), which may involve either corporate or limited recourse finance. Limited recourse financing tends to cover only large projects involving the construction of dams, highways, power plants, and the like, so measures of private finance restricted to limited recourse financing may underestimate the flow of funds to finance infrastructure.

Infrastructure investments are defined as those in construction and heavy engineering, power (including electricity generation and electric and energy utilities), telecommunications (communications infrastructure and services), transport (all modes, as well as transport companies, such as subway or motorway operators), and water and sewerage (all activities relating to water supply and treatment, waste management infrastructure and services, sanitation and drainage, and the like). Mining and oil and gas are considered separately under the extraction sector. Sectoral aggregations are based on the sector of the borrower.

Table 2.1 Infrastructure financing raised by developing countries by type of borrower and instrument, 1986–95

(millions of U.S. dollars)

Type of borrower and instrument	1986	1987	1988	1989	1990	1991	1992	1993	1994	1995
Total	1,351	2,543	910	3,503	2,641	6,312	8,835	18,027	23,314	22,297
Sovereign	286	850	143	0	0	6	116	0	0	205
Loans	286	850	143	0	0	6	116	0	0	205
Bonds	0	0	0	0	0	0	0	0	0	0
Other public sector	965	1,529	630	2,587	640	2,798	2,963	5,759	7,580	6,485
Loans	847	1,476	549	2,448	306	2,013	1,682	2,571	2,185	2,188
Bonds	118	53	81	139	334	748	1,030	3,034	1,003	2,035
Equity	0	0	0	0	0	36	251	154	4,391	2,262
Private sector	100	165	137	917	2,002	3,509	5,756	12,267	15,734	15,607
Loans	100	165	137	767	1,380	126	1,536	6,271	6,007	11,086
Bonds	0	0	0	150	500	740	1,155	3,867	5,810	3,262
Equity	0	0	0	0	121	2,643	3,065	2,130	3,918	1,259

Note: Amounts refer to amounts covered by closed transactions, not necessarily to disbursements.
Source: Euromoney Loanware and Bondware and World Bank staff estimates.

Although preliminary figures suggest that the volume of project financing slowed somewhat in 1996, the inherent "lumpiness" of project finance (transactions are infrequent but involve large amounts) makes it difficult to draw any clear inferences about the long-run trend (table 2.2). A sample of transactions illustrates the variety of project finance in 1996: a $300 million financing by Avance de Telecommunicaciónes Latinoamericano for a fiber optic network in Mexico, a $399 million loan for an Indonesian toll road, and several Chinese power projects cofinanced by the World Bank.

The distribution of funds raised is uneven across regions (figure 2.1). Over the past decade East Asia has raised the most (led by China, Indonesia, the Republic of Korea, Malaysia, the Philippines, and Thailand), followed by Latin America (led by Argentina, Brazil, Chile, and Mexico). And while the Middle East and North Africa and Sub-Saharan Africa have raised only small amounts, Europe and Central Asia has attracted substantial volumes since 1993, particularly Hungary, Poland, and Turkey.

Not only the amounts but also the terms of borrowing have varied widely across regions (figure 2.2). Over the past decade infrastructure loans to developing countries have averaged about $100 million, with a maturity of just under ten years. But the Middle East receives much smaller loans on average with somewhat shorter maturities, and

Sub-Saharan Africa does much worse on both counts. And neither region issued any bonds for infrastructure in the past decade.

The sectoral distribution of external financing of infrastructure is dominated by power, telecommunications, and transport (figure 2.3). During the 1990s telecommunications has become increasingly prominent, with especially large borrowings by the Philippine Long Distance Telephone company, PT Telekomunikasi Indonesia, Thai Telephone and Telecommunications, Telex Chile, and Indonesian- and Chinese-sponsored satellite companies. In the power sector the Indonesian Paiton I 1,230-megawatt coal-fired power project raised financing of $1.82 billion in 1995 through four term loans ranging in maturity from four and a half to sixteen and a half years. In telecommunications the APT Satellite, a consortium of mainly Chinese companies, raised $232 million in 1995. And in transport Citra Bhakti Margatama Persada received a $399 million twelve-year loan to build part of an Indonesian toll road.

Private sector outpacing the public

In a reversal since the 1980s the private sector has become a much more important borrower of external infrastructure funds (including privatizations) than the public sector, raising almost twice as much in the 1990s. Compared with the public

Table 2.2 Infrastructure financing raised by developing countries by region and type of instrument, 1986–95
(millions of U.S. dollars)

Region and instrument	1986	1987	1988	1989	1990	1991	1992	1993	1994	1995
All developing countries	1,351	2,543	910	3,503	2,641	6,312	8,835	18,027	23,314	22,297
Loans	1,233	2,490	829	3,215	1,686	2,145	3,334	8,841	8,192	13,479
Bonds	118	53	81	289	834	1,488	2,185	6,901	6,813	5,297
Equity	0	0	0	0	121	2,679	3,316	2,284	8,309	3,521
East Asia and the Pacific	935	693	260	2,210	1,798	1,188	3,831	9,329	10,786	13,712
Loans	817	640	260	2,210	1,525	797	2,489	5,987	4,146	7,598
Bonds	118	53	0	0	250	215	480	2,377	2,557	2,809
Equity	0	0	0	0	23	175	863	965	4,083	3,306
Europe and Central Asia	369	1,162	316	466	334	862	448	2,496	1,662	3,657
Loans	369	1,162	235	328	0	464	148	1,673	963	3,124
Bonds	0	0	81	139	334	398	300	764	253	506
Equity	0	0	0	0	0	0	0	59	445	27
Latin America and the Caribbean	0	382	284	243	392	3,841	4,431	5,630	7,543	2,248
Loans	0	382	284	93	44	462	578	890	1,579	811
Bonds	0	0	0	150	250	875	1,405	3,580	4,003	1,437
Equity	0	0	0	0	98	2,504	2,448	1,160	1,961	0
Middle East and North Africa	47	206	50	0	0	0	4	41	474	370
Loans	47	206	50	0	0	0	4	16	474	370
Bonds	0	0	0	0	0	0	0	0	0	0
Equity	0	0	0	0	0	0	0	25	0	0
South Asia	0	93	0	583	117	415	120	489	2,850	1,914
Loans	0	93	0	583	117	415	115	234	1,030	1,576
Bonds	0	0	0	0	0	0	0	180	0	150
Equity	0	0	0	0	0	0	5	75	1,820	188
Sub-Saharan Africa	0	7	0	0	0	6	0	42	0	396
Loans	0	7	0	0	0	6	0	42	0	0
Bonds	0	0	0	0	0	0	0	0	0	396
Equity	0	0	0	0	0	0	0	0	0	0
Memo item										
Project financing for all developing countries through loan syndications	7,027	6,297	6,672	7,149	8,704	14,922	16,046	19,566	22,654	27,403

Source: Euromoney Loanware and Bondware and World Bank staff estimates.

Figure 2.1 East Asia leads in raising external funds for infrastructure

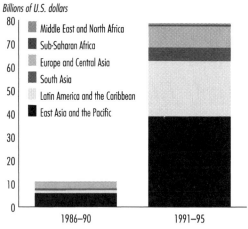

Billions of U.S. dollars

Legend:
- Middle East and North Africa
- Sub-Saharan Africa
- Europe and Central Asia
- South Asia
- Latin America and the Caribbean
- East Asia and the Pacific

Source: Euromoney Loanware and Bondware and World Bank staff estimates.

sector, the private sector tends to rely more on loans than on bonds or equity offerings (see table 2.1).

The level of private sector activity varies greatly across regions. Latin America and East and South Asia have experienced rapid growth in private sector financing in the past decade (figure 2.4). So have Europe and Central Asia recently, though data for 1986–95 tend to understate the level of activity because the change in transition economies began during that period. By contrast, there is almost no private sector borrowing in the Middle East and North Africa and Sub-Saharan Africa. These variations reflect the relative speed with which governments have addressed the need to engage the private sector (discussed further in chapter 3).

Figure 2.2 The size and terms of infrastructure borrowing vary across developing regions

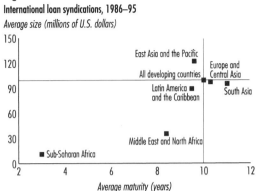

Source: Euromoney Loanware and Bondware and World Bank staff estimates.

Public sector borrowing is accounted for almost entirely by public corporations rather than sovereign borrowers. But the data on public sector borrowing do not fully reflect the public sector's contribution to raising funds for infrastructure. Host country governments have issued guarantees covering 20 percent of all infrastructure loans to the private sector over the past decade (figure 2.5). Of the $11.1 billion in syndicated loans to the private sector for infrastructure in developing countries in 1995, some $3.8 billion was covered by public guarantees.

Guarantees reduce uncertainty, but no substitute for good policies

Governments typically offer a range of guarantees, comfort letters, and other forms of insurance to mitigate a variety of risks faced by project sponsors, ranging from regulatory risks to commercial risks of nonpayment to transfer risk—the risk that the sponsor will be unable to convert domestic currency to foreign exchange. In addition to

explicit contractual guarantees, governments provide implicit guarantees—for example, by guaranteeing tariff rates for a public utility. Implicit guarantees probably outweigh explicit ones, because governments are a party to most infrastructure concession contracts. The creditworthiness of such transactions is often determined by the public utility purchasing the service provided. Governments are obliged to offer implicit guarantees because of the general lack of creditworthiness of public utilities. Most bonds used to raise finance for infrastructure are not guaranteed.

While guarantees can play an important and legitimate role in reducing future policy uncertainties, there is a danger that host country guarantees may be used as a substitute for correcting sectoral distortions. To obtain financing for desired projects, for example, governments may offer generous

Figure 2.3 Power, telecommunications, and transport attract the most financing in developing countries

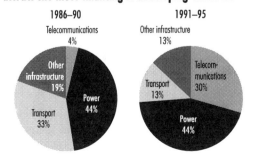

Source: Euromoney Loanware and Bondware and World Bank staff estimates.

Figure 2.4 Private sector borrowing for infrastructure showed rapid growth in Asia and Latin America in 1986–95 (cumulative)

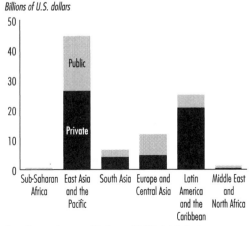

Source: Euromoney Loanware and Bondware and World Bank staff estimates.

Figure 2.5 Host country government guarantees covered a fifth of all infrastructure loans to the private sector in developing countries in 1986–95

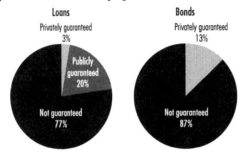

Loans

Bonds

Note: Refers only to guarantees on the borrower's side.
Source: Euromoney Loanware and Bondware and World Bank staff estimates.

price and regulatory concessions (for example, undertakings to underwrite fixed exchange rates) rather than directly addressing the market distortions that increase project costs and give rise to the demand for such concessions. Yet removing distortions, such as by liberalizing consumer prices, would both attract more unguaranteed private finance, domestic and foreign, and reduce the need for it. An estimate based on the power, water, and railway sectors suggests that reducing subsidies could produce fiscal savings equivalent to nearly 10 percent of total government revenue in developing countries.[1] Privatization offers even greater scope for savings, with gains from improved technical efficiency estimated to be equivalent to roughly a quarter of the annual costs of infrastructure investment in developing countries.

Creditor governments also support private finance for infrastructure through guarantees issued by export credit agencies. While solid estimates of the aggregate support for infrastructure provided by export credit agencies are hard to come by because of the uncertainties surrounding data reported on a commitment basis, it seems probable that the great majority of large loan syndications have been covered by export credit agency guarantees.

The continued high share of project loans covered by export credit agency guarantees has led to lower spreads. These guarantees generally cover about 75 percent of country risk on loans. Sometimes coverage is even higher. It was 95 percent for the Nkossa oilfield project undertaken by Elf Congo–though, strictly speaking, this project is in the extraction rather than the infrastructure sector. Export credit agencies have provided greater support in the past two years as project

finance departments have been set up in the Canadian, French, U.K., and U.S. export credit agencies and upgraded in the Dutch and Japanese agencies. In the past two years they have also begun financing private infrastructure on a limited recourse basis, without borrower guarantees.

A comparison of the spreads on guaranteed and nonguaranteed loans provides some insight into commercial banks' price-risk tradeoffs and their willingness to accept lower spreads in exchange for lower country risk exposure. The Birecik hydroelectric dam project in Turkey, for example, initiated in late 1995, received two loans. The first, a nonguaranteed loan, was a DM 400 million seven-and-a-half-year loan at 230 basis points over LIBOR. The second, supported by guarantees from the Austrian, Belgian, French, and German export credit agencies, was a DM 1.4 billion fifteen-year export credit at 100 basis points over LIBOR. The difference in the size and price of these loans illustrates the premiums that banks require to accept country risk exposure and the key role that export credit agency guarantees can play in larger projects.

Another example, the Paiton project in Indonesia, shows how host and creditor governments can work together to alleviate investors' concerns about risk in order to secure project financing. Among investors' major concerns during the development and construction phases of infrastructure projects are contracting, the granting of permits, and the resolution of environmental and resettlement issues. During the operational phase concerns center on changes in contractual arrangements, prompt receipt of payments due, and transfer risk. For the Paiton project the Indonesian government issued a letter of support, the export credit agencies bore a measure of construction risk, and the Overseas Private Investment Corporation, the U.S. official insurance agency, lent $200 million and provided an additional $200 million in commercial and political risk insurance.

Although third-party guarantees complicate negotiations on the price of financing, guarantees by multilateral agencies can play a useful role in reducing the uncertainties surrounding the future policy regime. Even if the government establishes a schedule of charges for the telephone industry, for example, or commits to a formula for electricity tariffs, private lenders may still fear that such decisions will be reversed. Agencies such as the World Bank can support transactions by placing their influence and financial resources behind the government's commitment. A recent case in which the World Bank promoted infrastructure investment through guarantees is the Uch power project in Pakistan, for which the financing was closed in mid-1996. The World Bank Group, both IBRD and IFC, provided support through partial guarantees and loans as part of a complex web of agreements (figure 2.6). The legal and financial structure of such deals is indeed complex and not easily replicable.

The Uch project is a $690 million, 586-megawatt gas-fired plant in Pakistan's Baluchistan Province that will rely entirely on an indigenous fuel source, the nearby Uch gas field. In support of the project, the World Bank issued a partial risk guarantee covering debt service payments for some commercial lenders in the Bank's syndicate. The guarantee would be triggered by a debt service default resulting from the government's failure to ensure the convertibility of foreign exchange or to make good on its guarantee of payments by the state utility company for the purchase of power. The guarantee also covers any legal changes that would result in the government or the project company being unable to fulfill its obligations to

the project, force majeure events arising from political or natural causes, and other default actions such as expropriation of the project company. The Bank's guarantee helped to ensure a $75 million syndicated loan for an unusually long term of fifteen years.

In addition, a World Bank loan provided through Pakistan's Private Sector Energy Development Fund (a government fund) helped catalyze bilateral donor funding of some $188 million. The IFC provided an A-loan, a B-loan syndicated with commercial lenders, and an interest rate swap for the B-loan and Bank-guaranteed lenders; thus the IFC's risk management facility backs up both the B-loan syndicate and the World Bank's syndicate. The U.S. Export-Import Bank provided further support through a $153 million guarantee against certain political risks during construction. And the government of Pakistan assumed sovereign and political risks through a series of agreements. This complex web of agreements was critical to securing private finance for the project.

Note

1. World Bank, *World Development Report 1994: Infrastructure for Development*, New York: Oxford University Press, 1994.

Figure 2.6 The Uch power project in Pakistan shows the role of World Bank Group guarantees

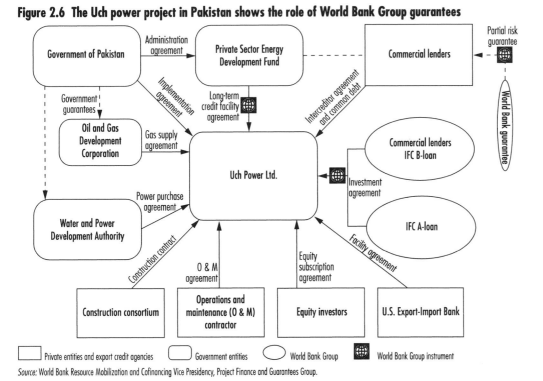

Source: World Bank Resource Mobilization and Cofinancing Vice Presidency, Project Finance and Guarantees Group.

CHAPTER 3

 Foreign direct investment and global integration

Foreign direct investment (FDI) forms one of the most important economic links between developing and industrial countries and, increasingly, among developing countries. FDI flows to developing countries have increased nearly fourfold in the 1990s, surpassing other types of capital flows and averaging about 1.7 percent of GNP for these countries. This increase has been spurred by two main factors: developing countries' liberalization of their economies, particularly the lifting of restrictions on FDI, and multinational corporations' shift toward more integrated global investment and production strategies.

What are the structural characteristics of the growth in FDI? What are the economic effects of FDI on the host country? And what are the prospects for sustained FDI flows? This chapter concludes that:

Foreign direct investment has continued to grow and to reach a broader range of countries. Like trade, it provides an important channel for global integration and technology transfer. Many developing countries are opening their investment regimes and enhancing the credibility of earlier trade and investment reforms.

The chapter describes the emerging characteristics of FDI, the benefits of FDI, and the opening of investment regimes. Its main messages:

• FDI is an important means of increasing global integration and can play an important role in privatization and in the provision of infrastructure.

• Research provides growing evidence of economic spillovers from FDI, such as transfers of managerial and technological expertise to the host country. But in a highly distorted private sector FDI may simply transfer monopolistic profits to foreign multinational corporations.

• FDI not only is linked to growth in trade, it also can promote an export orientation in host countries.

• Multilateral and bilateral investment agreements continue to evolve, embodying a fundamental and hard-to-reverse shift in attitude from prohibiting or restricting foreign-owned businesses to liberalizing their entry and taking a more hands-off approach to their ownership and operation.

Changing characteristics of foreign direct investment flows

FDI is an important means of increased global integration: it links capital and labor markets and it tends to bring wages and the productivity of capital in the recipient country closer to levels in the source country. From a long-term perspective FDI can be viewed as a substitute for migration, which is far more constrained today than it was a century ago.

Much of the FDI in the 1970s and early 1980s appears to have been motivated by "tariff jumping." More recently the strategies of multinational corporations have undergone a major shift as falling transport and communication costs and other technological changes have permitted truly regional or even global strategies (in contrast to the "multicountry" strategy of subsidiaries operating independent of one another, each behind the tariff walls of its host country). The liberalization of trade and the lifting of restrictions on FDI have supported this shift, which has increased competitive pressures among multinational corporations.

The share of FDI in global economic activity—as measured by the ratio of FDI flows to gross domestic fixed capital formation—doubled in the past two decades to 4 percent in 1995. The dollar value of sales by foreign affiliates of transnational corporations has also grown considerably and now exceeds the dollar value of global exports of goods and services. In 1993 (the most recent year for which data are available) world sales totaled $6 trillion, equivalent to 128 percent of world exports of goods and nonfactor services. Sales by foreign affiliates in developing countries were $1.3 trillion, equivalent to 130 percent of imports into these countries.

FDI flows to developing countries have grown rapidly in the 1990s and now account for roughly 40 percent of all global FDI flows (figure 3.1). In 1996 net FDI flows to developing countries were estimated to have reached some $110 billion. Following a decade of strong and uninterrupted growth, aggregate growth continued strong in 1996. China experienced a $6.5 billion increase in inward flows to $42.3 billion, while Chile and Hungary experienced declines from their previously high levels.

The recent surge in global FDI has been fueled by cross-border mergers and acquisitions in industrial countries. But foreign investors have been increasingly attracted to privatization projects in developing countries—particularly in Latin America and Eastern Europe. Generating the most interest has been infrastructure privatizations, which averaged about $2.2 billion a year in FDI support in 1990–95 (appendix 6). The scope for further external financing of privatizations would appear to be large, although it should be acknowledged that for many countries, privatization is not a mere economic issue, but rather a more complex political and social one.

The distribution of FDI among developing regions continues to be uneven (table 3.1). East

Figure 3.1 FDI flows to developing countries account for a growing share of global flows

Billions of U.S. dollars

Source: IMF, *International Financial Statistics*, various years; and World Bank Debtor Reporting System.

Asia and Latin America still take the lion's share—together, some $87 billion. Brazil, Indonesia, Malaysia, and Mexico each attracted inflows of more than $5 billion, thanks to improved economic performance. In a notable development FDI flows to Europe and Central Asia (led by Hungary and Poland) have risen rapidly in the past two years, reaching $15 billion. In South Asia, India's efforts in liberalizing its investment regime and creating a healthier climate for the private sector are beginning to bear fruit, with substantial investor interest evident. The Middle East and North Africa attracts few inflows. In Sub-Saharan Africa foreign direct investment is confined largely to natural resource sectors in a few countries.

FDI flows as a share of GNP also vary widely across regions (table 3.2), although less sharply than absolute FDI flows. For developing countries as a group FDI inflows ranged from 1.5 to 1.9 percent of total GNP in the past four years. Among the largest recipients of FDI on this basis are Malaysia and Vietnam, with inflows equivalent to about 6.5 percent of GNP in 1996. East Asia has sustained inflows equivalent to more than 4 percent of GNP (thanks largely to China), while South Asia and the Middle East and North Africa receive inflows equivalent to only about 0.5 percent of GNP (although flows to South Asia are increasing rapidly). Sub-Saharan Africa receives inflows equivalent to 0.8 percent of GNP but largely because of only a few countries, including Ghana and Nigeria.

The uneven distribution of FDI as a share of GNP can be explained in part by proximity to large markets (including the host country's domestic markets) and in part by progress in implementing structural reforms and removing regulatory impediments, particularly those to the free repatriation of profits and capital.

The sectoral distribution of foreign direct investment in developing countries is not well documented, but it seems that in recent years services have increased their share to more than one third, while manufacturing has declined to less than one-half, with the remainder accounted for by agriculture and mining. Within services financial services are a major component, with trade, construction, and tourism also important. Within manufacturing the trend has been to move from lower-technology or labor-intensive industries (food, textiles, paper and printing, rubber, plas-

Table 3.1 Net foreign direct investment in developing countries, 1990–96
(billions of U.S. dollars)

Country or country group	1990	1991	1992	1993	1994	1995	1996ª
All developing countries	24.5	33.5	43.6	67.2	83.7	95.5	109.5
Sub-Saharan Africa	0.9	1.6	0.8	1.6	3.1	2.2	2.6
East Asia and the Pacific	10.2	12.7	20.9	38.1	44.1	51.8	61.1
South Asia	0.5	0.5	0.6	0.8	1.2	1.8	2.6
Europe and Central Asia	2.1	4.4	6.3	8.4	8.1	17.2	15.0
Latin America and the Caribbean	8.1	12.5	12.7	14.1	24.2	22.9	25.9
Middle East and North Africa	2.8	1.8	2.2	4.2	3.0	−0.3	2.2
Income group							
Low-income countries	4.5	7.1	13.9	32.0	39.1	41.6	49.5
Middle-income countries	20.0	26.3	29.8	35.2	44.6	53.9	60.0
Major recipient countries							
China	3.5	4.4	11.2	27.5	33.8	35.8	42.3
Mexico	2.5	4.7	4.4	4.4	11.0	7.0	6.4
Malaysia	2.3	4.0	5.2	5.0	4.3	5.8	6.2
Brazil	1.0	1.1	2.1	1.3	3.1	4.9	5.5
Indonesia	1.1	1.5	1.8	2.0	2.1	4.3	5.8
Thailand	2.4	2.0	2.1	1.8	1.4	2.1	2.9
Argentina	1.8	2.4	2.6	3.5	0.6	1.3	2.0
Hungary	0.0	1.5	1.5	2.4	1.1	4.5	1.7
Poland	0.1	0.3	0.7	1.7	1.9	3.7	4.2
Chile	0.6	0.5	0.7	0.8	1.8	1.7	2.2
Memo item							
Low-income countries excluding China	1.0	2.7	2.7	4.5	5.3	5.8	7.2

a. Preliminary.
Source: World Bank Debtor Reporting System.

Table 3.2 Net foreign direct investment as a share of GNP by region and income group, 1990–96
(percent)

Country group	1990	1991	1992	1993	1994	1995	1996ª
All developing countries	0.6	0.8	1.0	1.5	1.8	1.8	1.9
Sub-Saharan Africa	0.3	0.6	0.3	0.6	1.2	0.8	0.8
East Asia and the Pacific	1.6	1.8	2.6	4.5	4.4	4.2	4.2
South Asia	0.1	0.1	0.2	0.2	0.3	0.3	0.5
Europe and Central Asia	0.1	0.3	0.5	0.8	0.8	1.6	1.2
Latin America and the Caribbean	0.8	1.2	1.1	1.1	1.6	1.5	1.6
Middle East and North Africa	0.6	0.4	0.5	0.9	0.6	−0.1	0.3
Income group							
Low-income countries	0.5	0.7	1.4	3.2	3.4	3.0	3.0
Middle-income countries	0.6	0.8	0.9	1.0	1.2	1.4	1.4
Memo item							
Low-income countries excluding China	0.2	0.5	0.5	0.8	0.9	0.8	0.9

a. Preliminary.
Source: World Bank Debtor Reporting System.

tics) to higher-technology industries (electronics, chemicals, pharmaceuticals).

Among developing countries China continues to be by far the largest recipient of FDI inflows, with $42 billion in 1996, although some of this probably represents roundtripping by domestic investors and a once-for-all surge in 1996 to take advantage of exemptions from import duties that have since been withdrawn. The country's strong macroeconomic fundamentals and large domestic markets have been important factors in attracting these large FDI inflows. China has undertaken progressive policy changes to afford equal treatment to foreign and domestic firms. Since 1994

China has worked to unify its conflicting tax codes. Foreign firms no longer enjoy tax advantages from the central government, provinces, or cities, with the important exception of corporate income tax, nor do they enjoy exemption from import duties on capital goods. More generally, countries with macroeconomic stability and a sound business climate have been able to attract FDI.

Multinational enterprises in industrial countries, led by those in the United States and Japan, remain the largest source of FDI, accounting for more than 90 percent of recent flows and about 95 percent of the stock of FDI (figure 3.2). In the past decade Japan has emerged as the largest supplier of direct investment capital. Its annual outflows of FDI rose from an average of $3.3 billion in 1971–80 to $27.4 billion in 1981–89. While this trend was reversed during 1989–92, reflecting the adverse business conditions faced by Japanese firms in domestic and foreign markets, Japanese FDI has begun to bounce back and is increasingly directed to fast-growing Asian economies. In 1995 Japan's outflows of FDI reached $52 billion,[1] and in the past decade its share of the global FDI stock doubled to 14 percent.

In recent years developing countries also have generated substantial outflows, with the largest shares coming from Brazil, Chile, China, and Thailand (figure 3.3). Motivating these flows has been the search for a supply of key raw materials (such as minerals and logs) and for lower labor costs in less developed economies as domestic industries in the home countries become technology intensive.

Falling transport and communications costs and the associated flexibility in the location of production have helped to drive FDI. So has the search for larger markets, at least in manufacturing and services, and lower production costs. But among the countries that offer large and growing markets, macroeconomic stability and regulatory policy tend to determine which countries get the most FDI.

Concerns have been raised that some countries that received large inflows of FDI in the past might now begin to experience negative net transfers as those investments mature and yield profits. The cash-flow impact of FDI on the balance of payments (net transfers) is hard to measure because profit remittances are poorly reported in balance of payments data. In principle profit remittances should be recorded as an outflow and any reinvestment of earnings as a new inflow. But in practice many countries (both source and host) do not report reinvested earnings. The presumption is that profit remittances are recorded on a net basis, though whether reinvested earnings are captured in data reporting new FDI varies from country to country and is generally not known. Studies of particular countries have suggested that a large share of profits is reinvested in the host country, accounting on average for a third of total FDI flows.[2] In 1996, against net FDI flows of $110 billion to developing countries, profit remittances were an estimated $30 billion.

Nevertheless, because FDI can contain a large share of debt financing (mainly intercompany

Figure 3.2 U.S. and Japanese multinationals continue to lead in FDI

FDI stocks by home country, 1973–93
Billions of U.S. dollars

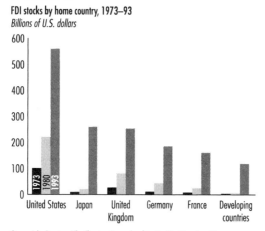

Source: John Dunning, "The Changing Geography of Foreign Direct Investment," paper presented at international workshop on Foreign Direct Investment, Technology Transfers, and Export Orientation in Developing Countries, Maastricht, the Netherlands, November 1996.

Figure 3.3 Some developing countries have begun generating larger FDI flows

Billions of U.S. dollars

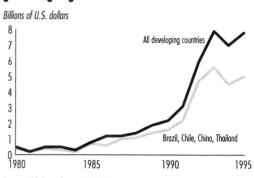

Source: IMF balance of payments statistics.

loans), sudden reversals in inflows could occur, perhaps as a result of policy uncertainties. This possibility underscores the need for host governments to follow sound macroeconomic policies and to encourage higher foreign equity participation by improving long-term growth prospects.

From data for recipient countries a stylized view has emerged of the stages of FDI's effects on net cash transfers to the host economy. In the preliminary stage a high import content can offset cash inflows. In the intermediate stage exports generate a cash offset to import costs. And in the mature stage profits tend to be high, but the rate of repatriation low. This scenario presumes that the host country is following sound macroeconomic policies, maintaining a stable exchange rate, low inflation, and an open capital account that permits conversion of foreign exchange and repatriation of invested funds. Economies pursuing such policies can reasonably expect to attract growing foreign investment.

Economic benefits of foreign direct investment

Foreign direct investment can bring substantial gains to recipient economies, contributing to physical capital formation, human capital development, transfer of technology and know-how (managerial skills), and expansion of markets and foreign trade. In part because of these benefits and in part because fast-growing countries attract a lot of foreign investment, there is a positive correlation between FDI and growth (figure 3.4). FDI benefits from a sound enabling environment,

helped by state investment in social sectors (such as education) where there is a substantial divergence between private and social returns.

The correct way to gauge the influence of FDI is by its impact on the real economy of the host country, rather than merely as a net financial flow. Just as with trade countries should be concerned less with the balance of exports over imports than with the stimulus to competition, the allocation of resources at international prices, and the like, so with FDI the real economy effects are what matter. In a highly distorted private sector, FDI may simply transfer monopolistic profits to foreign multinational corporations. But evidence has shown that FDI can boost technological development, exports, and growth in recipient economies.

FDI can promote technological changes in developing countries in a number of ways. It can have a direct impact through its contribution to higher factor productivity, changes in product and export composition, research and development practices, and employment and training. And it can have an indirect impact through collaboration with local research and development institutions, technology transfer to local downstream and upstream producers, and the effects of the presence of foreign affiliates on the composition of production and the efficiency of local producers. While the evidence does not conclusively demonstrate the existence of technology spillovers, it does suggest that it is likely that FDI generates substantial economic benefits and at least some spillover effects (box 3.1).

Links between foreign direct investment and export orientation

FDI has also been shown to promote exports and provide access to export markets. The export propensity of U.S. foreign affiliates, measured by the ratio of exports to outputs, nearly tripled in the past two decades. In Latin America this ratio reached 39 percent in 1993, more than doubling from the low point at the onset of the debt crisis.[3] In Asia the U.S. affiliates' propensity has remained high, ranging from about 30 percent in the Republic of Korea to more than 80 percent in Malaysia, and has been particularly high in such sectors as electronics.

Figure 3.4 FDI is positively correlated with growth
Ratio of FDI to GDP

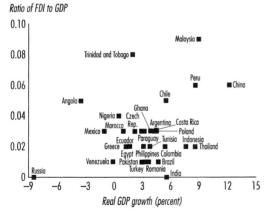

Real GDP growth (percent)

Note: Calculations are based on averages for 1993–95.
Source: World Bank Debtor Reporting System and other data.

Box 3.1 The evidence on technology spillovers

One goal in liberalizing the rules governing FDI has been to capture the benefits of the technology spillovers associated with direct investment and the operations of affiliates of transnational firms in local economies. The literature on such spillovers is extensive, but evidence of the benefits—believed to be significant—is difficult to pin down.

A technology spillover is a special case of a positive externality. For example, a horizontal technology spillover might arise from research and development that leads to a new technology copied by other firms. The technology spillover is horizontal because benefits are realized (or generated) by firms that compete with the firm that created the technology. A vertical technology spillover can occur if, for example, a manufacturing firm transfers technology to input supply firms that enables these firms to deliver inputs at a lower cost, and these lower costs are then passed on to customers of firms other than the original firm.

A 1995 study of sixty-nine developing countries presented circumstantial evidence that FDI generates technology spillovers.[1] First, it found that FDI contributes to economic growth and has a larger impact on growth than domestic investment does. This finding is consistent with other studies indicating that FDI to developing countries is associated with the transfer of technology.[2] Second, it found that, beyond a minimum threshold, higher FDI inflows are associated with higher productivity of human capital for the economy as a whole, indicating that FDI may have some positive spillover effects through the training of workers. Third, it found that FDI does not crowd out domestic investment, but instead seems to supplement it—a finding consistent with vertical spillovers leading to increased capital investment by suppliers and distributors.

These findings are consistent with another recent study showing that productivity tends to be higher in developing countries that have strong links with OECD countries than in those that do not.[3] The difference is attributed to technology embodied in imports from OECD countries by the high-productivity developing countries. But because FDI flows from OECD to developing countries are highly correlated with trade flows, the productivity could be associated with technology transfer through FDI rather than trade.

Another study provides evidence that FDI has produced technology spillovers in China.[4] Using data covering 434 urban areas in China during 1988–90, the study showed that of the three types of firms in China (state-owned, township-and-village, and foreign-invested), the foreign-invested firms grew the fastest. Moreover, the study found that the share of foreign-invested firms and the depreciated stock of FDI were important in explaining differences in growth among urban areas.

1. E. Borenzstein, J. de Gregorio, and J. Lee, "How Does Foreign Direct Investment Affect Growth?" NBER Working Paper 5057, National Bureau of Economic Research, Cambridge, Mass., 1995.
2. See, for example, Magnus Blomström, Robert Lipsey, and Mario Zejan, "What Explains Developing Country Growth?" NBER Working Paper 4132, National Bureau of Economic Research, Cambridge, Mass., 1992.
3. David Coe, Elhanan Helpman, and Alexander Hoffmaister, "North-South R & D Spillovers," Discussion Paper 1133, Centre for Economic Policy Research, London, 1995.
4. Shang-jin Wei, "Foreign Direct Investment in China: Sources and Consequences," in Takatoshi Ito and Anne O. Kreuger, eds., "Financial Deregulation and Integration in East Asia," Chicago: University of Chicago Press, forthcoming.

The export orientation of Japanese affiliates also has been increasing, most notably in East Asia, where their exports accounted for 34 percent of total sales in 1993. Japanese affiliates in China exported 53 percent of their sales in 1992, up from less than 10 percent in 1986, directing 43 percent of their sales to home markets in Japan.

Empirical studies generally support the notion that FDI promotes economic growth in host developing countries, perhaps in part by encouraging additional domestic investment. But the macroeconomic impact of FDI varies by country and region, depending on the policy regime in the host economy: benefits tend to be greater where policy distortions are fewer. For example, one study found that FDI had a positive effect on growth in eight Pacific Basin economies where distortions were low, whereas the effect was negative in a control group of developing economies.[4]

The benefits of FDI seem to be linked to the growth in trade: trade acts as a channel for mediating benefits, and the liberalization of trade and the opening of investment regimes have often gone hand in hand in recent years (as discussed below). In principle, trade may promote FDI or substitute for it (and vice versa). Much of FDI during the 1970s and early 1980s appeared to be motivated by "tariff jumping" efforts to circumvent actual or potential trade barriers, including voluntary export restraints. By contrast, most FDI in the late 1980s and in the 1990s appears to be driven by increased competition, arising in part from trade liberalization.

While the links are far from easy to trace, the close association between trade and FDI is evidenced by the high share of intrafirm transactions in a country's total trade—trade between a parent multinational corporation and its affiliates or between affiliates. Data for the 1980s and earlier show that for three major source countries (the United States, Japan, and the United Kingdom) trade associated with multinational corporations was typically in the range of 25–40 percent of total trade. A more recent study estimates the 1993 share of intrafirm exports in total U.S. exports at 36 percent. By any reckoning intrafirm trade, and thus FDI, is an important part of world trade.

Similarly, the link between FDI and exporting is shown by the high share of foreign affiliates in the exports of such developing countries as China, Malaysia, Mexico, the Philippines, and Thailand. In Malaysia it is estimated that foreign affiliates accounted for 46 percent of exports and 32 percent of corresponding employment in the late 1980s—and for 60 percent of exports and 49 percent of corresponding employment in manufacturing. In China foreign affiliates' share in total exports rose from 6 percent in 1989 to nearly 28 percent in 1993.

The opening of investment regimes during the 1990s

Investment regimes in many developing and industrial countries have undergone tremendous liberalization over the past six years, with an effect on investment flows comparable to that of the Uruguay Round on trade. Indeed, investment and trade liberalization have frequently gone hand in hand.

The changes in investment regimes have been embodied in new investment laws, bilateral treaties, and multilateral instruments. During the 1990s some fifty countries have enacted new laws on investment. More dramatic still has been the growth in the number of bilateral treaties on the promotion and protection of investment: such treaties increased almost threefold during the 1990s, to about 1,100.

Multilateral instruments with provisions on investment have also appeared. Early examples include the 1981 Agreement of the Organization of the Islamic Conference and the 1987 Association of Southeast Asian Nations (ASEAN) Agreement on Investment. The first multilateral instrument to be adopted in the 1990s was the World Bank's Guidelines on the Treatment of Foreign Direct Investment, issued in September 1992 by the World Bank's Development Committee and the IMF Board of Governors. As the name suggests, the guidelines, unlike laws and treaties, are not binding on governments but were intended to influence the formulation of new laws and treaties. Since the adoption of the guidelines, several more multilateral instruments dealing with investment have appeared, including the 1994 Asia-Pacific Economic Cooperation Non-Binding Investment Principles and several regional multilateral treaties that, of course, are binding once they enter into force. These treaties include the 1992 North American Free Trade Agreement and the 1994 Energy Charter Treaty, which also deal with trade issues, and the two 1994 investment protocols to the trade agreement establishing Mercosur.

The investment provisions of the laws, treaties, and instruments of the 1990s have much in common. They all cover a broad range of foreign investment, including portfolio and direct investment, and investment in both tangible and intangible assets. To encourage the flow of private investment, such laws, treaties, and instruments typically provide for high standards of protection for investment and liberal arrangements for entry. Investment is protected by legal guarantees ranging from the general (such as "fair and equitable treatment" and "constant protection and security") to the particular (such as the proscription of uncompensated expropriation or similar measures and the right to transfer investment-related funds into and out of the host country).

The laws enacted during the 1990s have either relaxed or eliminated screening requirements for the establishment of new investments and acquisitions of existing investments by foreign investors. Some of the treaties extend most-favored-nation and even national treatment to the establishment or acquisition of investment by investors from one signatory country in the territory of another, excluding only sectors specified in annexes to the treaties. Under these agreements countries may remove sectors from, but not add sectors to, the list of those excluded from national treatment regarding entry.

These laws, treaties, and instruments also have in common provisions governing the submission to international arbitration of disputes between investors and their host states. Some of the investment laws and most of the treaties require arbitration under the auspices of the International Centre for Settlement of Investment Disputes, one of the five international organizations belonging to the World Bank Group. Many treaties also allow investors to pursue international arbitration while simultaneously making claims under investment insurance arrangements, such as those offered by the Multilateral Investment Guarantee Agency, another member of the World Bank Group.

As part of the 1994 World Trade Organization Agreement resulting from the Uruguay Round trade negotiations, three binding instruments that are relevant to investment were concluded: the Agreement on Trade-Related Investment Measures (TRIMs), the Agreement on Trade-Related Aspects of Intellectual Property Rights (TRIPs), and the General Agreement on Trade in Services (GATS). Although these instruments deal only with certain aspects of the treatment of investment, their provisions take much the same approach as the laws, treaties, and instruments discussed above. The TRIPs agreement contains general provisions on protecting and enforcing intellectual property rights, commonly mentioned in treaties as one of the forms of covered investments. And the TRIMs agreement and the GATS set forth the general principles of most-favored-nation and national treatment, also found in investment treaties.

Countries, particularly transition economies, continue to liberalize their investment laws and conclude bilateral and multilateral treaties dealing with investment. The OECD member countries are negotiating a comprehensive Multilateral Agreement on Investment scheduled to be completed by mid-1997. Although negotiated by OECD members, the agreement is expected to be open to accession by any other country.

The widespread opening up of investment regimes embodies the broad changes in attitude and practice toward FDI over the past decade. Its importance lies in the hard-to-reverse nature of the laws and treaties: once made the changes can have a powerful effect on the credibility of the host country in the eyes of potential foreign investors. To ensure the greatest gains from FDI, developing countries need to continue with domestic price liberalization and sectoral reforms.

Notes

1. Figures are based on notification, as compiled by the Japanese Ministry of Finance.
2. UNCTAD, *World Investment Report,* New York: United Nations, 1996.
3. Robert E. Lipsey, "The Internationalization of U.S. MNEs and Its Impact in Developing Countries," paper presented at international workshop on Foreign Direct Investment, Technology Transfers, and Export Orientation in Developing Countries, Maastricht, the Netherlands, November 1996.
4. Maxwell Fry, "Foreign Direct Investment in a Macroeconomic Framework: Finance, Efficiency, Incentives, and Distortions," Policy Research Working Paper 1141, World Bank, International Economics Department, International Finance Division, Washington, D.C., 1993.

CHAPTER 4

The changing face of aid

Aid and donor attitudes toward it stand at a crossroads. Following a sharp fall in 1993 and a partial recovery in 1994, official development assistance (ODA) dropped by nearly 10 percent in real terms (that is, adjusted for inflation and exchange rates) in 1995. Moreover, the composition of ODA has shifted, with a significant portion being used to fund emergency relief and peacekeeping activities and less going toward long-term development needs. The shift is even more pronounced when aid to middle-income transition economies (Eastern Europe and the former Soviet republics), which is not classified as ODA, is taken into account.

ODA now accounts for about one-fifth of net flows to developing countries, compared with one-half in 1990, reflecting mainly a surge in private capital flows. The reordering of geopolitical priorities since the end of the Cold War has led to sharp cuts in aid budgets and a shift away from long-term development and poverty reduction efforts at the very time that many developing countries have become more receptive to market-based reform. Some of the reduction in assistance has been to countries that lack access to private capital markets. Many of these countries have no realistic external financing alternative in the short to medium term. Prospects for an increase in aid are limited, and donors have become more selective in their allocation of aid. Some potential recipients have performed poorly and suffered reduced aid flows. But whether due to weak donor commitments or to poor recipient performance, aggregate aid to traditional low-income claimants has fallen. What is needed now is a new vision of aid.

Given this difficult environment, in which aid lacks strong domestic constituencies in the face of donor budget constraints, can aid donors and recipients refocus their programs?

This chapter argues that:
The traditional role of aid in promoting long-term development and alleviating poverty—as distinct from funding emergency relief and assisting transition economies—has borne the brunt of aid cutbacks in the 1990s. Donors need to renew their vision of aid as a means of helping poor countries create an enabling environment for private sector development and ensure that the resulting growth reaches all segments of society.

Ailing official development assistance

In nominal terms net ODA flows hovered near $60 billion in 1994–95 (figure 4.1).[1] In real terms, however, ODA fell about 9 percent in 1995, according to data from the OECD's Development Assistance Committee (DAC). Of this drop, 7 percentage points represented a decline in amounts calculated in donors' currencies (offset in dollar-equivalent terms by the decline of the U.S. dollar); the rest represented the adjustment for inflation.

In nominal terms sharp cuts in ODA from the United States and Italy were partly offset by an increase from Japan. In 1995 the United States became the fourth-largest donor—behind Japan, France, and Germany despite real cuts in the ODA programs of France and Germany. Japan contributed $14.5 billion, France $8.4 billion, Germany $7.5 billion, and the United States $7.4 billion.

Among DAC members, ODA as a share of donor GNP fell to a weighted average of 0.27 percent, its lowest level in forty-five years (figure 4.2). As a share of GNP, ODA fell in fifteen of twenty-one DAC member countries, including all the G-7 countries. ODA remained unchanged in Austria and increased in Ireland and some countries that had made earlier cuts.

Figure 4.1 Nominal ODA has held steady in recent years; real ODA has been slipping

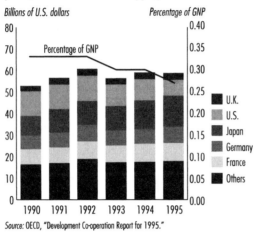

Source: OECD, "Development Co-operation Report for 1995."

Figure 4.2 In 1995 net ODA from industrial countries dropped to its lowest level in half a century

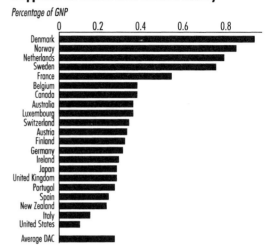

Source: OECD, "Development Co-operation Report for 1995."

Pressures on OECD governments for fiscal consolidation and the lack of domestic constituencies to protect aid have been the most important factors driving the decline in aid budgets. Countries with large deficits (Finland, Italy, and Sweden) have cut aid, while those with small deficits (Ireland, Japan, and Norway) have increased it. Assistance from European Union (EU) countries in particular will remain constrained as they seek to meet the fiscal targets for monetary union. In the view of some donors, the case for aid has been undercut by poor policy performance in recipient countries. In addition, the public and policymakers in some countries—notably the United States—have started to question the effectiveness of aid. In just three years U.S. ODA has fallen by a third, from 0.15 percent of GNP in 1993 to 0.10 percent in 1995.

Aid from Arab donors (not included in figures 4.1 and 4.2, which show DAC donors only) fell to less than $1 billion, its lowest level in many years. Nevertheless, Kuwait remained the leading donor as measured by share of GNP, with a ratio well above 1 percent, and cumulative aid from Kuwait, Saudi Arabia, and the United Arab Emirates remains substantial. Since the early 1970s, for example, Saudi Arabian aid has totaled $71 billion. Other significant non-DAC donors include Greece, the Republic of Korea, and Turkey.

Shifting composition of aid

Overall ODA figures tell only part of the story of the retrenchment in long-term development assis-

tance. In recent years ODA, traditionally used to alleviate poverty and foster development, has also been used to fund substantial increases in refugee relief and other emergency aid, notably in the former Yugoslav republics and Rwanda. Bilateral emergency aid (excluding food aid) was about $3 billion in 1995, down from $3.5 billion in 1994. Multilateral emergency aid—mostly representing the activities of United Nations agencies—fell to just over $2 billion in 1995, from more than $2.5 billion in 1994. Thus in 1994–95 some $5–6 billion a year of ODA was used for emergency aid (including peacekeeping activities).[2]

By way of example of the shifts in composition, estimates of aid flows to Bosnia and Herzegovina (much of it emergency aid) from bilateral and multilateral sources are roughly $600 million in 1993, $650 million in 1994, $550 million in 1995, and a projected $700 million in 1996. These figures exclude technical cooperation grants, which are projected to contribute an additional $100 million in 1996.

The uses to which this money has been devoted have high humanitarian value. Their value is not the issue. The issue is that funding for other aid categories has been cut, putting a tight squeeze on aid for long-term economic development.

The position of aid is worse than it appears in one further respect: the sizable cut by bilateral donors in their commitments to multilateral concessional lending windows. In 1990–95 multilateral aid disbursements cushioned the overall decline (described below), rising from 26 percent to 32 percent of total aid disbursements. The outlook, however, is less promising, because while multilateral disbursements are rising, donor commitments are falling. This is true for the International Development Association (IDA), the World Bank's concessional lending arm, and there are signs that budgetary pressures could affect the European Commission's multilateral facilities.

Donor commitments to IDA have dropped significantly, by about $7 billion during 1994–96 (although IDA commitment authority has not declined). Because of the lag between donor commitments and disbursements, cash flows to IDA have not yet declined. But they will decline eventually unless donors increase commitments (or accelerate disbursements).

There is one respect in which aid has fared better than appearances might suggest: the significant concessional loans and grants flowing to transition economies (the mostly middle-income postcommunist economies of Eastern Europe and the former Soviet Union). These flows are classified as official aid rather than ODA because the recipient countries are not on the DAC Part 1 list of countries eligible for ODA. In 1995 net official aid rose by $1.6 billion to $9.0 billion; in 1990 it was $2.2 billion. Thus during 1990–95 ODA and official aid taken together actually rose in nominal terms (figure 4.3). Assistance to Eastern Europe and the former Soviet Union has been comparatively modest in absolute amounts, however, with the cumu-

lative totals for 1990–95 being $8.5 billion for Russia, $11.9 billion for Poland, and $2.2 billion for Ukraine.

Although the concessional flows allocated to transition economies typically are determined separately from donors' ODA budgets, so that there is no mechanical link between increases in one and decreases in the other, the overall figures indicate donor capacity for providing concessional assistance. Moreover, they shed light on the argument sometimes made that donors are losing confidence in the effectiveness of aid. To the extent that confidence is dwindling, it seems to vary considerably by country, between different channels of aid, and among groups within donor countries concerned with formulating policies on aid. The special needs of the transition economies elicit substantial support on concessional terms. Such support does not, however, fall under the traditional aid rubric of supporting long-term development in the poorest countries.

The regional distribution of concessional aid has not changed much during the 1990s (figure 2, overview) except for the sizable increase to Europe and Central Asia (which went from $166 million in 1989 to an estimated $8.9 billion in 1996). In 1996 Sub-Saharan Africa received 34 percent (against 40 percent in 1989), Europe and Central Asia received 20 percent (against 1 percent), South Asia received 14 percent (against 17 percent), East Asia received 14 percent (against 22 percent), the Middle East and North Africa remained unchanged at 10 percent, and Latin America received 8 percent (against 11 percent). (Data for 1996 are estimated.)

During this period the biggest increases in aid (in absolute U.S. dollars) went to the former Yugoslav republics (notably Bosnia and Herzegovina), Algeria, Cambodia, Egypt, Haiti, Pakistan, Poland, Russia, Rwanda, South Africa, Ukraine, Vietnam, and Zambia. In Europe, the surge in assistance to Poland and Russia at the start of the decade has now flattened out, while Ukraine and Bosnia and Herzegovina gained substantially in 1996. It is harder to identify countries that have lost aid because the set is more diffuse, but substantial reductions have occurred for Cuba, Jamaica, Sudan, Syria, and Zaire. In addition to the former Yugoslav republics, the biggest aid recipients in 1995 were Bangladesh, China, Egypt, India, Mozambique, Pakistan, Poland, Russia, and Vietnam.

Figure 4.3 Official aid to transition economies accounts for the only increase in recent aid flows

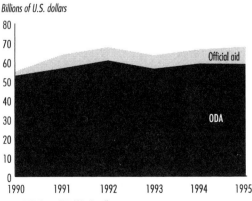

Billions of U.S. dollars

Source: OECD data and World Bank staff estimates.

Refocusing aid

The share of concessional flows (net aid flows, both ODA and official aid) going to low-income countries has fallen in the 1990s (figure 4.4). In 1990 low-income countries received 60 percent of aid flows; by 1995 that share had fallen to 52 percent.

ODA has retained its low-income focus. The share of ODA going to low-income countries has remained constant—69 percent in 1990 and 70 percent in 1995. There has been some redistribution of funds, however. For example, ODA to Malaysia and the Republic of Korea (middle- and high-income countries) has been cut, while ODA to Cambodia, the Lao People's Democratic Republic, and Vietnam (low-income countries) has increased sharply. Sub-Saharan Africa contin-

ues to take the largest share of ODA—about 34 percent. In 1995 ODA to high-income countries fell significantly to $1.1 billion, a small fraction of the total.

Concentrating aid on low-income countries does not guarantee that the funds will be used to reduce poverty. But it does make such a focus more likely, while aid directed to middle- or even high-income countries suggests that other objectives are being pursued. A larger portion of aid from multilateral sources goes to low-income countries than from bilateral sources. In 1995, 65 percent of aid from multilateral sources went to low-income recipients; for bilateral sources the share was 46 percent (figure 4.5). No multilateral aid goes to high-income countries.

The main sectoral shift in bilateral aid over the past fifteen years has been toward the social sectors. Education, the largest recipient sector, accounts for about 18 percent of bilateral aid commitments. Water supply and sanitation receives about 8 percent of concessional assistance, a share that has risen sharply in recent years. Less ODA is being devoted to physical infrastructure, reflecting the ability of some countries to attract external project finance for large-scale infrastructure (see chapter 2). One exception, however, has been ODA in support of rural roads. Traditionally, little ODA goes to the services sector, but in recent years significant aid has been directed to banking system reform.

Pressures on aid budgets and shifts in donor priorities have led to a reexamination of the objectives of aid. One central objective should remain, how-

Figure 4.4 Low-income countries are receiving a smaller share of concessional aid flows

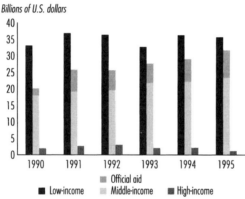

Billions of U.S. dollars

- Low-income
- Official aid / Middle-income
- High-income

Note: Data are the same as those presented in figure 4.3 except that multilateral disbursements are shown rather than donor contributions to multilateral institutions.
Source: OECD data and World Bank staff estimates.

Figure 4.5 A larger share of multilateral than bilateral concessional aid flows to low-income countries

Multilateral
Billions of U.S. dollars

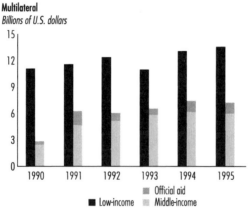

- Low-income
- Official aid / Middle-income

Bilateral
Billions of U.S. dollars

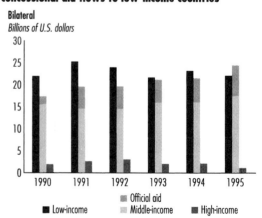

- Low-income
- Official aid / Middle-income
- High-income

Source: OECD and World Bank staff estimates.

Box 4.1 Linking IDA lending to country performance

Multilateral institutions, including the World Bank, play a unique role in advising developing countries on policy reform, evaluating results on the ground and disseminating best practice, and coordinating aid and strengthening partnerships. This support can help concentrate aid flows in countries where they can be most effective and, through coordination, ensure that governments make the best use of aid.

Lending commitments by the International Development Association (IDA)—the concessional lending arm of the World Bank—have increasingly reflected the emphasis placed on country performance. Annual performance ratings for IDA recipient countries reflect evaluations of their macroeconomic stability, structural reforms, poverty reduction efforts, and the quality of the loan portfolio under implementation. Because of these criteria, IDA lending is closely correlated with country performance (box table).

Annual IDA lending commitments are closely linked to country performance
(U.S. dollars per capita)

Performance quintile	IDA-9 (fiscal 1990–93)		IDA-10 (fiscal 1994–96)		Share of IDA lending (percent)
	Number of countries	Per capita amount	Number of countries	Per capita amount	
Top	10	10.4	11	13.4	31
Upper	10	11.5 [a]	11	8.7	25
Middle	9	8.7	11	8.5	28
Lower	9	6.9	11	6.2	14
Lowest	9	1.5	10	1.1	2
Total/average	47	7.9	54	7.7	100

Note: Based on data for IDA-only countries, excluding countries with fewer than 500,000 people.
a. This relatively high level reflects extraordinary levels of support provided for debt workouts to Guyana, Nicaragua, and Zambia.
Source: World Bank, "The Pursuit of Sustained Poverty Reduction: Review of the IDA-10 Program FY94-96," Washington, D.C., 1997.

ever—to quickly reduce poverty in recipient countries. In so doing, aid will also promote the economic and strategic interests of donor countries. In an increasingly competitive global economy, aid should create healthy private sectors, facilitate global integration, and ensure that growth reaches all segments of society. These rationales require that aid support policy reform (box 4.1), infrastructure development, the provision of social services, and the creation of social safety nets.

The declining trend in traditional aid flows is obliging recipient countries to use aid resources more effectively. It is hoped that the more effective use of aid will itself make the case for enlarged resources.

Notes

1. Unlike table 4 in the overview, these figures include technical cooperation grants (about $20 billion in 1995), high-income countries on the DAC Part 1 list (about $1 billion in 1995), and bilateral contributions to multilateral institutions (as opposed to multilateral disbursements to recipient countries).
2. About $3 billion a year was also spent on military activities in support of peacekeeping and security. These funds do not, however, count as aid.

CHAPTER 5

 # Removing the debt overhang of the heavily indebted poor countries

The plight of heavily indebted poor countries (HIPCs) has gained increasing international attention over the past two years.[1] In the fall of 1995 the Development Committee of the World Bank and the Interim Committee of the IMF acknowledged the need to address this issue and one year later endorsed the HIPC Debt Initiative. This initiative provides a framework for international support to adjustment and reform efforts in the world's poorest and most heavily indebted countries to ensure that their debt is reduced to sustainable levels.

All creditors are expected to participate in the initiative in a coordinated and concerted way. The World Bank has established a HIPC Trust Fund and has allocated $500 million as its initial contribution. The IMF will participate in the initiative through special Enhanced Structural Adjustment Facility operations. And the Paris Club of official creditors has agreed to go beyond Naples terms, which reduce eligible debt by two-thirds in present value terms, offering debt reductions of up to 80 percent. Other multilateral creditors have endorsed the initiative and are working out the details of their participation. The HIPC Debt Initiative is now being implemented, and work is under way on some half-dozen countries.

Action in this area has been stimulated by debate over the need to reduce debt burdens, the best way to go about it, and how to pay for it. What is the nature of the debt problem in countries that take in far more cash from their creditors than they pay out? What are the prospective benefits of reducing debt stocks, and how can they be realized? How can the international community best respond to the needs of HIPCs? These straightforward questions deserve straightforward answers.

This chapter argues that:

Removing the debt overhang is a necessary but not a sufficient condition for successful reform, particularly in countries that must reinvigorate (or create) the private sector and stimulate domestic investment. Restoring (or establishing) country creditworthiness will take time and depend on the continued efforts of these countries to address economic and social problems. Thus continued official support for adjustment is essential, and the HIPC Debt Initiative is an important instrument for helping poor countries with a high level of debt achieve sustainable growth and reduce poverty.

What is the debt problem?

Annual GDP growth in HIPCs averaged 2.2 percent during 1985–90 but fell to an average of just 1.0 percent during 1990–95 (table 5.1). Average export receipts fell during 1980–85, though they grew by more than 2 percent a year during 1985–95 as adjustment programs went into effect and commodity prices recovered. Still, the weak growth and export performance of HIPCs stands in sharp contrast to that of other developing countries.

Much of this poor performance can be attributed to civil disturbances, weak governance, poor macroeconomic policies, and deep-seated structural problems, including neglected physical infrastructure, inadequate health care and nutrition, unskilled workforces, and weak institutions. In addition, HIPCs suffered large external shocks in the 1980s. These countries rely on primary commodities for their export earnings and were hit particularly hard by a large and sustained decline in non-oil commodity prices from their peak levels at the end of the 1970s. Although commodity prices have recovered over the past three years, overall these countries have suffered large terms of trade losses since 1980.

Table 5.1 Growth and export performance of heavily indebted poor countries and developing countries, 1980–95

(annual percentage growth in constant 1987 prices)

Category	1980–85	1985–90	1990–95	1980–95
Exports				
Heavily indebted poor countries[a]	−0.8	2.7	2.2	1.5
Other developing countries	3.5	6.9	6.3	5.5
GDP				
Heavily indebted poor countries[a]	1.3	2.2	1.0	1.6
Other developing countries	2.6	3.8	3.4	3.3

a. Excludes Nigeria.
Source: World Bank staff estimates.

Figure 5.1 Heavily indebted poor countries have received sizable net flows and net transfers from creditors

Percentage of recipient GNP

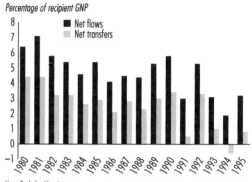

Note: Excludes Nigeria.
Source: World Bank Debtor Reporting System.

Figure 5.2 Grants and foreign direct investment in heavily indebted poor countries are growing

Percentage of recipient GNP

Note: Excludes Nigeria.
Source: World Bank Debtor Reporting System.

Falling commodity prices in the early 1980s prompted many poor countries to increase their external borrowing, both to finance domestic investment and to cushion their economies against the associated loss of foreign exchange earnings. Most commercial banks stopped lending to these countries once the debt crisis began, however, and most of the new lending came from official sources. As a result, nearly all HIPCs received large net flows and net transfers from external creditors (figure 5.1). Over the past fifteen years net resource flows—inflows of finance net of principal repayments—averaged 2–7 percent of recipient GNP. Net transfers from creditors, which are inflows net of both principal and interest payments, were usually 1–5 percent of recipient GNP, although net transfers were slightly negative in 1994. HIPCs have received far more financial support from creditors than they have repaid, and official creditors have provided substantial resources to finance domestic investment and consumption in these countries.

In addition to net transfers from creditors, HIPCs have received substantial grants from donors as well as foreign direct investment (figure 5.2). Grants have increased sharply since the late 1980s and recently averaged 7–8 percent of GNP. Foreign direct investment flows also have increased, to about 1 percent of GNP. Over the past fifteen years net transfers from creditors and donors totaled about 7 percent of GNP.

Despite high net transfers, all the HIPCs, except the Lao People's Democratic Republic, Myanmar, Rwanda, and Sâo Tomé and Principe, have rescheduled their debt since 1980. The surge in borrowing, coupled with increasing reliance on rescheduling and refinancing, increased the nominal stock of debt of HIPCs from $55 billion in 1980 to $183 billion in 1990. Since 1990 the stock of debt has grown more slowly, though by the end of 1995 it had reached $215 billion. The slowdown reflected a shift toward greater provision of grants, concessional rescheduling of loans, commercial bank debt reduction, and widespread forgiveness of official development assistance loans. Still, the external debt stock of HIPCs was more than twice the average value of their exports in 1993–95, and in several countries was more than ten times the value of exports.

Unlike the debt of middle-income countries, however, a sizable portion of the debt of most HIPCs has been contracted on concessional terms, so the interest rate charged on these loans is below prevailing market rates. Because of concessionality, the face value of external debt relative to exports overstates the debt burden. The ratio of the present value of future debt service obligations to exports is a better indicator of these countries' debt burdens.

In early 1996 World Bank and IMF staff assessed the outlook for debt sustainability in HIPCs (table 5.2). The analysis projected the likely economic performance of HIPCs if they followed sound economic policies and continued structural reforms. Projections included an assessment of the likely availability of external finance—including new concessional lending, aid flows, and private flows—for each country and the estimated effects of concessional debt relief (under Naples terms) from the Paris Club and comparable treatment from other bilateral and commercial creditors.

Countries were classified as having sustainable debt burdens if the projections indicated that within five years the ratio of the net present value of debt to exports would fall below 200 percent and the ratio of debt service to exports would fall below 20 percent. Countries were rated as having unsustainable debt burdens if their debt ratios exceeded 250 percent and 25 percent after ten years. The group of countries falling between these categories was classified as possibly stressed. Three countries—Liberia, Nigeria, and Somalia—were not assessed. It is important to note that this classification does not constitute an assessment of debt sustainability under the HIPC Debt Initiative. Under that initiative debt sustainability will be determined through joint analysis by the World Bank, the IMF, and the country concerned (box 5.1).

This preliminary assessment did not attempt to identify the ways in which large debt overhangs undermine growth and economic performance. Still, it is widely accepted that a large external debt burden constrains economic growth by removing incentives for investment and discouraging policy reforms. For countries whose stock of debt exceeds their repayment capacity, future debt service levels will depend on future output levels. The higher is the level of output, the more the country will be expected to pay. This implicit tax can discourage private investment. At the same time policymakers

---

Box 5.1 Determining a country's debt sustainability

• A debt sustainability analysis will be prepared by World Bank and IMF staff, together with the officials of the debtor country, to determine if the country faces an unsustainable debt burden after the full application of Naples terms and comparable treatment by other creditors.
• Sustainable debt levels will be defined as a ratio of debt to exports (on a present value basis) of 200–250 percent and a ratio of debt service to exports of 20–25 percent, by the completion point.
• Specific targets will be based on country vulnerability factors, such as the concentration and variability of exports, with particular attention to fiscal indicators of the burden of debt service.

Table 5.2 Preliminary assessments of debt sustainability for heavily indebted poor countries

Sustainable	Possibly stressed	Unsustainable	Not assessed
Angola	Bolivia	Burundi	Liberia
Benin	Cameroon	Guinea-Bissau	Nigeria
Burkina Faso	Congo	Mozambique	Somalia
Central African Republic	Côte d'Ivoire	Nicaragua	
Chad	Ethiopia	Sâo Tomé and Principe	
Equatorial Guinea	Guyana	Sudan	
Ghana	Madagascar	Zaire	
Guinea	Myanmar	Zambia	
Honduras	Niger		
Kenya	Rwanda		
Lao PDR	Tanzania		
Mali	Uganda		
Mauritania			
Senegal			
Sierra Leone			
Togo			
Vietnam			
Yemen, Rep. of			

Note: As of January 1996.
Source: IMF and World Bank staff estimates.

are likely to find it difficult to implement policy reforms if foreign creditors receive most of the benefits in the form of higher debt repayments. By permanently reducing the value of future claims, lifting the debt overhang improves the incentive to invest and broadens domestic support for policy reforms.

A second argument in favor of debt reduction is that repeated debt reschedulings create considerable uncertainty about future debt service burdens. Such uncertainty may generate instability in the indebted economy, discouraging domestic investment.[2]

In many HIPCs the negative impact of external debt seems to come more from the growing debt stock rather than from the excessive burden of debt service actually paid. Nearly all HIPCs continue to receive large positive net flows and net transfers from external creditors and donors. Thus there is a basic difference between the commercial bank debt crisis of the 1980s and the (largely) official debt problem of HIPCs. Once debt restructuring packages were in place, most commercial banks stopped providing credit to countries saddled by debt (at least until the restoration of commercial creditworthiness). But official agencies, both bilateral donors and multilateral institutions, continue to provide financial support for the reform efforts of poor countries that have poor chances of accessing private capital markets. Thus debt relief for HIPCs must support the continuing role of official creditors and donors in providing concessional assistance to debtors.

What is the HIPC Debt Initiative?

The HIPC Debt Initiative is a program designed to facilitate a comprehensive resolution to the debt problems of heavily indebted poor countries that are eligible to borrow only from the International Development Association (IDA), have a track record of sustained economic reform, and are found to have an unsustainable debt burden even after traditional debt relief mechanisms are applied. Because the initiative requires participation by all relevant creditors, debt relief efforts will have to be closely coordinated.

The initiative is guided by six principles:
• The objective is to achieve overall debt sustainability, allowing each country to exit from continuous rescheduling.

• Action will be undertaken only when a debtor has proved its ability to make good use of whatever exceptional support is provided.
• New measures will build, as much as possible, on existing mechanisms for dealing with payment difficulties (such as Paris Club procedures).
• Actions will be coordinated among all creditors, with broad and equitable participation.
• Any debt relief provided by multilateral creditors will preserve their financial integrity and preferred creditor status.
• New external finance for HIPCs will be on appropriately concessional terms.

Thus the initiative can be viewed as an evolution of the widely accepted debt relief strategy that emphasizes providing all debtors with assistance in reducing debt to a sustainable level in present value terms. Implementation for each country is necessarily complex and will correspond to country performance (figure 5.3).

In the first stage HIPCs are expected to establish a three-year track record of good economic performance, which is needed to qualify for a stock-of-debt (that is, debt reduction) operation on Naples terms from Paris Club creditors. During the third year of the first stage of the initiative, a preliminary agreement on the country's medium-term macroeconomic framework and debt sustainability analysis will be reached between the government and World Bank and IMF staff. Based on that agreement an assessment will be made on whether the country is likely to be eligible to take part in the initiative (see box 5.1).

If the analysis shows that a rescheduling on Naples terms by Paris Club creditors and comparable treatment by other bilateral and commercial creditors is sufficient to achieve debt sustainability within three years (the completion point), the debtor country will seek a stock-of-debt operation and exit from further rescheduling.

If the analysis shows that the country faces an unsustainable debt burden, Bank and IMF staff will assess the amount of assistance needed to achieve a sustainable debt position at the completion point. In most cases the completion point is about three years later, although in exceptional cases this period may be shortened to take into account a country's track record of sustained performance.

Figure 5.3 How does the HIPC Debt Initiative work?

First stage

- *Paris Club* provides flow rescheduling on Naples terms (up to 67 percent reduction, on a net present value basis).
- *Other* bilateral and commercial creditors provide comparable treatment.
- *Multilateral institutions* continue to provide adjustment support in the framework of Bank- and IMF-supported adjustment program.
- *Country* establishes first three-year track record of good performance.

Decision point

- Paris Club stock-of-debt operation on Naples terms and comparable treatment by other bilateral and commercial creditors is adequate for the country to achieve sustainability by the completion point — country not eligible for HIPC Debt Initiative.

- Paris Club stock-of-debt operation (on Naples terms) is not sufficient for the country's overall debt to become sustainable by the completion point — country requests additional support under the HIPC Debt Initiative, and executive boards determine eligibility.

- Where there is doubt about whether sustainability would be achieved by the completion point under a Paris Club stock-of-debt operation (on Naples terms), the country receives a further flow rescheduling on Naples terms.
  If the outcome at the completion point is better than or as projected, the country receives a stock-of-debt operation on Naples terms from Paris Club creditors.
  If the outcome at the completion point is worse than projected, the country could receive additional support under the HIPC Debt Initiative.

Second stage

- *Paris Club* provides more concessional flow rescheduling as needed (up to 80 percent reduction in debt on a net present value basis).
- *Other* bilateral and commercial creditors provide comparable treatment.
- *Donors and multilateral institutions* provide enhanced support.
- *Country* establishes a second track record of good performance under Bank- and IMF-supported programs.

Completion point

- *Paris Club* provides deeper stock-of-debt reduction as needed (up to 80 percent reduction in debt on a net present value basis).
- *Other* bilateral and commercial creditors provide comparable treatment.
- *Multilateral institutions* take such additional measures, as needed, for the country to reach a sustainable level of debt, choosing from a menu of options and ensuring broad and equitable participation.

Source: World Bank staff.

Bank and IMF staff will consult with other creditors to determine the level of funding that could be made available under the HIPC initiative.

After the consultations IMF and Bank staff will make a recommendation to their boards on the country's eligibility for assistance under the initiative, appropriate targets for key debt indicators at the completion point, and the contributions from multilateral institutions needed to achieve these targets.[3]

Once the Bank and IMF boards determine that a country is eligible for support under the initiative, arrangements will be put in place to secure financing for the program. The country will seek support from Paris Club creditors and comparable relief from other bilateral and commercial creditors. Multilateral institutions will be expected to confirm their willingness to provide assistance at the completion point, and donor financing for the initiative will be mobilized. The country's progress on macroeconomic and structural reforms and sound policies will be kept under review.

As a country approaches the completion point, the government and IMF and World Bank will update the debt sustainability analysis to reflect the country's debt burden based on exports at that time.

- *Results within the target range.* If debt indicators fall into the ranges established at the decision point, creditors will begin taking the measures promised at that time.

• *Better or worse than expected outcomes.* If debt indicators are higher than initially projected (by more than a small margin), creditors will be expected to increase their support to reach the debt sustainability targets. If debt indicators are lower than projected because of an extraordinary improvement in the country's economic circumstances due to external events rather than to the country's own policy performance, creditor support may be reduced, consistent with achieving the original targets.

Bank and IMF staff have estimated that full implementation of the initiative may require debt relief of $5.5 billion, with more than $3 billion coming from multilateral institutions. These estimates, however, are extremely sensitive to assumptions about the targets set for countries to be judged as having sustainable debt burdens—especially projected export growth. For example, a 2 percentage point reduction in the growth of export earnings below the baseline projections might raise the cost of the initiative by more than $2 billion, with most of the additional costs borne by multilateral creditors.

In conclusion, the HIPC Debt Initiative maps out a way to achieve debt sustainability for the poorest, most heavily indebted countries, based on the indispensable element of a track record of adjustment and continued reform of domestic policies. Debt sustainability analyses are now well advanced for about half a dozen HIPCs that could move to a decision point during the first half of 1997.

Notes

1. Forty-one countries are classified as heavily indebted poor countries: Angola, Benin, Bolivia, Burkina Faso, Burundi, Cameroon, Central African Republic, Chad, Congo, Côte d'Ivoire, Equatorial Guinea, Ethiopia, Ghana, Guinea, Guinea-Bissau, Guyana, Honduras, Kenya, Lao People's Democratic Republic, Liberia, Madagascar, Mali, Mauritania, Mozambique, Myanmar, Nicaragua, Niger, Nigeria, Rwanda, Sâo Tomé and Principe, Senegal, Sierra Leone, Somalia, Sudan, Tanzania, Togo, Uganda, Vietnam, Republic of Yemen, Zaire, and Zambia. Of these, thirty-two are classified as severely indebted low-income countries, seven have received concessional treatment from the Paris Club, and two are lower-middle-income countries that have recently become International Development Association (IDA)–only countries (Angola and Congo). Nigeria has been excluded from the aggregate data on heavily indebted poor countries reported on in this chapter because it is not an IDA-only country and has never received concessional debt rescheduling from the Paris Club.

2. Stijn Claessens, Daniel Oks, and Sweder Van Wijnbergen, 1993. "Interest Rates, Growth, and External Debt: The Macroeconomic Impact of Mexico's Brady Deal," Policy Research Working Paper 1147, World Bank, International Economics Department, Washington, D.C.

3. For borderline cases where there is uncertainty that a stock-of-debt operation on Naples terms would result in a sustainable debt burden, countries would have the option of seeking a further flow rescheduling of debt service falling due from Paris Club creditors and deferring action on a stock-of-debt operation for three additional years. This option would leave open the possibility of receiving additional assistance from creditors if it were needed to meet debt sustainability targets.

Part II

Appendixes

Debt burden indicators and country classifications

The 136 countries that report debt data to the World Bank's Debtor Reporting System (DRS) are classified by degree of indebtedness, which is measured using debt and debt service data taken from Bank DRS files and GNP and export data as shown in the country tables in volume 2. Export figures are earnings from goods and services, including worker remittances. Data on official grants are not included, although they may be a stable source of foreign exchange in some countries.

World Debt Tables 1992–93 introduced a new methodology for country classification. Until then, three-year averaged ratios were used based on scheduled debt service and nominal value of debt. The new methodology uses present (rather than nominal) value of scheduled debt service in order to account for differing borrowing terms on the country's long-term liabilities (see *World Debt Tables 1993–94*, volume 1, appendix 4). This methodology was used again this year by calculating the average of the ratios for 1993, 1994, and 1995. This approach provides a broad sense of the relative rankings of countries, but the results are sensitive to the precise methodology used for calculating present value ratios. This methodology is being refined in the context of the Debt Initiative for the Heavily Indebted Poor Countries (HIPCs). The impact of these refinements on country classifications will be taken into account in next year's *Global Development Finance*.

Indebtedness is classified based on two ratios, the ratio of present value of total debt service to GNP and the ratio of present value of total debt service to exports. These ratios cast a country's level of indebtedness in terms of two important aspects of its potential capacity to service the debt: exports (because they provide foreign exchange to service debt) and GNP (because it is the broadest measure of the income generation in an economy).

Classification of countries for 1996

If either of these ratios for a particular country exceeds a critical value—80 percent for present value of debt service to GNP and 220 percent for present value of debt service to exports—the country is classified as severely indebted. These ratios have been set on the basis of country experience with debt servicing difficulties. If the critical value is not exceeded but either ratio is three-fifths or more of the critical value (that is, 48 percent for the present value of debt service to GNP and 132 percent for the present value of debt service to exports), the country is classified as moderately indebted. If both ratios are less than three-fifths of the critical value, the country is classified as less indebted. Countries are further classified as low income if 1995 GNP per capita is $765 or less and as middle income if 1995 GNP per capita is more than $765 but less than $9,386.

Combining these criteria leads to the identification of severely indebted low-income countries (SILICs), severely indebted middle-income countries (SIMICs), moderately indebted low-income countries (MILICs), moderately indebted middle-income countries (MIMICs), less-indebted low-income countries (LILICs), and less-indebted middle-income countries (LIMICs; table A1.1).

The use of critical values for defining the boundaries between indebtedness categories means that changes in country classifications should be interpreted with caution. If a country has an indicator that is close to the critical value, a small change in the indicator may trigger a change in indebtedness classification even though economic fundamentals may not have changed significantly. Accordingly, the use of critical values for defining the boundary points between the indebtedness classifications implies a greater degree of precision in the exercise than is warranted by their

Table A1.1 Income and indebtedness classification criteria

	Indebtedness classification		
Income classification	PV/XGS higher than 220 percent or PV/GNP higher than 80 percent	PV/XGS less than 220 percent but higher than 132 percent or PV/GNP less than 80 percent but higher than 48 percent	PV/XGS less than 132 percent and PV/GNP less than 48 percent
Low-income: GNP per capita less than $765	Severely indebted low-income countries	Moderately indebted low-income countries	Less-indebted low-income countries
Middle-income: GNP per capita between $766 and $9,386	Severely indebted middle-income countries	Moderately indebted middle-income countries	Less-indebted middle-income countries

Note: PV/XGS is present value of debt service to exports of goods and services. PV/GNP is present value of debt service to GNP.
Source: World Bank.

capacity to signal discrete changes in the burden of country indebtedness.

Moreover, these indicators do not represent an exhaustive set of useful indicators of external debt. They may not, for example, adequately capture the debt servicing capacity of countries in which government budget constraints are key to debt service difficulties. Governments can face budget difficulties that are related to service of external public debt but are not necessarily reflected in balance of payments data. But rising external debt may not necessarily imply payment difficulties, especially if debt obligations are incurred by the private sector or if there is a commensurate rise in the country's debt servicing capacity. These indicators should be used in the broader context of a country-specific analysis of debt sustainability.

Discount rates used in calculating present value are interest rates charged by OECD countries for officially supported export credits. They represent, on average, the most favorable terms for fixed-rate nonconcessional debt that countries are able to contract in international loan markets. The rates are specified for G-7 currencies—British pounds, Canadian dollars, French francs, German marks, Italian lire, Japanese yen, and U.S. dollars. IBRD loans and IDA credits are discounted by the most recent IBRD lending rate; IMF loans are discounted at the SDR lending rate. For debt denominated in other currencies, discount rates are the average of interest rates on export credits charged by other OECD countries (see *World Debt Tables 1993–94* for methodology of present value calculations).

In present value calculations, debt service on fixed-rate loans is determined and each payment discounted to compute its present value. For variable-rate loans, for which the future debt service

payment cannot be precisely determined, debt service is calculated using the rate as of the end of 1995 for the base specified for the loan.

Classification of low-income countries

Applying the *World Debt Tables 1992–93* present value methodology to 1993–95 data, thirty-seven countries are classified as SILICs, twelve as MILICs, and eleven as LILICs (table A1.2). There are four changes from last year in the indebtedness classification of low-income countries: Malawi joined the severely indebted group (because of a decline in GNP and exports), Burkina Faso joined the moderately indebted group (because of an increase in the ratio of present value of debt to exports), and Albania and Nepal joined the less indebted group (because of improvements in debt to exports ratios).

Classification of middle-income countries

In the middle-income group, twelve countries are classified as SIMICs, nineteen as MIMICs, and forty-three as LIMICs. There were eight changes in the indebtedness classification since last year. Five countries joined the moderately indebted group: Algeria and Poland (because of declines in present value of debt to exports ratios) and Macedonia FYR, St. Vincent, and Trinidad and Tobago (because of increases in present value of debt to exports ratios). Cape Verde and the Dominican Republic moved to the less indebted category (because of declines in present value of debt to exports ratios). In addition, the Republic of Korea, previously classified as a LIMIC, was reclassified as a high-income country, and thus is no longer included in *Global Development Finance.*

Table A1.2 Classification of DRS economies

Severely indebted low-income	Severely indebted middle-income	Moderately indebted low-income	Moderately indebted middle-income	Less-indebted low-income	Less-indebted middle-income
Angola[a]	Argentina	Bangladesh	Algeria[b]	Albania[b]	Barbados
Burundi	Bolivia	Benin	Egypt, Arab Rep.[a]	Armenia	Belarus
Cambodia	Brazil	Burkina Faso[c]	Chile	Azerbaijan	Belize
Cameroon	Bulgaria	Chad	Colombia	Bhutan	Botswana
Central African Rep.	Ecuador	Comoros	Hungary	China	Cape Verde[b]
Congo	Gabon	Gambia, The	Indonesia	Georgia	Costa Rica
Côte d'Ivoire	Jamaica	Haiti	Macedonia, FYR[c]	Kyrgyz Rep.	Croatia
Equatorial Guinea	Jordan	India	Morocco	Mongolia	Czech Rep.
Ethiopia	Mexico	Lao PDR	Papua New Guinea	Nepal[b]	Djibouti
Ghana	Panama	Pakistan	Philippines	Sri Lanka	Dominica
Guinea	Peru	Senegal	Poland[b]	Tajikistan	Dominican Republic[b]
Guinea-Bissau	Syrian Arab Rep.	Zimbabwe	Russian Federation		El Salvador
Guyana			St. Vincent[c]		Estonia
Honduras			Trinidad and Tobago[c]		Fiji
Kenya			Tunisia		Grenada
Liberia			Turkey		Guatemala
Madagascar			Uruguay		Iran, Islamic Republic
Malawi[c]			Venezuela		Kazakstan
Mali			Western Samoa		Latvia
Mauritania					Lebanon
Mozambique					Lesotho[a]
Myanmar					Lithuania
Nicaragua					Malaysia
Niger					Maldives
Nigeria					Malta
Rwanda					Mauritius
São Tomé and Principe					Moldova
Sierra Leone					Oman
Somalia					Paraguay
Sudan					Romania
Tanzania					Seychelles
Togo					Slovak Republic
Uganda					Slovenia
Vietnam					Solomon Islands
Yemen Republic					St. Kitts and Nevis
Zaire					St. Lucia
Zambia					Swaziland
					Thailand
					Tonga
					Turkmenistan
					Ukraine
					Uzbekistan
					Vanuatu

a. Countries whose income classification has changed.
b. Countries whose indebtedness has decreased.
c. Countries whose indebtedness has increased.
Note: This table classifies all World Bank member economies with populations of more than 30,000. Economies are divided among income groups according to 1995 GNP per capita, calculated using the *World Bank Atlas* method. Income groups are defined as follows: low-income, $765 or less; lower-middle-income, $766–3,035; upper-middle-income, $3,036–9,385; and high-income, $9,386 or more. Estimates for economies of the former Soviet Union are preliminary, and their classification will be kept under review. The table excludes Bosnia and Herzegovina and the Federal Republic of Yugoslavia because of lack of data over a three-year period.
Source: World Bank Debtor Reporting System.

Table A1.3 Classification of non-DRS economies

Severely indebted low-income	Severely indebted middle-income	Moderately indebted middle-income	Less-indebted middle-income	
Afghanistan	Cuba	Gibraltar	Antigua and Barbuda	Namibia
	Iraq	Greece	Bahrain	Saudi Arabia
			Kiribati	South Africa
			Korea, Dem. Rep.	Suriname
			Libya	

Note: This table classifies all World Bank member economies with populations of more than 30,000. Economies are divided among income groups according to 1995 GNP per capita, calculated using the *World Bank Atlas* method. Income groups are defined as follows: low-income, $765 or less; lower-middle-income, $766–3,035; upper-middle-income, $3,036–9,385; and high-income, $9,386 or more.
Source: World Bank Debtor Reporting System.

Table A1.4 Major economic indicators, 1995

(millions of U.S. dollars)

Country	EDT	PV	TDS	INT	XGS	GNP
Albania	709	720	7	6	761	2,245
Algeria	32,610	25,078	4,380	1,831	12,345	39,265
Angola	11,482	10,859	458	130	3,653	4,176
Argentina	89,747	83,044	9,732	5,372	28,027	271,408
Armenia	374	291	9	8	313	2,122
Azerbaijan	321	277	10	10	—	3,475
Bangladesh	16,370	9,153	729	186	5,490	29,069
Barbados	597	598	119	42	—	1,683
Belarus	1,648	1,330	180	72	4,946	20,803
Belize	261	220	37	11	302	555
Benin	1,646	920	49	23	577	2,013
Bhutan	87	43	9	2	—	297
Bolivia	5,266	3,899	372	173	1,284	5,810
Bosnia and Herzegovina	—	—	—	—	381	2,323
Botswana	699	559	92	28	2,908	4,278
Brazil	159,139	151,853	22,328	11,177	58,989	663,589
Bulgaria	10,887	10,295	1,256	594	6,680	11,790
Burkina Faso	1,267	646	48	19	366	2,305
Burundi	1,157	523	39	12	140	1,051
Cambodia	2,031	1,436	6	2	989	2,762
Cameroon	9,350	7,482	423	211	2,763	7,516
Cape Verde	213	134	6	3	183	383
Central African Rep.	944	504	16	6	234	—
Chad	908	442	16	6	268	1,117
Chile	25,562	24,410	5,150	1,487	20,014	59,059
China	118,090	107,890	15,066	5,996	152,781	685,874
Colombia	20,760	19,878	3,778	1,380	14,966	73,705
Comoros	203	110	1	1	106	228
Congo	6,032	5,357	181	97	1,252	1,649
Costa Rica	3,799	3,534	646	250	3,945	8,930
Côte d'Ivoire	18,952	16,596	1,046	421	4,527	7,530
Croatia	3,662	3,255	419	153	7,375	17,998
Czech Republic	16,576	16,104	2,569	915	24,579	44,750
Djibouti	260	157	10	5	212	—
Dominica	93	60	7	2	112	218
Dominican Republic	4,259	3,855	428	193	3,315	11,657
Ecuador	13,957	12,573	1,416	666	5,298	16,597
Egypt	34,116	25,860	2,395	1,400	16,397	46,525
El Salvador	2,583	2,103	281	123	3,164	9,569
Equatorial Guinea	293	217	2	1	85	150
Estonia	309	286	21	14	2,801	4,604
Ethiopia	5,221	3,435	155	63	1,140	5,227
Fiji	253	225	67	16	1,141	1,805
Gabon	4,492	3,587	442	226	2,802	3,694
Gambia, The	426	214	25	5	181	—
Georgia	1,189	1,022	20	20	—	2,303
Ghana	5,874	3,776	370	97	1,603	6,179
Grenada	113	85	7	2	—	267
Guatemala	3,275	2,796	342	148	3,226	14,708
Guinea	3,242	2,104	181	47	715	3,553
Guinea-Bissau	894	582	16	6	48	253
Guyana	2,105	1,583	109	35	641	558
Haiti	807	396	94	32	209	2,026
Honduras	4,567	3,707	553	217	1,787	3,664
Hungary	31,248	31,060	7,021	2,111	17,939	42,924
India	93,766	75,019	13,123	4,624	46,600	331,941
Indonesia	107,831	103,202	16,419	6,219	53,134	189,370
Iran	21,935	20,403	—	—	19,140	—
Jamaica	4,270	3,895	673	233	3,770	3,165
Jordan	7,944	6,822	610	271	4,850	6,296

(table continues on next page)

53

Table A1.4 Major economic indicators, 1995 (continued)
(millions of U.S. dollars)

Country	EDT	PV	TDS	INT	XGS	GNP
Kazakstan	3,712	3,437	243	139	6,110	15,771
Kenya	7,381	5,466	765	257	2,974	7,557
Kyrgyz Republic	610	451	60	24	—	3,028
Lao PDR	2,165	743	26	7	453	1,734
Latvia	462	430	34	24	2,151	6,047
Lebanon	2,966	2,883	245	141	1,942	11,646
Lesotho	659	385	40	15	606	1,479
Liberia	2,127	1,963	2	2	—	—
Lithuania	802	705	44	31	3,243	7,976
Macedonia, FYR	1,213	1,044	32	11	1,450	1,844
Madagascar	4,302	3,189	70	27	765	3,037
Malawi	2,140	1,018	108	40	428	1,284
Malaysia	34,352	31,079	6,532	1,591	84,212	80,585
Maldives	155	92	11	4	152	252
Mali	3,066	1,805	80	25	656	2,324
Malta	955	911	75	42	3,198	—
Mauritania	2,467	1,685	116	38	538	1,014
Mauritius	1,801	1,631	216	73	2,402	3,920
Mexico	165,743	159,221	23,556	11,126	97,201	237,090
Moldova	691	622	69	30	865	3,874
Mongolia	512	329	47	10	511	833
Morocco	22,147	19,923	3,541	1,377	11,022	31,203
Mozambique	5,781	4,429	173	83	485	1,303
Myanmar	5,771	4,688	250	70	—	—
Nepal	2,398	1,180	94	33	1,211	4,497
Nicaragua	9,287	8,194	282	87	730	1,575
Niger	1,633	1,016	58	15	286	1,791
Nigeria	35,005	32,948	1,571	762	12,754	24,912
Oman	3,107	2,949	486	204	6,442	10,531
Pakistan	30,152	23,401	3,145	1,197	11,692	60,932
Panama	7,180	7,681	373	202	9,614	7,083
Papua New Guinea	2,431	2,057	626	113	3,014	4,559
Paraguay	2,288	2,120	284	129	4,256	7,784
Peru	30,831	29,739	1,182	663	7,717	56,938
Philippines	39,445	37,802	5,328	2,327	32,398	76,566
Poland	42,291	35,740	4,069	1,789	33,215	117,057
Romania	6,653	6,253	967	292	9,098	34,180
Russian Federation	120,461	111,632	6,303	3,028	95,100	320,297
Rwanda	1,008	480	20	9	153	1,131
São Tomé and Principe	277	142	2	1	13	40
Senegal	3,845	2,510	296	74	1,714	4,676
Seychelles	164	134	21	7	292	479
Sierre Leone	1,226	768	77	21	105	768
Slovak Republic	5,826	5,432	1,083	270	11,188	17,377
Slovenia	3,489	3,368	723	191	10,487	18,680
Solomon Islands	157	107	8	2	—	350
Somalia	2,678	2,213	1	1	—	—
Sri Lanka	8,230	5,570	409	160	5,866	12,777
St. Kitts and Nevis	56	40	7	2	—	209
St. Lucia	128	99	12	6	376	525
St. Vincent	206	177	10	6	144	246
Sudan	17,623	16,206	69	15	—	—
Swaziland	251	170	23	6	1,038	1,048
Syrian Arab Republic	21,318	18,699	293	201	6,329	15,810
Tajikistan	665	627	—	—	657	1,902
Tanzania	7,333	5,389	218	86	1,253	3,536
Thailand	56,789	57,480	7,533	2,831	74,093	162,686
Togo	1,486	917	30	12	320	1,227
Tonga	70	42	3	1	—	172

(table continues on next page)

Table A1.4 Major economic indicators, 1995 (continued)

(millions of U.S. dollars)

Country	EDT	PV	TDS	INT	XGS	GNP
Trinidad and Tobago	2,555	2,489	431	181	2,906	4,772
Tunisia	9,938	8,928	1,490	542	8,778	17,331
Turkey	73,592	67,178	11,476	4,443	41,396	166,740
Turkmenistan	393	368	99	24	—	3,919
Uganda	3,564	1,868	137	38	642	5,597
Ukraine	8,434	7,881	922	501	17,337	78,963
Uruguay	5,307	5,117	865	379	3,679	16,380
Uzbekistan	1,630	1,494	223	74	4,618	21,590
Vanuatu	48	25	2	1	129	213
Venezuela	35,842	34,242	4,867	2,403	22,406	73,184
Vietnam	26,495	23,319	386	169	6,691	20,351
Western Samoa	162	73	5	2	108	197
Yemen, Republic of	6,212	5,109	102	37	3,234	4,002
Yugoslavia	13,839	13,574	—	—	—	—
Zaire	13,137	11,630	25	24	—	5,147
Zambia	6,853	4,963	2,616	549	1,296	3,581
Zimbabwe	4,885	4,016	651	240	—	6,190

— Not available

Note: Exports of goods and services have been adjusted to reflect staff estimates of exports, reexports, or worker remittances in order to present a clearer picture of debt servicing capacity for Comoros (adjusted exports $0.06 billion), Haiti (adjusted exports $0.4 billion), and Mexico (adjusted exports $53.4 billion). For definition of indicators, see *Sources and Definitions* section.

Source: World Bank Debtor Reporting System.

Table A1.5 Key indebtedness ratios, 1993–95

(percent)

Country	EDT/XGS	PV/XGS	EDT/GNP	PV/GNP	TDS/XGS	INT/XGS
Albania	140	128	44	41	1	1
Algeria	247	208	71	59	51	14
Angola	341	318	300	280	9	3
Argentina	359	325	30	27	34	19
Armenia	94	82	12	10	2	2
Azerbaijan	—	—	4	4	—	—
Bangladesh	349	187	60	32	14	4
Barbados	66	65	36	35	12	5
Belarus	37	29	6	4	3	1
Belize	74	60	41	34	9	3
Benin	293	157	88	47	7	4
Bhutan	89	46	33	17	8	2
Bolivia	427	321	88	66	31	14
Bosnia and Herzegovina	—	—	—	—	—	—
Botswana	27	21	17	13	4	1
Brazil	289	273	29	27	31	14
Bulgaria	210	197	108	101	13	6
Burkina Faso	319	163	52	27	12	5
Burundi	996	439	113	50	35	11
Cambodia	354	264	79	58	3	2
Cameroon	346	262	106	80	18	8
Cape Verde	124	75	53	32	4	2
Central African Rep.	456	240	85	45	8	4
Chad	379	184	80	38	8	4
Chile	154	146	46	44	23	8
China	84	75	19	17	10	4
Colombia	148	142	30	29	28	10
Comoros	320	168	82	43	3	2
Congo	479	412	329	283	26	12
Costa Rica	112	102	48	43	16	6
Côte d'Ivoire	504	429	271	231	31	13
Croatia	46	42	21	19	6	2
Czech Republic	57	58	32	33	10	3
Djibouti	105	62	—	—	4	2
Dominica	80	49	43	26	6	2
Dominican Republic	142	128	43	39	13	6
Ecuador	322	299	95	88	24	11
Egypt	204	146	77	55	14	8
El Salvador	89	69	28	21	12	5
Equatorial Guinea	415	300	210	152	2	1
Estonia	11	10	5	5	1	1
Ethiopia	563	362	95	61	13	5
Fiji	27	24	17	15	7	2
Gabon	153	118	108	84	11	6
Gambia, The	201	103	117	61	13	3
Georgia	—	—	44	39	—	—
Ghana	384	242	87	55	25	8
Grenada	88	67	48	36	6	2
Guatemala	116	96	24	20	12	5
Guinea	430	275	93	60	17	6
Guinea-Bissau	1,857	1,250	351	235	22	8
Guyana	346	254	447	328	17	6
Haiti	330	187	45	25	8	3
Honduras	291	232	130	104	30	12
Hungary	211	205	69	68	42	13
India	249	191	33	25	27	11
Indonesia	208	193	58	54	32	12
Iran	116	110	32	31	20	6
Jamaica	133	116	116	102	19	7

(table continues on next page)

Table A1.5 Key indebtedness ratios, 1993–95 (continued)
(percent)

Country	EDT/XGS	PV/XGS	EDT/GNP	PV/GNP	TDS/XGS	INT/XGS
Jordan	179	149	135	113	14	6
Kazakstan	57	53	15	14	2	1
Kenya	274	201	116	85	28	11
Kyrgyz Republic	—	—	14	11	—	—
Lao PDR	—	165	—	42	—	—
Latvia	19	17	6	5	1	1
Lebanon	122	119	20	20	12	7
Lesotho	101	56	44	25	6	2
Liberia	408	373	137	125	3	1
Lithuania	20	18	7	6	2	1
Macedonia, FYR	80	75	60	56	5	1
Madagascar	630	457	135	98	11	4
Malawi	512	236	140	65	22	8
Malaysia	45	40	43	39	9	2
Maldives	83	49	58	35	6	2
Mali	501	287	128	73	15	5
Malta	30	28	28	26	2	1
Mauritania	502	340	244	165	25	9
Mauritius	65	57	40	35	8	3
Mexico	343	327	43	41	56	22
Moldova	72	65	12	11	4	2
Mongolia	101	67	63	42	8	2
Morocco	217	194	75	67	34	13
Mozambique	1,338	1,003	444	333	34	17
Myanmar	526	407	—	—	14	8
Nepal	224	109	54	26	8	3
Nicaragua	2,050	1,863	726	657	36	16
Niger	563	338	90	53	25	7
Nigeria	284	262	123	114	14	8
Oman	49	46	30	28	9	3
Pakistan	260	196	50	37	29	10
Panama	82	80	111	107	4	2
Papua New Guinea	94	79	58	49	27	5
Paraguay	58	52	26	23	8	3
Peru	431	395	56	51	30	13
Philippines	157	147	59	55	20	9
Poland	188	159	45	38	12	5
Romania	74	69	18	17	8	3
Russian Federation	152	134	48	43	5	2
Rwanda	745	346	87	40	9	5
São Tomé and Principe	2,227	1,160	620	321	23	12
Senegal	246	161	83	55	14	4
Seychelles	59	48	35	28	7	2
Sierre Leone	991	682	196	137	62	23
Slovak Republic	49	45	32	29	9	3
Slovenia	29	27	17	16	6	2
Solomon Islands	60	40	51	34	4	1
Somalia	6,404	5,191	303	246	1	1
Sri Lanka	157	101	66	43	8	3
St. Kitts and Nevis	41	28	29	20	4	1
St. Lucia	32	24	23	17	3	1
St. Vincent	—	91	—	50	—	3
Sudan	2,703	2,464	290	265	5	1
Swaziland	24	16	24	16	2	1
Syrian Arab Republic	361	304	146	123	6	4
Tajikistan	97	91	25	23	—	—
Tanzania	726	525	205	148	22	10
Thailand	82	80	35	34	12	4
Togo	533	330	128	79	10	4

(table continues on next page)

Table A1.5 Key indebtedness ratios, 1993–95 (continued)

(percent)

Country	EDT/XGS	PV/XGS	EDT/GNP	PV/GNP	TDS/XGS	INT/XGS
Tonga	101	58	37	21	5	2
Trinidad and Tobago	100	96	51	49	24	7
Tunisia	125	109	60	52	19	7
Turkey	203	182	44	39	29	12
Turkmenistan	—	—	8	8	—	—
Uganda	929	495	82	43	43	11
Ukraine	34	32	7	6	3	1
Uruguay	150	144	34	33	19	9
Uzbekistan	35	31	6	6	3	1
Vanuatu	39	20	24	12	2	1
Venezuela	188	176	60	56	21	11
Vietnam	509	429	163	138	9	3
Western Samoa	191	96	99	49	6	3
Yemen, Republic of	212	170	169	135	4	1
Yugoslavia	—	—	—	—	—	—
Zaire	701	605	230	199	1	1
Zambia	572	441	200	154	89	23
Zimbabwe	194	157	80	65	27	10

— Not available

Note: Exports of goods and services have been adjusted to reflect staff estimates of exports, reexports, or worker remittances in order to present a clearer picture of debt servicing capacity for Comoros (adjusted exports $0.06 billion), Haiti (adjusted exports $0.4 billion), and Mexico (adjusted exports $53.4 billion), and indebtedness ratios have been adjusted accordingly. For definition of indicators, see *Sources and Definitions* section.
Source: World Bank Debtor Reporting System.

Table A1.6 Classification of economies by income and region, 1997

Income group	Subgroup	Sub-Saharan Africa East and Southern Africa	West Africa	Asia East Asia and Pacific	South Asia	Europe and Central Asia Eastern Europe and Central Asia	Rest of Europe	Middle East and North Africa Middle East	North Africa	Americas

Low-income		Angola
		Burundi
		Comoros
		Eritrea
		Ethiopia
		Kenya
		Madagascar
		Malawi
		Mozambique
		Rwanda
		Somalia
		Sudan
		Tanzania
		Uganda
		Zaire
		Zambia
		Zimbabwe
			Benin
			Burkina Faso
			Cameroon
			Central Afri-
			  can Republic
			Chad
			Congo
			Côte d'Ivoire
			Equatorial Guinea
			Gambia, The
			Ghana
			Guinea
			Guinea-Bissau
			Liberia
			Mali
			Mauritania
			Niger
			Nigeria
			São Tomé
			  and Principe
			Senegal
			Sierra Leone
			Togo
				Cambodia
				China
				Lao PDR
				Mongolia
				Myanmar
				Vietnam
					Afghanistan
					Bangladesh
					Bhutan
					India
					Nepal
					Pakistan
					Sri Lanka
						Albania
						Armenia
						Azerbaijan
						Bosnia and
						  Herzegovina
						Georgia
						Kyrgyz Republic
						Tajikistan
								Yemen, Rep.		Guyana
										Haiti
										Honduras
										Nicaragua

Middle-income	Lower	Botswana
		Djibouti
		Lesotho
		Namibia
		Swaziland
			Cape Verde	Fiji
				Indonesia
				Kiribati
				Korea, Dem.
				  Rep.
				Marshall Islands
				Micronesia,
				  Fed. Sts.
				Papua New
				  Guinea
				Philippines
				Solomon Islands
				Thailand
				Tonga
				Vanuatu
				Western Samoa
					Maldives	Belarus
						Bulgaria
						Estonia
						Kazakstan
						Latvia
						Lithuania
						Macedonia,
						  FYR
						Moldova
						Poland
						Romania
						Russian
						  Federation
						Slovak Republic
						Turkmenistan
						Ukraine
						Uzbekistan
						Yugoslavia,
						  Fed. Rep.[a]
							Turkey	Iran, Islamic
								  Rep.
								Iraq
								Jordan
								Lebanon
								Syrian Arab
								  Republic
								West Bank
								  and Gaza
									Algeria
									Egypt, Arab
									  Rep.
									Morocco
									Tunisia
										Belize
										Bolivia
										Colombia
										Costa Rica
										Cuba
										Dominica
										Dominican
										  Republic
										Ecuador
										El Salvador
										Grenada
										Guatemala
										Jamaica
										Panama
										Paraguay
										Peru
										St. Vincent
										  and the
										  Grenadines
										Suriname
										Venezuela

	Upper	Mauritius
		Mayotte
		Seychelles
		South Africa
			Gabon	American
				  Samoa
				Malaysia
						Croatia
						Czech
						  Republic
						Hungary
						Slovenia
							Greece
							Isle of Man
							Malta
								Bahrain
								Oman
								Saudi Arabia
									Libya	Antigua and
										  Barbuda
										Argentina
										Barbados
										Brazil
										Chile
										Guadeloupe
										Mexico

(table continues on next page)

Table A1.6 Classification of economies by income and region, 1997 (continued)

Income group	Subgroup	Sub-Saharan Africa		Asia		Europe and Central Asia		Middle East and North Africa		Americas
		East and Southern Africa	West Africa	East Asia and Pacific	South Asia	Eastern Europe and Central Asia	Rest of Europe	Middle East	North Africa	
										Puerto Rico St. Kitts and Nevis St. Lucia Trinidad and Tobago Uruguay
Subtotal	158	26	23	21	8	27	4	10	5	34
High-income	OECD			Australia Japan Korea, Rep.b New Zealand			Austria Belgium Denmark Finland France Germany Iceland Ireland Italy Luxembourg Netherlands Norway Portugal Spain Sweden Switzerland United Kingdom			Canada United States
	Non-OECD	Reunion		Brunei French Polynesia Guam Hong Kong Macao New Caledonia N. Mariana Islands Singapore Taiwan, China			Andorra Channel Islands Cyprus Faeroe Islands Greenland Liechtenstein Monaco	Israel Kuwait Qatar United Arab Emirates		Aruba Bahamas, The Bermuda Cayman Islands French Guiana Martinique Netherlands Antilles Virgin Islands (U.S.)
Total	210	27	23	34	8	27	28	14	5	44

Note: This table classifies all World Bank member economies with populations of more than 30,000. Economies are divided among income groups according to 1995 GNP per capita, calculated using the *World Bank Atlas* method. Income groups are defined as follows: low-income, $765 or less; lower-middle-income, $766–3,035; upper-middle-income, $3,036-9,385; and high-income, $9,386 or more. Estimates for economies of the former Soviet Union are preliminary, and their classification will be kept under review.

For operational and analytical purposes, the World Bank's main criterion for classifying economies is gross national product (GNP) per capita. Classification by income does not necessarily reflect development status, although low-income and middle-income economies are usually referred to as developing economies. The use of the term is convenient; it is not intended to imply that all economies in the group are experiencing similar development or that other economies have reached a preferred or final stage of development.

a. Federal Republic of Yugoslavia (Serbia and Montenegro).

b. Republic of Korea became a member of OECD on December 12, 1996.

Source: World Bank data.

61

Table A1.7 Classification of economies by major export category and indebtedness, 1997

| | Low- and middle-income | | | | | | | High-income | |
| | Low-income | | | Middle-income | | | | | |
Group	Severely indebted	Moderately indebted	Less indebted	Severely indebted	Moderately indebted	Less indebted	Not classified by indebtedness	OECD	Non-OECD
Exporters of manufactures		India Pakistan	Armenia China Georgia Kyrgyz Republic	Bulgaria	Russian Federation	Belarus Czech Republic Estonia Korea, Dem. Rep. Latvia Lebanon Lithuania Malaysia Moldova Romania Thailand Ukraine Uzbekistan		Canada Finland Germany Ireland Italy Japan Sweden Switzerland	Hong Kong Israel Korea, Rep. Macao Singapore Taiwan, China
Exporters of nonfuel primary products	Burundi Côte d'Ivoire Equatorial Guinea Ghana Guinea Guinea-Bissau Guyana Honduras Liberia Madagascar Malawi Mali Mauritania Myanmar Nicaragua Niger Rwanda São Tomé and Principe Somalia Sudan Tanzania Togo Uganda Vietnam Zaire Zambia	Chad Zimbabwe	Albania Mongolia	Bolivia Cuba Peru	Chile	Botswana Namibia Solomon Islands Suriname Swaziland Islands	American Samoa Guadeloupe	Iceland New Zealand	Faeroe Islands French Guiana Greenland Reunion
Exporters of fuels (mainly oil)	Angola Congo Nigeria			Gabon Iraq	Algeria Trinidad and Tobago Venezuela	Bahrain Iran, Islamic Rep. Libya Oman Saudi Arabia Turkmenistan			Brunei Qatar United Arab Emirates
Exporters of services	Cambodia Ethiopia Mozambique Yemen, Rep.	Benin Burkina Faso Comoros Gambia, The	Bhutan Nepal	Jamaica Jordan Panama	Egypt, Arab Rep. Greece Morocco	Antigua and Barbuda Barbados Belize		United Kingdom	Aruba Bahamas, The Bermuda Cayman Islands

(table continues on next page)

Table A1.7 Classification of economies by major export category and indebtedness, 1997 (continued)

Group	Low- and middle-income							High-income	
	Low-income			Middle-income					
	Severely indebted	Moderately indebted	Less indebted	Severely indebted	Moderately indebted	Less indebted	Not classified by indebtedness	OECD	Non-OECD
		Haiti		Western Samoa		Cape Verde Djibouti Dominican Republic El Salvador Fiji Grenada Kiribati Lesotho Maldives Paraguay Seychelles St. Kitts and Nevis St. Lucia Tonga Vanuatu			Cyprus French Polynesia Kuwait Martinique Monaco
Diversified exporters	Afghanistan Cameroon Central African Republic Kenya Sierra Leone	Bangladesh Lao PDR Senegal	Azerbaijan Sri Lanka Tajikistan	Argentina Brazil Ecuador Mexico Syrian Arab Republic	Colombia Hungary Indonesia Papua New Guinea Philippines Poland St. Vincent and the Grenadines Tunisia Turkey Uruguay	Costa Rica Dominica Guatemala Kazakstan Malta Mauritius South Africa	Yugoslavia, Fed. Rep.ª	Australia Austria Belgium Denmark France Luxembourg Netherlands Norway Portugal Spain United States	Netherlands Antilles
Not classified by export category				Macedonia, FYR	Croatia Slovak Republic Slovenia	Bosnia and Herzegovina Eritrea Isle of Man Marshall Islands Mayotte Micronesia, Fed. Sts. Puerto Rico West Bank and Gaza			Andorra Channel Islands Guam Liechtenstein New Caledonia N. Mariana Islands Virgin Islands (US)
Number of economies 210	38	12	11	14	20	52	11	22	30

Note: This table classifies all World Bank member economies, plus all other economies with populations of more than 30,000.

Major export category: Major exports are those that accounted for 50 percent or more of total exports of goods and services from one category during 1990–93. The categories are nonfuel primary (SITC 0,1,2,4, plus 68), fuels (SITC 3), manufactures (SITC 5 to 9, less 68), and services (factor and nonfactor service receipts plus worker remittances). If no single category accounts for 50 percent or more of total exports, the economy is classified as *diversified.*

Indebtedness: Standard World Bank definitions of severe and moderate indebtedness, averaged over three years (1993–95), are used to classify economies in this table. *Severely indebted* means either present value of debt service to GNP exceeds 80 percent or present value of debt service to exports exceeds 220 percent. *Moderately indebted* means either of the two key ratios exceeds 60 percent of the critical levels but does not reach them. For economies that do not report detailed debt statistics to the World Bank Debtor Reporting System (DRS), present value calculation is not possible. Instead the following methodology is used: *severely indebted* means that three of the following four key ratios (averaged over 1993–95) are above critical levels: debt to GNP (50 percent), debt to exports (275 percent), debt service to exports (30 percent), and interest to exports (20 percent). *Moderately indebted* means that three of the four key ratios exceed 60 percent of but do not reach the critical levels. All other classified low- and middle-income economies are listed as *less indebted.*

a. Federal Republic of Yugoslavia (Serbia and Montenegro).

Source: World Bank data.

External debt trends in 1995

This appendix examines trends in the external debt of developing countries in 1995. The country tables in volume 2 and the aggregate tables in this volume are based on loan-by-loan reporting of public and publicly guaranteed long-term debt of 136 countries in the World Bank Debtor Reporting System (DRS). Private nonguaranteed debt is reported by some countries and is estimated by World Bank staff for the remainder (see *Sources and Definitions* section for details).

Fourteen low- and middle-income countries do not report to the DRS (see table A1.3 in appendix 1). These include countries that are members of the World Bank but that have not had an active lending program for several years (Afghanistan and Iraq, for example); countries that are members of the World Bank but that have income levels that make them ineligible to borrow from the World Bank (Greece and Saudi Arabia); and countries that are not members of the World Bank (Cuba and the Democratic Republic of Korea). External debt data for these countries are compiled by the OECD, and these data are reflected in the aggregate tables in this volume. The most notable change in country coverage this year is the exclusion of the Republic of Korea, which is now classified as a high-income country.

Developing country debt

Total debt of developing countries reached $2,065.7 billion at the end of 1995 (table A2.1). This represents an increase of $138.8 billion, or 7.2 percent, over the total debt outstanding at the end of 1994 ($1,926.9 billion).

Exposure to currency rate changes varied considerably across regions and income groups. The movement of the U.S. dollar against other major currencies was mixed in 1995. The dollar continued to weaken (by an average of 8 percent) relative to most European currencies, which increased the dollar-measured debt stock for developing

Table A2.1 Nominal and currency-adjusted rates of growth of external debt, 1995

Country group	Total debt (billions of U.S. dollars)		Growth of debt (percent)	
	1994	1995	Nominal	Currency-adjusted
All developing countries	1,926.9	2,065.7	7.2	6.6
Region				
Sub-Saharan Africa	211.2	226.5	7.2	5.2
East Asia and the Pacific	362.3	404.5	11.6	11.9
Europe and Central Asia	396.5	425.3	7.3	5.7
Latin America and the Caribbean	585.7	636.6	8.7	8.2
Middle East and North Africa	210.2	216.0	2.8	1.6
South Asia	161.1	156.8	–2.7	–0.4
Income classification				
Low-income	512.2	534.8	4.4	4.4
Middle-income	1,414.8	1,530.9	8.3	7.4
Memo item				
Heavily indebted poor countries	207.8	214.9	3.4	2.0

Source: World Bank Debtor Reporting System.

countries with external debt denominated in key European currencies. In Sub-Saharan Africa valuation changes increased the total stock of outstanding debt by 2 percent because of the relatively high (19 percent) share of debt denominated in French francs and deutsche marks. By contrast, countries with a large share of yen-denominated debt saw their dollar-measured debt stock fall as a consequence of the 9 percent appreciation of the U.S. dollar relative to the yen in 1995. Debt stocks fell by 0.3 percent in East Asia and 2.3 percent in South Asia as a result of valuation changes. For all developing countries the rise in total external debt in 1995, after adjusting for the overall depreciation of the U.S. dollar, was 6.6 percent (see table A2.1).

Net flows on debt accounted for almost 96 percent of the rise in debt stock in 1995, with exchange rate changes and debt restructuring accounting for the rest (table A2.2). Positive net flows to developing countries—including long-term debt, net use of IMF credits, and short-term debt—totaled $133 billion. Valuation changes associated with movements of the dollar against other major currencies increased the dollar value of developing countries' external debt denominated in currencies other than the dollar by $11.6 billion. Capitalization of interest through debt rescheduling added $5.2 billion, and accumulation of interest arrears added $0.8 billion. This increased debt stock was partly offset by voluntary debt reduction efforts (debt buybacks, debt exchanges, debt-for-equity swaps, and outright debt forgiveness), which reduced the debt stock by $6.0 billion. Unidentified changes (the residual) totaled –$5.8 billion.

Net flows on debt rose 61 percent in 1995, to $133 billion. Net long-term lending from official sources (excluding the IMF) rebounded to $20.4 billion, equivalent to 15.3 percent of the total net flows on debt in 1995, up more than 54 percent from the net inflow ($13.2 billion) provided by official sources in 1994. This rise was driven by the large international rescue package for Mexico in the first quarter of 1995, however, and masks the underlying trend in official flows. When the $10.3 billion from official sources (excluding the IMF) to Mexico is excluded, net long-term lending from official sources fell $3.1 billion, or 23 percent, in 1995.

This decline (for countries other than Mexico) was driven by a sharp increase in payments to bilateral creditors by Argentina, Brazil, India, and the Russian Federation. Payments by Latin American countries to Paris Club creditors rose as maturities started to fall due under rescheduling arrangements. India made large payments in kind (worth $1.2 billion) under the arrangement it concluded with Russia to restructure defense debt, and Russia paid $0.5 billion to its Arab creditors.

By contrast, net inflows from multilateral creditors (excluding the IMF) rose 7 percent in 1995, reaching $11.0 billion. The increase came despite large prepayments by several borrowers, most notably Chile (to the World Bank and the Inter-American Development Bank) and Hungary and Russia (to the European Investment Bank). The rise was helped by a turnaround in net inflows from the World Bank, which increased from zero in 1994 to $1.4 billion in 1995. China, Russia, and Ukraine were the main beneficiaries.

The net flow of funds from the IMF soared by $15.2 billion to $16.8 billion in 1995. Much of this increase was accounted for by the $12.1 billion provided to Mexico as part of the international rescue package. Net IMF flows of $5.5 billion to the Russian Federation and $1.2 billion to Ukraine supported structural reform. Net IMF

Table A2.2 Sources of change in total debt, 1995

(billions of U.S. dollars)

Source	All countries	Middle-income countries	Low-income countries	Heavily indebted poor countries
Net flows on debt	133.0	108.8	24.3	4.4
Cross-currency valuation effects	11.6	11.7	–0.1	2.9
Voluntary debt reduction	–6.0	–3.0	–3.1	–3.0
Rescheduled interest	5.2	4.3	0.9	0.8
Net increase in interest arrears	0.8	–1.2	2.0	1.0
Unidentified changes	–5.8	–4.5	–1.3	1.0
Net change in debt stock	138.9	116.1	22.6	7.1

Source: World Bank Debtor Reporting System.

flows to Argentina in support of stabilization measures reached $1.9 billion. By contrast, India repaid $1.7 billion and Poland repaid $1.4 billion to the IMF in 1995.

Net long-term lending to developing countries by private creditors rose by $11.7 billion to $56.6 billion in 1995, led by a surge in commercial bank lending. Most of this increase went to private borrowers, who accounted for 60 percent of flows from private creditors, up from 53 percent in 1994. East Asia, Europe and Central Asia, and Latin America received 92 percent of these flows. Commercial banks reached $26.4 billion and portfolio debt flows $28.5 billion, with other private credits (primarily guaranteed export credits) reaching $1.6 billion.

Short-term lending also rose sharply, from $23.3 billion to $39.2 billion. The overall increase masks sharp divergences across countries, however. The net inflow of short-term capital to East Asian borrowers rose to $15.4 billion, up from $1.7 billion in 1994. Indonesia recorded the largest inflow ($5.2 billion), followed by China ($4.8 billion) and Thailand ($4.3 billion). Short-term borrowing in Europe and Central Asia also rose sharply in 1995, with Turkey driving the trend. Net inflows totaled $10.6 billion, compared with –$0.8 billion in 1994. By contrast, short-term liabilities declined in other regions. In Latin America net inflows of short-term capital dropped from $13.1 billion in 1994 to $5.0 billion in 1995, largely because of the decline in lending to Brazil and Mexico.

The $0.8 billion in interest arrears in 1995 marked the first year since 1992 that interest arrears have accumulated. Interest arrears fell sharply in some Latin America countries, notably Brazil ($0.5 billion), Ecuador ($2.3 billion), and Nicaragua ($0.5 billion), but these declines were more than offset by the build-up of arrears in Sub-Saharan Africa ($2.2 billion, including $1 billion by Nigeria alone), the Russian Federation ($1 billion), Vietnam ($0.2 billion), the countries of the former Soviet Union ($0.2 billion) and some countries in the Middle East ($0.3 billion).

Capitalized interest (an implicit net flow from partially financing interest due or in arrears) resulting from debt and debt service reduction programs fell to $5.2 billion in 1995, one-third the 1994 level. Ecuador, which capitalized $1.8 billion under the agreement it concluded with its commercial bank creditors, accounted for more than

one-third of the total. Interest rescheduled under other agreements included $1.1 billion for Russia, $0.4 billion for Algeria, and $0.8 billion for Sub-Saharan Africa. Most of the rescheduling was done through Paris Club agreements on Naples terms.

Debt reduction and outright debt forgiveness reduced outstanding debt by $6.0 billion in 1995 (net of the cost of debt buybacks accounted for in net flows), a much smaller reduction than the $18.9 billion recorded in 1994. The reduction in private source debt came primarily through officially supported comprehensive debt and debt service reductions, market buybacks, and debt-for-equity swaps. In Latin America debt declined by $4.1 billion ($0.9 billion in Argentina, $1.2 billion in Ecuador, and $1.5 billion in Nicaragua). Among low-income countries the IDA Debt Reduction Facility enabled Albania to reduce its debt to commercial creditors by $116 million and Sierra Leone to reduce its debt by $202 million net of the cost of the buyback.

Debt forgiveness by official creditors reduced the debt of low-income countries by $3.1 billion, all of which went to heavily indebted poor countries. Most of the debt relief was provided by France, which continued to support CFA franc countries following the devaluation of the CFA franc in 1994. Official debt forgiveness to middle-income countries was largely restricted to the $300 million debt forgiveness Jordan received from the United States.

Debt indicators

The 7.2 percent rise in developing country debt stocks in 1995 was more than offset by the rise in developing country exports and their combined gross national product (GNP). As a result aggregate debt indicators for developing countries continued to improve, with the ratio of debt to exports falling from 170.3 percent in 1994 to 151.4 percent in 1995 (table A2.3) and the ratio of debt to GNP falling from 40.8 percent in 1994 to 39.6 percent in 1995. The ratio of debt service to exports (computed on the basis of debt service payments actually made) fell from 17.5 percent in 1994 to 17 percent in 1995 (see table A2.3).

Debt to export ratios fell in all regions in 1995, but the differences across regions were significant. Although Sub-Saharan Africa's debt to export ratio fell to 241.7 percent (down from 262.4 percent in 1994) as a result of buoyant export earnings for

Table A2.3 Debt indicators by income group and region, 1990–95

(percent)

Country group	Share of 1996 total debt	Debt to exports ratio						Debt service to exports ratio					
		1990	1991	1992	1993	1994	1995	1990	1991	1992	1993	1994	1995
All developing countries	100.0	165.1	175.0	175.0	179.8	170.3	151.4	18.3	18.3	18.0	17.9	17.5	17.0
Indebtedness classification													
Severely indebted	38.6	332.2	351.2	332.6	338.9	314.9	283.3	24.4	24.9	25.7	26.6	24.9	25.7
Low-income	11.2	432.8	472.3	468.8	498.5	495.3	421.2	21.8	21.9	20.7	16.3	18.4	18.6
Middle-income	27.4	297.8	312.2	292.1	296.1	270.6	248.8	25.3	25.8	27.2	29.4	26.5	27.5
Moderately indebted	40.5	187.2	208.2	210.0	215.8	206.0	174.3	24.8	26.6	23.9	23.7	23.0	21.5
Other countries	20.8	58.2	61.7	66.0	71.3	71.1	68.3	9.1	8.4	9.1	8.9	9.5	9.0
Region													
Sub-Saharan Africa	10.8	226.6	239.7	236.1	249.3	262.4	241.7	18.0	16.5	15.8	15.0	14.6	14.5
East Asia and the Pacific	20.7	136.1	132.6	125.7	122.8	108.7	98.3	17.5	16.0	15.8	16.0	13.9	12.8
South Asia	7.4	317.0	312.7	318.3	284.1	265.5	218.7	28.1	25.6	25.3	22.9	24.6	24.6
Europe and Central Asia	20.8	102.9	127.5	147.6	158.7	153.5	130.7	14.3	16.5	13.2	11.9	14.8	13.8
Latin America and the Caribbean	30.2	255.9	261.1	252.9	255.3	233.4	212.3	24.4	24.3	26.3	28.4	25.4	26.1
Middle East and North Africa	10.1	118.0	121.0	115.6	130.8	141.7	133.4	15.7	15.9	15.9	15.4	15.7	14.9
Memo item													
Heavily indebted poor countries	9.8	489.9	529.1	532.4	550.9	518.9	446.5	21.1	21.4	17.2	17.3	18.6	20.4

a. Preliminary
Note. Based on (nominal) debt stock at year-end.
Source: World Bank Debtor Reporting System.

some countries, it was still higher than any other region's. South Asia had the second highest debt-export ratio (218.7 percent in 1995, down from 265.5 percent in 1994) followed by Latin America (212.3 percent in 1995, down from 233.4 percent in 1994). East Asia had the lowest debt-export ratio (98.3 percent, down from 108.7 percent in 1994).

The debt service to export ratio also varied significantly across regions. Ratios of 26.1 percent in Latin America and 24.6 percent in South Asia were roughly comparable. In Sub-Saharan Africa the debt service to export ratio was 14.5 percent, and the payments made by African borrowers represented only a fraction of the amounts falling due. In East Asia the debt service to export ratio was 12.8 percent, and borrowers were servicing all debt on schedule.

Lending terms to developing countries

Overall, there was a marked hardening of the terms of lending to developing countries in 1995.

The average interest rate on new loans rose to 6.3 percent, up from 5.5 percent in 1994, and average maturities fell to 13.5 years, down from 16.2 years in 1994. Some of the deterioration in terms can be attributed to the Mexican financing package, which was extended on short terms (five years) at a rate of interest 3.75 percent over LIBOR.

Lending terms by private creditors also hardened for developing countries, although less severely than those of official creditors. The average interest rate rose to 6.6 percent (from 6.3 percent in 1994), and the average maturity fell to 7.5 years (from 8.3 years in 1994). But again, there were wide differences in the lending terms offered to individual countries, with East Asian borrowers offered interest rates that averaged almost 1 percentage point less than Latin American borrowers (6.3 percent compared with 7.1 percent) and average maturities that were, on average, more than twice as long (9.7 years compared with 4.5 years).

APPENDIX 3

 Official external debt restructuring

Debt relief arrangements for official bilateral debt are established largely in the framework of the Paris Club, where creditor governments agree on common terms on which to reschedule arrears and payments falling due. Most Paris Club debts are export credit loans—commercial debts at market interest rates that, upon default by the debtor, become official debt after export credit agencies have paid out claims to the private policyholders who had insured their commercial loans against nonpayment. Paris Club agreements cover government-guaranteed debt and direct government-to-government loans, including aid loans. During the period under review, July 1995 to December 1996, five stock-of-debt operations and nine flow reschedulings were made on Naples terms for the poorest countries (box A3.1). In the context of the Heavily Indebted Poor Countries Debt Initiative the Paris Club agreed to increase the maximum debt reduction available to 80 percent of eligible debt (in present value terms). Since June 1995 seven Paris Club agreements were made on nonconcessional terms, including the club's largest ever deal, the comprehensive restructuring of more than $40 billion in debt owed by the Russian Federation.

Poor countries

Until the late 1980s official creditors addressed the repayment difficulties of the poorest and most highly indebted countries by helping them overcome their liquidity problems. The debt relief granted was a rescheduling or refinancing of (a part of) arrears and of payments falling due during the period of an IMF-supported adjustment program—usually between one and three years. Repeated rescheduling and the refinancing of interest falling due on pre-cutoff date debt, however, contributed to a steady increase in the stock

of outstanding debt for many of the poorest countries.

In the late 1980s, as middle-income countries began to benefit from market-based debt and debt service reduction deals with the commercial banks, which were their main creditors, Paris Club creditors recognized that in some of the poorest countries the problem was not one of liquidity but one of solvency, and that some of these debts were unlikely to be repaid in full. In October 1988, following an agreement at the 1988 Toronto summit of the Group of Seven (G-7) industrial countries, Paris Club creditors started to provide debt relief on concessional terms to the poorest rescheduling countries by forgiving up to a third of debt payments rescheduled or by reducing the interest rate charged on rescheduled amounts to below the prevailing market rate. At the same time many creditor governments forgave some or all of the development aid debts owed by the poorest countries and increasingly provided new development aid on grant rather than loan terms.

In response to the increasingly difficult situation of the poorest countries, G-7 leaders agreed at the 1991 London summit to increase the degree of concessionality in reschedulings for the poorest countries. In December 1991 Paris Club creditors adopted the London terms, under which maximum available debt relief on eligible pre-cutoff date debt was increased from one-third to one-half in present value terms. Following the G-7 summit in Naples in 1994, the Paris Club creditors agreed that, where necessary, concessionality could be increased to two-thirds on debt eligible for restructuring. These terms are known as Naples terms (box A3.1).

Creditors also agreed in principle to go beyond repeated flow rescheduling and to restructure the full stock of eligible (pre-cutoff date) debt out-

Box A3.1 Paris Club Naples terms

Key elements of the Naples terms, which have replaced the previous (Toronto or London) concessional terms for low-income countries, include:

• *Eligibility.* Determined by creditors on a case-by-case basis according to a country's income and level of indebtedness. Countries that have previously received concessional reschedulings (on Toronto or London terms) are eligible for Naples terms.

• *Concessionality.* Most countries receive a reduction in eligible non-ODA debt of 67 percent in net present value terms. Some countries with per capita incomes of more than $500 and a ratio of debt to exports of less than 350 percent in present value terms may receive a 50 percent net present value reduction, to be determined on a case-by-case basis.

• *Coverage.* Coverage (inclusion in the rescheduling agreement) of non-ODA pre-cutoff date debt is determined on a case-by-case basis in light of balance of payments need. Debt previously rescheduled on concessional terms may be subject to further rescheduling to top up the amount of concessionality granted. Under the top up the net present value reduction is increased from the original level given under Toronto or London terms to the level agreed under Naples terms.

• *Choice of options.* Creditors have a choice of two concessional options for achieving a 67 (or 50) percent net present value reduction,[1] the debt reduction option under which repayment is made over twenty-three years with a six-year grace period, and the debt

service reduction option, under which the net present value reduction is achieved by concessional interest rates (with repayment in less than thirty-three years).[2] There is also a commercial, or long maturities, option that provides for no net present value reduction and repayment over forty years with a twenty-year grace period. Creditors choosing this option undertake best efforts to change to a concessional option at a later date when feasible.

• *Official development assistance (ODA) credits.* Pre-cutoff date credits are rescheduled on interest rates at least as concessional as the original interest rates over forty years with a sixteen-year grace period (thirty years maturity with a twelve-year grace period for 50 percent net present value reduction). Creditors can also choose an option reducing the net present value of ODA debt by 67 (or 50) percent.

• *Flow reschedulings* provide for the rescheduling of debt service on eligible debt falling due during the consolidation period (generally in line with the period of the IMF arrangement).

• *Stock-of-debt operations,* under which the entire stock of eligible pre-cutoff date debt is rescheduled concessionally, are reserved for countries with a satisfactory track record for a minimum of three years with respect to both payments under rescheduling agreements and performance under IMF arrangements. Creditors must be confident that the country will be able to respect the debt agreement as an exit rescheduling (with no further reschedulings required).

1. For a 50 percent net present value reduction, the debt service reduction option provides for repayment over twenty-three years with a six-year grace period; the long maturities option provides for repayment over twenty-five years with a sixteen-year grace period.

2. For flow reschedulings there is no grace period; for stock-of-debt operations the grace period is three years. There is, in addition, a capitalization of moratorium interest option, which also achieves the net present value reduction by a lower interest rate over the same repayment (and grace) periods as the debt service reduction option.

standing for poor countries that established a three-year track record of good macroeconomic adjustment policies and debt service payments. The aim of such stock-of-debt operations is to allow a debtor to exit the rescheduling process and manage its future debt service obligations without additional relief. Although payments requested from the debtor are not necessarily higher under a stock operation than under a flow rescheduling, a stock-of-debt deal may require an increase in the level of actual payments being made to creditors as debtors forgo the opportunity to negotiate regular comprehensive flow rescheduling of payments falling due. Thus an important motivation for a debtor to negotiate such a deal is that it reduces

uncertainty about future levels of external debt service to be paid and so reduces the concern that foreign creditors might appropriate some of the benefits accruing from stronger future growth. Through the reduction of uncertainty—and by making an eventual return to creditworthiness a real possibility—stock-of-debt deals improve the ability of a country to fully implement its economic adjustment program.

Creditors have implemented this exit option only since 1995 (on Naples terms). By December 1996 six such operations—for Uganda, Bolivia, Mali, Guyana, Burkina Faso, and Benin—had been approved covering more than $2 billion. In addition, nineteen flow reschedulings have been

Table A3.1 Paris Club agreements on Naples terms, 1995–96

Country	Signature date	Cutoff date	Amount rescheduled (US$ millions)	Eligible concessionality level (percentage of present value)	Consolidation period start date	Length (months)	Earliest month for consideration of stock of debt rescheduling
Benin	24 Oct 96	31 Mar 89	209	67	Debt stock rescheduling	n.a.	n.a.
Bolivia	24 Mar 95	31 Dec 85	482	67	1 Jan 95ª	36	n.a.
Bolivia	15 Dec 95	31 Dec 85	881	67	Debt stock rescheduling	n.a.	n.a.
Burkina Faso	20 Jun 96	1 Jan 91	n.a.	67	Debt stock rescheduling	n.a.	n.a.
Cambodia	26 Jan 95	2 Jan 86	249	67	1 Jan 95ª	30	—ᵇ
Cameroon	16 Nov 95	31 Dec 88	1129	50	1 Oct 95	12	Oct 98
Chad	28 Feb 95	30 Jun 89	24	67	1 Apr 94ª	12	—ᵇ
Chad	14 Jun 96	30 Jun 89	—	67	1 Jan 96	32	—ᵇ
Congo	16 Jul 96	1 Jan 86	1522	67	11 Jul 96ª	36	Jul 99
Guinea	25 Jan 95	1 Jan 86	156	50	1 Jan 95ª	12	—ᶜ
Guinea-Bissau	23 Feb 95	31 Dec 86	195	67	1 Jan 95ª	36	Feb 98
Guyana	23 May 96	31 Dec 88	793	67	Debt stock rescheduling	n.a.	n.a.
Haiti	30 May 95	1 Oct 93	177	67	1 Mar 95ª	13	—ᶜ
Honduras	19 Feb 96	1 Jun 90	112	50	1 Jan 95ª	12	Jan 99
Mali	20 May 96	1 Jan 88	33	67	Debt stock rescheduling	n.a.	n.a.
Mauritania	28 Jun 95	31 Dec 84	66	67	1 Jan 95ª	36	Dec 97
Mozambique	21 Nov 96	1 Feb 84	664	67	1 Nov 96	36	Nov 99
Nicaragua	22 Mar 95	1 Nov 88	848	67	1 Apr 94ª	27	Jun 97
Niger	19 Dec 96	1 Jul 83	128	67	1 Dec 96ª	31	Jun 99
Senegal	20 Apr 95	1 Jan 83	169	67	1 Apr 94ª	29	Aug 97
Sierra Leone	28 Mar 96	1 Jul 83	39	67	1 Jan 95ª	24	Jan 98
Togo	23 Feb 95	1 Jan 83	237	67	1 Jan 95ª	33	Feb 98
Uganda	20 Feb 95	1 Jul 81	110	67	Debt stock rescheduling	n.a.	n.a.
Yemen, Rep.	24 Sep 96	1 Jan 93	113	67	1 Sept 96ª	12	—ᶜ
Zambia	28 Feb 96	1 Jan 83	566	67	1 Jan 96ª	36	Feb 99

n.a. Not applicable.
— Not available.
a. Arrears as of beginning of consolidation period also rescheduled.
b. In accordance with normal Paris Club practice to base reschedulings on agreed terms of reference when the number of creditors involved is very small, the reschedulings for Cambodia (1995) and Chad (1995) were not based on full-fledged agreed minutes. Cambodia and Chad obtained Naples terms, but no date for stock-of-debt operation was specified in the terms of reference.
c. The goodwill clauses in the Guinea, Haiti, and Republic of Yemen agreements provided for continuation of debt rescheduling if certain conditions were met.
Source: World Bank Debtor Reporting System and Paris Club data.

made on Naples terms (table A3.1), covering about $7 billion. Two of these flow reschedulings—for Cambodia and Haiti—dealt with a large volume of arrears, which constituted the bulk of outstanding debt.

While Naples terms provide for a net present value reduction of up to 67 percent on eligible debt, the effective net present value reduction on total debt to Paris Club creditors is typically lower, for two reasons. First, post-cutoff date and short-term debts are normally excluded from eligible debt (although when warranted, creditors may grant exceptional treatment on these debt categories). Second, official development assistance (ODA) debt is treated differently from non-ODA debt under Naples terms. Under the ODA debt option, debt is rescheduled over forty years, with

sixteen years' grace at a rate at least as concessional as the original loan rate. The net present value reduction on rescheduled ODA debt depends on the level of the interest rate applicable to the rescheduled debt compared with the interest rate on the original loan and the current market interest rate, as well as the remaining maturity of the loan. A number of creditors have systematically forgiven all ODA claims, resulting in substantial debt relief for poor countries and more debt relief than required under Naples terms.

Topping up

Depending on the financing needs of a rescheduling country, Paris Club reschedulings on Naples terms typically involve a comprehensive restructuring of pre-cutoff date debts including, where necessary, arrears and debts outstanding as the result of earlier rescheduling agreements with Paris Club creditors (known as previously rescheduled debt). Some previously rescheduled debt may already have been treated concessionally, under either Toronto terms (up to 33 percent net present value reduction) or London terms (up to 50 percent net value reduction). Naples terms agreements often grant an additional reduction in order to raise the total net present value reduction granted on previously rescheduled debt (including nonconcessional previously rescheduled debt) to 67 percent. The coverage of the agreement and extent of topping up are negotiated on a case-by-case basis. All the stock-of-debt agreements during the period under review provided for such topping up.

Enhanced debt relief for the heavily indebted poor countries

In November 1996, following the Lyon Summit of the G-7 in June 1996, the Paris Club creditors agreed (in the context of the Heavily Indebted Poor Countries Debt Initiative) to provide debt relief on a case-by-case basis of up to 80 percent in net present value terms where such relief would be necessary for a debtor country to achieve external debt sustainability.

Middle-income countries

In addition to the Naples terms agreements for poor countries described above, seven nonconcessional reschedulings were approved by Paris Club creditors during the eighteen months ending December 1996. Debt repayments falling due under those agreements are rescheduled or refinanced at market-related interest rates. The largest of these agreements was the rescheduling of $40.2 billion of debt owed by the Russian Federation in April 1996, the largest rescheduling in the history of the Paris Club; $7.3 billion of debt owed by Algeria in July 1995; and $6.7 billion of debt owed by Peru in July 1996.

To smooth future debt service profiles the agreements with the Russian Federation and Peru included comprehensive restructurings of payments falling due at the end of the IMF arrangements and were closely tied to good performance

under those arrangements. Under the agreement with the Russian Federation, rescheduled amounts due between January 1996 and March 1999 as well as debt to be restructured in April 1999 are to be repaid between 2002 and 2020, with a gradually rising repayment profile. The agreement is considered to be an exit rescheduling. Unlike previous Paris Club agreements with the Russian Federation, there is no capitalization of moratorium interest. The agreement included a termination clause linked to the IMF arrangement under the extended fund facility (EFF), which allows creditors to terminate the agreement if the scheduled 1996 quarterly reviews under the IMF arrangement are not completed. A trigger clause links the continued application of the agreement to approval of the annual arrangements under the EFF for 1997 and 1998, and to completion of the final review under the EFF arrangement.

The agreement with Peru included the rescheduling of a declining portion of debt falling due between April 1996 and December 1998 and a reprofiling of a limited portion of the stock of debt (amounts outstanding as of January 1999 that resulted from the 1991 rescheduling agreement with Paris Club creditors). A trigger clause links the continued implementation of the agreement to approval of the annual arrangements for 1997 and 1998 under Peru's extended arrangement with the IMF. As a precondition for the restructuring, Peru also agreed that following the present extended arrangement it would maintain a close relationship with the IMF for three years, during which time it will agree to enhanced surveillance and reporting of its economic policies and performance.

Swap arrangements

Since 1990 Paris Club creditors have incorporated provisions into agreements with lower-middle and low-income countries that allow some debtors to use part of the debt covered by a Paris Club agreement in debt-equity, debt for nature, development, and other local currency debt swaps. Participation in such agreements is voluntary on the part of both debtor and creditor. All ODA debts are eligible for swaps; for non-ODA obligations a limit of 10 percent of the debt covered by a rescheduling agreement or $10 million, whichever is larger, was set by creditors. The setting of a limit reflected a general concern among Paris Club creditors that large creditors of a particular country should not be encouraged to exit from a rescheduling country by swapping most of its debt stock for other assets. In June 1996 creditors agreed to double the amount of commercial debt that can be swapped in future agreements to 20 percent of the rescheduled commercial debts, or SDR 15-30 million (decided case by case), whichever is greater. The July 1996 Paris Club agreement with Peru reflected this change in allowing up to 20 percent of rescheduled debt to be swapped, on a voluntary basis, for local currency obligations.

Graduation from Paris Club rescheduling

The work of the Paris Club is now increasingly concentrated on poor countries. As of December 1996 only five middle- and lower middle-income countries (Gabon, Jordan, Peru, Algeria, and the Russian Federation) had rescheduling agreements in effect with Paris Club creditors. Most of the other twenty five lower- middle- and middle-income countries that had previously rescheduled their debts to Paris Club creditors are not expected to require further debt relief.

Among poor countries, however, in addition to the six countries that have benefited from stock-of-debt exit deals on Naples terms, another sixteen countries have flow rescheduling agreements in effect. Eleven other countries do not have a current arrangement but have not yet graduated from the rescheduling process.

Debt owed to the Russian Federation

After the collapse of the Soviet Union, the Russian Federation, along with other former Soviet republics, signed the so-called "zero option" agreements, under which Russia assumed all the pre-1991 claims of the former Soviet Union. Comprehensive data on the extent of Russian claims on developing countries have never been officially published, but according to preliminary data on state claims provided by the Russian

authorities, the total value of Russian claims (including military debt) on developing countries, was about $173 billion at the end of 1993. Russian claims are heavily concentrated on a small group of developing countries that were viewed by the former Soviet Union as "strategic partners." The Russian authorities valued the ruble claims at the Gosbank exchange rate at the end of 1993 of 0.64 rubles to the dollar. Many debtors disagree with this valuation method and exchange rate.

Russian debt can be classified as civilian or military and concessional ("state") or nonconcessional ("commercial"). State debt has long grace periods and maturities and carries low fixed interest rates. Commercial debt is similar to suppliers credits and is held by state-owned foreign trade companies. While a significant portion of commercial debt is denominated in U.S. dollars, deutsche marks, and Swiss francs, the bulk of Russian claims—up to 90 percent—is made up of state claims denominated in rubles.

Since 1991 the Russian Federation has signed debt rescheduling agreements or rollover agreements with several debtor countries, and it continues to negotiate with others. The Russian Federation has not yet taken part as a creditor in Paris Club agreements, although discussions continue regarding future Russian participation. Agreements during the period under review include the first debt-for-equity deal agreed on by the Russian Federation, concluded with Tanzania in October 1995. The debt covered was held by a Russian foreign trade company which agreed to a cash payment of 50 cents on the dollar of face value, spread over a five-year period, and a 25 percent stake in the hotel the investor planned to build in Dar es Salaam. The Russian Federation also reached a preliminary rescheduling agreement with Nicaragua in April 1996. That agreement was based on the Gosbank ruble exchange rate of 0.64 rubles to the dollar for the valuation of Nicaragua's outstanding ruble debt and provided for 90 percent forgiveness of the $3.4 billion of ruble-denominated debt and a rescheduling of the remaining debt over fifteen years at a commercial interest rate, with some graduation of payments during the first five years.

Table A3.2 Multilateral debt relief agreements with official creditors, January 1980–December 1996

Country and date of agreement	Contract cutoff date	Consolidation period for current maturities		Consolidation includes		Share of debt consolidated (percent)	Amount consolidated (US$ millions)	Repayment terms[a]	
		Start date	Length (months)	Arrears	Previously rescheduled debt			Maturity (years/ months)	Grace (years/ months)
Albania*									
1 Dec 93	30 Sep 93	Arrears as of 30 Sep 93		y		100	35	9/3	2/9
Algeria									
1 Jun 94	30 Sep 93	1 Jun 94	12			100	5,250	14/6	3/0
21 Jul 95	30 Sep 93	1 Jul 95	36			100	7,035	13/0	1/6
Angola									
20 Jul 89	31 Dec 86	1 Jul 89	15	y		100	365	9/6	6/0
Argentina									
16 Jan 85	10 Dec 83	1 Jan 85	12	y		90	1,535	9/6	5/0
20 May 87	10 Dec 83	1 May 87	14	y		100	1,198	9/5	4/11
21 Dec 89	10 Dec 83	1 Jan 90	15	y	y	100	1,798	9/4	5/10
19 Sep 91	10 Dec 83	1 Oct 91	9	y	y	100	750	9/9	6/3
21 Jul 92	10 Dec 83	1 Jul 92	33		y	100	2,589	13/8	1/2
Benin									
22 Jun 89	31 Mar 89	1 Jun 89	13	y		100	199	Menu	Menu
18 Dec 91	31 Mar 89	1 Jan 92	19	y		100	116	Menu	Menu
27 Jun 93	31 Mar 89	1 Aug 93	29		y	100	37	Menu	Menu
24 Oct 96	31 Mar 89	24 Oct 96	Stock		y	100	209	Menu	Menu
Bolivia									
18 Jul 86	31 Dec 85	1 Jul 86	12	y		100	424	9/6	5/0
14 Nov 88	31 Dec 85	1 Oct 88	15	y	y	100	230	9/5	5/1
15 Mar 90	31 Dec 85	1 Jan 90	24		y	100	485	Menu	Menu
24 Jan 92	31 Dec 85	1 Jan 92	18		y	100	248	Menu	Menu
24 Mar 95[b]	31 Dec 85	1 Jan 95	36		y	100	502	Menu	Menu
14 Dec 95	31 Dec 85	31 Dec 95	Stock		y	100	881	Menu	Menu
Brazil									
23 Nov 83	31 Mar 83	1 Aug 83	17	y		85	2,338	9/0	5/0
21 Jan 87	31 Mar 83	1 Jan 85	30			100	2,831	5/6	3/0
29 Jul 88	31 Mar 83	1 Aug 88	20	y		100	4,066	9/6	5/0
26 Feb 92	31 Mar 83	1 Jan 92	20	y		100	6,881	13/4	1/10
Bulgaria									
17 Apr 91	1 Jan 91	1 Apr 91	12	y		100	573	10/0	6/6
14 Dec 92	1 Jan 91	1 Dec 92	5	y		100	148	9/10	6/4
13 Apr 94	1 Jan 91	1 Apr 94	13	y		100	349	9/5	5/11
Burkina Faso									
15 Mar 91	1 Jan 91	1 Mar 91	15	y		100	53	Menu	Menu
7 May 93	1 Jan 91	1 Apr 93	33	y		100	36	Menu	Menu
20 Jun 96	1 Jan 91	20 June 96	Stock		y	100	64	Menu	Menu
Cambodia									
26 Jan 95	31 Dec 85	1 Jan 95	30	y	y	100	258	Menu	Menu
Cameroon									
24 May 89	31 Dec 88	1 Apr 89	12	y		100	621	9/6	6/0
23 Jan 92	31 Dec 88	1 Jan 92	9	y		100	935	19/5, 14/8	9/11, 8/2
24 Mar 94	31 Dec 88	1 Apr 94	18	y	y	100	1,343	Menu	Menu
15 Nov 95	31 Dec 88	1 Oct 95	12		y	100	1,129	Menu	Menu
Central African Republic									
12 Jun 81	1 Jan 81	1 Jan 81	12	y		85	28	8/6	4//0
9 Jul 83	1 Jan 83	1 Jan 83	12	y		90	15	9/6	5//0
22 Nov 85	1 Jan 83	1 Jul 85	18		y	90	17	9/3	4/9
14 Dec 88	1 Jan 83	1 Jan 89	18		y	100	39	Menu	Menu
15 Jun 90	1 Jan 83	1 Jan 90	12	y	y	100	11	Menu	Menu
12 Apr 94	1 Jan 83	1 Apr 94	12	y	y	100	30	Menu	Menu

Table A3.2 Multilateral debt relief agreements with official creditors, January 1980–December 1996 (continued)

Country and date of agreement	Contract cutoff date	Consolidation period for current maturities		Consolidation includes		Share of debt consolidated (percent)	Amount consolidated (US$ millions)	Repayment terms[a]	
		Start date	Length (months)	Arrears	Previously rescheduled debt			Maturity (years/ months)	Grace (years/ months)
Chad									
24 Oct 89	30 Jun 89	1 Oct 89	15	y		100	33	Menu	Menu
28 Feb 95	30 Jun 89	1 Apr 95	12	y		100	24	Menu	Menu
14 Jun 96	30 Jun 89	1 Jan 96	32	y	y	100	n/a	Menu	Menu
Chile									
17 Jul 85	1 Jan 85	1 Jul 85	18			65	140	6/3	2/9
2 Apr 87	1 Jan 85	15 Apr 87	21			85	164	6/2	2/7
Congo, Republic of									
18 Jul 86	1 Jan 86	1 Aug 86	20	y		95	463	9/2	3/8
13 Sep 90[c]	1 Jan 86	1 Sep 90	21	y	y	100	1,011	14/3	5/9
30 Jun 94[c]	1 Jan 86	1 Jul 94	11	y	y	100	1,138	19/7, 14/7	10/1, 5/1
16 Jul 96	1 Jan 86	30 Jun 96	36	y	y	100	1,750	Menu	Menu
Costa Rica									
11 Jan 83	1 Jul 82	1 Jul 82	18	y		85	67	8/3	3/9
22 Apr 85	1 Jul 82	1 Jan 85	15	y		90	78	9/5	4/11
26 May 89	1 Jul 82	1 Apr 89	14	y	y	100	155	9/5	4/11
17 Jul 91	1 Jul 82	1 Jul 91	9	y	y	100	191	9/7	5/1
22 Jun 93	1 Jul 82	Arrears as of 31 Jun 93		y		100	30	6/6	2/0
Côte d'Ivoire									
4 May 84	1 Jul 83	1 Dec 83	13			100	265	8/6	4/0
25 Jun 85	1 Jul 83	1 Jan 85	12			100	215	8/6	4/0
27 Jun 86	1 Jul 83	1 Jan 86	36			Var.	157	8/7	4/1
18 Dec 87	1 Jul 83	1 Jan 88	16	y	y	100	931	9/4	5/10
18 Dec 89	1 Jul 83	1 Jan 90	16	y	y	100	1,116	13/4	5/10
20 Nov 91	1 Jul 83	1 Oct 91	12	y	y	100	768	14/6	8/0
22 Mar 94	1 Jul 83	1 Mar 94	37	y	y	100	1,943	Menu	Menu
Croatia									
21 Mar 95	2 Dec 82	1 Jan 95	12	y	y	100	861	13/7	2/1
Cuba									
1 Mar 83		1 Sep 82	16			100	426		
19 Jul 84	1 Sep 82	1 Jan 84	12			100	204	9/0	5/6
18 Jul 85	1 Sep 82	1 Jan 85	12			100	156	9/0	5/6
16 Jul 86	1 Sep 82	1 Jan 86	12		y	100	—	9/6	5/6
Dominican Republic									
21 May 85	30 Jun 84	1 Jan 85	15	y		90	289	9/5	4/11
22 Nov 91	30 Jun 84	1 Oct 91	18	y	y	100	876	14/3	7/9
Ecuador									
28 Jul 83	1 Jan 83	1 Jun 83	12			85	155	7/6	3/0
24 Apr 85	1 Jan 83	1 Jan 85	36	y		Var	265	7/6	3/0
20 Jan 88	1 Jan 83	1 Jan 88	14	y		100	397	9/5	4/11
24 Oct 89	1 Jan 83	1 Nov 89	14	y	y	100	395	9/5	5/11
20 Jan 92	1 Jan 83	1 Jan 92	12	y	y	100	361	19/5, 14/6	9/11, 8/0
27 Jun 94	1 Jan 83	1 Jul 94	6	y	y	100	289	19/9, 14/9	10/3, 8/3
Egypt									
22 May 87	31 Oct 86	1 Jan 87	18	y		100	5,563	9/3	4/9
25 May 91	31 Oct 86	Balances: 30 Jun 91		y		100	20,700	Menu	Menu
El Salvador									
17 Sep 90[c]	1 Sep 90	1 Sep 90	13	y		100	156	19/6, 14/6	10/0, 8/0
Equatorial Guinea									
22 Jul 85	1 Jul 84	1 Jan 85	18	y		100	44	9/0	4/6
1 Mar 89	1 Jul 84	Arrears as of 31 Dec 88		y	y	100	12	Menu	Menu

(table continues on next page)

Table A3.2 Multilateral debt relief agreements with official creditors, January 1980–December 1996 (continued)

Country and date of agreement	Contract cutoff date	Consolidation period for current maturities		Consolidation includes		Share of debt consolidated (percent)	Amount consolidated (US$ millions)	Repayment terms[a]	
		Start date	Length (months)	Arrears	Previously rescheduled debt			Maturity (years/ months)	Grace (years/ months)
2 Apr 92*	1 Jul 84	1 Jan 92	12	y	y	100	32	Menu	Menu
15 Dec 94*	1 Jul 84		21	y	y	100	51	Menu	Menu
Ethiopia									
16 Dec 92	31 Dec 89	1 Dec 92	35	y		100	371	Menu	Menu
Gabon									
21 Jan 87	1 Jul 86	21 Sep 86	15			100	474	9/5	3/11
21 Mar 88	1 Jul 86	1 Jan 88	12			100	315	9/6	5/0
19 Sep 89	1 Jul 86	1 Sep 89	16	y		100	520	10/0	4/0
24 Oct 91[d]	1 Jul 86	1 Oct 91	15	y	y	100	498	8/0	2/0
15 Apr 94	1 Jul 86	1 Apr 94	12	y	y	100	1,250	14/6	2/0
12 Dec 95	1 Jul 86	1 Dec 95	36	y	y	100	1,176	13/6	1/0
Gambia, The									
19 Sep 86	1 Jul 86	1 Oct 86	12	y		100	19	9/6	5/0
Ghana									
29 Mar 96	1 Jan 93	Arrears as of 01 Jul 95				100	93	4/5	1/0
15 Apr 96									
Guatemala									
25 Mar 93	1 Jan 91	Arrears as of 31 Mar 93				100	375	19/6, 14/6	10/0, 8/0
Guinea									
18 Apr 86	1 Jan 86	1 Jan 86	14	y		95	232	9/4	4/11
12 Apr 89	1 Jan 86	1 Jan 89	12	y	y	100	161	Menu	Menu
18 Nov 92	1 Jan 86	Arrears as of 31 Dec 92		y	y	100	169	Menu	Menu
25 Jan 95	1 Jan 86	01 Jan 95	12	y	y	100	163	Menu	Menu
Guinea Bissau									
27 Oct 87	31 Dec 86	1 Jul 87	18	y		100	24	19/3	9/9
26 Oct 89	31 Dec 86	1 Oct 89	15	y	y	100	40	Menu	Menu
23 Feb 95	31 Dec 86	1 Jan 95	36	y	y	100	150	Menu	Menu
Guyana									
23 May 89	31 Dec 88	1 Jan 89	14	y		100	179	19/5	9/11
12 Sep 90	31 Dec 88	1 Sep 90	35	y	y	100	140	Menu	Menu
6 May 93	31 Dec 88	1 Aug 93	17	y	y	100	55	Menu	Menu
23 May 96	31 Dec 88	23 May 96	Stock	y	y	100	793	Menu	Menu
Haiti									
30 May 95	1 Oct 93	31 Mar 95	12	y		100	117	Menu	Menu
Honduras									
14 Sep 90[c]	1 Jun 90	1 Sep 90	11	y		100	364	19/7, 14/7	8/1, 8/1
26 Oct 92	1 Jun 90	1 Oct 92	34	y	y	100	200	Menu	Menu
29 Feb 96	1 Jun 90	30 Jan 95	12	y	y	100	112	Menu	Menu
Jamaica									
16 Jul 84	1 Oct 83	1 Jan 84	15	y		100	132	8/5	3/11
19 Jul 85	1 Oct 83	1 Apr 85	12			100	60	9/6	4/0
5 Mar 87	1 Oct 83	1 Jan 87	15	y		100	112	9/5	4/11
24 Oct 88	1 Oct 83	1 Jun 88	18		y	100	158	9/3	4/9
26 Apr 90	1 Oct 83	1 Dec 89	18		y	100	138	9/3	4/9
19 Jul 91[c]	1 Oct 83	1 Jun 91	13		y	100	139	19/6, 14/6	8/9, 6/0
25 Jan 93[c]	1 Oct 83	1 Oct 92	36		y	100	404	18/6, 13/6	9/0, 5/0
Jordan									
19 Jul 89	1 Jan 89	1 Jul 89	18	y		100	500	9/3	4/9
28 Feb 92	1 Jan 89	1 Jan 92	18	y		100	763	19/5, 14/3	9/11, 7/9
28 Jun 94[c]	1 Jan 89	1 Jul 94	35	y	y	100	1.147	18/7, 16/7	9/1, 2/1

Table A3.2 Multilateral debt relief agreements with official creditors, January 1980–December 1996 (continued)

Country and date of agreement	Contract cutoff date	Consolidation period for current maturities		Consolidation includes		Share of debt consolidated (percent)	Amount consolidated (US$ millions)	Repayment terms[a]	
		Start date	Length (months)	Arrears	Previously rescheduled debt			Maturity (years/ months)	Grace (years/ months)
Kenya									
19 Jan 94	31 Dec 91	Arrears as of 31 Dec 93		y		100	517	7/9	1/3
Liberia									
19 Dec 80	1 Jan 80	1 Jul 80	18			90	21	7/9	3/3
16 Dec 81	1 Jan 80	1 Jan 82	18			90	24	7/11	3/3
22 Dec 83	1 Jan 83	1 Jul 83	12			90	18	8/6	4/0
17 Dec 84	1 Jan 83	1 Jul 84	12			90	13	9/6	5/0
Macedonia, FYR									
17 Jul 95	2 Dec 82	1 July 95	12	y	y	100	323	14/7	3/1
Madagascar									
30 Apr 81	1 Jan 81	1 Jan 81	18	y		85	172	8/3	3/9
13 Jul 82	1 Jan 82	1 Jul 82	12	y		85	107	8/3	3/9
23 Mar 84	1 Jul 83	1 Jul 83	18		y	95	389	10/3	4/9
22 May 85	1 Jul 83	1 Jan 85	15		y	100	141	10/5	4/11
23 Oct 86	1 Jul 83	1 Apr 86	21		y	100	181	9/2	4/8
28 Oct 88	1 Jul 83	1 Apr 88	21	y	y	100	236	Menu	Menu
10 Jul 90	1 Jul 83	1 Jun 90	13	y	y	100	111	Menu	Menu
Malawi									
22 Sep 82	1 Jan 82	1 Jul 82	12			85	26	8/0	3/6
27 Oct 83	1 Jan 82	1 Jul 83	12			85	15	8/0	3/6
22 Apr 88	1 Jan 82	1 Apr 88	14	y	y	100	43	19/5	9/11
Mali									
27 Oct 88	1 Jan 88	1 Jul 88	16	y		100	48	Menu	Menu
22 Nov 89	1 Jan 88	1 Nov 89	26		y	100	33	Menu	Menu
29 Oct 92	1 Jan 88	1 Oct 92	35	y	y	100	107	Menu	Menu
20 May 96	1 Jan 88	20 May 96	Stock	y	y	100	33	Menu	Menu
Mauritania									
27 Apr 85	31 Dec 84	1 Jan 85	15	y		90	40	8/3	3/9
16 May 86	31 Dec 84	1 Apr 86	12			95	36	8/6	4/0
15 Jun 87	31 Dec 84	1 Apr 87	14			95	39	14/5	5/0
19 Jun 89	31 Dec 84	1 Jun 89	12	y	y	100	66	Menu	Menu
25 Jan 93	31 Dec 84	1 Jan 93	24	y	y	100	211	Menu	Menu
28 Jun 95	31 Dec 84	1 Jan 95	36		y	100	72	Menu	Menu
Mexico									
22 Jun 83*	20 Dec 82	1 Jul 83	6	y		90	1,367	5/6	3/0
7 Sep 86	31 Dec 85	22 Sep 86	18			100	1,807	8/3	3/9
30 May 89	31 Dec 85	1 Jun 89	36			100	2,256	9/7	6/1
Morocco									
25 Oct 83	1 May 83	1 Sep 83	16	y		85	1,228	7/3	3/9
17 Sep 85	1 May 83	1 Sep 85	18	y		90	1,083	8/3	3/9
6 Mar 87	1 May 83	1 Mar 87	16		y	100	1,074	9/3	4/9
26 Oct 88	1 May 83	1 Jul 88	18		y	100	1,100	9/3	4/9
11 Sep 90[c]	1 May 83	1 Jan 90	15		y	100	1,809	19/5, 14/5	9/11, 7/11
27 Feb 92[c]	1 May 83	1 Feb 92	11	y	y	100	1,320	19/5, 14/7	9/11 , 8/1
Mozambique									
25 Oct 84	1 Feb 84	1 Jul 84	12	y		95	317	10/6	5/0
16 Jun 87	1 Feb 84	1 Jun 87	19	y		100	429	19/3	9/9
14 Jun 90	1 Feb 84	1 Jul 90	30	y	y	100	739	Menu	Menu
23 Mar 93	1 Feb 84	1 Jan 94	24	y	y	100	343	Menu	Menu
21 Nov 96	1 Feb 84	1 Nov 96	36	y	y	100	664	Menu	Menu

(table continues on next page)

76

Table A3.2 Multilateral debt relief agreements with official creditors, January 1980–December 1996 (continued)

Country and date of agreement	Contract cutoff date	Consolidation period for current maturities		Consolidation includes		Share of debt consolidated (percent)	Amount consolidated (US$ millions)	Repayment terms[a]	
		Start date	Length (months)	Arrears	Previously rescheduled debt			Maturity (years/ months)	Grace (years/ months)
Nicaragua									
17 Dec 91	1 Nov 88	1 Jan 92	15	y	y	100	389	Menu	Menu
21 Mar 95	1 Nov 88	1 Apr 95	27	y	y	100	848	Menu	Menu
Niger									
14 Nov 83	1 Jul 83	1 Oct 83	12			90	37	8/6	4/6
30 Nov 84	1 Jul 83	1 Oct 84	14			90	44	9/5	4/11
21 Nov 85	1 Jul 83	1 Dec 85	12			90	48	9/6	5/0
20 Nov 86	1 Jul 83	3 Dec 86	12			100	34	9/6	5/0
21 Apr 88	1 Jul 83	5 Dec 87	13			100	34	19/6	10/0
16 Dec 88	1 Jul 83	1 Jan 89	12			100	57	Menu	Menu
18 Sep 90	1 Jul 83	1 Sep 90	28	y	y	100	151	Menu	Menu
4 Mar 94	1 Jul 83	1 Jan 94	15	y	y	100	194	Menu	Menu
19 Dec 96	1 Jul 83	1 Dec 96	31	y	y	100	128	Menu	Menu
Nigeria									
16 Dec 86	1 Oct 85	1 Oct 86	15	y		100	5,898	6/6	2/0
3 Mar 89	1 Oct 85	1 Jan 89	16	y		100	4,747	9/4	4/10
18 Jan 91[c]	1 Oct 85	1 Jan 91	15	y		100	3,023	19/5, 14/5	9/11, 7/11
Pakistan									
14 Jan 81*	1 Jul 80	15 Jan 81	18			90	263	Variable	Variable
Panama									
19 Sep 85	31 Dec 84	15 Sep 85	16			50	16	7/4	2/10
14 Nov 90[e]	31 Dec 84	1 Nov 90	17	y	y	100	176	9/4	4/10
Peru									
26 Jul 83	1 Jan 83	1 May 83	12			90	424	7/6	3/0
5 Jun 84	1 Jan 83	1 May 84	15			90	1,000	8/5	4/11
17 Sep 91[c]	1 Jan 83	1 Oct 91	15	y	y	100	5,749	19/5, 145	9/11, 7/11
4 May 93[c]	1 Jan 83	1 Jan 93	39		y	100	2,032	18/5, 13/5	8/11, 6/11
20 Jul 96	1 Jan 83	30 April 96	Stock			100	6,724	17/0, 19/3	0/6, 2/0
Philippines									
21 Dec 84	1 Apr 84	1 Jan 85	18	y		100	994	9/3	4/9
22 Jan 87	1 Apr 84	1 Jan 87	18			100	988	9/3	4/9
26 May 89	1 Apr 84	1 Jun 89	25	y		100	1,642	9/0	5/6
20 Jun 91[c]	1 Apr 84	1 Jul 91	14		y	100	1,682	19/5, 14/5	9/11, 7/11
19 Jul 94[d]	1 Apr 84	1 Aug 94	17	y	y	100	586	19/4, 14/4	9/10, 7/10
Poland									
27 Apr 81*	1 Jan 80	1 May 81	8	y		90	2,254	7/6	4/0
15 Jul 85*	1 Jan 84	1 Jan 82	36	y		100	10,300	10/6	5/0
19 Nov 85*	1 Jan 84	1 Jan 86	12			100	1,910	9/2	4/8
16 Dec 87*	1 Jan 84	1 Jan 88	12	y	y	100	9,027	9/0	4/6
16 Feb 90	1 Jan 84	1 Jan 90	15	y	y	100	9,400	13/9	8/3
21 Apr 91	1 Jan 84	Balances: 30 Mar 91		y	y	100	30,504	Menu	Menu
Romania									
9 Jul 82	1 Jan 82	1 Jan 82	12	y		80	234	6/0	3/0
18 May 83	1 Jan 82	1 Jan 83	12			60	195	6/0	3/0
Russian Federation									
2 Apr 93[f]	1 Jan 91	1 Jan 93	12	y		100	14,497	10/0	6/0
2 Jun 94	1 Jan 91	1 Jan 94	12			100	7,100	15/2	2/9
3 Jun 95	1 Jan 91	1 Jan 95	12			100	6,400	15/4	2/10
15 Apr 96	1 Jan 91	1 Jan 96	Stock			100	40,200	21/5	2/11
Senegal									
13 Oct 81	1 Jul 81	1 Jul 81	12			85	77	8/6	4/0
29 Nov 82	1 Jul 81	1 Jul 82	12			85	84	8/9	4/3

Table A3.2 Multilateral debt relief agreements with official creditors, January 1980–December 1996 (continued)

Country and date of agreement	Contract cutoff date	Consolidation period for current maturities		Consolidation includes		Share of debt consolidated (percent)	Amount consolidated (US$ millions)	Repayment terms[a]	
		Start date	Length (months)	Arrears	Previously rescheduled debt			Maturity (years/ months)	Grace (years/ months)
21 Dec 83	1 Jan 83	1 Jul 83	12			90	64	8/6	4/0
18 Jan 85	1 Jan 83	1 Jan 85	18	y		95	140	8/3	3/9
21 Nov 86	1 Jan 83	1 Jul 86	16			100	92	9/4	4/10
17 Nov 87	1 Jan 83	1 Nov 87	12			100	74	15/6	6/0
24 Jan 89	1 Jan 83	1 Nov 88	14		y	100	184	Menu	Menu
12 Feb 90	1 Jan 83	1 Jan 90	12	y	y	100	111	Menu	Menu
21 Jun 91	1 Jan 83	1 Jul 91	12	y	y	100	126	Menu	Menu
3 Mar 94	1 Jan 83	1 Jan 94	15	y	y	100	250	Menu	Menu
20 Apr 95	1 Jan 83	1 Apr 95	29		y	100	169	Menu	Menu
Sierra Leone									
8 Nov 80	1 Jul 79	1 Jul 79	30	y		90	39	9/6	4/0
8 Feb 84	1 Jul 83	1 Jan 84	12	y	y	90	88	10/0	5/0
19 Nov 86	1 Jul 83	1 Jul 86	16	y	y	100	65	9/4	4/10
20 Nov 92	1 Jul 83	1 Nov 92	16	y	y	100	276	Menu	Menu
20 Jul 94	1 Jul 83	1 Aug 94	17	y	y	100	47	Menu	Menu
25 Apr 96	1 Jul 83	1 Jan 96	24	y	y	100	39	Menu	Menu
Somalia									
6 Mar 85	1 Oct 84	1 Jan 85	12	y		95	126	9/6	5/0
22 Jul 87	1 Oct 84	1 Jan 87	24	y	y	100	95	19/0	9/6
Sudan									
18 Mar 82	1 Jul 81	1 Jul 81	18	y	y	90	211	9/6	4/6
4 Feb 83	1 Jan 83	1 Jan 83	12		y	100	546	15/0	5/6
2 May 84	1 Jan 84	1 Jan 84	12		y	100	231	15/6	6/0
Tanzania									
18 Sep 86	30 Jun 86	1 Oct 86	12	y		100	676	9/6	5/0
13 Dec 88	30 Jun 86	1 Jan 89	6	y	y	100	236	Menu	Menu
16 Mar 90	30 Jun 86	1 Jan 90	12	y	y	100	245	Menu	Menu
21 Jan 92	30 Jun 86	1 Jan 92	30	y	y	100	779	Menu	Menu
Togo									
20 Feb 81	1 Jul 80	1 Jan 81	24			85	120	8/6	4/0
12 Apr 83	1 Jan 83	1 Jan 83	12	y	y	90	125	9/6	5/0
6 Jun 84	1 Jan 83	1 Jan 84	16		y	95	67	9/4	4/10
24 Jun 85	1 Jan 83	1 May 85	12			95	25	10/6	5/0
22 Mar 88	1 Jan 83	1 Jan 88	15	y	y	100	118	15/5	7/11
20 Jun 89	1 Jan 83	16 Apr 89	14		y	100	82	Menu	Menu
9 Jul 90	1 Jan 83	1 Jul 90	24		y	100	101	Menu	Menu
19 Jun 92[d]	1 Jan 83	1 Jul 92	24		y	100	50	Menu	Menu
23 Feb 95	1 Jan 83	1 Feb 95	33	y	y	100	246	Menu	Menu
Trinidad and Tobago									
25 Jan 89	1 Sep 88	1 Jan 89	14	y		100	250	9/5	4/11
27 Apr 90	1 Sep 88	1 Mar 90	13			100	170	8/4	3/10
Turkey									
23 Jul 80*	30 Jun 80	1 Jul 80	36	y	y	90	2,600	9/0	4/6
Uganda									
18 Nov 81	1 Jul 81	1 Jul 81	12	y		90	63	9/0	4/6
1 Dec 82	1 Jul 81	1 Jul 82	12			90	16	9/0	4/6
19 Jun 87	1 Jul 81	1 Jul 87	12	y	y	100	102	14/6	6/0
26 Jan 89	1 Jul 81	1 Jan 89	18	y	y	100	86	Menu	Menu
17 Jun 92	1 Jul 81	1 Jul 92	17	y	y	100	172	Menu	Menu
20 Feb 95	1 Jul 81	1 Feb 95	Stock	y	y	100	110	Menu	Menu

(table continues on next page)

Table A3.2 Multilateral debt relief agreements with official creditors, January 1980–December 1996 (continued)

| Country and date of agreement | Contract cutoff date | Consolidation period for current maturities | | Consolidation includes | | Share of debt consolidated (percent) | Amount consolidated (US$ millions) | Repayment terms[a] | |
		Start date	Length (months)	Arrears	Previously rescheduled debt			Maturity (years/ months)	Grace (years/ months)
Vietnam									
14 Dec 93	1 Jan 90	Arrears as of 31 Dec 93		y		100	849	Menu	Menu
Yemen									
24 Sep 96	1 Jan 93	01 Sep 96	10	y		100	113	Menu	Menu
Yugoslavia									
22 May 84*	2 Dec 82	1 Jan 84	12			100	568	6/6	4/0
24 May 85*	2 Dec 82	1 Jan 85	16			90	399	8/4	3/10
13 May 86*	2 Dec 82	16 May 86	23			85	863	8/6	4/0
13 Jul 88*	2 Dec 82	1 Apr 88	15		y	100	894	9/5	5/11
Zaire									
9 Jul 81	1 Jan 79	1 Jan 81	24			90	276	9/6	4/0
20 Dec 83	30 Jun 83	1 Jan 84	12	y	y	95	1,417	10/6	5/0
18 Sep 85	30 Jun 83	1 Jan 85	15		y	95	385	9/5	4/11
15 May 86	30 Jun 83	1 Apr 86	12		y	100	425	9/6	4/0
18 May 87	30 Jun 83	1 Apr 87	13	y	y	100	740	14/6	6/0
23 Jun 89	30 Jun 83	1 Jun 89	13	y	y	100	1,602	Menu	Menu
Zambia									
16 May 83	1 Jan 83	1 Jan 83	12	y		90	302	9/6	5/0
20 Jul 84	1 Jan 83	1 Jan 84	12	y	y	100	263	9/6	5/0
4 Mar 86	1 Jan 83	1 Jan 86	12	y	y	100	355	9/6	5/0
12 Jul 90	1 Jan 83	1 Jul 90	18	y	y	100	1,174	Menu	Menu
23 Jul 92	1 Jan 83	1 Jul 92	33	y	y	100	874	Menu	Menu
27 Feb 96	1 Jan 83	1 Jan 96	36	y	y	100	566	Menu	Menu

* The rescheduling was concluded outside of formal Paris Club auspices.
Note: The figures in this table are commitment values (amounts of debt relief agreed to). They correspond to the disbursement figures (minus debt forgiveness, when applicable) for debt restructuring shown in the country tables of volume 2. All agreements shown in this table were negotiated through the Paris Club, except those indicated with an asterisk. Figures for 1993 and 1994 agreements are estimated.
a. Maturity is measured from the end of the consolidation period to the date of the final amortization payment; the grace period is the time between the end of the consolidation period and the date of the first amortization payment. The secretariat of the Paris Club measures grace and maturity from the midpoint of the consolidation period. "Menu" terms refer to the options agreed to at the 1988 Toronto economic summit meeting; for agreements under the enhanced Toronto terms, the consolidation period comes into effect in stages, according to preestablished conditions. For agreements starting in 1995, "menu" terms refers to Naples terms, agreed on in December 1994.
b. Agreement signed in March 1995 covered a thirty-six month period, but a new agreement was signed in December 1995 covering the stock of debt, starting twelve months after the beginning of the consolidation period of the previous agreement.
c. Agreement with a Paris Club–designated lower-middle-income country with heavy official debt. These agreements also allow for debt conversions, subject to the limit for each creditor country (for non-ODA debt) of $10 million or 10 percent of the debt outstanding as of the beginning of the consolidation period, whichever is higher. Where two sets of figures for repayment terms (maturity and grace) are given, the first set represents official development assistance debt (ODA) and the second non-ODA debt.
d. Agreement was canceled.
e. Agreement was implemented in 1991 because of the agreement's conditionality on an IMF program, which took place in 1991.
f. Agreement follows the deferral signed in January 1992 by the former Soviet republics.
Source: World Bank Debtor Reporting System and International Monetary Fund data.

APPENDIX 4

Commercial debt restructuring

Since 1989 the restructuring of developing country debt to commercial banks has occurred largely through officially supported debt and debt service reduction programs ("Brady-type" operations) for middle-income countries[1] and through buybacks supported by the World Bank's Debt Reduction Facility for low-income countries eligible for borrowing only from the International Development Association (IDA).[2] These programs have helped resolve long-standing concerns of debtors and commercial bank creditors and have improved these countries' creditworthiness, in some cases contributing to the restoration of market access. Some countries have recently come full circle, voluntarily entering the market to retire collateralized Brady bonds through swaps for uncollateralized instruments and through debt buybacks.

Officially supported programs and associated market swap operations reduced developing countries' debt to commercial banks by $46.5 billion between 1989 and December 1996. This reduction, equivalent to nearly 22 percent of the $212.2 billion of eligible commercial bank debt (including interest arrears), was eliminated through buybacks, cash payments, and writeoffs. Since 1989 thirty countries have completed thirty-three debt and debt service reduction operations under the aegis of the Brady Plan, the Debt Reduction Facility and, most recently, voluntary swap operations (by the Philippines and Mexico). Fifteen middle-income countries have eliminated 20 percent of their $207.7 billion in commercial bank debt, and thirteen low-income countries have extinguished $4.3 billion of eligible principal and interest arrears due to commercial banks at a cost of $367.1 million under the Debt Reduction Facility.

Financing costs of officially supported operations—funds expended for buybacks and other

cash payments and for principal and interest collateral needed to guarantee the debt exchanges—have totaled $23.2 billion. Financing, net of the $3.7 billion of concerted new money provided by commercial banks, came in almost equal shares from debtor countries and official lenders. The World Bank's participation amounted to $4.6 billion, or about 37 percent of foreign financing requirements net of concerted commercial bank lending.

Recent developments

Seven agreements between debtor countries and their commercial bank creditors were concluded in 1996, restructuring $16.9 billion in debt and reducing outstanding debt by $5.5 billion (table A4.1). Among middle-income countries, Mexico and the Philippines retired $4.4 billion of Brady bonds through swaps for uncollateralized bonds and through a debt buyback. Panama and Peru restructured $11.9 billion under the Brady initiative. Among low-income countries, Ethiopia, Mauritania, and Senegal bought back $356.0 million at an average price of 9 cents per dollar in deals supported by the Debt Reduction Facility.

In November 1995 Côte d'Ivoire reached a debt and debt service reduction agreement with commercial banks to restructure $7.2 billion of commercial bank debt, including $4.6 billion of interest in arrears. For eligible principal the menu of options includes buyback, discount bonds, and front-loaded interest reduction bonds. Interest payments of $30.0 million will be made by closing, with the remainder settled by past-due interest bonds and a writeoff stemming from the recomputation of penalty interest at a lower interest rate. The cost of the operations, including the buyback, debt service collaterals, and interest

Table A4.1 Debt and debt service reduction, 1989–96
(billions of U.S. dollars)

Type of operation	Country	Closing date	Gross amount restructured[a]	Face value of debt reduction[b]	Face value of restructured debt
Debt and debt	Cumulative, 1995		191.3	37.2	154.2
service reductions	Panama	Apr 96	3.9	0.8	3.2
	Peru	Nov 96	8.0	3.2	4.8
	Cumulative, 1996		203.3	41.1	162.1
Buybacks funded	Cumulative, 1995		3.9	3.8	0.1
by the Debt Reduction	Ethiopia	Jan 96	0.3	0.3	0.0
Facility	Mauritania	Aug 96	0.1	0.1	0.0
	Senegal	Dec 96	0.1	0.1	0.0
	Cumulative, 1996		4.5	4.3	0.1
Associated debt and	Cumulative, 1995		0.0	0.0	0.0
debt service	Mexico	Apr 96	3.6	0.8	2.8
reduction	Philippines	Sep 96	0.8	0.1	0.7
market swaps	Cumulative, 1996		4.4	1.0	3.4
Total	Cumulative, 1995		195.3	41.0	154.3
	Operations, 1996		16.9	5.5	11.4
	Cumulative, 1996		212.2	46.5	165.7

Note: Totals may not add up because of rounding.
a. Includes past-due interest.
b. Includes buybacks, discounts, down payment on PDI, and forgiveness.
Source: World Bank Debtor Reporting System and Euromoney Bondware.

downpayment, is estimated at $280.0 to $300.0 million, depending on which options participating banks choose. As a result of the accord, Côte d'Ivoire's debt with commercial banks is expected to decline by about $4.8 billion. The deal is expected to close by June 1997.

Swaps in middle-income countries

A significant new development in 1996 was the swap by Mexico and the Philippines of Brady bonds for uncollateralized long-term bonds. These voluntary deals show the renewed confidence of foreign investors in these countries' prospects, particularly significant in the case of Mexico following the uncertainties of 1995. The attractiveness of the swaps for debtor countries is twofold. First, collateral associated with the Brady bonds, including interest earned on escrow accounts, is released and can be used by the country to meet other obligations. Second, because the exchange is effected at a discount based on secondary market prices, the level of debt outstanding is commensurately reduced. The advantage to the original holder of the bond lies in higher yields on the uncollateralized bonds.

Mexico. Between January and September 1996 Mexico undertook two operations to retire $3.6

billion of Brady bonds at an average 24 percent discount. In effect, these operations were equivalent to prepaying Brady bonds at a discount funded by new issues. Savings of about $1.2 billion resulted from the differential between the par and the market values of these securities ($0.8 billion) and from the pro rata release of the collateral of the Brady bonds ($0.4 billion). In the first exchange, in May, Mexico swapped $2.4 billion of Brady bonds for a $1.8 billion thirty-year uncollaterized bond at an annual interest rate of 11.5 percent. In September Mexico bought back $1.2 billion of Brady bonds at a cost of 81 cents per dollar. This operation was funded by a $1.0 billion twenty-year bond at an interest rate of 445 basis points above U.S. Treasury rates.

The Philippines. In September, 1996 the Philippines issued a $0.7 billion eurobond in exchange for Brady bonds originally issued in 1989 to replace commercial bank debt. This exchange was the first step in the government's plans to retire $1.9 billion of Brady bonds. The eurobond was issued in the form of a twenty-year note at an annual interest rate of 8.75 percent.

Future deals. Other middle-income countries—notably Argentina, Brazil, and Venezuela—are reportedly considering whether to launch similar initiatives. Whether the market for these types of voluntary transactions expands in the near term will depend, among other things, on investors' confidence, secondary market prices, spreads on the new instruments, and accounting rules. Accounting rules limited demand for the Mexican issue by domestic banks, which, in accordance with accounting guidelines list Brady bonds as assets at face value rather than as tradable instruments. As a result, the books of any Mexican banks participating in the swap showed a loss equal to the difference between the face value and the market value of the transaction.

Debt and debt service reduction operations in middle-income countries

Panama. In April 1996 Panama closed a debt and debt service reduction agreement to restructure $3.9 billion of debt owed to commercial banks, including $1.9 billion of past-due interest (table A4.2). Eligible principal of $2.0 billion was rescheduled according to a menu of choices, with $87.8 million in discount bonds (45 percent discount), $268.0 million in par bonds, and $1,612.1 million in front-loaded interest reduction bonds. Creditors choosing the new money option purchase debt conversion bonds equal to the full face amount of the principal tendered and commit to purchase new money bonds equal to 10 percent of the principal tendered. By the closing date $130 million of past-due interest was paid, of which $30 million was paid prior to closing, $590.4 million was forgiven following recalculation of interest at a lower spread and the waiving of penalty interest, and $1,247.6 million was exchanged for past-due interest bonds.

The principal component of the discount and the par bonds was collateralized by thirty-year U.S. Treasury zero-coupon bonds delivered at closing. Payment of nine months of interest is guaranteed on a rolling basis by cash or permitted investments. Panama will pledge additional amounts so that twelve months of interest would be guaranteed by year two for discount bonds and year three for par bonds. The principal component of front-loaded interest reduction bonds is not collateralized, but payment of six months of interest will be collateralized on a rolling basis by cash or permitted investments until year seven.

As a result of these operations Panama's debt with commercial banks was reduced by $0.8 bil-

lion in nominal terms. Taking into account interest service savings and cash payments as a result of bond collateral, the debt reduction value of the debt and debt service reduction (excluding additional official lending) totaled $1.2 billion, equivalent to 31 percent of the nominal amount restructured.[3] The operation, including cash payments and bond collateral, cost $226.3 million, of which about 60 percent was funded from Panama's own resources. The balance was provided in roughly equal shares by the Inter-American Development Bank , the IBRD, and the IMF.

Peru. In November 1996 Peru completed a debt and debt service reduction accord to restructure $8.0 billion of debt owed to commercial banks (table A4.3). Of the $4,181 million of eligible principal, Peru bought back $1,266 million at 38 cents per dollar and exchanged $947 million at a 45 percent discount, $189 million at par, and $1,779 million for front-loaded interest reduction bonds. The $3,809 million in past-due interest was restructured so that $308 million was to be paid in cash by closing, $1,217.0 million was to be repurchased at 38 cents per dollar, and $2,284.0 million was exchanged for past-due interest bonds.

The principal component of the discount and the par bonds is collateralized by thirty-year U.S. Treasury zero-coupon bonds delivered at closing. Payment of six months of interest is guaranteed on a rolling basis by cash or permitted investments at an annual interest rate of 7.0 percent for the discount bonds and 3.0 percent for the par bonds. The principal component of the front-loaded interest reduction bonds is not guaranteed, but six months of rolling interest is secured by cash or permitted investments until the eleventh year. Neither principal nor interest securitization is required in the past-due interest bonds. Moreover, for the first six years Peru may choose to capitalize the difference between LIBOR plus $13/_{16}$ and 4 percent a year.

The debt and debt service reduction accord allowed Peru to reduce its debt with commercial banks by $3.2 billion in nominal terms. Taking into account interest service savings and cash payments on account of bond collateral, debt reduction (excluding additional official lending) amounted to $4.5 billion, equivalent to 56.1 percent of the nominal amount restructured. The operation, including cash payments, buyback, and bond collateral, cost

Table A4.2 Terms of Panama's debt and debt service reduction agreement, April 3, 1996

Instrument	Debt retired (millions of U.S. dollars)	Share (percent)	Maturity/grace (years)	Interest rate (percent)	Comments
Principal subject to the menu approach	1,968	100.0			
Discount bonds (45 percent discount)	87.8	4.5	30/bullet	LIBOR +$^{13}/_{16}$	Principal collateralized with 30-year U.S. Treasury zero-coupon bonds. Nine months of rolling interest guarantee at an annual interest rate of 7 percent, increasing in 2 years to cover 12 months at an annual rate of 7.5 percent secured by cash or permitted investments.
Par bonds with reduced fixed interest rates	268.0	13.6	30/bullet	Year 1 3.00 2 3.25 3 3.50 4 3.75 5–6 4.25 7–8 4.75 9–10 5.25 11–30 5.5	Principal collateralized with 30-year U.S. Treasury zero-coupon bonds. Nine months of rolling interest guarantee at an annual interest rate of 3.07 percent, increasing in 3 years to cover 12 months at an annual rate of 4.25 percent secured by cash or permitted investments.
Front-loaded interest reduction bonds	1,612.1	81.9	18/5	Year 1 3.50 2 3.75 3 4.00 4 4.25 5 4.50 6 4.75 7 5.00 8–18 LIBOR +$^{13}/_{16}$	No principal collateral. Six months of rolling interest guarantees up to year 7 at an assumed annual interest rate of 3.55 percent, increasing by reinvestment of interest collateral to cover 12 months at an annual rate of 5 percent secured by cash or permitted investments.
Memo item					
New money debt conversion par bonds	—	—	20/9.5	Year 1 4.50 2–4 4.75 5–6 5.75 7–20 LIBOR +$^{13}/_{16}$	No principal or interest collateral.
Debt conversion bonds	—	—	15/7.5	LIBOR +$^{13}/_{16}$	No principal or interest collateral.
Past-due interest	1,968.0				
Down payment prior to closing	30.0				
Down payment at closing	100.0				
Past-due interest par bonds	1,247.6		20/10	LIBOR +$^{13}/_{16}$	No principal or interest collateral. Graduated amortization schedule. For the first 6 years Panama may choose to capitalize interest accruing from the difference, if positive, between LIBOR +$^{13}/_{16}$ and 4 percent.
Forgiveness	590.4				
Total amount restructured	3,936.0				

— Not applicable.
Source: Republic of Panama, "1995 Financing Plan."

$1.4 billion, of which about 45.0 percent was funded from Peru's own resources, 6.9 percent by Eximbank-Japan, and the remainder by the Inter-American Development Bank, the IBRD, and the IMF, in equal shares.

The Russian Federation. In November 1995 an agreement in principle was reached with foreign commercial banks to reschedule $33.0 billion of the Russian Federation's debt, including $7.5 billion of interest arrears.[4] Eligible principal will be

Table A4.3 Terms of Peru's debt and debt service reduction agreement, November 8, 1996

Instrument	Debt retired (millions of U.S. dollars)	Share (percent)	Maturity/grace (years)	Interest rate (percent)	Comments
Principal subject to the menu approach	4,181.0	100.0			
Discount bonds (45 percent discount)	947.0	22.7	30/bullet	LIBOR +$^{13}/_{16}$	Principal collateralized with 30-year U.S. Treasury zero-coupon bonds. Six-month rolling annual interest guarantee at a rate of 7 percent secured by cash or permitted investments.
Par bonds with reduced fixed interest rate	189.0	4.5	30/bullet	Yrs 1–14 3.00 / 15–24 4.00 / 25–30 5.00	Principal collateralized with 30-year U.S. Treasury zero-coupon bonds. Six-month rolling annual interest guarantee at a rate of 3 percent secured by cash or permitted investments.
Front-loaded Interest reduction bonds	1,779.0	42.5	20/8	Year 1 3.25 / 2–3 3.75 / 4–5 4.00 / 6–7 4.50 / 8–9 5.00 / 10–20 LIBOR +$^{13}/_{16}$	No principal collateral. Six-month rolling interest guarantee until year 11 at an annual rate of 3.25 percent secured by cash or permitted investments. Graduated amortization schedule.
Buyback (38 cents per dollar)	1,266.0	30.3			
Past-due interest	3,809.0				
Cash payments prior to closing	83.0				
Cash payments at closing	225.0				
Past-due interest par bonds	2,284.0		20/10	LIBOR +$^{13}/_{16}$	No principal or interest collateral. Graduated amortization schedule. For six years, Peru may choose to capitalize interest accrued from the difference between LIBOR +$^{13}/_{16}$ and 4.0 percent on average.
Buyback (38 cents per dollar)	1,217.0				
Total amount restructured	7,990.0				

Source: Republic of Peru, "1996 Financing Plan".

repaid over twenty-five years, including a seven-year grace period. A graduated amortization plan will result in annual payments of about 2 percent a year for the first two to three years following expiration of the grace period, peaking at 15 percent in years nine and ten and declining thereafter. Interest due will be calculated at LIBOR plus $^{13}/_{16}$, with actual payments rising from about 25 percent of the amount due in 1996 to full payment beginning in 2002. The shortfall in interest payments will be covered by issuance of interest notes with a fourteen-year payment profile. About $2.0 billion will be paid up-front into escrow accounts toward the past-due interest arrears. The accord is being implemented in phases. In September 1996 the government announced that the London Club had agreed to complete the rescheduling of $20.0 billion and that it expects the remaining $13.0 billion to be rescheduled in the first quarter of 1997.

Debt buybacks in low-income countries

Ethiopia. In January 1996 Ethiopia concluded an agreement sponsored by the Debt Reduction Facility to purchase $226.0 million of eligible principal owed to commercial banks (table A4.4). About 80 percent of the debt due to commercial banks was bought back at 8 cents per dollar. As with other restructuring accords sponsored by the Debt Reduction Facility, past-due interest arrears, including penalties, were written off. The operation cost $18.8 million, of which $6.2 million was provided by the IBRD. The remainder was provided by other bilateral donors.

Mauritania. In August 1996 Mauritania concluded an agreement sponsored by the Debt Reduction Facility to restructure $92.0 million due to commercial banks, including the writeoff of $37.0 million in past-due interest and the buyback of $55.0 million at 10 cents per dollar. A significant portion of this debt consisted of liabilities assumed by the government following the privatization of a development bank. Financing required for the repurchase totaled $5.3 million, of which $3.2 million was provided by the IBRD.

Senegal. In December 1996 Senegal closed an operation sponsored by the Debt Reduction Facility to restructure its debt to commercial banks. Debt eligible under the proposed operation totaled $118.0 million, $75.0 million in principal and $43.0 million in past-due interest arrears. Senegal purchased the debt for 16 cents per dollar of principal of eligible debt. The commercial banks also exchanged part of the debt for long-term non–interest bearing notes issued by the government. The notes are collateralized by U.S. Treasury notes of similar maturity with a present value equivalent to that of the buyback option. Total financing required for the operation if all debt were tendered was placed at $13.4 million, of which some $7.7 million would come from the IBRD.

Debt conversion programs

The number of countries participating in debt conversions and the face value of debt restructured increased rapidly after May 1985, when Chile established the first institutionalized debt-for-

equity swap program. Since 1985 debt-equity conversions have totaled $45.2 billion (table A4.5).

Debt conversion activities have declined since 1992, however. Debt-for-equity swaps totaled only $200 million in 1995, and debt-for-development swaps totaled less than $100 million. Several factors have contributed to the drop in debt conversions. Investor interest in debt conversion programs has declined as rising secondary market prices of several countries' commercial bank debt have reduced the discount that can be captured. A significant amount of debt conversion activity has been linked to specific privatization programs that have been winding down or have turned to other instruments. At the same time, Brady operations, which have enabled debtor countries to regularize relations with commercial bank creditors, have permitted more flexibility in debt management and reduced some governments' interest in conversion programs.

Debt for equity

Debt-for-equity swaps generally involve the purchase of debt by the investor at a discount in the secondary market and the sale of the debt to the central bank for funds that are used to acquire public assets or invest in private equity. Debt-for-equity conversions can be a useful tool for accelerating a country's privatization program, as has

Table A4.4 Completed operations financed by the IDA Debt Reduction Facility as of December 1996
(millions of U.S. dollars)

Country	Date completed	Principal extinguished	Price (cents per dollar)[a]	Percentage of eligible principal extinguished	Total resources[b]	IBRD resources[b]
Niger	March 1991	107.0	18.0	99.0	19.4	8.4
Mozambique	December 1991	123.8	10.0	64.0	13.4	5.9
Guyana	November 1992	69.2	14.0	100.0	10.2	10.0
Uganda	February 1993	153.0	12.0	89.0	22.6	10.2
Bolivia	May 1993	170.0	16.0	94.0	27.3	9.8
São Tomé and Principe	August 1994	10.1	10.0	87.0	1.3	1.3
Zambia	September 1994	199.7	11.0	78.0	24.9	11.7
Albania	July 1995	371.3	26.0	99.0	97.4	26.0
Sierra Leone	September 1995	234.7	13.0	73.0	31.3	21.0
Nicaragua	December 1995	1,100.0	8.0	81.0	88.8	40.0
Ethiopia	January 1996	226.0	8.0	80.0	18.83	6.2
Mauritania	August 1996	53.0	10.0	98.0	5.90	3.3
Senegal	December 1996	71.0	20.0[c]	95.0	15.4	6.6
Total		2,888.06	13.0[d]	84.4[d]	377.3	161.2

a. Of original face value of principal.
b. Includes technical assistance grants.
c. 16 cents for cash buy back and 20 cents for long-term bonds.
d. Weighted average.
Source: World Bank staff estimates.

85

been done in Argentina, Mexico, and the Philippines.

Debt-for-equity swaps were negligible in 1995, however. The only two sizable operations were in Latin America, both in Peru. The privatization of EDEGEL (the electric utility company of Lima) generated $524 million, of which $100 million was debt for equity. The privatization of Banco Continental brought in $255 million to the Peruvian Treasury, of which $60 million was converted debt.

Debt-for-equity swaps were also used on a small scale in Mexico as part of the debt relief and recapitalization measures adopted by the government in 1995–96 to contain the banking crisis. Through these swaps banks acquired major shares of several companies including Mexicana and Aeromexico (airlines) and Grupo Gigante (retail). Two small debt-equity operations in Macedonia FYR accounted for $ 0.1 million.

Debt for development

In debt-for-development swaps an international organization (usually an NGO) purchases sovereign debt in the secondary market at a deep discount and then exchanges the debt at a redemption price negotiated with the country. The funds are then used for a development project approved by the country and managed by the NGO.

Debt for nature. Debt-for-nature operations are used to reduce developing countries' debt and allocate funds to the protection of nature preserves. Since 1987, when Conservation International and Bolivia signed the first debt-for-nature agreement, sixteen countries have retired $159 million in face value of debt though such programs, at an average discount of 62 percent

(table A4.6). Since 1994 Mexico has converted $1.9 million in face value of debt through five debt-for-nature transactions.

The importance of debt-for-nature swaps has been declining over time, however. Only one debt-for-nature swap operation took place in 1996—conversion of $391,000 in face value of Mexican debt.

Other debt-for-development swaps. Three organizations—Finance for Development, New York Bay, and the United Nations Childrens Fund (UNICEF)—have been the main participants in debt-for-development swaps that provide local currency funds for projects other than nature preserves. Finance for Development and New York Bay have swapped $391 million since 1992, of which $29.7 million was swapped in the first half of 1996 (table A4.7). The organizations have invested in various sectors, including health, population, agriculture, ecotourism, and low-income housing.

UNICEF, a pioneer in debt-for-development swaps, has continued its debt-for-child-development swap program. By 1996 UNICEF had completed twenty-two transactions, generating almost $53 million in local currency while helping participating countries reduce external debt stock by $199 million (table A4.8). A wide range of entities has been involved in the transactions, including an IDA Debt Reduction Facility operation for Zambia. The funds used come from national committees for UNICEF in industrial countries. These funds help finance programs for primary education, women in development, children in especially difficult circumstances, primary health, and water supply and sanitation. UNICEF is planing additional debt conversion operations in developing countries.

Table A4.5 Types of debt conversion instruments, 1985–95
(millions of U.S. dollars)

Instrument	1985	1986	1987	1988	1989	1990	1991	1992	1993	1994	1995	Total	Share (percent)
Debt equity swaps	570	882	3,577	7,567	6,981	9,624	2,823	8,148	4,586	248	200	45,206	32
Debt buyback or exchange	0	0	0	1,830	1,011	12,347	1,006	9,026	7,106	20,033	8,963	61,322	44
Local currency conversions	156	438	796	1,535	1,512	1,540	1,443	1,217	127	3	88	8,855	6
Local currency payments	0	63	87	3,580	2,269	5,242	800	342	0	2	0	12,385	9
Private sector restructuring	89	279	3,454	4,341	3,113	337	788	371	293	0	0	13,065	9
Total	815	1,662	7,914	18,853	14,886	29,090	6,860	19,104	12,112	20,286	9,251	140,833	100

Source: Institute for International Finance and World Bank Debtor Reporting System.

Role of the Debt Reduction Facility in debt conversions. Through the IDA Debt Reduction Facility, the World Bank has expanded the menu of debt reduction options to include provision for debt-for-development swaps. Under this provision commercial banks can choose to donate or tender debt to be repurchased by NGOs (at the same price as the debt buyback option). NGOs can then convert the debt into local currency to finance development projects. Two countries, Bolivia (1993) and Zambia (1994), have implemented such options. No debt-for-development swap has been concluded through the Debt Reduction Facility since 1994.

Notes

1. For details, see box A2.2, *World Debt Tables 1994–95.*
2. For details, see page 27, *World Debt Tables 1990–91.*
3. For details of the debt reduction equivalent concept, see box 2.2, *World Debt Tables 1993–94.*
4. Details of this agreement, previewed in *World Debt Tables 1996,* are revisited here to present additional details not available previously.

Table A4.6 Debt-for-nature swaps
(thousands of U.S. dollars)

Date	Country	Purchaser	Face value of debt[a]	Cost to donor[b]	Conservation funds[c]
1996	Mexico	CI	391	191.6	254
1995	Mexico	CI	488	246	336.5
1994	Mexico	CI	290	248.4	290
1994	Mexico	CI	480	399.4	480
1994	Mexico	CI	280	236	280
1994	Madagascar [d]	CI/WWF	2,000	50	2,000
1993	Madagascar	CI/WWF	5,000	3,200	5,000
1993	Philippines	WWF	1,900	13,000	17,700
1993	Mexico	CI	252	208	252
1992	Ecuador	Japan	n.a.	n.a.	1,000
1992	Brazil	TNC	2,200	746	2,200
1992	Bolivia [d]	TNC/WWF/JP Morgan	11,500	n.a.	2,800
1992	Guatemala	CI/USAID	1,300	1,200	1,300
1992	Panama	TNC	n.a.	n.a.	30,000
1992	Ecuador	WWF	1,000	n.a.	n.a.
1992	Philippines [e]	WWF	9,900	5,000	8,800
1992	Mexico	CI/USAID	44.1	355	441
1991	Ghana [f]	DDC/CI/SI	1,000	250	1,000
1991	Jamaica	TNC/USAID	437	300	437
1991	Guatemala [g]	TNC	100	75	90
1991	Mexico [h]	CI	250	n.a.	250
1991	Nigeria	NCF	149	65	93
1991	Philippines	USAID/WWF	n.a.	n.a.	8,000
1991	Mexico [h, i]	CI	250	183	250
1991	Costa Rica [j, g]	Rainforest Alliance	600	360	540
1991	Madagascar [k]	CI/UNDP	119	59	119
1990	Madagascar	WWF	919	446	919.4
1990	Philippines	WWF	900	439	900
1990	Madagascar	CI	5,000	n.a.	5,000
1990	Costa Rica	WWF/TNC/Sweden	10,800	1,900	9,600
1990	Dominican Rep.	TNC/PRCT	582	116	582
1990	Poland	WWF	n.a.	n.a.	50
1989	Zambia	WWF	2,300	454	2,300
1989	Madagascar	WWF	2,100	950	2,100
1989	Ecuador	WWF/TNC/MBG	9,000	1,100	9,000
1989	Costa Rica	Sweden	24,500	3,500	17,100
1989	Costa Rica	TNC	5,600	784	1,700
1989	Philippines [l]	WWF	390	200	390
1988	Costa Rica [m]	Holland	33,000	5,000	9,900
1988	Costa Rica	CI/WWF	5,400	918	5,400
1987	Ecuador	WWF	1,000	354	1,000
1987	Bolivia	CI	650	100	250

n.a. Not applicable.

CI = Conservation International, DDC = Debt for Development Coalition, MBG = Missouri Botanical Gardens, SI = Smithsonian Institute, TNC = The Nature Conservancy, UNDP = United Nations Development Programme, USAID = U.S. Agency for International Development, WWF = World Wildlife Fund.

a. Expenditures by environmental agency to acquire sovereign debt.

b. Equals expenditures by environmental agency to acquire the debt.

c. Value in dollar equivalent to the local currency part of the swap (either face value of the environmental bond or local currency equivalent). Overhead fees charged by government are not deducted.

d. Debt donated by JP Morgan.

e. Face value of debt includes $200,000 debt donation by Bank of Tokyo.

f. Involves buying blocked local currency funds from multinational organizations; includes Midwest universities, Consortium for International Activities, and U.S. Committee of the International Council on Monuments and Sites.

g. Purchase of Central American Bank for Economic Integration debt.

h. Total amount of program is $4 million.

i. Debt donated by Bank of America.

j. WWF contributed $1.5 million on top of the swap.

k. Total amount of program is $5 million.

l. Total amount of agreement is $3 million.

m. Includes $250,000 donated by Fleet National Bank of Rhode Island.

Source: World Wildlife Fund, Nature Conservancy, Conservation International, and World Bank.

Table A4.7 Face value of debt conversions originated by Finance for Development and New York Bay, 1992–96
(millions of U.S. dollars)

Country	1992	1993	1994	1995	Mid-1996
Mexico	4.2	15.4	92.1	37.5[a]	22.5
Philippines	7	8	13	3	0
Nigeria	0	1.7	1.5	6.8	7.2
South Africa	0	7.4	18.8	0	0
Tanzania	0	4.4	0	9.6	0
Kenya	1.5	8.6	0	0	0
Ghana	1	0	0	0	0
Zambia	0	0.1	86.9[a]	0	0
Bolivia	0	0	0	32.7	0
Total	13.7	45.6	212.3	89.6	29.7

a. Includes special conversion transactions.
Source: New York Bay Company and Finance for Development.

Table A4.8 UNICEF debt-for-child-development swaps, 1989–95
(thousands of U.S. dollars)

Country	Year	Sector	Face value	Cost	Development funds[a]	Purchase price (percent)
Mexico	1995	UNICEF programs	6,400	3,647	4,935	57.00
Madagascar	1994	Emergency	2,000	1,000	2,000	50.00
	1994	Water/education/health	1,200	576	950	48.00
Peru[b]	1994	UNICEF programs	10,880	0	2,720	0.00
Zambia[c]	1994	UNICEF programs	66,614	7,328	10,990	11.00
Mexico	1994	Health/education	1,870	1,015	1,902	54.30
Philippines[d]	1993	Education	250	0	180	0.00
Philippines	1993	Education	1,226	864	1,000	70.50
Bolivia	1993	Education/institutions	15,000	2,400	3,600	47.00
Madagascar	1993	Water/education/health	2,000	940	2,000	16.00
Senegal	1993	Water/education/health	24,000	6,000	11,000	25.00
Jamaica[e]	1992	Health/street children	4,000	2,877	4,000	71.90
Madagascar[f]	1992	Health/education/nutrition	4,000	2,000	4,000	50.00
Philippines	1992	Children in armed conflict	486	245	329	50.40
Sudan[g]	1992	Water/sanitation/health	38,068	0	1,200	0.00
	1991	Water/sanitation/health	5,000	0	460	0.00
	1991	Water/sanitation/health	3,000	0	276	0.00
	1990	Water/sanitation/health	7,023	0	801	0.00
	1989	Water/sanitation/health	2,732	0	244	0.00
	1989	Water/sanitation/health	2,732	0	225	0.00
	1989	Water/sanitation/health	800	0	80	0.00
Total or average			199,281	28,892	52,892	14.5

a. Value in dollar equivalent to the local currency part of the swap (either face value of the bond or local currency equivalent).
For bonds, the figure does not include interest earned over the life of the bond.
b. Debt donated.
c. IDA Debt Reduction Facility operation.
d. Donation of Brady bonds.
e. Primary health care, women in development, and children in especially difficult circumstances.
f. Health, nutrition, education, social mobilization, and area-based UNICEF programs.
g. UNICEF water, sanitation, and health education programs in rural areas.
Source: UNICEF and World Bank.

Table A4.9 Multilateral debt relief agreements with commercial banks, January 1980–December 1996

Country and date of agreement	Consolidation period Start date	Length (months)	Amount restructured (US$ millions) Deferment[a]	Rescheduling[b]	Other assistance (US$ millions) New long-term money[c]	Short-term credit maintenance[d]	Maturity (years/months)	Grace (years/months)	Interest (margin)[e]
Algeria									
February 1992	See notes			1,500			5-8/0	3/0	$1\,^1/_2/1\,^3/_8$
June 1995	March 1994			3,200			12/6-16	6/6	$^{13}/_{16}$
Albania									
July 1995	Debt buypack (see notes)								
Argentina									
January 1983	1 January 1983	12			1,300		1/2	0/7	$1\,^1/_4$
August 1983					500		4/6	3/0	$2\,^1/_4$
August 1985	1 January 1982	48		9,777	3,593	3,100	10/0	3/0	$1\,^3/_8$
August 1987	See notes			24,286	1,253	3,500	19/0	7/0	$^{13}/_{16}$
April 1993	DDSR agreement (see notes)								
Bolivia									
December 1980	1 August 1980	8	200				1/0	1/0	$1\,^3/_4$
April 1981	1 April 1981	24		411			6/0	3/0	$2\,^1/_4$
July 1988	Buyback arrangement (see notes)								
July 1992	DDSR agreement (see notes)								
May 1993	Debt buypack (see notes)								
Brazil									
February 1983	1 January 1983	12		4,800	4,195	15,675	8/0	2/6	$2\,^1/_4$
January 1984	1 January 1984	12		5,900	6,510	15,100	9/0	5/0	2
July 1986	1 January 1985	12	9,600	6,552		14,750	6/3	4/3	$1\,^1/_4$
November 1988	1 January 1987	84		61,482	5,200	14,833	20/0	8/0	$^{13}/_{16}$
July 1992	Interest arrears end-1990 (see notes)								
April 1994	DDSR agreement (see notes)								
Bulgaria									
July1994	DDSR agreement (see notes)								
Chile									
July 1983	1 January 1983	24		2,151	1,294	1,700	8/0	4/0	$2\,^1/_4$
January 1984	Short-term debt only			1,204			8/0	4/0	$2\,^1/_4$
June 1984					785		9/0	5/0	$1\,^3/_4$
November 1984						1,700	0/6	0/6	
November 1985	1 January 1985	36		3,891	1,037	1,700	12/0	6/0	$1\,^3/_8$
June 1987	1 January 1988	48		9,732		1,700	15/6	5/0	1
August 1988	Modification of terms (see notes)								$^{13}/_{16}$
December 1990	1 January 1991	48		4,173	320		8-12/0	4/0	$^{13}/_{16}$
Colombia									
December 1985					1,000		8/6	3/0	$1\,^1/_2$
June 1989					1,640		11/0	5/6	$^7/_8$
April 1991							12/6	7/6	1
Congo									
October 1986*	See notes								
Costa Rica									
September 1983	1 January 1983	24		706	202	202	8/0	4/0	$2\,^1/_4$
May 1985	1 January 1985	24		470	75		10/0	3/0	$1\,^5/_8$
May 1990	DDSR agreement (see notes)				1,457				

(table continues on next page)

Table A4.9 Multilateral debt relief agreements with commercial banks, January 1980–December 1996 (continued)

Country and date of agreement	Consolidation period — Start date	Length (months)	Amount restructured (US$ millions) — Deferment[a]	Rescheduling[b]	Other assistance (US$ millions) — New long-term money[c]	Short-term credit maintenance[d]	Repayment terms (consolidation portion only) — Maturity (years/ months)	Grace (years/ months)	Interest (margin)[e]
Côte d'Ivoire									
March 1985	1 December 1983	25		485	104		8/0	3/0	$1\,^7/_8$
November 1986	1 January 1986	48		851			9/0	3/0	$1\,^5/_8$
April 1988*	See notes								
Cuba									
December 1983	1 September 1982	28		130		490	5/6	2/0	$2\,^1/_{14}$
December 1984	1 January 1984	12		103		490	7/0	2/6	$1\,^7/_8$
July 1985	1 January 1985	12		90		490	10/0	6/0	$1\,^1/_2$
Dominican Republic									
December 1983	1 December 1982	13		500			5/0	1/0	$2\,^1/_4$
February 1986	1 January 1985	60		787			13/0	3/0	$1\,^3/_8$
August 1994	DDSR agreement (scc notes)								
Ecuador									
October 1983	1 November, 1982	14		2,770	433	700	7/0	1/0	$2\,^1/_4$
December 1985	1 January 1985	60		4,219	200	700	12/0	3/0	$1\,^3/_8$
November 1987*	See notes								
February 1995*	DDSR agreement (see notes)								
Gabon									
December 1987	1 September 1986	16		27			10/0	4/6	$1\,^3/_8$
December 1991	1 January 1989	36		75			13/0	3/0	$^7/_8$
May 1994	10 July 1994	6		187			10/0	2/6	$^7/_8$
Gambia, The									
February 1988	Balance as of 18 December 1986				19		8/0	3/6	$1\,^1/_4$
Guinea									
April 1988	Short-term debt only			28			3/0	0/6	$1\,^3/_4$
Guyana									
August 1982	11 March 1982	13	14						$2\,^1/_2$
June 1983	1 July 1983	7	12						$2\,^1/_2$
July 1984	1 August 1984	12	11						$2\,^1/_2$
July 1985	1 August 1985	18	15						$2\,^1/_2$
July 1988			8						
November 1992	Debt buypack (see notes)								
Honduras									
June 1987*	1 April 1987	33		248			8/0	6/0	$1\,^1/_8$
August 1989	See notes			101					
Iran, Rep. of									
March 1993	Balance as of March 1993			2,800			1/1	1/0	$^{13}/_{16}$
December 1994	Balance as of December 1994			10,900			6/0	2/0	$^{13}/_{16}$

Table A4.9 Multilateral debt relief agreements with commercial banks, January 1980–December 1996 (continued)

Country and date of agreement	Consolidation period Start date	Length (months)	Amount restructured (US$ millions) Deferment[a]	Rescheduling[b]	Other assistance (US$ millions) New long-term money[c]	Short-term credit maintenance[d]	Repayment terms (consolidation portion only) Maturity (years/ months)	Grace (years/ months)	Interest (margin)[e]
Jamaica									
April 1981	1 April 1979	24		126			5/0	2/0	2
June 1981	1 July 1981	21		89	89		5/0	2/0	2
June 1984	1 July 1983	21		164			5/0	2/0	2 $^1/_2$
September 1985	1 April 1985	24		359			10/0	3/0	1 $^7/_8$
May 1987	1 January 1987	39		366			12/6	9/0	1 $^1/_4$
June 1990	1 January 1990	24		315			14/0	0/6	$^{13}/_{16}$
Jordan									
September 1989*	1 January 1989	30		580			11/0	5/0	$^{13}/_{16}$
November 1989*	1 January 1989	18			50	50	10/6	4/0	$^{13}/_{16}$
December 1993	See notes.								
Liberia									
December 1982	1 July 1981	24		29			6/0	2/9	1 $^3/_4$
June 1983	See notes			26					
Madagascar									
November 1981	Arrears only			155			3/6	0/0	1 $^1/_2$
October 1984	See notes			379			8/0	2/6	2
June 1987	See notes						9/0	0/0	1 $^5/_8$
May 1990*	1 April 1990	69		49			12/0	0/2	$^7/_8$
Malawi									
March 1983	1 September 1982	24		59			6/6	3/0	1 $^7/_8$
October 1988	Balance as of 21 August 1987			36			8/0	4/0	1 $^1/_4$
Mauritania									
August 1996	Debt buypack (see notes)								
Mexico									
August 1983	23 April 1982	28		23,280	5,007		8/0	4/0	1 $^7/_8$
April 1984					3,873		10/0	5/6	1 $^1/_2$
March 1985	1 January 1987	48		28,000			14/0	0/0	1 $^1/_4$
August 1985	1 January 1985	72		20,256			14/0	1/0	1 $^1/_4$
October 1985			950						
March 1987				44,216	7,439		20/0	7/0	$^{13}/_{16}$
August 1987				9,700			20/0	7/0	$^{13}/_{16}$
March 1988	Debt exchange (see notes)								
March 1990	DDSR agreement (see notes)			48,231	1,091				
May/September 1996	Voluntary debt swap (see notes)								
Morocco									
February 1986	9 September 1983	16		531		610	7/ 0	3/0	1 $^1/_4$
September 1987	1 January 1985	48		2,415			11/0	4/0	1 $^3/_{16}$
September 1990	Balance as of 31 December 1989			3,200			18/4	8/10	$^{13}/_{16}$
Mozambique									
May 1987	Entire stock of debt			253			15/0	8/0	1 $^1/_4$
December 1991	Debt buypack (see notes)								

(table continues on next page)

Table A4.9 Multilateral debt relief agreements with commercial banks, January 1980–December 1996 (continued)

Country and date of agreement	Consolidation period		Amount restructured (US$ millions)		Other assistance (US$ millions)		Repayment terms (consolidation portion only)		
	Start date	Length (months)	Deferment[a]	Rescheduling[b]	New long-term money[c]	Short-term credit maintenance[d]	Maturity (years/ months)	Grace (years/ months)	Interest (margin)[e]
Nicaragua									
December 1980	Arrears			582			12/0	5/0	$3/_4$
December 1981	See notes			192			12/0	5/0	$3/_4$
March 1982	See notes			100			12/0	5/0	$3/_4$
February 1984	1 July 1983	12		145			8/0	0/0	$1\,1/_4$
December 1995	Debt buypack (see notes)								
Niger									
March 1984	1 October 1983	29		29			7/6	3/6	2
April 1986	1 October 1985	39		36			8/6	4/0	2
March 1991	Debt buypack (see notes)				107				
Nigeria									
November 1987	1 April 1986	21		4,714			9/0	3/0	$1\,1/_4$
March 1989	Short-term debt only			5,671			20/0	3/0	$7/_8$
January 1992	DDSR agreement (see notes)			5,436					
Panama									
September 1983					278	217	6/0	3/0	$2\,1/_4$
October 1985	1 January 1985	24		578	60	190	12/0	3/6	$1\,3/_8$
April 1996	DDSR agreement (see notes)								
Peru									
January 1980	1 January 1980	12		364			5/0	2/0	$1\,1/_4$
July 1983	7 March 1983	12		432	650	2,000	8/0	3/0	$2\,1/_4$
November 1996	DDSR agreement (see notes)								
Philippines									
January 1986	17 October 1983	38		5,885	925	2,974	10/0	5/0	$1\,5/_8$
December 1987	1 January 1987	72		9,010		2,965	17/0	7/6	$7/_8$
January 1990	DDSR agreement (see notes)			1,337	715				
December 1992	DDSR agreement (see notes)				135		17/0	5/0	$13/_{16}$
September 1996	Voluntary debt swap (see notes)								
Poland									
April 1982	26 March 1981	9		1,956			7/0	4/0	$1\,3/_4$
November 1982	1 January 1982	12		2,225			7/6	4/0	$1\,3/_4$
November 1983	1 January 1983	12		1,254			10/0	4/6	$1\,7/_8$
July 1984	1 January 1984	48		1,480		335	10/0	5/0	$1\,3/_4$
September 1986	1 January 1986	24		1,940			5/0	5/0	$1\,3/_4$
July 1988	1 January 1988	72		8,310		1,000	15/0	0/0	$15/_{16}$
June 1989*	1 May 1989	20	206						
October 1994	DDSR agreement (see notes)		206		138				
Romania									
December 1982	1 January 1982	12		1,598			6/5	3/0	$1\,3/_4$
June 1983	1 January 1983	12		567			6/5	3/6	$1\,3/_4$
September 1986	1 January 1986	24		800			5/6	4/0	$1\,3/_8$
September 1987*	1 January 1986	24		800			5/6	4/0	$13/_{16}$
Russian Federation									
December 1991	See notes								
July 1993	See notes								
November 1995	Balance as of 15 November 1995			32,500			25/0	7/0	$13/_{16}$

Table A4.9 Multilateral debt relief agreements with commercial banks, January 1980–December 1996 (continued)

Country and date of agreement	Consolidation period: Start date	Consolidation period: Length (months)	Amount restructured (US$ millions): Deferment[a]	Amount restructured (US$ millions): Rescheduling[b]	Other assistance (US$ millions): New long-term money[c]	Other assistance (US$ millions): Short-term credit maintenance[d]	Repayment terms (consolidation portion only): Maturity (years/months)	Repayment terms (consolidation portion only): Grace (years/months)	Repayment terms (consolidation portion only): Interest (margin)[e]
São Tomé and Principe									
August 1994	Debt buypack (see notes)								
Senegal									
February 1984	1 May 1981	38		96			6/0	3/0	2
May 1985	1 July 1984	24		20			7/0	3/0	2
January 1989				37			9/0	0/0	7/8
December 1996	Debt buypack (see notes)								
Sierra Leone									
January 1984	Principal arrears			25			7/0	2/0	1 3/4
August 1995	Debt buypack (see notes)								
South Africa									
September 1985	28 August 1985	7	13,628						
March 1986	28 August 1985	22		650			1/3	Bullet/variable	
March 1987	1 July 1987	36		4,500			3/0	Bullet/variable	
October 1989	1 July 1990	42		7,500					
September 1993	See notes			5,000			8/0	0/6	1 1/8
Sudan									
November 1981	1 January 1980	28		593			7/0	3/0	1 3/4
March 1982	Interest arrears only			3			0/9	0/5	1 3/4
April 1983	See notes			702			6/0	2/0	1 3/4
October 1985	See notes			1,037			8/0	3/0	1 1/4
Togo									
March 1980	See notes			69			3/6	1/0	
October 1983	See notes			84			7/3	0/0	2
May 1988	See notes			48			8/0	4/0	1 3/8
Trinidad and Tobago									
December 1989	1 September 1988	48		473			12/6	4/6	15/16
Turkey									
March 1982	See notes			2,269			10/0	5/0	1 3/4
Uganda									
February 1993	Debt buypack (see notes)								
Uruguay									
July 1983	1 January 1983	24		555	240		6/0	2/0	2 1/4
July 1986	1 January 1985	60		1,720			12/0	3/0	1 3/8
March 1988	1 January 1990	24		1,512			17/0	3/0	7/8
February 1991	DDSR agreement (see notes)			1,284	89				
Venezuela									
February 1986	1 January 1983	72		21,089			12/6	0/0	1 1/8
November 1987	See notes				100		14/0	1/0	7/8
September 1988	See notes			20,388			13/0	0/0	7/8
December 1990	DDSR agreement (see notes)			19,598	1,212				

(table continues on next page)

Table A4.9 Multilateral debt relief agreements with commercial banks, January 1980–December 1996 (continued)

Country and date of agreement	Consolidation period — Start date	Length (months)	Amount restructured (US$ millions) — Deferment[a]	Rescheduling[b]	Other assistance (US$ millions) — New long-term money[c]	Short-term credit maintenance[d]	Repayment terms (consolidation portion only) — Maturity (years/ months)	Grace (years/ months)	Interest (margin)[e]
Yugoslavia, former									
October 1983	1 January 1983	12		1,300	600	800	6/0	3/0	$1\,^7/_8$
May 1984	1 January 1984	24		1,330			7/0	4/0	$1\,^5/_8$
December 1985	1 January 1985	48		4,004			10/6	4/0	$1\,^1/_4$
September 1988	1 January 1988	24		7,000		300	18/0	6/0	$^{13}/_{16}$
Zaire									
April 1980	See notes			402			10/0	5/0	$1\,^7/_8$
January 1983	1 January 1983	12	58				10/0	0/0	2
June 1984	1 January 1984	16	64				10/0	0/0	2
May 1985	1 May 1985	12	61				10/0	0/0	2
May 1986	1 May 1986	12	65				10/0	0/0	2
May 1987	1 May 1987	12	61				10/0	0/0	2
June 1989	See notes		61						
Zambia									
December 1984	1 January 1985			74					
September 1994	Debt buypack (see notes)								

* Agreement in principle.
DDSR = Officially supported debt and debt service reduction agreement (Brady initiative); DRF = IDA Debt Reduction Facility; FLIRB = Front loaded interest reduction bonds; MYRA = Multiyear rescheduling agreement; PDI = Past due interest.
a. Short-term rollover of current maturities.
b. Consolidation of debt into new long-term obligations; may include arrears as well as future maturities; interest and short-term debt included only if indicated in country notes. For DDSR agreements, figures include face value of buybacks and of all debt exchanges.
c. Loans arranged for budgetary or balance of payments support in conjunction with debt rescheduling, usually in proportion to each creditor bank's exposure; sometimes referred to as concerted lending.
d. Understanding by banks to maintain the size of existing trade or other short-term credit facilities, arranged in conjunction with debt rescheduling.
e. The percentage points above LIBOR.
Sources: World Bank Debtor Reporting System, Institute of International Finance, and IMF.

Country Notes

Algeria
Feb 92 1991–93 Financing Facility designed to refinance maturities falling due between October 1991 and March 1993. Tranche A covers debts with a maturity of 2 years or more and is repayable in 8 years, including 3 years grace bearing interest at LIBOR $+1\,^1/_2$ percent. Tranche B covers debts with a maturity of more than 360 days and less than 2 years, and is repayable in 5 years, including 3 years grace.

Albania
Jun 95 Restructuring of $501 million due to commercial banks. $371 million bought back for $96.5 million funded by grants from IDA DRF and other donor countries; $130 million converted into long-term bonds.

Argentina
Jan 83 Bridge loan.
Aug 83 New money initially $1.5 billion.
Aug 85 Agreed in principle December 1984.
Aug 87 Agreement extended maturity and lowered spreads on 1983 and 1985 agreements. Also includes noncollateralized debt exchange with interest reduction ($15 million).
Apr 93 DDSR agreement in which outstanding stock of $19.3 billion exchanged for 30-year bonds yielding a market interest rate (LIBOR $+^{13}/_{16}$ percent) at a 35 percent discount or 30-year par FLIRBs. First-year interest rate 4 percent, rising to 6 percent in year 7 and remaining there until maturity. Both bonds collateralized for principal and contain rolling 12-month guarantee. Agreement also included $9.3 billion of past due interest of which $0.7 billion was paid in cash at closing, $400 million was written off, and the remainder was exchanged for bonds (17-year maturity, 7 years grace), repayable in rising installments and yielding LIBOR $+^{13}/_{16}$ percent.

Bolivia
Dec 80 Includes short-term debt.
Apr 81 Includes debt deferred in August 1980.
Jun 88 Ongoing program in which commercial bank debt retired through a buyback ($272 million) and a local currency bond exchange ($72 million). Applies only to previously deferred loans.
Jul 92 DDSR term sheet. Cash buyback at 84 percent discount; collateralized interest-free 30-year bullet-maturity par bonds; short-term discount bonds (84 percent) convertible on maturity into local currency assets at a 1:1.5 ratio, exchangeable into investments for special projects. Past-due interest canceled under all options. Value recovery clause based on price of tin.
May 93 Buyback of $170 million commercial bank debt, funded by grants from IDA DRF and other donor countries.

Brazil
Jul 86 Includes deferment of 1986 maturities.
Nov 88 Includes broad package of creditor options.
Jul 92 Interest arrears: December 31, 1990. Cash payment during 1992: $863 million. Balance converted into 10-year bonds (3 years grace), bearing market interest rates.
Apr 94 DDSR agreement under which four components of debt, totaling $48 billion, were restructured (a) debt to foreign banks under the 1988 multiyear deposit facility agreement ($32.5), (b) debt to Brazilian banks under the MDFA, (c) debt resulting from the 1988 new money facilities ($8.1 billion), and (d) interest arrears accruing from 1991–94 ($6.0 billion). The first category of debt was restructured following a six-choice menu: (a) discount bonds, 35 percent discount, 30-year bullet maturity yielding LIBOR $+^{13}/_{16}$ percent with principal collateral and a 12-month rolling interest guarantee ($11.2 billion); (b) par bonds with a reduced fixed-rate interest (yielding 4 percent in the first year, gradually rising to 6

percent in year 7), 30-year bullet maturity, with principal collateral and a 12-month rolling interest guarantee. ($10.5 billion); (c) FLIRBs ($1.7 billion), with interest rising from a fixed rate of 4 percent in year 1 to 6 percent in years 5 and 6 and then reverting to LIBOR +$^{13}/_{16}$ percent from year 7 to maturity, 15 years maturity including 9 years grace, 12-month rolling interest guarantee; (d) C-bonds, par reduced interest rate bonds with capitalization of interest ($7.1), with repayment terms of 20 years maturity, including 10 years grace, interest beginning at 4 percent and the applicable rates in the first 6 years being capitalized, no collateral; (e) conversion bonds ($1.9 billion) combined with new money bonds in a 1:5.5 ratio, interest at LIBOR +$^7/_8$ percent, 18-year maturity, including 10 years grace, for the conversion bonds and 15 years, including 7 years grace, for the new money bonds, no collateral; (f) interest reduction loan with capitalization, maturity of 20 years including 10 years grace, interest rising from 4 percent in year 1 to 5 percent in year 6 to LIBOR +$^{13}/_{16}$ from year 7 to maturity.

Bulgaria

Jul 94 DDSR agreement under which creditors agreed to restructuring of $8.3 billion in public external debt, including about $2.1 billion in PDI. The menu for the original debt includes (a) buyback at 0.25 cent per dollar ($.8 billion); (b) discount bond 50 percent discount on face value (30-year bullet maturity, market rate, $3.7 billion), with the discount bonds collateralized for principal; and (c) FLIRBs, 18 years maturity, including 8 years grace, interest beginning at 2 percent, rising to 3 percent in the 7 year and thereafter LIBOR +$^{13}/_{16}$ ($1.7 billion). FLIRBs have 1 year's interest rolling interest guarantee. PDI includes cash payment of about 3 percent, a buyback ($.2 billion), write-off of $0.2 billion, and PDI par bonds ($1.6 billion) having a 17-year maturity, including 7 years grace, and a yield of LIBOR +$^{13}/_{16}$ percent.

Chile

Jan 84 Short-term debt consolidated.

Nov 84 Short-term debt rolled over to June 30, 1985.

Nov 85 Short-term trade credit rolled over to 1990.

Aug 88 Interest spread reduced to $^{13}/_{16}$ percent. Also cash buybacks ($439 million).

Dec 90 New money bonds not tied to existing banks' exposure. Rescheduling includes previously rescheduled debt.

Colombia

December 85 New money without restructuring.

June 89 New money without restructuring.

April 91 New money without restructuring.

Congo

Oct 86 Agreement in principle, never concluded, to restructure 1986–88 maturities, repayable in 9 years, including 3 years grace, bearing interest at LIBOR +2 $^7/_8$ percent. Approximately $200 million of debt would have been restructured. In addition, there was a new money provision of $60 million.

Costa Rica

Sep 83 Includes principle arrears.

May 85 Includes deferment of revolving credit ($2 million).

May 90 DDSR agreement including cash buyback at 84 percent discount ($992 million), debt-for-bond-exchange ($579 million), and write-off of $29 million of PDI.

Côte d'Ivoire

Nov 86 MYRA.

Apr 88 Agreement designed to replace MYRA. Includes new money to refinance interest. Interest on the new money portion was LIBOR +1$^1/_2$ percent. Agreement was not put into effect because interest arrears were not cleared, and current interest payments were suspended in April 1988.

Dominican Rep.

Dec 83 Includes short-term debt.

Feb 86 MYRA. Includes arrears as of December 31, 1984.

Aug 94; DDSR agreement covering principal and PDI ($1.2 billion). The agreement has a menu consisting of (a) buybacks ($.4 billion); (b) discount exchange bonds ($.5 billion), 35 percent discount, 30-year bullet maturity, interest rate of LIBOR +$^{13}/_{16}$ percent; and (c) PDI bonds ($171 million) bearing interest at LIBOR +$^{13}/_{16}$ percent, with 3 years grace and 15 years maturity. The accord also included a write-off of $112 million of PDI, and $52 million paid in cash at closing.

Ecuador

Dec 85 MYRA.

Nov 87 Replaces MYRA.

Feb 95 DDSR agreement restructuring $7.8 billion of principal and PDI. For principal, creditors agreed to exchange $2.6 billion for discount bonds (45 percent discount) yielding LIBOR +$^{13}/_{16}$ percent and $1.9 billion for par reduced-interest rate bonds. Both bonds have a 30-year bullet maturity, are collateralized for principal, and have a 12-month rolling interest guarantee. The interest rate on the par bonds is 3 percent for the first year, rising to 5 percent in year 11. For PDI, $75 billion is to be settled in cash at closing, $2.3 billion was exchanged for bonds with a 20-year maturity (no grace period) repayable on a graduated amortization schedule, $191 million was exchanged for interest equalization bonds, and $582 million was written off.

Ethiopia

Jan 96 Debt buyback at 8 cents per dollar of $226.0 million owed to commercial banks. Funding for the operation provided by the IDA DRF.

Gabon

May 94 Rescheduled principal due through 1994 on debt contracted prior to September 20, 1986 (debt covered by the 1991 agreement, which had not been implemented). Ten-year maturity including 2$^1/_2$ years grace, interest at LIBOR +$^7/_8$ percent. Arrears of interest and arrears of post cut-off maturities as of July 1, 1994, are to be repaid between 1994 and 1996.

Guyana

Aug 82 One-year deferment.

Jun 83 Extension of 1982 deferment.

Jul 84 Extension of previous deferment.

Jul 85 Extension of previous deferment.

Nov 92 Buyback of $69 million under the IDA DRF at 14 cents per dollar.

Honduras

Jun 87 Two agreements, in 1983 and 1984, were not implemented; this agreement incorporated 1981–85 maturities but was not signed.

Aug 89 Bilateral rescheduling of debt to two commercial banks. The agreement includes interest arrears. Grace period varied from 7 to 10 years. Interest rates were fixed, ranging from 4 to 6$^1/_2$ percent.

Jamaica

May 87 Includes reduced spreads on earlier agreements.

Jun 90 Agreement also includes a reduction of spreads on earlier agreements to $^{13}/_{16}$ percent.

Jordan

Dec 93 DDSR agreement restructuring $736 million of principal and $153 million of PDI. For restructured principal, a small amount was repurchased at 39 cents per dollar, $243 million was exchanged for discount bonds (35 percent discount), and $493 million was exchanged for par fixed interest bonds. Both bonds have a 30-year bullet maturity with principal collateral and a 6-month rolling interest guarantee. The discount bonds yield LIBOR +$^{13}/_{16}$ percent interest; the yields on par bonds begin at 4 percent in the first year, rising to 6 percent in year 7. At closing $29 million in PDI was paid; $91 million was exchanged for noncollateralized bonds with a 12-year maturity, including 3 years grace, yielding LIBOR +$^{13}/_{16}$ percent; and $33 million was written off. Up-front costs totaled $147 million, all of which was provided from Jordan's own resources.

(table continues on next page)

Liberia
1983   Consolidation of oil facility debt.

Madagascar
Oct 81   Restructuring of entire stock of debt, including arrears.
Nov 81   Arrears on overdrafts consolidated into long-term debt.
Jun 87   Modified terms of October 1984 agreement.

Malawi
Oct 88   Rescheduled balances as of August 21, 1987.

Mauritania
Aug 96   Debt buyback of $53.0 million, at a 90 percent discount.
          Funding for operation provided by the IDA DRF.

Mexico
Mar 85   MYRA covering previously rescheduled debt.
Aug 85   MYRA covering debt not previously rescheduled.
Oct 85   Deferment of first payment under March 1985 agreement.
Mar 87   Modification of terms of earlier agreements.
Aug 87   Private sector debt restructured.
Mar 88   Exchange of debt for 20-year zero-coupon collateralized bonds ($556 million).
Mar 90   DDSR agreement. In addition to new money of $1 billion, the agreement provides for the exchange of $20.5 billion of debt for bonds at a 35 percent discount, an exchange of $22.4 billion of debt at par for reduced interest rate bonds, and conversion bonds totaling $5.3 billion. Conversion bonds are not collateralized and have a 15-year maturity, including 7 years grace, and an interest rate of LIBOR $+^{13}/_{16}$. The total base also includes $693 million not committed to any option.
May/   On May 7 Mexico swapped $2.4 billion of Brady bonds for a
Sep 96 $1.8 billion 30-year uncollaterized bond at an interest rate of 11.5 percent. On September 24 Mexico bought back $1.2 billion of Brady bonds at a cost of 81 cents per dollar. This operation was funded by a $1.0 billion 20-year bond at an interest rate of 445 basis points above U.S. Treasury rates.

Morocco
Feb 86   Agreement in principle initiated August 1983.
Jun 90   Phase one of this agreement restructures debt; phase two is a DDSR arrangement that will take effect if Morocco signs an EFF agreement with the IMF by December 31, 1991.

Mozambique
May 87   Outstanding balance consolidated, including interest arrears.
Dec 91   Buyback of $124 million of outstanding commercial bank debt at a 90 percent discount, funded by grants from the IDA DRF and from France, the Netherlands, Switzerland, and Sweden.

Nicaragua
Dec 80   Covers government debt, all maturities, including arrears.
Dec 81   Covers nationalized bank debts, all maturities, including arrears.
Mar 82   Covers debts of nonfinancial enterprises, all maturities, including arrears.
Feb 84   Deferment of service on rescheduled debt.
Dec 95   Buyback of $1.1 billion of outstanding commercial bank debt at 8 cents per dollar.

Niger
Mar 91   Buyback of all commercial bank debt at 82 percent discount ($107 million). Resources provided by grants from the DRF ($10 million), Switzerland ($3 million), and France ($10 million).

Nigeria
Nov 87   Includes short-term debt.
Mar 89   Includes line of credit arrears.
Jan 92   DDSR agreement providing for a cash-back at 60 percent discount on $3.3 billion and debt exchanges on $2 billion for collateralized 30-year bullet maturity par bonds with reduced interest rates of 5.5 percent for the first 3 years, 6.25 percent thereafter. Creditor selections: 62 percent for the buyback, 38 percent for the debt-reduction bond. A third option, new money combined with conversion bonds, was not selected by participating creditor banks.

Panama
Apr 96   DDSR agreement under which creditors agreed to restructuring of $3.9 billion in public external debt, including $2.0 billion in PDI. The menu for the principal includes (a) discount bonds at a 45 percent discount of face value (30 years bullet maturity, market rate, $87.8 million); (b) par bonds with reduced interest rates and a 30-year bullet repayment ($268.0 million); and (c) FLIRBs for $1,612.2 million with 18 years maturity, including 5-year grace period. The discount and the par bonds are collateralized with respect to the principal by U.S. Treasury zero-coupon bonds and with respect to interest in the form of a nine month rolling interest rate guarantee in the first year rising to 12 months in years 2–3. The FLIRBs do not require guarantee for the capital, but include a 6 month rolling interest guarantee. PDI settlement includes progress payments of $30.0 million, a payment at closing of $100.0 million, a write-off of $590.4 million arising from the recalculation of penalty interest at a lower interest rate, and PDI par bonds of $1,247.6 million with 20-year maturity, including 7 years grace, and an interest rate of LIBOR $+^{13}/_{16}$ percent. Neither principal nor interest is guaranteed, and Panama may capitalize for the first 6 years any positive differences between LIBOR $+^{13}/_{16}$ and 4.0 percent.

Peru
Nov 96   DDSR agreement under which creditors agreed to restructure $8.0 billion in public external debt, including $3.8 billion in PDI. The menu for the principal includes (a) discount bonds at a 45 percent discount of face value (30 year bullet maturity, market rate, $947.0 million); (b) par bonds with reduced interest rates and a 30 year bullet repayment ($189 million); (c) FLIRBs for $1,779.0 million with a 20-year maturity, including 8 years grace period; and (d) a buyback of $1,266.0 million at 38 cents per dollar. The discount and the par bonds are collateralized with respect to the principal by U.S. Treasury zero-coupon bonds and with respect to interest in the form of a 6-month rolling interest rate guarantee secured by cash or permitted investments. The FLIRBs do not require guarantee for the capital, but include a 6-month rolling interest guarantee. PDI settlement includes progress payments of $83.0 million, a payment at closing of $225.0 million, a buyback of $1,217.0 million at 38 cents per dollar, and PDI par bonds of $2,284.0 million with a 20-year maturity, including 10 years grace, and an interest rate of LIBOR $+^{13}/_{16}$ percent. Neither principal nor interest is guaranteed, and Peru may capitalize for the first 6 years, the difference between LIBOR $+^{13}/_{16}$ and 4.0 percent a year.

Philippines
Jan 90   DDSR agreement provided for $1,337 million of buybacks at 50 percent discount.
Dec 92   DDSR agreement: Following implementation of a cash buyback of $1.3 billion on May 14, 1992, banks selected debt exchanges from three options: (a) FLIRBs; yielding LIBOR $+^{13}/_{16}$ percent from year 7 to maturity (15 years for series A and $15^1/_2$ year for series B, both including 7 years grace); (b) collateralized step-down/step-up interest reduction bonds yielding 6.5 percent from year 6 to maturity (25-year bullet maturity for series A and $25^1/_2$ year for series B); and (c) new money combined with conversion bonds in a 1:4 ratio, with both bonds attaining $17^1/_2$ (series A) or 17-year (series B) maturity, including 5 years grace and yielding LIBOR $+^{13}/_{16}$ percent. Interest payments on both interest-reduction bonds covered by a rolling 14-month guarantee. Creditor choices ($4.4 billion, 96 percent total eligible debt): buybacks, $1.3 billion (27.5 percent): option (a) $0.8 billion (46.3 percent), option (b) $1.9 billion (41.1 percent), option (c) $0.5 billion, (11.7 percent).
Sep 96   Philippines issued $0.7 billion eurobond in exchange for Brady bonds originally issued to replace commercial bank debt in 1989. The Eurobond was issued in the form of a 20-year note at an annual interest rate of 8.75 percent.

Poland

Jul 84   Includes some short-term trade credits.

Sep 86   Covers debt rescheduled in 1982.

Jul 88   MYRA. Also improved terms of earlier agreements.

Jun 89   Principal due May 1989-December 1990 deferred until
December 1991; in October the $145 million in interest due
in the fourth quarter of 1989 was deferred until the second
quarter of 1990.

Oct 94   DDSR agreement under which creditors restructured $14.4
billion. Three categories of debt were affected: (a) long-term
debt covered by the 1988 restructuring agreement ($8.9 bil-
lion), (b) debt due under the Revolving Short-Term
Arrangement ($1.2 billion), and (c) PDI not otherwise
restructured ($4.3 billion). The first category was subject to a
menu approach, with $2.1 billion of long-term debt repur-
chased at 41 cents per dollar and $0.3 billion of RSTA debt
repurchased at 38 cents per dollar. For the remaining long-
term debt, creditors chose between (a) discount bonds at 45
percent discount ($5.4 billion), (b) par reduced fixed interest
bonds ($0.9 billion), and (c) conversion bonds combined with
new money bonds equal to 35 percent of the amount converted ($0.4 billion). The discount bonds and par bonds have 30-
year bullet maturities and feature collateralization of principal
only. Interest on the discount bonds is LIBOR +$^{13}/_{16}$ percent.
Interest on the par bonds is 2.75 percent for the first year, rising to 5 percent in year 21. The conversion bonds have a 25-
year maturity, including 20 years grace period. Yield in year 1
is 4.5 percent, rising to 7.5 percent in year 11. New money
bonds have a 15-year maturity, including 10-year grace, and
yield LIBOR +$^{13}/_{16}$ percent. New money and conversion
bonds are not collateralized. RSTA debt not repurchased
($0.9 billion) is exchanged for 30-year bullet maturity fixed
interest bonds, with similar (but slightly different) step-
down/step-up arrangements as the par bonds, starting at 2.75
percent in year 1 and gradually rising to 5 percent in year 21.
For PDI $.8 billion was repurchased with related long-term
and RSTA principal. A portion is to be settled with cash payments at closing ($63 million), a portion was written off ($0.8
billion), and the remainder ($2.7 billion), was converted into
fixed-interest rate bonds yielding 3.25 percent in year 1, rising
to 7 percent in year 9. Maturity is 20 years, including 7 years
grace. Amortization is graduated.

Romania

Sep 86   Covers previously rescheduled debt only.

Russian Federation

Dec 91   Deferment of principal due between December 1991 and
March 1992 on pre-1991 debt. Deferment was extended for
each consecutive quarter until the end of 1993.

Jul 93   Agreement in principle to R reschedule the stock of debt of
the former Soviet Union to commercial banks contracted
prior to January 1, 1991 ($24 billion), to be repaid with 15-
year maturity, including 5 years grace. In the fourth quarter
of 1993, $500 million was to be paid on interest accruing
during 1993. At the end of 1993, all remaining unpaid interest (estimated at $3 billion) would then be consolidated and
repaid with 10-year maturity including 5-year grace. The
1993 interest payments were not made, and; the agreement
was not implemented, mainly because of Russian rejection of
refusal to accept the waiver of bankers' requirement that sovereign immunity be waived. On October 5, 1994 However,
an agreement was signed understanding was reached on 5-
Oct-94 that in which the banks would dropped their insis-
tence on the waiver of sovereign immunity and that the
Vneshekonombank (or another public sector entity) committed to would guarantee the restructured debts. The Signing
and payment of the $500 million in interest arrears was final-
ly is made in spring 1995, opening the way to a comprehensive rescheduling agreement.expected by end-1994.

Nov 95   Agreement in principle. Heads of terms were signed for a
comprehensive rescheduling of the debt of the former USSR
in the amount of $25.5 billion in principal outstanding and
$7.5 billion in accrued interest due. This total of $33 billion
was to be repaid over 25 years, with 7 years grace, beginning
December 15, 1995, in 37 semi-annual payments on a graduated schedule at LIBOR +$^{13}/_{16}$ percent a year. It was further

agreed that an interest note would be issued with a 20-year
maturity and 7 years grace from December 15, 1995, that
would bear the same interest rate, listed on the Luxembourg
Stock Exchange. The remaining $1.5 billion in interest
arrears was paid over 1995–96. By September 1996 the minimum subscribership by individual commercial banks of $20
billion in outstanding principal was reached, which triggered
the Russian agreement to the rescheduling package.

São Tomé and Principe

Aug 94   Buyback under the IDA DRF at 10 cents per dollar
extinguished $10.1 million of principal (87 percent of eligi-
ble debt).

Senegal

Dec 96   Debt buyback under the IDA DRF at 8 cents per dollar of
$80.0 million owed to commercial banks.

Sierra Leone

Jan 84   Covers arrears as of December 31, 1983.

Aug 95   Buyback at 13 cents on average per dollar of $235 million
due to commercial banks. Funded by grants from IDA DRF
and other donor countries.

Sudan

Nov 81   Includes arrears of principal and some short-term debt.

Mar 82   Covers arrears of interest and modifies 1981 agreement.

Apr 83   Modification of 1981 agreement.

Oct 85   Covers arrears of interest.

Togo

Mar 80   Balance of debts to French banks, including arrears of principal. Interest rates vary by currency.

Oct 83   Covers all commercial bank debt, including debt previously
rescheduled.

May 88   Restructuring of 1983 agreement.

Turkey

Mar 82   Improved the terms of the August 1979 agreement.

Uganda

Feb 93   Buyback of $153 million commercial bank debt, funded by
grants from IDA DRF and other donor countries.

Uruguay

Jul 86   MYRA.

Mar 88   Improved terms of July 1986 agreement.

Feb 91   DDSR agreement provided for cash buyback at a 44 percent
discount ($628 million), collateralized debt reduction bonds
($535 million), and new money ($89 million) combined
with debt conversion notes ($447 million). Repayment terms
are 30-year bullet maturity and 6.75 percent fixed interest for
the interest reduction bonds, 16-year maturity, including 7
years grace, with LIBOR +$^{7}/_{8}$ percent interest for the conversion notes, and 15-year maturity including seven years grace
with LIBOR +1 percent interest for the new money notes.

Venezuela

Feb 86   MYRA. Agreed in principle in September 1984.

Nov 87   Reduced spread and extended maturities of 1986 agreement.

Sep 88   Reduced spread on February 1986 agreement.

Dec 88   Exchange of debt for bonds outside the framework of the
main negotiations.

Dec 90   DDSR agreement featuring buybacks in the form of 91-day
collateralized short-term notes ($1,411 million), exchange for
bonds at 30 percent discount ($1,810 million), exchange at
par for reduced fixed-rate interest bonds ($7,457 million),
exchange for bonds at par with temporary step-down interest
rates ($3,027 million), and new money combined with debt
conversion bonds ($6,022 million).

Yugoslavia, former

Oct 83   Includes a 1-year rollover of short-term bonds.

Dec 85   MYRA.

(table continues on next page)

Zaire

Apr 80 Covered stock of debt as of end-1979, including arrears.
Jan 83 Rescheduled principal due under April 1980 agreement.
Jun 84 Rescheduled principal due under April 1980 agreement.
May 85 Rescheduled principal due under April 1980 agreement.
May 86 Rescheduled principal due under April 1980 agreement.
May 87 Rescheduled principal due under April 1980 agreement.
Jun 89 Financed monthly payments on outstanding claims, mainly interest on arrears.

Zambia

Dec 84 Includes arrears as of February 28, 1983.
Sep 94 Buyback under the IDA DRF at 11 cents per dollar extinguished $200 million of principal (75 percent of eligible debt), using $10.5 million of IDA resources and $22.3 million from other donors.

APPENDIX 5

 # Portfolio investment in developing countries

Portfolio flows to developing countries increased to $81 billion in 1995 from $78 billion in 1994 but remained below the peak of $95 billion recorded in 1993.[1] Strong growth in equities and debt is estimated to have raised portfolio flows to a record $134 billion in 1996 (table A5.1; see data discussion in box A5.1).

Since 1990 an improved regulatory environment in developing countries and increased confidence from international investors have helped many countries gain greater access to international capital markets. Portfolio flows accounted for 30 percent of net resource flows in 1995–96, up from 5 percent in 1990. Portfolio flows also rose as a share of total private flows (figure A5.1).

About two-thirds of portfolio investments for 1995 were made in the second half of the year, as returns in stock and bond markets in industrial countries declined and investor confidence in emerging markets grew. Equity flows accounted for 40 percent of these investments, or $32 billion.[2] An increasing share of foreign funds was invested in local equity markets directly rather than through depository receipts or other cross-border private equity placements. Strong overall performance in emerging equity markets relative to developed markets, high economic growth in many developing countries, and attractive valuation of securities compared with developed markets and historical levels in emerging markets

Table A5.1 Gross portfolio flows to developing countries by region, 1990–96
(billions of U.S. dollars)

Region	1990	1991	1992	1993	1994	1995	1996[a]
All developing countries	8.5	17.8	34.1	94.6	78.1	80.9	134.3
Debt	5.3	10.6	23.1	49.6	45.4	48.8	88.6
Equity	3.2	7.2	11.0	45.0	32.7	32.1	45.7
Sub-Saharan Africa	0.0	0.0	0.9	0.2	2.3	6.4	5.2
Debt	0.0	0.0	0.7	0.0	1.4	1.5	1.7
Equity	0.0	0.0	0.1	0.2	0.9	4.9	3.5
East Asia and the Pacific	2.3	1.5	4.4	23.6	25.4	26.9	35.7
Debt	0.6	0.8	2.3	8.9	15.3	12.2	22.8
Equity	1.7	0.7	2.1	14.6	10.1	14.7	12.9
South Asia	0.4	0.2	0.4	2.6	7.3	3.1	6.9
Debt	0.3	0.2	0.0	0.6	1.1	0.8	1.5
Equity	0.1	0.0	0.4	2.0	6.2	2.3	5.4
Europe and Central Asia	1.9	0.8	7.5	14.6	9.8	12.2	18.9
Debt	1.6	0.8	7.5	13.6	7.5	9.4	12.2
Equity	0.2	0.0	0.1	1.0	2.3	2.8	6.7
Latin America and the Caribbean	3.8	15.0	20.8	53.7	32.6	31.0	65.9
Debt	2.7	8.7	12.6	26.5	19.5	23.8	49.4
Equity	1.1	6.2	8.2	27.2	13.2	7.2	16.5
Middle East and North Africa	0.1	0.0	0.0	0.0	0.8	1.2	1.7
Debt	0.1	0.0	0.0	0.0	0.7	1.0	1.0
Equity	0.0	0.0	0.0	0.0	0.1	0.2	0.7

a. Preliminary.
Note: Portfolio debt figures refer to gross capital raised by developing countries through international bonds, certificates of deposit, and commercial paper issues. Portfolio equity refers to gross funds raised through international equity issues and net foreign investments in local equity markets.
Source: Euromoney Bondware, Micropal, central banks, national stock and securities exchanges, various market sources, and World Bank staff estimates based on net asset value of stocks of investment funds adjusted for price movements in individual equity markets.

increased portfolio equity investment to an estimated $46 billion in 1996.

Debt instruments—mainly international bonds—have always accounted for most portfolio flows to emerging markets. Strong issuance activity in the second half of 1995 brought portfolio debt flows for the year to $49 billion, only slightly lower than the peak level recorded in 1993. Low yields in industrial countries coupled with investor interest in diversifying their portfolios toward developing countries pushed debt flows to a record $89 billion in 1996, with international bond issues accounting for more than 90 percent of the total.

Regional trends

By mid-1995 investors had reassessed the general fundamentals of emerging market risk in the aftermath of the Mexican peso crisis. Flows increased in all regions in the second half of 1995, accounting for two-thirds of annual flows.

• The largest volume of portfolio funds was invested in *Latin America and the Caribbean* although the $31 billion inflow in 1995 was slightly below the 1994 level. As market sentiment improved during 1995, both debt and equity

activity picked up. Equity flows through depository receipts and direct investments by institutional investors increased significantly in 1996, with total flows expected to reach a record $66 billion.

• Flows to *East Asia and the Pacific* continued their upward trend, rising to about $27 billion in 1995 and an estimated $36 billion in 1996. Equity flows (including more than $8 billion flowing directly into stock markets) accounted for more than half the total in 1995, and bond issuance increased strongly in 1996. The level of depository receipts and private issues declined in 1996 because of smaller volumes from Indonesia, Malaysia, and the Philippines.

• Following the downturn in 1994, portfolio investment flows to *Europe and Central Asia* recovered to about $12.2 billion in 1995, as the volume of international equity issues and direct investment in local stock markets rose. Portfolio flows increased to an estimated $19 billion in 1996 as a result of increased activity in international equity markets by the Czech Republic, Greece, Poland, and Russia. A decline in equity market activity was observed in Hungary.

• Strong inflows to the South African stock market helped portfolio investment to *Sub-Saharan*

Box A5.1 A word about the data

Both official and market sources are used to compile data on portfolio flows. Gross statistics on international bond and equity issues are arrived at by aggregating individual transactions reported by market sources. Information on foreign investments in local equity markets is gathered from national authorities, investment positions of mutual funds, and other market sources. To compile portfolio flows the World Bank uses Euromoney databases and publications; Micropal Inc.; Lipper Analytical Services; published reports of private investment houses, central banks, national securities and exchange commissions, and national stock exchanges; and the World Bank's Debtor Reporting System.

The volume of portfolio investment figures reported by the World Bank generally differs from data reported by other sources, in part because the Republic of Korea, Hong Kong, Singapore, and Taiwan (China) are not considered developing countries in the World Bank's country classification (for the World Bank classification of countries, refer to appendix 1). The sources and methodology used to collect information also differ for data on foreign investments in local markets because of the lack of clear, comprehensive, and

regular reporting by many developing countries. Significant portfolio investment flows to developing countries are a relatively new phenomenon, however, and some countries have recently improved the recording and reporting of these flows.

The World Bank has strengthened its efforts to collect comprehensive information on international capital flowing directly into local equity markets. As a result the data in this report differ significantly from those reported in the *World Debt Tables 1996*. Most of the information in this volume is collected directly from national sources or reliable published reports. Where such information is not available, the stock of net holdings of investment funds is used as a proxy. The net holdings of assets of investment funds are adjusted for valuation effects, using the IFC's local market price index to arrive at flow figures.

Capital flowing through international debt and equity instruments has been accurately recorded in the past. Differences between reporting here and elsewhere stem primarily from differences in country classifications, exchange rates, and inclusion or omission of particular tranches of transactions and certain offshore issuing activity.

Figure A5.1 Net development financing and portfolio investments to developing countries, 1989–96

1989–92   1993–96

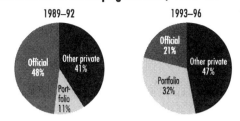

Billions of U.S. dollars

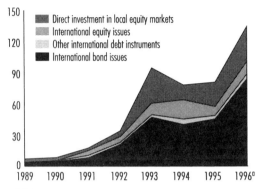

a. Preliminary.
Note: Data for direct investments in local equity markets are on a net basis; all other data are on a gross basis for funds raised in international capital markets.
Source: World Bank Debtor Reporting System.

Africa reach a record $6.4 billion in 1995. South Africa also accounted for almost all the international bond issues from the region. The volume of portfolio flows for the region is estimated to have declined in 1996, as a slight increase in flows to Côte d'Ivoire and Ghana only partly compensated for a decline in flows to South Africa as a result of weak market conditions and a decline in the issuance of international bonds.

• Although portfolio flows to *South Asia* picked up midway through the year, flows to the region declined to about $3.1 billion in 1995, down from a peak of $7.3 billion in 1994. The decline was primarily the result of lower foreign investment in local markets in India and Pakistan and a decline in international offerings. Debt flows are estimated to have reached record levels in 1996, however, and equity flows rebounded as equity investors turned toward the Indian stock markets and global depository receipts. Bond issues from the subcontinent are estimated to have risen to more than $1 billion in 1996.

• Portfolio flows to the *Middle East and North Africa* increased to $1.2 billion in 1995, primarily because of international bond issues by Lebanon and Tunisia. Although equity investment doubled, it accounted for a small portion of total flows. The

volume of bond flows remained stable in 1996 (with Lebanon, Morocco, and Tunisia the primary issuers from the region), while equity flows increased as a result of investments in Egyptian and Moroccan securities.

International equity issues and foreign investment in local equity markets

Portfolio equity flows, which include international equity issues and investment by foreigners in local equity markets, are estimated to have rebounded from $32–33 billion in 1994 and 1995 to a record $46 billion in 1996 (table A5.2). Equity flows declined during the first half of 1995 as a result of the Mexican peso crisis, which caused investors to temporarily reevaluate the share of emerging markets in their portfolios. At the same time spectacular performance in the U.S. equity market in 1995 provided an attractive alternative to investment in emerging markets. Nevertheless, emerging markets continued to attract a significant share of global capital (table A5.3).[3] Several factors boosted investor interest in developing country equity markets in 1995, including:

• Continuing low international interest rates.

• The availability of securities at low prices (in Eastern Europe, for example) compared with both historical levels and the valuations of securities in developed markets.

• Relatively high economic growth prospects in developing countries—estimated at more than 6 percent in 1996 compared with 2.5 percent for industrial economies—with sharp improvements in some countries, including Mexico and Argentina.

• Increased liquidity as investments in U.S. mutual funds surged in early 1996, nearly doubling their share of funds invested abroad.

• The general trend among European asset managers to diversify investments from domestic to foreign markets.

Depository receipts and direct investment in local equity markets

Depository receipts—American and global—and privately placed cross-border equity issues accounted for about a quarter of portfolio equity flows to developing countries during 1994–96, with three-quarters of these funds channeled through direct

Table A5.2 Composition of portfolio equity flows to developing countries by region, 1990–96
(billions of U.S. dollars)

Region	1990	1991	1992	1993	1994	1995	1996[a]
All developing countries	3.2	7.2	11.0	45.0	32.7	32.1	45.7
International issues	0.1	4.7	5.7	11.0	18.5	8.7	—
Direct investment	3.1	2.5	5.3	34.0	14.2	23.4	—
Sub-Saharan Africa	0.0	0.0	0.1	0.2	0.9	4.9	3.5
International issues	0.0	0.0	0.1	0.1	0.6	0.4	—
Direct investment	0.0	0.0	0.0	0.0	0.2	4.5	—
East Asia and the Pacific	1.7	0.7	2.1	14.6	10.1	14.7	12.9
International issues	0.0	0.0	1.3	2.6	6.8	6.3	—
Direct investment	1.7	0.7	0.8	12.0	3.3	8.4	—
South Asia	0.1	0.0	0.4	2.0	6.2	2.3	5.4
International issues	0.0	0.0	0.2	0.3	4.3	0.3	—
Direct investment	0.1	0.0	0.1	1.7	2.0	2.1	—
Europe and Central Asia	0.2	0.0	0.1	1.0	2.3	2.8	6.7
International issues	0.0	0.0	0.0	0.2	0.7	0.9	—
Direct investment	0.2	0.0	0.1	0.8	1.5	1.9	—
Latin America and the Caribbean	1.1	6.2	8.2	27.2	13.2	7.2	16.5
International issues	0.1	4.7	4.0	7.7	6.0	0.8	—
Direct investment	1.0	1.5	4.3	19.5	7.1	6.3	—
Middle East and North Africa	0.0	0.0	0.0	0.0	0.1	0.2	0.7
International issues	0.0	0.0	0.0	0.0	0.0	0.0	—
Direct investment	0.0	0.0	0.0	0.0	0.1	0.2	—

— Not available.

a. Preliminary.

Note: International issues refer to issuance of American depository receipts, global depository receipts, and private placement of equity issues in international markets. Direct investment refers to acquisition of securities by foreigners directly in the local equity markets.

Source: Euromoney Bondware, Micropal, central banks, national stock and securities exchanges, various market sources, and World Bank staff estimates based on net asset value of stocks of investment funds adjusted for price movements in individual equity markets.

investment in local stock markets. Many of these direct investments are made through international brokerage houses that have extended their local networks to serve as a bridge between foreign institutional investors and local equity markets. Other factors influencing flows include the overall increase in liquidity in emerging markets and direct dealings by seasoned investors with interests in particular markets and investments.

Depository receipts offer some advantages over direct investments. To the issuer they provide the opportunity to tap the widest possible pool of investors and to attract the capital of new investors and retail investors who are unwilling to go directly to the markets or are prevented from doing so by legal restrictions. To the investor depository receipts offer convenience, liquidity, elimination of settlement risks, and a safer regulatory environment.

American depository receipts (ADRs) achieved record trading volumes of about $278 billion in 1995 and $179 billion in the first half of 1996. Although ADRs have been more popular than global depository receipts (GDRs), GDRs are becoming more popular with developing country issuers because of their ability to reach a broader investor base and the less stringent regulatory criteria that govern their use.

The dollar volume of international issues by developing countries declined in 1995 (figure A5.2). The IFC Total Return Index fell 12 percent, creating an unfavorable environment for launching equity issues in the international markets. The peso crisis had a more pronounced and lasting effect on the volume of equity issued in Latin America, which declined by 87 percent. Activity picked up in the second half of the year but remained restricted to East Asia. In 1996 the volume of international equity issues is estimated to have increased to $12 billion, representing about a quarter of total equity flows.

Regional trends

Sub-Saharan Africa. Sub-Saharan Africa, which accounted for a negligible share of portfolio equity flows to developing countries until 1994, accounted for about 15 percent in 1995. However, 94 percent of these flows went to South Africa. The dollar volume of investments is estimated to have declined in 1996, as the South African mar-

Table A5.3 Foreign investments in local equity markets of developing countries, 1995–96

(millions of U.S. dollars)

Region and country	1995	1996 trend	Region and country	1995	1996 trend
All developing countries	23,357				
Sub-Saharan Africa	4,475	downward	**East Asia and the Pacific**	8,398	upward
South Africa	4,240	downward	Indonesia	2,749	upward
Ghana	204	downward	China	2,141	downward
Zimbabwe	18	downward	Thailand	1,519	downward
Nigeria	6	downward	Malaysia	1,049	upward
Mauritius	4	downward	Philippines	770	upward
Other	3	upward	Vietnam	155	upward
			Other	16	downward
South Asia	2,059	upward	**Middle East and North Africa**	168	upward
India	1,243	upward	Morocco	150	upward
Pakistan	729	downward	Jordan	11	upward
Sri Lanka	61	upward	Oman	5	upward
Bangladesh	26	upward	Egypt	2	upward
			Other	1	upward
Latin America and the Caribbean	6,345	upward	**Europe and Central Asia**	1,912	upward
Brazil	3,955	upward	Poland	703	upward
Peru	1,611	upward	Turkey	463	upward
Mexico	520	upward	Bulgaria	400	upward
Argentina	210	upward	Hungary	149	upward
Colombia	60	upward	Russian Federation	119	upward
Panama	20	downward	Czech Republic	50	upward
Venezuela	7	upward	Other	28	upward
Other	–38	upward			

Source: Central banks, national stock and securities exchanges, Micropal, various market sources, and World Bank staff estimates based on net asset value of stocks of investment funds adjusted for price movements in individual equity markets.

ket struggled with the effects of the depreciating rand. Through mid-1996 Ghana and South Africa were the only countries in the region to have placed international equity issues.

About $4 billion in foreign flows was invested directly into the *South African* capital market in 1995, and more than half of the trading on the Johannesburg stock exchange is by foreign investors. In 1996 investments declined owing to uncertainty about the depreciation of the rand, which had lost a quarter of its value against the dollar by the middle of the year. Foreign investment in the *Ghana* stock exchange was estimated at about $200 million in 1995. About 60 percent of the shares on the exchange are held by foreigners, with the remaining shares held by a small number of pension funds and insurance companies. About $30 million of direct investment in the region's stock markets went to *Côte d'Ivoire, Mauritius, Nigeria,* and *Zimbabwe.*

Lack of securities, slow settlement, low liquidity, few local investors, antiquated systems, and the slow pace of privatization continue to constrain foreign investment in the local equity markets of

the region, and flows in 1996 are estimated to have declined. African countries are taking steps to attract foreign portfolio investments, however. *Ghana* is allowing a capital gains tax holiday through 2000 and has abolished certain other duties, seven francophone West African countries plan to convert *Côte d'Ivoire's* stock exchange into a regional bourse to take advantage of economies

Figure A5.2 Facilities used by developing countries for international equity issuance

Billions of U.S. dollars

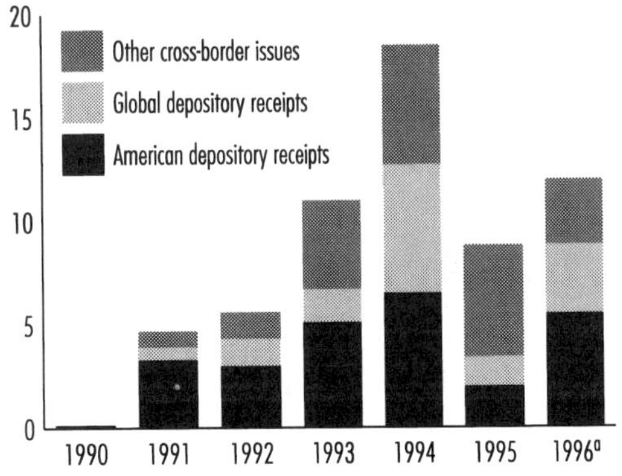

a. Preliminary.
Source: Euromoney Bondware and World Bank staff estimates.

of scale, and *Nigeria* has relaxed regulations on foreign participation in the stock market. On the investor side, the $60 million Africa Fund was established in 1996 to invest in newly privatized and growing companies in Africa.

East Asia and the Pacific. Portfolio equity flows to East Asia and the Pacific reached a record $15 billion in 1995. The region, the largest recipient of portfolio equity flows to developing countries, increased its share of total portfolio equity flows from 32 percent during 1989–94 to 46 percent in 1995. Thirty-eight percent of the region's portfolio equity flows were raised through international equity issues; the rest was raised through direct investment in local exchanges. Inflows in 1996 are estimated to have fallen to about $13 billion, primarily because of a decline in international equity issues from Indonesia, Malaysia, and the Philippines. Funds flowing directly into stock markets, however, are estimated to have increased by about 15 percent in 1996.

Foreign investment in local stock markets rose in 1995 as *China, Malaysia,* the *Philippines,* and *Thailand* recorded strong growth in the volume of inflows. In 1996 funds flowing into the region are estimated to have increased to about $10 billion. Foreign investment in these markets comes from industrial countries and from within the region itself. About one-fifth of such investments are estimated to have been intraregional in 1995.[4]

Foreign investment in the *Chinese* equity market usually takes place in the Shenzen B-shares market (34 stocks), denominated in Hong Kong dollars; the Shanghai B-shares market (38 stocks), denominated in U.S. dollars; and the H-share market of stocks, which is listed in Hong Kong.

After poor performance for many years, the *Indonesian* market outperformed all other markets in the region at the beginning of 1996. About 80 percent of trading on the Jakarta exchange is done by foreigners, and investments remain concentrated in large capitalized companies. *Malaysia* is planning to broaden and deepen the Kuala Lumpur stock exchange and encourage international portfolio investments by allowing the foreign listings of stocks. The *Philippine* stock exchange is recovering from two years of correction and has grown rapidly since mid-1995. Despite the lackluster performance of the *Thai* stock market, foreign

investment recovered from a negative flow in 1994, and about 18 percent of investment is estimated to be by foreigners.[5] *Vietnam* still lacks a stock exchange and attracts foreign investment only through joint ventures, since investment in local companies by foreigners is not permitted.

South Asia. The volume of international equity issues to South Asia fell sharply in 1995 as depository receipt placement by Indian issuers declined. Activity resumed in the euro-issue market in 1996, and foreign investment in 1996 is estimated to have increased over 1995 levels. Only about 3 percent of market capitalization is accounted for by foreigners. The success of the $200 million GDR by *India's* Industrial Credit and Investment Corporation highlighted investor demand for quality borrowers from that country. A sharp pickup in activity by Indian issuers brought the volume for the region to about $1.5 billion in 1996.

Bangladesh, which accounted for less than 2 percent of foreign funds flowing into regional stock markets in 1995, is seeking to attract greater volumes through a broad economic reform program that includes specific measures to encourage foreign investment. Foreigners are now permitted to invest independently in all sectors except defense-related industries; previously, foreign investment was limited to joint ventures with local investors. The government also has lifted the one-year holding period imposed on foreign investors in the stock market.

Investments in *Pakistan's* stock market are estimated to have declined moderately in 1996 because of uncertainty over the course of economic policy.

Europe and Central Asia. After rising modestly to $2.8 billion in 1995, portfolio equity flows to Europe and Central Asia increased sharply in 1996, with a major boost coming from the increased volume of international equity issues driven by privatization programs in the *Czech Republic, Greece, Hungary, Poland,* and the *Russian* Federation and by the first-time issue from *Croatia. Lithuania* was the only new issuer in the region in 1995, with a $4.3 million privately placed international offering by a private bank.

International investment in the region increased in 1996 as markets became more liquid and less volatile and political risk in the region declined. *Poland,* which has the most transparent and well-regulated stock exchange in the region, received the largest inflow of foreign funds ($703 million). In 1995 an estimated 80 percent of privatization offerings there were purchased by foreigners. Many investors use the Warsaw stock exchange as a center for Eastern European operations. Investments likely increased in 1996 as the privatization of attractive companies and modernization of the stock exchange got under way.

Foreign funds began to flow to the *Russian Federation's* stock market in 1995, although volumes remained low compared with many other emerging markets. Initial investors were mainly speculative hedge funds and high-turnover private investors. This profile is changing as international investors begin to focus on the planned offering of securities through the privatization of blue-chip companies. Direct investment in 1996 is estimated to have increased considerably.

Despite a volatile stock market, *Turkey* attracted the second-largest portfolio equity flows in the region.

Latin America and the Caribbean. Portfolio equity flows to Latin America and the Caribbean declined in 1995, primarily as a result of a fall in the volume of international equity issues as demand dried up following the increase in U.S. interest rates and the contagion effects of the Mexican peso crisis. Direct investment in local stock markets was also lower than in 1994. The decline was less significant than in equities, as restoration of investor confidence toward the end of 1995 made up for weak inflows at the beginning of the year. The volume of international equity issues and direct acquisition of stocks rebounded in 1996.

Despite high volatility in early 1996, the performance of the Merval index of the *Argentine* market attracted substantial foreign money into the market, which by mid-year was perceived by investors to have achieved greater stability and liquidity. Although regulations on that market impose fewer restrictions on foreign investment than in Chile, the limited availability of blue-chip stocks outside the oil and gas sector has constrained investment.

Of all Latin American countries, *Mexico* and *Brazil* have attracted the largest volume of foreign equity funds. Investors' reassessment of Mexico's share in their portfolio holdings toward the end of

1994 caused an outflow of funds from the market and a sharp decline in volumes for 1995. Investors began feeling comfortable with the market in the second half of 1995, however, and net investments picked up. Recent data indicate that foreign investment increased in 1996, fueled by the reestablishment of Mexican borrowers in international capital markets, improved corporate earnings, a stable exchange rate, and controlled inflation.[6]

Peru is a major destination in the region for international equity capital, and *Colombia* and *Venezuela* account for large shares of investment flowing to the region's stock markets.

Middle East and North Africa. The first international equity issue from the Middle East and North Africa was made in 1995, with a GDR issue from Lebanon. All other portfolio equity flows to the region were invested directly in local equities. The region is likely to have reached record levels of investment in 1996 as a result of issues from Egypt, Lebanon, and Morocco.

Morocco accounted for 89 percent of the capital invested by mutual funds in the region in 1995. *Jordan,* where foreign investment is largely by U.K. and U.S. residents, had the second highest share. Strong investor interest is also reported in *Lebanon,* where analysts see potential interest in restructuring local companies and offering them to international investors.[7] International interest in *Egypt's* stock market increased in 1996, with the share of foreign investment increasing threefold in the first six months of the year. Major investors are from the United States, United Kingdom, some Gulf states, and Singapore. A closed-end fund (the Egypt Investment Company) was also established.

International bond issues from developing countries

Portfolio debt flows to developing countries—essentially bond issues in the international capital markets—reached a record $49 billion in 1995.[8] These flows are estimated to have increased more than 80 percent in 1996, to $89 billion. Developing country activity in international bond markets was adversely affected in the early part of 1995 by the Mexican peso crisis. Recovery in the bond markets began in the second quarter

Table A5.4 Average spreads on international bond issues by developing countries, 1993–96
(basis points)

Country	Sovereign issuers				Public sector issuers				Private sector issuers			
	1993	*1994*	*1995*	*1996*[a]	*1993*	*1994*	*1995*	*1996*[a]	*1993*	*1994*	*1995*	*1996*[a]
Argentina	316	242	399	406	440	283	395	262	441	429	549	439
Barbados	—	425	—	—	—	—	—	—	—	—	—	—
Bolivia	—	—	—	—	—	—	—	—	—	500	—	—
Brazil	—	—	385	305	518	463	415	318	536	419	448	419
Chile	—	—	—	—	—	138	—	90	190	125	140	106
China	89	85	69	151	101	124	30	363	—	—	—	—
Colombia	215	154	200	199	263	240	—	218	—	290	290	—
Czech Republic	272	—	—	—	—	115	—	—	—	—	—	98
Ecuador	—	—	—	—	—	—	—	—	—	—	579	647
Estonia	—	—	—	221	—	—	—	—	—	—	—	—
Greece	157	198	—	90	—	—	145	—	345	—	—	—
Hungary	248	232	245	—	324	195	—	—	—	—	—	—
India	—	—	—	—	—	—	—	170	—	—	190	267
Indonesia	—	—	—	100	—	—	—	—	407	466	488	358
Jamaica	—	—	—	—	—	—	—	—	—	200	—	—
Kazakstan	—	—	—	360	—	—	—	—	—	—	—	—
Lebanon	—	325	320	295	—	—	—	278	—	—	350	318
Lithuania	—	—	445	—	—	—	—	—	—	—	—	—
Malaysia	—	—	—	—	110	—	85	60	—	89	110	96
Malta	—	—	—	—	—	115	—	—	—	—	—	—
Mexico	208	—	407	422	212	163	302	314	374	369	216	465
Morocco	—	—	—	48	—	—	—	—	—	—	—	340
Pakistan	—	385	—	—	—	—	—	—	—	—	—	—
Panama	—	—	—	—	—	—	—	—	—	—	—	385
Philippines	320	—	—	225	255	250	204	170	380	270	305	210
Poland	—	—	185	65	—	—	—	88	—	—	—	—
Romania	—	—	—	293	—	—	—	—	—	—	—	—
Russian Federation	—	—	—	345	—	—	—	—	—	—	—	318
Slovak Republic	—	—	—	115	—	325	—	—	—	—	—	—
Slovenia	—	—	—	58	—	—	—	—	—	—	—	—
South Africa	—	193	—	175	—	—	—	—	—	—	162	—
Thailand	—	—	—	—	—	—	—	85	—	—	112	124
Trinidad and Tobago	495	425	—	175	—	—	—	—	—	—	—	—
Tunisia	—	—	162	—	—	—	—	—	—	—	—	—
Turkey	256	—	297	277	—	—	—	—	—	265	—	—
Uruguay	228	158	236	160	—	—	—	—	300	—	285	375
Venezuela	330	—	352	440	222	—	—	—	465	—	—	399
All developing countries	268	251	296	292	257	194	179	202	445	397	350	334
Sub-Saharan Africa	—	193	—	175	—	—	—	—	—	—	162	—
East Asia and the Pacific	166	85	69	155	164	156	108	109	396	312	301	193
South Asia	—	385	—	—	—	—	—	170	—	—	190	267
Europe and Central Asia	239	226	272	221	324	173	145	88	345	265	—	141
Latin America and the Caribbean	316	264	361	368	313	275	355	286	451	405	393	398
Middle East and North Africa	—	325	241	172	—	—	—	278	—	—	350	325

— Not available.

Note: Average spread is based on comparable government securities in the currency in which the bond is denominated and is calculated based on the transactions for which the launch spread information was available. For the Republic of Korea, now classified as a high-income country, the comparable spreads (in basis points) for public sector issuers were 77 in 1993, 66 in 1994, 53 in 1995, and 73 in 1996. For private sector issuers the spreads were 97, n.a., 94, and 77, respectively.

Source: Euromoney Bondware and World Bank staff estimates.

a. Based on information available as of June.

of 1995, however, led by a return of Latin American and Eastern European borrowers. Increased selectivity and risk aversion by investors was reflected in shorter maturities and increased spreads on transactions (table A5.4). The volume of issuance gathered speed in the second half of the year, as investor confidence in emerging markets returned and borrowers that had postponed borrowing began tapping the markets. Borrowings through issuance of commercial paper and certificates of deposit accounted for less than 8 percent of total debt flows. Estimates for increased bond volumes by developing countries in 1996 are driven by:

• Low rates of returns on conventional investments in industrial countries.

• Increased liquidity in international capital markets (as a result of maturing investments), leading to a favorable environment in global bond markets (including tighter spreads and increased transaction sizes) for developing country financing of borrowing needs.[9]

• Increased levels of risk tolerance by investors, leading to a diversified and expanded investor base as conservative investors join the pool of emerging market investors.

Attributes

Sovereign borrowers, particularly from Latin America, led the reestablishment of developing country access to international bond markets in 1995. Borrowing increased to make up for postponed borrowings required to service maturing obligations and to establish benchmarks for other

borrowers from the country. The share of sovereign borrowings in total bond issues from developing countries increased by 18 percentage points in 1995, with more than 80 percent of sovereign issues coming from Latin America. Sovereign borrowings continued to dominate volumes in 1996, as Argentina and Mexico continued to borrow on a large scale. Private borrowers followed sovereign borrowers, with major issues from Indonesia and Thailand in East Asia and Argentina, Brazil, and Mexico in Latin America. The Philippines and Chile also contributed to private sector volumes in 1996.

The Mexican peso crisis had the largest impact on Latin American borrowers, for whom borrowing costs rose sharply in 1995. Spreads for other borrowers declined, however, and overall spreads remained at 1995 levels through mid-1996. The secondary market spreads on Brady bonds for Argentina, Brazil, and Mexico also rose sharply at the beginning of 1995. By the end of 1996 spreads in Argentina and Brazil had returned to the levels that had prevailed before the peso devaluation. Mexican spreads remained high, however.[10] Spreads in East Asia were lower in 1995 than in 1994. However, issues of longer maturity bonds—which require more compensation for investors—increased spreads in 1996. Europe and Central Asia also experienced an increase of about 50 basis points in the cost of borrowing in 1995, although spreads had declined by mid-1996.

In an effort to reduce costs, compensate for declining investor interest (especially on the part of U.S. investors for Latin American issues), and take advantage of the preferences for longer maturities in

Figure A5.3 Currencies used for international bond issuance by developing countries, 1994–96

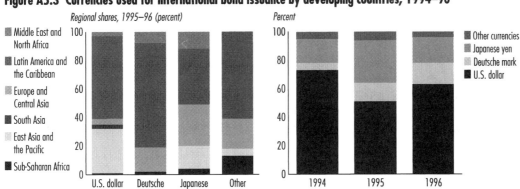

Note: 1996 figures are for January through mid-September.
Source: Euromoney Bondware and World Bank staff estimates.

108

some nondollar markets compared with the U.S. market, borrowers diversified their investor base and currency of issuance in 1995. The share of dollar-denominated bonds fell about 23 percentage points; the share of deutsche mark-denominated bonds went up 8 percentage points; and the share of yen-denominated bonds rose 15 percentage points in 1995, with much of the change caused by Latin American issues. These currencies retained a significant share of all issues in 1996, although the share of yen-denominated issues declined (figure A5.3). German and Japanese retail investor interest in high-yielding Latin debt securities was driven by low domestic interest rates and the scarcity of emerging market securities from other regions. The cultural ties of some Latin borrowers also helped them tap the lira market.

After falling in 1995, the average maturity of international bond issues from developing countries rose in 1996. About 40 percent of the bonds carried a maturity of six to ten years, up from 28 percent in 1995 (table A5.5). The share of issues with maturities longer than fifteen years almost doubled, from 5 percent to 9 percent. In the deutsche mark and yen sectors more than 50 percent of issues had maturities between six and ten years and about 12 percent had maturities longer than ten years. China and Malaysia were able to issue bonds with 100-year maturities.

In 1995–96 convertible issues accounted for about 5 percent of the bond volume by developing countries. Because they provide a fixed income and rights to acquire stocks at predetermined prices, convertible bonds appeal to both debt and equity investors. The coupon on a convertible bond, although lower than on a conven-

tional bond of comparable risk, serves as a hedge against a decline in the stock market, and exposure to the stock market provides potential for capital gains. East Asian borrowers have been the main issuers of these bonds; Latin issuers prefer securitized bonds. Given the comparatively high yields offered by fixed-rate emerging market issuers, investors preferred to lock in rates through fixed-rate instruments. Floating-rate notes represented only about one-fifth of total issuances in 1995–96.

Regional trends

Sub-Saharan Africa. Bond issues from Mauritius and South Africa brought the volume of bond issues from Sub-Saharan Africa to just over $1 billion in 1995, and volume is estimated to have edged up slightly in 1996. *Mauritius* issued its first international bond to finance infrastructure. The size of the five-year issue was increased by 50 percent to $150 million and priced at 90 basis points above LIBOR. Most of the region's volume was accounted for by *South Africa*, which is expected to remain the largest issuer from the region in 1996 despite slightly lower volume. *Ghana* had a landmark convertible bond offering from Ashanti Goldfields, the size of which was increased from $175 million to $250 million in response to strong investor demand. Major investors in the issue were U.S. institutional investors.

East Asia and the Pacific. With bond issues of more than $10 billion in 1995, East Asia and the Pacific was second only to Latin America in volume of international bond issues. Strong issues by China, Indonesia, the Philippines, and Thailand are estimated to have doubled the volume of the region's

Table A5.5 Maturity classification of international bond issues by developing countries, 1995–96
(*percentage share of regional volumes*)

Region	1–5 years 1995	1996ᵃ	6–10 years 1995	1996ᵃ	11–15 years 1995	1996ᵃ	More than 15 years 1995	1996ᵃ
All developing countries	62	48	28	40	5	3	5	9
Sub-Saharan Africa	47	20	42	80	0	0	11	0
East Asia and the Pacific	36	34	48	53	0	2	16	10
South Asia	5	35	95	36	0	0	0	29
Europe and Central Asia	38	56	34	30	21	6	6	8
Latin America and the Caribbean	79	53	16	36	4	2	0	9
Middle East and North Africa	88	46	12	36	0	17	0	0

a. Based on information available as of September—
Source: Euromoney Bondware and World Bank staff estimates.

bond issues to $20 billion in 1996. Favorable international capital market conditions, a positive investor outlook toward regional issuers, and a scarcity of long-term funds in the Asian domestic markets helped increase volume.[11]

In 1996 *China* returned to the dollar bond market after a two-year absence with a two-tranche deal of $300 million and $100 million. The second tranche, termed a "century bond," had a maturity of 100 years. *Indonesia* accounted for 25 percent of the region's bond volume in 1995. *Malaysia's* Tenaga Nasional Bhd. issued a $150 million, 100-year bond, the first century bond to be issued by an Asian borrower and only the second by a non-U.S. borrower in the U.S. market. The *Philippines,* considered one of the most financially innovative borrowers, issued eurobonds worth $690 million in exchange for Brady bonds to reduce debt service costs and increase maturities. The move has the potential to improve international investors' perceptions of the country's creditworthiness (now two notches below investment grade). *Thailand,* with its reputation as one of the most deregulated markets in Asia, was the region's third-largest borrower in the international bond markets in 1995 and is estimated to be the largest international bond issuer among Asian countries in 1996.

South Asia. India continued its presence in the global bond markets in 1995, raising $770 million. The market response to a handful of bonds issued toward the end of the year was limited, as the outstanding international bonds from the country performed poorly in the secondary market. In *Sri Lanka* the Bank of Ceylon, a public bank, issued a $12 million three-year bond (with a put option) in a privately placed deal in the euromarket. *Pakistan* raised $100 million with its first floating-rate note issue. The note carried a maturity of four and a half years and had put and call options attached.

Europe and Central Asia. Greece, Hungary, and Turkey remain the major issuers from Europe and Central Asia, accounting for 90 percent of bond issues from the region in 1995. Strong issuance by Greece and Turkey in 1996 is estimated to have edged up volumes for the year. All the bonds from these countries were issued by either sovereign or public borrowers. *Greek* issuers were Hellenic Republic, Hellenic Railways Organization SA, and Public Power Corporation.

The National Bank of *Hungary* and the government of *Turkey* remained the sole borrowers from those countries until mid-1996. The Turkish $500 million eurodollar bond met with strong investor demand, and the size of the deal was increased twice. First-time issuers from the region in 1995 were *Croatia,* where a public finance company raised $60 million in a privately placed issue in the euromarket; *Latvia,* which issued a yen-denominated $45 million equivalent two-year issue, also placed privately in the euromarket; *Lithuania,* which paid a spread of 445 basis points over the U.S. Treasury rate to borrow $60 million for two years; and *Poland,* which launched a $250 million five-year deal at a 185 basis point spread. *Romania* reestablished itself in international capital markets by launching its debut issue, a fixed-rate 52 billion yen ($496 million) three-year bond in the samurai market at a spread of 280 basis points. *Estonia* also made its debut, through a DM 60 million ($40.5 million) three-year issue.

Latin America and the Caribbean. Issuers from Latin America and the Caribbean were the most affected by the international investor community's temporary reassessment of emerging market risks in early 1995. Confidence started returning to the bond markets in the second half of 1995, led by the most creditworthy countries from the region, and bond volume from the region reached a record high in 1996.

Ecuador was the only newcomer from the region in 1995, with a $10 million two-year privately placed transaction by a private bank in the euromarket at a spread of 579 basis points. In 1996 *Argentina* issued its third lira deal, which carried the longest maturity (five years) of any developing country bond issued in Italy. Argentina lengthened its already established yield curve in the deutsche mark sector by issuing a fifteen-year bond, the longest by any issuer from the region. Argentina was also the first to launch a public guilder-denominated bond, tapping one of the world's most conservative markets. Taking advantage of one of the most lucrative sources of funding in Europe, *Brazil* became the second country from Latin America to successfully tap the eurolira market. Brazil also diversified its investor base by issuing in the samurai, eurosterling, and Portuguese navigator bond sectors. *Colombia's* $200 million twenty-year Yankee bond was launched at a spread of 263 basis points. In 1996 Colombia also became the first Latin American country to make a public yen-denominated offering.

In January 1996 *Mexico* returned to the U.S. institutional investor market with a $1 billion, five-year global bond issue, its first sovereign issue since 1993. In May United Mexican States issued a $1.75 billion thirty-year global bond at a spread of 552 basis points above the U.S. Treasury rate in exchange for its collateralized Brady bonds, held principally by U.S. institutional investors. By July the sovereign's $6 billion floating rate note carried an investment grade rating from Moody's and Standard & Poor's as a result of the support provided by oil revenues from Petróleos Mexicanos (Pemex). The issue met with strong investor demand, and its size was doubled from $3 billion.

Middle East and North Africa. Bond volumes from the Middle East and North Africa set records in 1995, as *Jordan* and *Tunisia* made their debut in international bond markets, joining Lebanon, the main issuer from the region. Volume from the region is estimated to be slightly lower in 1996, with issues coming from Lebanon, Morocco, and Tunisia. Investor interest in *Lebanese* debt paper remains strong, as reflected in the republic's issue of a $100 million four-year bond launched at 295 basis points, down from 320 basis points in 1995. *Morocco* made its debut in the euromarket with a French franc issue equivalent to $290 million, guaranteed by Caisse Francaise de Development. The issue was priced at 48 basis points over comparable risk-free securities and carried a maturity

of six years. The issue was placed primarily with European institutional investors. The Central Bank of *Tunisia* issued a fifteen-year samurai bond worth $137 million.

Notes

1. It should be noted that the historical numbers presented in this year's publication have been adjusted because the Republic of Korea is no longer classified as a developing country.
2. This figure differs from the estimate for 1995 presented in the *World Debt Tables 1996* because of the inclusion of additional countries in the database and more comprehensive information on other countries. Investments by open- and closed-end funds in developing countries have been used as proxies for countries for which information was not available from national sources. Estimates of such investments are based on the value of total net assets held by such funds in developing countries after taking into account changes in the International Finance Corporation's (IFC) index of stock prices.
3. According to the IFC's Emerging Markets Database, developing countries accounted for almost 11 percent of world market capitalization at the end of 1995.
4. Reported by ING Barings.
5. Reported by Jardine Fleming.
6. Reported by Banco de México and Goldman Sachs.
7. Reported by Middle East Capital Group.
8. Portfolio debt investments in developing countries also take place through foreign investment in local debt instruments, albeit at much lower levels than investment in international debt issues. Because of the lack of coherent, comprehensive, and organized statistics on these local debt investments, the volume of portfolio debt flows given in this report understates the total volume of foreign investment taking place through portfolio debt flows in developing countries.
9. Euromoney reports that $115 billion worth of dollar bonds were due to mature in 1996.
10. Reported by Salomon Brothers.
11. Reported by Bankers Trust.

Table A5.6 International bond issues by developing countries, 1993–96

(millions of U.S. dollars)

Region and country	1993	1994	1995	1996[a]
All developing countries	47,104	40,874	45,456	81,669
Sub-Saharan Africa	0	1,317	1,242	1,220
Botswana	0	0	0	0
Congo	0	492	0	0
Côte d'Ivoire	0	0	0	0
Ghana	0	0	0	250
Liberia	0	0	0	0
Mauritius	0	0	150	0
Nigeria	0	0	0	0
South Africa	0	825	1,092	970
Zimbabwe	0	0	0	0
East Asia and the Pacific	7,714	13,028	10,156	19,629
China	3,184	3,602	1,611	3,783
Indonesia	485	1,960	2,479	4,910
Malaysia	958	2,345	2,580	2,572
Myanmar	0	0	0	0
Papua New Guinea	0	0	0	0
Philippines	970	1,264	1,131	3,237
Thailand	2,117	3,856	2,355	5,127
Vietnam	0	0	0	0
South Asia	556	1,078	782	1,357
Bangladesh	0	0	0	0
India	556	883	770	1,107
Pakistan	0	195	0	250
Sri Lanka	0	0	12	0
Europe and Central Asia	13,605	7,218	9,410	11,534
Bulgaria	0	0	0	0
Croatia	0	0	0	54
Czech Republic	694	250	37	543
Estonia	0	0	0	61
Greece	4,237	3,964	2,817	4,294
Hungary	4,801	1,729	3,311	333
Kazakstan	0	0	0	200
Latvia	0	0	45	0
Lithuania	0	0	60	50
Malta	0	205	0	0
Poland	0	0	250	314
Romania	0	0	0	1,043
Russian Federation	0	0	347	1,100
Slovakia	0	275	64	328
Slovenia	0	0	0	325
Turkey	3,872	795	2,479	2,891

(table continues on next page)

Table A5.6 International bond issues by developing countries, 1993–96 (continued)

Region and country	1993	1994	1995	1996ᵃ
Latin America and the Caribbean	25,231	17,555	22,827	46,932
Argentina	5,611	5,166	6,354	13,865
Barbados	0	50	0	0
Bolivia	0	10	0	0
Brazil	6,255	3,848	6,761	9,920
Chile	322	155	500	2,020
Colombia	567	872	1,093	1,826
Costa Rica	0	50	0	0
Ecuador	0	0	10	0
Guatemala	60	0	0	0
Jamaica	0	55	0	0
Mexico	9,694	6,442	6,846	17,961
Panama	0	250	324	125
Peru	0	60	0	0
Trinidad and Tobago	125	150	0	150
Uruguay	140	200	211	100
Venezuela	2,457	248	729	965
Middle East and North Africa	0	678	1,038	998
Algeria	0	0	0	0
Bahrain	0	0	60	60
Egypt	0	0	0	0
Jordan	0	0	50	0
Lebanon	0	400	350	510
Morocco	0	0	0	290
Oman	0	0	0	0
Tunisia	0	278	578	137

a. Preliminary and not comprehensively inclusive of certain offshore transactions.
Source: Euromoney Bondware and World Bank staff estimates.

Table A5.7 International equity issues by developing countries, 1993–96

(millions of U.S. dollars)

Region and country	1993	1994	1995	1996[a]
All developing countries	10,980	18,482	8,730	11,754
Sub-Saharan Africa	126	638	393	761
Botswana	0	0	0	0
Congo	0	0	0	0
Côte d'Ivoire	0	0	0	0
Ghana	0	454	62	112
Kenya	0	0	0	12
Liberia	0	0	0	0
Mauritius	0	9	0	0
Nigeria	0	0	0	0
South Africa	126	176	331	636
Zimbabwe	0	0	0	0
East Asia and the Pacific	2,635	6,818	6,317	4,077
China	1,800	2,803	666	1,369
Indonesia	136	1,672	2,124	1,237
Malaysia	0	0	1,250	600
Myanmar	0	0	0	0
Papua New Guinea	0	0	450	187
Philippines	82	1,230	1,191	533
Thailand	617	1,062	635	151
Vietnam	0	52	0	0
South Asia	340	4,271	281	1,340
Bangladesh	0	26	7	0
India	340	3,029	274	1,340
Pakistan	0	1,183	0	0
Sri Lanka	0	33	0	0
Europe and Central Asia	191	717	860	1,506
Bulgaria	0	0	0	0
Croatia	0	0	0	111
Czech Republic	0	36	32	104
Estonia	0	7	3	0
Greece	0	30	20	167
Hungary	13	247	334	256
Latvia	0	0	0	0
Lithuania	0	0	4	21
Malta	0	0	0	0
Poland	0	0	218	17
Romania	0	1	0	10
Russian Federation	0	5	23	808
Slovak Republic	0	0	60	0
Turkey	178	391	167	12

(table continues on next page)

Table A5.7 International equity issues by developing countries, 1993–96 (continued)

Region and country	1993	1994	1995	1996 [a]
Latin America and the Caribbean	7,688	6,037	845	3,661
Argentina	3,604	1,065	0	217
Barbados	0	0	0	0
Bolivia	0	0	0	0
Brazil	0	1,475	456	387
Chile	288	808	318	297
Colombia	128	256	71	0
Costa Rica	0	0	0	0
Ecuador	0	0	0	0
Guatemala	0	0	0	0
Jamaica	0	0	0	0
Mexico	3,597	2,208	0	669
Panama	0	100	0	137
Peru	26	100	0	1,052
Trinidad and Tobago	0	0	0	0
Uruguay	0	23	0	0
Venezuela	44	0	0	904
Middle East and North Africa	0	0	34	410
Algeria	0	0	0	0
Bahrain	0	0	0	0
Egypt	0	0	0	233
Jordan	0	0	0	0
Lebanon	0	0	34	117
Morocco	0	0	0	60
Oman	0	0	0	0
Tunisia	0	0	0	0

a. Preliminary.
Source: Euromoney Bondware and World Bank staff estimates.

Progress on privatization

Narrowly defined, privatization is the sale or transfer of state-owned enterprises to private investors through auction, stock flotation, management-employee buyout, negotiated sale, stock distribution, or voucher or coupon privatization. Privatization can also be achieved through leasing, joint venture, management contract, or concession-type arrangements, such as build-operate-transfer (BOT), build-own-operate (BOO), and build-own-operate-transfer (BOOT), particularly for infrastructure projects.

In 1995 privatization revenues in developing countries exceeded $21 billion (figure A6.1). Hungary led the way with more than $3 billion in sales, mostly from divestiture of power and gas utilities. Privatization activity in other Eastern and Central European countries also continued apace. Latin American countries continued to suffer from the effects of the Mexican peso crisis, with privatization activity slowing in most countries as many large selloffs were postponed until 1996. In East Asia, Indonesia privatized PT Telekom and Malaysia privatized Petronas Gas in two of the biggest deals in the history of each country's privatization program. In South Asia, India's planned

Figure A6.1 Privatization revenues in developing countries, 1988–95

Billions of U.S. dollars

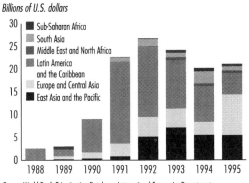

Source: World Bank Privatization Database, International Economics Department.

divestitures were slowed by the continued weak market for primary equity issues. In Africa privatization continued in Côte d'Ivoire, Ghana, and Zambia. In the Middle East and North Africa activity was concentrated in Egypt, Kuwait, Morocco, and Tunisia.

East Asia and the Pacific

East Asian and Pacific countries raised more than $5.4 billion from privatization activities in 1995, carried out mostly through private placements in U.S. markets (table A6.1). The leader was *Malaysia,* which generated almost $2.5 billion from state selloffs. The sale of Petronas Gas for $1.1 billion injected much-needed liquidity into the market and represented the first time that international investors were allowed to participate, through an American depository receipt placement, in a program hitherto restricted to domestic investors.

The largest privatization issue, however, was *Indonesia's* sale of PT Telekom, which raised $1.68 billion. The deal was originally expected to raise about $2.6 billion but was scaled down in size and price because of lower than expected demand.

China's H share market remained sluggish, and public offers by state-owned enterprises slowed to a trickle in 1995. Corporatization proceeds during 1995 were well under $1 billion, down from more than $2 billion in 1993 and 1994.

Privatization activity slowed in the *Philippines.* The sale of an additional stake in the Philippine National Bank was the largest deal of the year.

Latin America and the Caribbean

Latin American countries raised about $ 4.6 billion from privatization in 1995 (table A6.2). *Brazil's* slow-moving privatization program, which

Table A6.1 Privatization revenues in East Asia and the Pacific, 1988–95
(millions of U.S. dollars)

Country	1988	1989	1990	1991	1992	1993	1994	1995	Total
China	—	—	—	11	1,262	2,849	2,226	685	7,033
Indonesia	—	—	—	190	13.9	31.1	1,748	2,031	4,014
Malaysia	16	31	375	387	2,883	2,148	798	2,519	9,158
Philippines	—	80	—	244	754	1,638	494	208	3,417
Thailand	5	85	—	2	237.5	471	242	—	1,042
Other	—	—	1	0	9.8	17.8	—	5	33
Total	21	196	376	835	5,161	7,155	5,507	5,447	24,698

— Not available.
Source: World Bank Privatization Database, International Economics Department.

Table A6.2 Privatization revenues in Latin America and the Caribbean, 1988–95
(millions of U.S. dollars)

Country	1988	1989	1990	1991	1992	1993	1994	1995	Total
Argentina	28	—	3,841	1,981	5,567	4,732	890	1,208	18,247
Bolivia	—	—	—	—	9	13	—	789	810
Brazil	—	8	44	1,635	2,564	2,718	1,697	992	9,658
Chile	278	302	98	364	8	106	128	13	1,297
Mexico	1,915	971	3,160	11,289	6,924	2,132	766	167	27,324
Peru	—	—	—	2	212	127	2,840	1,276	4,457
Venezuela	—	—	10	2,278	140	36	8	39	2,511
Other	309	154	144	439	382	797	1,490	140	3,855
Total	2,530	1,436	7,297	17,989	15,797	10,646	7,818	4,623	68,136

— Not available.
Source: World Bank Privatization Database, International Economics Department.

had been concentrated in the steel and petrochemicals sectors, received a boost with the sale of Escelsa, the first electric utility in the country to be privatized and the first utility privatization on which foreigners were permitted to bid. Despite the Escelsa deal, total proceeds from privatization were the lowest since 1990. Only eight companies were sold in 1995, and several large sales were postponed until 1996, including Light (Electricity) Co., which eventually sold for $2.2 billion (making it the largest sale to date in Brazil). During the early years of Brazil's privatization program, noncash means of payments (including debt-for-equity swaps) were the principal method of settlement, with only a small share of total revenues generated in cash. As the perceived commercial viability of the enterprises offered has improved, however, cash sales have increased substantially, accounting for 32 percent of privatization proceeds in 1995.

In *Argentina* the fourth phase of privatization took off in 1995 with the sale of three hydropower utilities and two petrochemical plants for $1.2 billion. The weak primary market for bonds and equities, which effectively precluded the sale of enterprises through stock flotations, forced Argentina to sell off state-owned enterprises

directly, and poor market conditions kept Argentina from realizing its 1995 target of $2.4 billion in privatization revenue. The federal government is expected to conclude its divestiture program in the near future, although privatization is just beginning at the provincial level.

Bolivia launched its "capitalization" program in 1995. This method of privatization combines popular participation with investment capital and requires a potential investor to purchase a 50 percent stake in the privatized enterprise in return for management control. The remaining shares are distributed to the public through private pension funds. The state receives no revenue from the process since the investor's contribution remains with the company. The electricity company, ENDE, and a telecommunications firm, ENTEL, were sold under the program, which attracted $789 million in capital investment.

Peru continued to privatize quickly, leading the region in proceeds in 1995. Like Bolivia, Peru has used a capitalization program to raise the level of investment in its privatized enterprises. Peru's program goes farther, however, in that it requires investors to provide 50 percent of the company's value in cash and another 50 percent as an investment commitment. According to COPRI, the implementing agency, the program is aimed principally at improving efficiency rather than raising revenue. To broaden the distribution of ownership, Peru also introduced a citizen participation program under which small investors can purchase shares in utility companies.

In 1995 *Mexico* began a second wave of privatizations that included strategic infrastructure sectors (petrochemicals, natural gas, telecommunications, railways, ports, and airports). Despite earlier delays, the first of sixty-one secondary petrochemical plants operated by the state monopoly, Petroleos Mexicanos (Pemex), was auctioned in 1995. Oil and gas exploration and production will, however, remain the sole responsibility of Pemex. In the first round of auctions of key port concessions, the government awarded twenty-year concessions for upgrading and maintaining container terminals at four of the country's largest ports.

Ecuador initiated its privatization program in 1995 with the sale of the state-run airline, Ecuatoriana, to Brazil's VASP, also a newly privatized airline.

Europe and Central Asia

Countries in Eastern and Central Europe were very active in selling off state enterprises in 1995, raising almost $9 billion—a nearly threefold increase over 1994 (table A6.3). After a slow start, *Hungary* raised more than $3 billion from sales of state enterprises in 1995, more than twice the target of $1.2 billion. Since Hungary does not have a voucher program, minority stakes are sold to strategic investors, usually foreigners. The sale of MOL, the oil and gas company, for $190 million

was the largest international share offering by an Eastern European country.

The *Czech* Republic's voucher mass privatization program ended in March 1995. But another stage of privatization, using traditional methods, took off with the highly successful sale of SPT Telecom for more than $1.3 billion to a consortium of foreign investors. Because of the high asking price and new technology requirements, local firms were excluded from bidding.

A mass privatization program to be carried out using national investment funds got under way in *Poland* in 1995. Companies targeted for sale were allocated to the funds through a lottery scheme, with each fund holding strategic stakes in about thirty enterprises.

The new government of the Republic of *Slovakia* canceled the second wave of voucher privatizations, to have taken place in 1995, and proceeded to sell off state-owned companies through direct sales. The government's sale of the oil company, Slovnaft, for $329 million met with poor institutional investor response, and the European Bank for Reconstruction and Development (EBRD) took up most of the unsold shares.

The *Russian* Federation raised more than $1 billion in privatization revenues in 1995, far less than its target of $1.8 billion. In one of its first global offerings and its largest equity offering to date, the government sold a stake in Lukoil through a novel convertible bond issue that enabled it, in effect, to sell shares in advance of the authorized date. Of the total sale of $320 million, $250 million worth of shares were purchased by U.S.-based Arco, giving it a 6 percent stake in the company and making it the largest strategic investment by a U.S. corporation in the Russian oil sector.

Table A6.3 Privatization revenues in Europe and Central Asia, 1988–95
(millions of U.S. dollars)

Country	1988	1989	1990	1991	1992	1993	1994	1995	Total
Bulgaria	—	—	—	—	—	45	147	111	302
Czech Republic	—	—	—	—	—	645	7	1,645	2,297
Hungary	—	462	483	798	787	1,754	420	3,254	7,957
Poland	—	—	62	338	240	733	641	980	2,994
Russian Federation[a]	—	—	—	35	88	110	—	1,002	1,234
Slovak Republic	—	—	—	—	—	63	415	1,004	1,482
Turkey	27	216	437	212	780	483	354	572	3,081
Other	—	7	322	1,400	2,446	318	895	370	5,758
Total	27	685	1,304	2,783	4,341	4,151	2,879	8,937	25,107

— Not available.

a. Sources of data include *Privatization Yearbook 1996, Euroweek,* and other published sources.

Source: World Bank Privatization Database, International Economics Department.

Box A6.1 Privatization in Eastern and Central Europe

Privatization has been a key element in the economic transformation of transition economies. The speed and scope of privatization has differed widely across countries in the region, however, because of different privatization methods and their timing and sequencing.

The Czech Republic adopted mass privatization through vouchers to achieve a speedy transfer of ownership to the private sector. According to the State Property Fund, 98 percent of all property was in state hands in 1989. By 1995, however, only 25 percent of property was under state control, and 70 percent of GDP was being produced by the nonstate sector. Mass privatization has resulted in the formation of 1,680 joint stock companies worth a nominal 363,000 million crowns (nearly $14 billion at 1995 exchange rates). With the conclusion of the second and last voucher privatization in 1995, the government began selling off its remaining assets through traditional methods.

In contrast, Hungary chose a market-based approach over mass privatization. Until the middle of 1995 domestic investors could participate in privatization through management buyouts, installment payments, leasing, compensation coupons, and other mechanisms. Implementation was slow, however, and did not generate significant new capital for newly privatized enterprises. In June 1995 a new privatization law was passed aimed at both speeding up the process and finding buyers who would provide capital and technology to upgrade the new companies. The original list of so-called strategic companies was cut to allow the selloff of a large number of state-owned enterprises that had previously been ineligible for sale. In 1995 Hungary became the first transition economy to permit the large-scale privatization of public utilities. The strategy of encouraging foreign investment in strategic sales appears to have paid off. By the end of 1995 Hungary had the highest per capita foreign capital investment in the region, with cumulative foreign capital inflows of $12 billion—almost 40 percent of total foreign capital invested in the region.

The Polish model of privatization combined direct sales and mass privatization methods with capital privatization as a means of harnessing new capital and management skills. Capital privatization through initial public offerings, tenders, and bids has been used to privatize large companies. To implement its mass privatization program, Poland created fifteen national investment funds, each of which will act as a lead fund for some thirty companies. Voucher holders can exchange their certificates for shares in the funds. Foreign and local institutional, strategic, and private investors will be eligible to participate in the program by purchasing and trading share certificates once the funds have been listed on the Warsaw stock exchange.

Estonia has adopted a modified form of the German Treuhandanstalt model, although lack of financial and institutional resources has allowed only limited restructuring prior to sale. International tender followed by sales to strategic investors has been the dominant form of privatization. Vouchers have been used only to a limited degree.

Middle East and North Africa

Countries in the Middle East and North Africa raised $657 million from privatization in 1995 (table A6.4). Although many countries in the region have established or are setting up privatization programs, actual selloffs have been concentrated in only a few countries. Egypt and Morocco, the main focus of privatization activity in the past, saw progress slow in 1995, and several large selloffs were postponed. The largest deal for *Morocco,* whose program is considered one of the region's most successful, was the sale of BMCE, the country's second-largest bank. Several other sales, however, including the sale of Samir (refinery) and Sonasid (steel), were postponed until 1996 because of insufficient initial demand. Despite the slowdown in 1995, privatization has invigorated the Casablanca bourse.

The pace of privatization in *Egypt* remained slow, as the government continued to offer only partial stakes in state enterprises to outside investors, with a portion reserved for employee buyouts. No sales have been effected since 1994, when three companies were sold outright to foreign investors. Fear of unemployment has been one of the main causes of the slowdown in privatization. Despite the slowdown in 1995, however, shares of privatized enterprises were largely responsible for the dramatic increase in trading volume on the Cairo stock exchange.

Iran revived its moribund program, which had been suspended since mid-1994, with the sale of a 40 percent stake in a metal company. In *Algeria* a privatization program was put in place in 1995, but sales of enterprises did not commence until 1996. The *United Arab Emirates,* one of the few Arab countries without an official program, took the first step toward privatization by setting up a joint stock company, Dubai Investments, that will identify suitable enterprises for sale. *Jordan,* the first Middle Eastern country to receive a sovereign rating in 1995, also inaugurated its privatization program, with the sale of a 54 percent stake in the Intercontinental Hotel.

South Asia

Activity in South Asia slowed significantly in 1995 (table A6.5). In *India* only four of the ten public sector units earmarked for public offer were listed for sale. Because of unfavorable market conditions, the government sold only a fraction of planned allocations, although 5–10 percent of shares were set aside for public listing, and some issues had to be withdrawn. Total proceeds of $52 million represented less than 3 percent of the 1995 target of more than $2 billion. Unlike other governments on the subcontinent, the Indian government retains a controlling stake in all enterprises divested.

Pakistan's privatization program stalled in 1995 as a result of political uncertainty, and several large energy and utility divestitures were postponed. In *Sri Lanka* privatization gained momentum in 1995. The centerpiece of the program is the sell-off of the plantations sector, in which a controlling (51 percent) stake is to be sold to a strategic investor and the state is to retain a golden (19 percent) share. The first public utility put up for sale was bought by a foreign investor, who received a controlling share in the gas company.

Sub-Saharan Africa

With encouragement from donor agencies, African countries continued to sell off state-owned enterprises, raising $544 million in 1995 (table A6.6). Although the total value of privatization proceeds in Africa is low compared with other regions, African countries have been actively engaged in selling or liquidating state-owned enterprises. The absence of functioning stock markets in many African countries is one of the main obstacles to privatization.

In *Zambia* privatization and the liquidation of loss-making state enterprises continued apace during 1995. Chilanga Cement, privatized through a stock offering in 1995, became the first company to be listed on the Lusaka stock exchange, more than a year after its official opening. The potentially large sale of Zambia Consolidated Copper Mines was postponed, however.

Kenya raised the limit on foreign ownership in local companies from 20 percent to 40 percent in 1995, allowing KLM to purchase a 26 percent stake in state-owned Kenya Airways in December 1995. In 1996 another 48 percent of the airline's shares were sold to local and foreign institutional investors and to the public.

In *Zimbabwe* the government reduced its controlling stake in the largest company listed on the Zimbabwe stock exchange, Delta Corporation, through a private placement of shares. In prepara-

Table A6.4 Privatization revenues in the Middle East and North Africa, 1988–95

(millions of U.S. dollars)

Country	1988	1989	1990	1991	1992	1993	1994	1995	Total
Egypt	—	—	—	—	—	328	179	173	679
Morocco	—	—	—	—	—	273	347	240	860
Tunisia	7	14	2	17	60	—	—	32	133
Other	—	—	—	—	9	26	42	212	289
Total	7	14	2	17	70	627	567	657	1,961

— Not available.
Source: World Bank Privatization Database, International Economics Department.

Table A6.5 Privatization revenues in South Asia, 1988–95

(millions of U.S. dollars)

Country	1988	1989	1990	1991	1992	1993	1994	1995	Total
Bangladesh	—	1	—	—	—	43	12	5	61
India	—	—	—	931	1,098	861	1,505	52	4,447
Pakistan	—	—	11.3	63	343	17	1,106	36	1,577
Sri Lanka	—	3	18	2	106	52	42	65	288
Other	—	—	—	—	11	1	1	—	13
Total	—	3	29	996	1,557	974	2,666	159	6,384

— Not available.
Source: World Bank Privatization Database, International Economics Department.

tion for the sale, the company announced a ten-for-one share split to enable small investors to participate in the sale.

Sectoral distribution

Infrastructure-related selloffs accounted for 44 percent of privatization revenues in 1995, about the same as in 1994 (table A6.7). Two large sales by Indonesia and the Czech Republic boosted the value of telecommunications sales, although both deals were brought to the market with some difficulty. Telecommunications and energy utilities accounted for more than 20 percent each of privatization proceeds and more than 95 percent of infrastructure selloffs.

The petrochemicals sector also saw some activity in 1995, with the partial privatization of Brazil's Petrobras and the sale of shares in the Russian Federation's Lukoil.

Sales of airlines represented only a small share of total privatizations in 1995. Two of the Latin American airlines put up for sale, Ecuador's Ecuatoriana and Bolivia LAB, were bought by another regional airline. Regionalization of airlines is expected to increase as airline privatizations pick up pace.

Method of sale

Direct sales remain the most commonly used method of divestiture. In particular, direct sales targeted at prequalified strategic investors were the preferred means of transferring scarce management and technology skills to newly privatized medium- and large-scale enterprises in East Asia, Eastern Europe, and Latin America. Across all regions, however, stock markets continued to assist in and benefit from privatization activity. In the Middle East and North Africa, market capitaliza-

Table A6.6 Privatization revenues in Sub-Saharan Africa, 1988–95
(millions of U.S. dollars)

Country	1988	1989	1990	1991	1992	1993	1994	1995	Total
Côte d'Ivoire	—	—	—	10	6	5	14	120	154
Ghana	—	1	10	3	15	28	476	87	619
Mozambique	—	1	4	5	9	6	2	26	52
Nigeria	—	33	16	35	114	541	24	—	764
South Africa	—	632	—	5	—	—	—	—	637
Uganda	—	—	—	—	12	19	24	47	101
Zambia	—	—	—	—	—	—	—	69	69
Zimbabwe	—	—	—	—	—	—	232	75	307
Other	10	16	45	2	35	49	22	121	299
Total	10	683	74	60	191	648	792	544	3,002

— Not available.
Source: World Bank Privatization Database, International Economics Department.

Table A6.7 Privatization revenues by sector, 1988–95
(millions of U.S. dollars)

	1988	1989	1990	1991	1992	1993	1994	1995	Total
Infrastructure	798	693	6,005	6,796	9,810	4,245	9,381	9,351	47,079
Telecommunications	325	212	3,690	5,821	3,007	1,083	6,069	4,543	24,744
Energy	106	8	59	364	4,901	1,897	2,176	4,526	14,033
Industry	52	791	1,118	5,400	7,508	7,171	5,254	3,963	31,258
Steel	0	97	197	2,282	2,025	2,917	1,209	274	9,002
Chemicals	0	5	3	617	964	749	1,125	614	4,077
Construction	7	224	196	485	1,379	523	689	641	4,145
Other manufacturing	45	465	721	2,017	3,140	2,982	2,231	2,434	14,035
Primary sector	1,374	225	1,588	1,728	3,421	6,582	4,061	5,356	24,335
Petroleum	0	9	567	1,226	2,357	5,065	1,981	3,775	14,979
Mining	1,360	50	485	236	548	187	1,411	618	4,896
Financial services	8	241	47	7,810	5,259	3,514	971	1,891	19,740
Banking	8	175	47	7,522	5,099	2,608	734	1,113	17,306
Other services	362	1,068	256	924	763	2,688	561	555	7,176
Total	2,594	3,017	9,013	22,659	26,761	24,200	20,228	21,116	129,588

Source: World Bank Privatization Database, International Economics Department.

tion in Egypt, Kuwait, Morocco, and Tunisia has been enhanced by the sale of state enterprises through public offerings of shares. In Africa efforts are under way to establish bourses in Sudan and elsewhere that would help speed the privatization process. In India and China, however, where public offers are the primary means of divestiture, stock market weaknesses actually slowed privatization. Leases and concessions were the preferred method of divestiture for infrastructure and agriculture projects in Latin America and Africa; management and employee buyouts continued to be popular in Eastern Europe.

Foreign participation

Privatization continued to be an important source of foreign direct investment and equity participation in 1995. Total foreign financing raised from privatization fell to $10.5 billion, down from nearly $13 billion in 1994 (table A6.8). Nearly three-fourths of these funds were in the form of direct investment, with portfolio investment accounting for the remainder (table A6.9).

Latin America saw a decline in the volume of foreign finance following Mexico's financial crisis. But in percentage terms the decline was more pronounced in South Asia and the Middle East and North Africa. In East Asia and the Pacific portfolio

investment for privatization declined markedly as a result of the slowdown in issuing activity by China. Eastern and Central Europe was the main beneficiary of foreign investment. Sales to strategic foreign investors of energy utilities (Hungary) and telecommunications (Czech Republic) substantially increased direct investment in the region.

Sources of data for the World Bank's Privatization Database

Table A6.10 on privatization in developing countries in 1994–95 draws on the World Bank Privatization Database. Most of the information in this database is obtained from privatization agencies, other official sources, and other internal World Bank Group databases. Public reports, such as *Privatization International, Euromoney Bondware,* and *Middle East Economic Digest,* were also used to supplement data collection efforts. All data are in U.S. dollars as published or provided by official sources. In cases where sale amounts were provided in local currencies, the annual average exchange rate was used as a conversion factor. Where the buyer's identity has not been provided, the buyer is assumed to be domestic. The portfolio investment content is not estimated for public offers when the identity of investors is unknown or the number of shares purchased is indeterminate.

Table A6.8 Foreign exchange raised through privatization in developing countries, 1988–95
(millions of U.S. dollars)

Country	1988	1989	1990	1991	1992	1993	1994	1995	Total
East Asia and the Pacific	1	—	1	102	1,556	4,156	4,036	2,062	11,913
Europe and Central Asia	14	666	628	2,107	3,724	3,033	1,460	6,059	17,691
Latin America and the Caribbean	353	323	2,565	7,093	3,827	3,719	5,632	2,106	25,617
Middle East and North Africa	—	1	0	3	19	299	158	16	497
South Asia	—	—	11	4	44	16	997	38	1,110
Sub-Saharan Africa	—	14	38	11	61	573	663	269	1,630
All developing countries	368	1,004	3,243	9,321	9,231	11,797	12,946	10,549	58,458

— Not available.
Source: World Bank Privatization Database, International Economics Department, and World Bank staff estimates.

Table A6.9 Portfolio investment and foreign direct investment in privatization, 1988–95
(millions of U.S. dollars)

Country	1988	1989	1990	1991	1992	1993	1994	1995	Total
Foreign direct investment	368	1,004	3,132	5,778	6,470	6,711	6,098	8,076	37,636
Portfolio investment	0	0	111	3,542	2,761	5,086	6,848	2,473	20,822
Total	368	1,004	3,243	9,321	9,231	11,797	12,946	10,549	58,458

Source: World Bank Privatization Database, International Economics Department, and World Bank staff estimates.

Table A6.10 Privatization transactions in developing countries, 1994–95

(millions of U.S. dollars)

Year	Company	Country	Sector	Equity share Percent	Amount	Foreign exchange	Purchaser
1995	Amballazh Kartoni, Tirane	Albania	Paper products	100.0	0.4	0.0	Local investor
1995	Asfaltim Rruga, Fier	Albania	Road maintenance	78.3	0.5	0.0	Local investor
1995	Bloja, Tirane	Albania	Agribusiness	67.2	0.7	0.0	Local investor
1995	Bread factory, Tirana	Albania	Food	39.4	0.5	0.0	Local investor
1995	Brick factory, Elbasan	Albania	Bricks	100.0	0.9	0.0	Local investor
1995	Cartography printing, Tirana	Albania	Printing	89.7	0.2	0.0	Local investor
1995	Cereal silos and processing, Vlore	Albania	Storage	79.7	1.1	0.0	Local investor
1995	Cereal silos, Durres	Albania	Storage	70.3	0.1	0.0	Local investor
1995	Cereal silos, Peqin	Albania	Storage	82.2	0.1	0.0	Local investor
1995	Dajti metal factory, Tirana	Albania	Metallurgy	57.0	0.3	0.0	Local investor
1995	Electricity distribution, Elbasan	Albania	Electricity	30.0	1.3	0.0	Local investor
1995	Electricity distribution, Vlore	Albania	Electricity	30.0	1.4	0.0	Local investor
1995	Elektromjeksore, Tirane	Albania	Medical equipment	100.0	0.3	0.0	Local investor
1995	Flour factory, Tirana	Albania	Milling	89.0	0.5	0.0	Local investor
1995	Frigoriferi, Berat	Albania	Cold storage	90.2	0.1	0.0	Local investor
1995	Gozhde Bullonat, Kavaje	Albania	Manufacturing	91.8	0.3	0.0	Local investor
1995	Iliria Hotel, Korca	Albania	Hotel	98.3	0.9	0.0	Local investor
1995	Leather products, Tirana	Albania	Manufacturing	81.3	0.7	0.0	Local investor
1995	Machines and metals, Tirana	Albania	Metallurgy	96.2	0.5	0.0	Local investor
1995	Mekanike Bujqesore, Fier	Albania	Agricultural machinery	100.0	0.1	0.0	Local investor
1995	Mekanike e K.M., Elbasan	Albania	Equipment	100.0	0.7	0.0	Local investor
1995	Military and Agricultural, Berat	Albania	Manufacturing	83.5	0.8	0.0	Local investor
1995	Military construction, Fier	Albania	Construction	100.0	0.1	0.0	Local investor
1995	Ndert. Asfalt. Rruga, Tirane	Albania	Road construction	66.3	0.3	0.0	Local investor
1995	Ndert. Rip. Mak. Asfalti, Tirane	Albania	Services	70.6	0.2	0.0	Local investor
1995	Ndertim Rruga, Elbasan	Albania	Road maintenance	100.0	0.8	0.0	Local investor
1995	Ndertim Ura, Tirane	Albania	Construction	90.8	0.2	0.0	Local investor
1995	OAT, Tirane	Albania	Vehicle maintenance	100.0	0.1	0.0	Local investor
1995	Oil machinery repair	Albania	Repair service	100.0	0.2	0.0	Local investor
1995	Oil refinery, Patos	Albania	Oil production	100.0	0.6	0.0	Local investor
1995	Petrolimpex, Tirana	Albania	Petroleum	4.2	1.3	0.0	Local investor
1995	Plastic factory, Lushnje	Albania	Plastics	100.0	0.6	0.0	Local investor
1995	Printing enterprise, Tirana	Albania	Printing	91.4	0.6	0.0	Local investor
1995	Prodhim Karbonike, Elbasan	Albania	Equipment	100.0	0.4	0.0	Local investor
1995	Prodhim Vajra, Delvine	Albania	Oil production	75.9	0.2	0.0	Local investor
1995	Retail network, Korca	Albania	Retail	76.5	0.3	0.0	Local investor
1995	Road construction, Patos	Albania	Construction	86.4	0.4	0.0	Local investor
1995	Shtypshkronja "cajupi," Tirane	Albania	Printing	85.4	0.4	0.0	Local investor
1995	Tobacco factory	Albania	Tobacco	95.4	0.1	0.0	Local investor
1995	Trucking company, Tirana	Albania	Services	73.1	0.3	0.0	Local investor
1995	Trucking enterprise, Tirana	Albania	Services	55.7	0.2	0.0	Local investor
1995	Turizmi, Vlore	Albania	Tourism	50.6	1.5	0.0	Local investor
1995	Wood processing, Berat	Albania	Wood products	75.6	0.1	0.0	Local investor
1995	Wood processing, Korca	Albania	Wood products	74.6	0.1	0.0	Local investor
1995	Wood processing, Lac	Albania	Wood products	70.7	0.2	0.0	Local investor
1995	Edesur	Argentina	Electricity	39.0	390.0	390.0	Enersis of Chile
1995	Femesa—Mitre Line	Argentina	Transport	—	—	—	Local investor
1995	Femesa—Roca Line	Argentina	Transport	—	—	—	Local investor

Table A6.10 Privatization transactions in developing countries, 1994–95 (continued)

(millions of U.S. dollars)

Year	Company	Sector	Country	Equity share Percent	Equity share Amount	Foreign exchange	Purchaser
1995	Femesa—Sarmiento Lin	Transport	Argentina	—	—	—	Aluar Aluminio Argentino
1995	Hidroelectrica Futaleufu, SA	Power utility	Argentina	51.0	226.0	0.0	AES Rio Dimante SA and AEC Corp. (U.S.)
1995	Hidroelectrica Rio Juramento SA	Power utility	Argentina	98.0	41.1	—	Dow Chemicals Argentina SA (U.S.), YPF SA (Argentina), Itochu Argentina (Japan)
1995	Petroquimica Bahia Blanca, SA	Petrochemicals	Argentina	51.0	357.5	297.6	Dow Chemicals
1995	Polisur	Petrochemicals	Argentina	100.0	193.0	193.0	Dow Chemicals
1995	Vias Navegables	Transport	Argentina	—	—	—	LC:Sideco Americana
1994	Acceso Notre	Roads	Argentina	—	—	—	Benito Roggio y Otros, Grupo Mexicano de Desarrolos;Comp Brasileira de Projectos
1994	Acceso Oeste	Roads	Argentina	—	—	—	Huarte y Otros
1994	Acceso Ricchieri	Roads	Argentina	—	—	—	Leucadia National Corp.; Los W S.A., Banco Mercantil S.A.
1994	Caja Nacional de Ahorro y Seguro	Banking	Argentina	60.0	86.3	43.2	Incopp S.A., Frigorifico Bahia Blanca S.A.
1994	CAP Cuatreros	Food products	Argentina	100.0	1.9	0.0	Iate S.A., Federacion Argentina de Trabajadores de Luz y Fuerza
1994	Centrales Termicas del Litoral	Power utility	Argentina	100.0	0.5	0.0	80% foreign, 20% local investors
1994	Centrales Termicas Mendoza	Power utility	Argentina	100.0	10.1	8.1	Foreign and local investors
1994	Districoyo	Power utility	Argentina	—	20.2	10.0	Prudent International;Oceanbulk Maritime;Rare Shipping;Altamira;Seabound
1994	Empresa Lineas Maritimas Argentinas S.A.	Shipping	Argentina	100.0	14.8	14.8	Industria Argentina de Material Pirotecnico S.A.
1994	Fabrica Militar Pilar	Defense	Argentina	100.0	2.8	0.0	LC: Transportes Metropolitanos General San Martin; operated Bart & JART
1994	Ferrocarriles Metropolitanos(FEMESA):Linea San Martin	Railroads	Argentina	—	—	—	LC: Ferrovias SA
1994	Ferrocarriles Metropolitanos(FEMESA):Linea Belgano Norte	Railroads	Argentina	—	—	—	LC: Transportes Metropolitanos General San Martin
1994	Ferrocarrils Metropolitanos (FEMESA):Linea Belgano Sur	Railroads	Argentina	—	—	—	EDF International(50%), Nucleamiento Inversor, Banco de Galicia y Buenos Aires
1994	Hidroelectrica Diamante S.A.	Power utility-generation	Argentina	100.0	32.8	16.4	Uruguay's UTE and Chubut electricity cooperatives
1994	Hidroelectrica Ameghino	Power utility-dam	Argentina	59.0	14.2	14.2	
1994	Metrogas	Gas	Argentina	—	121.5	121.5	River Plate Container, Murchison S.A., Estibajes y Cargas, Roman Maritime
1994	Puerto Nuevo Ciudad de Buenos Aire: Terminal 1,2	Ports/Port Facilities	Argentina	—	—	—	Local investor
1994	Puerto Nuevo Ciudad de Buenos Aires: Terminals 1–6	Ports/Port Facilities	Argentina	—	3.0	0.0	LC: Fed. Argentina de Luz y Fuerza, Banco Feigin, IATE, Tecsa, Gestion Electrica
1994	Transnea	Power utility	Argentina	90.0	8.7	0.0	Local investors, and foreign through debt-equity swap
1994	Transnoa S.A.	Power utility	Argentina	51.0	20.8	10.4	Foreign and local investors
1994	Transpa S.A.	Power utility	Argentina	27.0	526.5	210.6	LC: Federacion Argentina de Trabajadores de Luz y Fuerza, Dragados y Obras
1994	Transportadora de Gas del Sur	Gas	Argentina		22.5	0.0	Contant Shipping Ltd., Global Marketing Systems
1994	Yacimientos Carboniferos Fiscales	Coal	Argentina		3.1	3.1	Jamaican Sandals
1994	YPF S.A.(5 tankers)	Petroleum/petrochemicals	Argentina		8.5	8.5	Local investors
1995	Le Meridien Royal Bahamian Hotel	Hotel	Bahamas	20.0	10.3	0.0	Local investor
1994	General trading and food processing company	Food	Bahrain	100.0	0.3	0.0	Local investor
1994	Barisal Textile Ltd	Textiles	Bangladesh	100.0	0.3	0.0	Local investor
1995	Jonfine Fabrics Ltd	Textiles	Bangladesh	100.0	4.5	0.0	Local investor
1995	Kohinoor Spinning Mills Ltd.	Textiles	Bangladesh	100.0	0.6	0.0	Local investor
1994	Bangladesh Cycle	Manufacturing	Bangladesh	51.0	0.6	0.0	Local investor
1994	Eagle Box and Cartoons Manufacturing	Packaging manufacturing	Bangladesh	100.0	0.3	0.0	Local investor
1994	Jofain Fabrics	Textiles	Bangladesh	100.0	2.4	0.0	Local investor
1994	Kishorganj Textile Mills Ltd.	Textiles	Bangladesh	100.0	2.0	0.0	Local investor
1994	Madaripur Textile	Textiles	Bangladesh	100.0	2.9	0.0	Local investor
1994	Sharmin Textiles Ltd	Textiles	Bangladesh	40.0	0.5	0.0	Local investor
1994	Squibb of Bangladesh	Pharmaceuticals	Bangladesh	51.0	2.9	2.9	Trinidad Cement Ltd.
1994	Arawak Cement Company Ltd.	Cement	Barbados	100.0	17.0	17.0	B.S. & T Resorts Ltd.
1994	Heywood Hotel	Tourism/hotels	Barbados	100.0	0.7	0.0	
1995	MAISERIE	Industry	Benin	100.0	0.2	0.0	
1995	US. CONC.TOM	Industry	Benin	100.0	0.3	0.0	
1995	US. NOIX CAJOU	Industry	Benin	100.0	0.2	0.0	
1995	US. JUS FRUITS	Industry	Benin				

(table continues on next page)

123

Table A6.10 Privatization transactions in developing countries, 1994–95 (continued)

(millions of U.S. dollars)

Year	Company	Country	Sector	Equity share Percent	Equity share Amount	Foreign exchange	Purchaser
1995	Bien Immeuble–Av. ARCE esq. M. Pinilla	Bolivia	Real Estate	100.0	0.8	0.0	Local investor
1995	Cadenas Andinas Sam— 1st Unit	Bolivia	Industry	100.0	0.0	0.0	Local investor
1995	Cadenas Andinas Sam—2nd Unit	Bolivia	Industry	100.0	0.0	0.0	Local investor
1995	Cadenas Andinas Sam—3rd Unit	Bolivia	Industry	100.0	0.0	0.0	
1995	Empresa de Luz y Fuerza S.A.M.	Bolivia	Electricity	100.0	50.3	50.3	Chilean company
1995	Empresa Nacional de Electricidad	Bolivia	Power utilities	50.0	104.8	104.8	Dominion Energy, Energy Initiatives, Constellation Energy
1995	Empresa Nacional de Telecomunicaciones	Bolivia	Telecommunications	50.0	610.0	610.0	Stet International(Italy)
1995	Fabrica de Vidrio Plano	Bolivia	Glass	100.0	1.3	0.0	
1995	Fondo Ganaderodel Beni y Pando	Bolivia	Livestock	30.0	0.0	0.0	
1995	Hotel Prefectural Coroico	Bolivia	Services	100.0	0.5	0.0	Local investor
1995	Hotel Prefectural de Chulumani	Bolivia	Services	100.0	0.1	0.0	
1995	Hotel Prefectural de Copacabana	Bolivia	Services	100.0	0.3	0.0	
1995	Hotel Prefectural de Urmiri	Bolivia	Services	100.0	0.2	0.0	
1995	Hotel Prefectural Sorata	Bolivia	Services	100.0	0.2	0.0	Local investor
1995	Hotel Prefectural Viscachani	Bolivia	Services	100.0	0.1	0.0	
1995	Industrial Metalicas—1st Unit	Bolivia	Metals	100.0	0.7	0.0	Local investor
1995	Linea Aerea Imperial	Bolivia	Airlines	100.0	0.7	0.0	SS Telecom Bolivia SRL
1995	Lloyd Aereo Boliviano	Bolivia	Airlines	50.0	5.0	5.0	VASP of Argentina
1995	Multiproposito Gran Chaco	Bolivia	Agriculture	25.0	0.0	0.0	
1995	Pait-Pl. Procesadora de Caranavi—1st Unit	Bolivia	Agriculture	100.0	0.1	0.0	Local investor
1995	Pait-Pl. Procesadora de Caranavi—2nd Unit	Bolivia	Agriculture	100.0	0.1	0.0	Local investor
1995	Pait-Pl. Procesadora de Chimate	Bolivia	Agriculture	100.0	0.1	0.0	Local investor
1995	Planta de Alimentos Balanc. Portachuelo—1st Unit	Bolivia	Agribusiness	100.0	0.1	0.0	Local investor
1995	Planta de Alimentos Balanceados, Tarija	Bolivia	Agribusiness	100.0	0.3	0.0	
1995	Planta Industrializadora de Leche Pil-Santa Cruz	Bolivia	Livestock	100.0	6.4	0.0	Employees (70%), suppliers (30%)
1995	Planta Industrializadora de Leche Pil-Sucre	Bolivia	Livestock	100.0	0.4	0.0	Suppliers (99%), employees (1%)
1995	Planta Industrializadora de Leche Pil-Tarija	Bolivia	Livestock	100.0	0.3	0.0	Suppliers
1995	Planta Laminadora de Goma Sam	Bolivia	Agriculture	100.0	0.2	0.0	Stockholders
1995	Produccion de Alimentos de Maiz Mairaina	Bolivia	Agribusiness	100.0	0.7	0.0	Local investor
1995	Terminal de Buses Cochabamba	Bolivia	Transport	100.0	3.4	0.0	Transportation syndicate
1995	Terminal de Buses Oruro	Bolivia	Transport	100.0	1.5	0.0	Transportation syndicate
1995	Brasiliera de Poliuretanos (CBP)	Brazil	Petrochemicals	23.7	0.0	0.0	Local investors
1995	Escelsa	Brazil	Power utility	50.0	387.4	0.0	Iven consortium (Brazilian banks and pension funds)
1995	Nitrocarbono S.A.	Brazil	Petrochemicals	33.4	29.6	0.0	Mariani Group
1995	Petroquimica de Camacari (CPC)	Brazil	Petrochemicals	20.8	99.6	1.2	Foreign participation involved
1995	Petroquimica do Nordeste (Copene)	Brazil	Petrochemicals	32.8	270.4	0.0	Nordeste Quimica SA, pension funds
1995	Pronor Petroquimica S.A.	Brazil	Petrochemicals	35.3	63.6	0.0	Mariani Group
1995	Quimica do Reconcavo (CQR)	Brazil	Petrochemicals	36.9	1.7	1.7	Foreign participation involved
1995	Salgema Industrias Quimicas S.A.	Brazil	Petrochemicals	29.3	139.2	1.2	Foreign participation involved
1994	Acrinor	Brazil	Petroleum/petrochemicals	17.7	12.1	4.5	Rhodia, Copene
1994	Araferril	Brazil	Agricultural supplies/fertilizers	33.3	10.8	5.4	Fertisul, Quimbrasil
1994	Brazilian Petroquimica Uniao(PQU)	Brazil	Petroleum/petrochemicals	50.3	287.5	57.5	Unipar 1.1% now holds 30.1%, Union Carbide 20%, Polibrasil 20%, employees 10%
1994	Caraiba	Brazil	Mining	100.0	5.8	0.0	Caraiba Metals
1994	Ciquine	Brazil	Petroleum/petrochemicals	31.4	23.7	23.7	Conepar, Mitsubishi, Nisshoiwai
1994	Companhia Vale do Rio Doce	Brazil	Steel	N/A	137.9	105.8	Local and foreign investors
1994	Coperbo	Brazil	Petroleum/petrochemicals	23.0	25.9	17.3	Petroflex,Copene
1994	Copesul	Brazil	Petroleum/petrochemicals	9.1	32.9	0.0	Local investors
1994	Cosipa	Brazil	Steel	21.3	216.2	12.2	

Table A6.10 Privatization transactions in developing countries, 1994–95 (continued)

(millions of U.S. dollars)

Year	Company	Country	Sector	Equity share Percent	Equity share Amount	Foreign exchange	Purchaser
1994	CSN	Brazil	Steel	8.8	210.3	0.0	Banco Bozano Simonsen 71% with unknown buyers
1994	Empresa Brasileira de Aeronautica(Embraer)	Brazil	Manufacturing/Aircraft	60.4	192.1	63.0	Conepar, Mitsubishi, Nisshoiwai
1994	Polialden	Brazil	Petroleum/petrochemicals	13.6	16.7	16.7	Conepar, Suzano, Sumitomo
1994	Politeno	Brazil	Petroleum/petrochemicals	24.9	44.9	44.9	Local and foreign investors
1994	Usiminas	Brazil	Steel	16.2	480.0	372.0	Biljana-1300
1995	A Hut Kindergarten	Bulgaria	Transport	100.0	0.2	0.0	Managers/employees
1995	Administrative Building (Sofia)	Bulgaria	Construction	100.0	0.5	0.0	Managers/employees
1995	Akvila	Bulgaria	Agribusiness	77.0	0.5	0.0	Albena Style-95
1995	Albena-Style	Bulgaria	Garments	75.0	3.0	0.0	Aluminium Joinery-95
1995	Aluminium joinery	Bulgaria	Metallurgy	70.0	0.5	0.0	Olympic Group
1995	Alvina	Bulgaria	Agribusiness	80.0	0.9	0.0	First Private Factor for Ready-Made Clothes
1995	Arda Rousse	Bulgaria	Garments	75.0	3.5	0.0	Daru Invest Ltd.
1995	Astika	Bulgaria	Brewery	80.0	5.0	5.0	Kano Trans
1995	Avrobaza Staro Orjahovo	Bulgaria	Transport	100.0	0.2	0.0	Bulgarian Tourist Holding
1995	Balkantourist	Bulgaria	Tourism	51.0	1.3	0.0	Barbukov
1995	Bilyana	Bulgaria	Agribusiness	80.0	0.7	0.0	Borella-94
1995	Borella-C	Bulgaria	Wood industry	80.0	0.3	0.0	Interbrew(Belgium)
1995	Bourgasko Pivo	Bulgaria	Brewery	67.0	5.0	5.0	Tom-Toma Bezhinarov
1995	Breza Confectionary	Bulgaria	Confectionary	100.0	0.2	0.0	Brilyant Invest
1995	Brilyant	Bulgaria	Garments	78.0	1.8	0.0	Bulfract
1995	Bulfracht	Bulgaria	Transport	80.0	2.4	0.0	Balkanfrut
1995	Bulgartsvet	Bulgaria	Agribusiness	58.0	0.3	0.0	Interbrew(Belgium)
1995	Burgasko Pivo	Bulgaria	Brewery	70.0	5.0	5.0	Chayka Engineering and Management
1995	Chayka	Bulgaria	Paper industry	80.0	1.3	0.0	Saga Distribution Service
1995	Coffee factory	Bulgaria	Food processing	100.0	2.0	2.0	Avco gruppa
1995	Delta-63	Bulgaria	Industry	80.0	0.4	0.0	Managers/employees
1995	Ecotherm Peria	Bulgaria	Machinery	100.0	0.3	0.0	Managers/employees
1995	Ekarissaj Dobrich	Bulgaria	Agribusiness	100.0	0.2	0.0	Management/employee buyout
1995	Electrostroeji Haskovo	Bulgaria	Power engineering	85.8	0.4	0.0	
1995	Fish Breeding Pool No. 1	Bulgaria	Agribusiness	100.0	0.2	0.0	Managers/employees
1995	Hellios Commercial Complex (Block A)	Bulgaria	Tourism	100.0	0.3	0.0	Hibriden Centar-Invest
1995	Hibriden Centar	Bulgaria	Agribusiness	80.0	0.6	0.0	Contraco
1995	Illinden	Bulgaria	Machinery	80.0	1.0	0.0	Management/employee buyout
1995	Industrial power engineering	Bulgaria	Power engineering	75.8	0.2	0.0	Management/employee buyout
1995	Industrial power engineering, Veliko Tarnovo	Bulgaria	Power engineering	100.0	0.2	0.0	T.B.S. Hotels
1995	Intercar-91	Bulgaria	Transport	80.0	0.4	0.0	ALG Ltd (80%), employees (0.4%)
1995	Interhotel Bulgaria	Bulgaria	Tourism	80.4	8.4	0.0	B. Balabanov-Capricornus
1995	Kabelcommerce	Bulgaria	Trade	75.0	3.0	0.0	Managers/employees
1995	Kamenets-91	Bulgaria	Wood	100.0	0.3	0.0	Interbrew (Belgium)
1995	Kameniisa	Bulgaria	Brewery	70.0	4.9	4.9	Pegas Budev
1995	Klon Kardjali	Bulgaria	Transport	100.0	0.2	0.0	Kofrajna Technika
1995	Kofrajna Technika	Bulgaria	Machinery	70.0	1.5	0.0	Plamen Naydenov
1995	Kopitoto Hotel Complex	Bulgaria	Tourism	100.0	0.3	0.0	Managers/employees
1995	Kora	Bulgaria	Agribusiness	100.0	0.2	0.0	Management/employee buyout
1995	Kumazit	Bulgaria	Construction	100.0	0.9	0.0	Milton Ltd
1995	Ljulin Shop (Sofcom)	Bulgaria	Tourism	100.0	0.2	0.0	
1995	Melnica-Mezdra	Bulgaria	Agribusiness	100.0	0.1	0.0	Managers/employees
1995	Messocombinat	Bulgaria	Agribusiness	100.0	0.2	0.0	

(table continues on next page)

Table A6.10 Privatization transactions in developing countries, 1994–95 (continued)

(millions of U.S. dollars)

Year	Company	Country	Sector	Equity share Percent	Equity share Amount	Foreign exchange	Purchaser
1995	Metal	Bulgaria	Machinery	80.0	1.5	0.0	Metal Invest
1995	MIP-91	Bulgaria	Construction	100.0	0.3	0.0	Managers/employees
1995	Motorest	Bulgaria	Machinery	100.0	0.2	0.0	Managers/employees
1995	Moura-Borovets	Bulgaria	Tourism	81.1	3.8	0.0	Almi-Tours Ltd
1995	Nadejda Autotransport	Bulgaria	Transport	100.0	0.6	0.0	Alfa Trucking
1995	Napredak	Bulgaria	Agribusiness	100.0	0.2	0.0	Managers/employees
1995	Nessebar Autotransport	Bulgaria	Transport	80.0	0.2	0.0	Perchemliev
1995	Oranjerii Levski	Bulgaria	Agribusiness	80.0	0.8	0.0	Timel Ltd
1995	Oranjerii Zvanichevo	Bulgaria	Agribusiness	60.0	0.7	0.0	Timel Ltd
1995	Pamporovo Ski	Bulgaria	Industry	78.0	0.5	0.0	Orion Ski
1995	Phoenix Recom	Bulgaria	Trade	78.0	1.1	0.0	S.B.R.
1995	Pigs-93	Bulgaria	Agribusiness	80.0	1.5	0.0	Pigs-95
1995	Pioneer Koynare	Bulgaria	—	100.0	0.4	0.0	
1995	Pirinska Moura	Bulgaria	Wood furniture	67.0	2.8	2.8	Evrotech Ld. (USA)
1995	Plodkonserv	Bulgaria	Agribusiness	65.0	0.6	0.0	Agro-Bio Konserv
1995	Podemplast	Bulgaria	Chemicals	100.0	0.2	0.0	Managers/employees
1995	Polmo Avto	Bulgaria	Automotive service	100.0	0.3	0.0	
1995	Prima Lacta	Bulgaria	Agribusiness	75.0	3.6	0.0	Nonex–Chr. Nonov
1995	Production workshop (Sofia)	Bulgaria	Construction	100.0	0.2	0.0	Simek Ltd.
1995	Proizvodstven Korpus PK-2	Bulgaria	Industry	100.0	2.8	0.0	Bulgarian National Bank
1995	Repair base (Jagodovo)	Bulgaria	Construction	100.0	0.5	0.0	Herku Ltd
1995	Repair base (Shoumen)	Bulgaria	Construction	100.0	0.2	0.0	Dimitar Alexandrov
1995	Reproductor po Svinevadstvo	Bulgaria	Agribusiness	64.1	0.6	0.0	Reproductor po Svinevadstvo
1995	Republika	Bulgaria	Agribusiness	70.0	0.8	0.0	Evroinvest 94
1995	Rezistori	Bulgaria	Industry	100.0	0.4	0.0	Chernomorski Bryag
1995	Rila	Bulgaria	Agribusiness	70.0	0.9	0.0	Pirin Plast STX
1995	Rilla	Bulgaria	Agribusiness	80.0	0.7	0.0	Krupkom
1995	Roussalka (weaving workshop)	Bulgaria	Textiles	100.0	0.2	0.0	Roussalka-Tex
1995	Russeproekt	Bulgaria	Construction	100.0	0.3	0.0	Managers/employees
1995	Semena-Shoumen	Bulgaria	Agribusiness	100.0	0.4	0.0	Managers/employees
1995	Shop N207 (fish exchange)	Bulgaria	Services	100.0	0.2	0.0	Vellessa
1995	Shtastlivesta Hotel	Bulgaria	Tourism	100.0	0.4	0.0	Milton Ltd
1995	Smesier	Bulgaria	Agribusiness	100.0	0.9	0.0	Multiagrex
1995	SMP	Bulgaria	Construction	100.0	0.3	0.0	Management/employee buyout
1995	Soreg	Bulgaria	Construction	100.0	0.3	0.0	Managers/employees
1995	Sozopol (holiday house)	Bulgaria	Hotel	100.0	0.3	0.0	Sozopol Hotel Ltd.
1995	Start	Bulgaria	Industry	51.2	1.0	0.0	BAT
1995	Storehouse, Shoumen	Bulgaria	Construction	100.0	0.2	0.0	Ficosota Ltd
1995	Storehouse, Sofia	Bulgaria	Construction	100.0	0.2	0.0	Industrial Commerce
1995	Storko	Bulgaria	Agribusiness	80.0	0.1	0.1	Luxcraft Trading (UK)
1995	Straldja Ceramika	Bulgaria	Construction	100.0	1.8	0.0	Management/employee buyout
1995	Strella Shop, Sofcom	Bulgaria	Tourism	100.0	0.2	0.0	Managers/employees
1995	Stroycomplekt	Bulgaria	Construction	100.0	0.2	0.0	Managers/employees
1995	Supermarket N104	Bulgaria	Services	100.0	0.3	0.0	Brulex-104
1995	Supermarket N205	Bulgaria	Services	100.0	0.2	0.0	Shipka Universal
1995	Supermarket N42	Bulgaria	Services	100.0	0.1	0.0	Dubrovnik Ltd
1995	Supermarket N60	Bulgaria	Services	100.0	0.3	0.0	Bolyari
1995	Svinevadstvo	Bulgaria	Agribusiness	80.0	0.6	0.0	Balkan Hotdog

126

Table A6.10 Privatization transactions in developing countries, 1994–95 (continued)

(millions of U.S. dollars)

Year	Company	Country	Sector	Equity share Percent	Amount	Foreign exchange	Purchaser
1995	Ticha-1	Bulgaria	Confectionary	100.0	0.2	0.0	Festa Ltd.
1995	Tompson	Bulgaria	Confectionary	75.0	2.5	2.5	Polly-eck Ltd
1995	Tourcommerce	Bulgaria	Tourism	100.0	0.4	0.0	Managers/employees
1995	Tunja	Bulgaria	Agribusiness	80.0	0.1	0.0	Russi Peychev
1995	Ustrem	Bulgaria	Agribusiness	51.0	0.6	0.0	Ustrem Invest
1995	Ustrem	Bulgaria	Agribusiness	80.0	0.2	0.0	
1995	Varna	Bulgaria	Agribusiness	70.0	0.8	0.0	Mill Complex
1995	Vaya-furaj	Bulgaria	Agribusiness	100.0	1.2	0.0	Vaya-Agro Ltd
1995	Vejen Tourist	Bulgaria	Tourism	100.0	0.2	0.0	Vulna M2
1995	Vida Style	Bulgaria	Garments	60.0	2.0	0.0	Vida-95
1995	Vinis	Bulgaria	Agribusiness	80.0	3.1	0.0	Vinis
1995	Vitavel	Bulgaria	Paper products	75.0	1.1	0.0	Vitavel-Invest
1995	Warehouse, Bakadjik	Bulgaria	Storage	100.0	0.5	0.0	Mill Combine HD-Sliven I Fenix
1995	Zagorets	Bulgaria	Agribusiness	79.0	1.5	0.0	Sky Group
1995	IPP I Isproekt JSC	Bulgaria	Communications	100.0	0.2	0.0	Terra Olympic
1994	Shumen Auto	Bulgaria	Trade	100.0	0.5	0.0	Mototechnica-Shumen
1994	Shipping agency	Bulgaria	Services	80.0	0.2	0.0	TCK 94 Ltd.
1994	AC Konsult-Building, Trojan	Bulgaria	Real estate	—	0.0	0.0	AC Konsult Ltd.
1994	Agromes I.rd.	Bulgaria	Agribusiness	100.0	0.0	0.0	GP Agropromstroi-BD & Partners
1994	Agroingenering Ltd.	Bulgaria	Agribusiness	80.0	2.6	0.0	The Economic Bank
1994	Agropromdein-Kavarzite Ltd.	Bulgaria	Agribusiness	100.0	0.1	0.0	Evrogroup Ltd.
1994	Alexander Dimitrov Ltd.	Bulgaria	Feed	79.0	0.4	0.0	MM-5
1994	Amfora Ltd., Dragoman	Bulgaria	Trade	100.0	1.9	0.0	Amfora 94 Ltd.
1994	Augusta Ltd.	Bulgaria	Agribusiness	100.0	0.0	0.0	GP Agropromstroi-BD & Partners
1994	Auto-Base	Bulgaria	Services/auto	—	0.3	0.0	Buts LSC
1994	Auto repair station	Bulgaria	Services/auto	100.0	0.3	0.0	Auto repair station
1994	Auto repair station, Drujba	Bulgaria	Services/auto	100.0	0.2	0.0	GP Stoichevi 5765
1994	Auto repair service and trade center	Bulgaria	Services/trade	—	0.4	0.0	Employees
1994	Auto repair station, Drujba	Bulgaria	Services/auto	100.0	0.1	0.0	Avrovest
1994	Auto repair station, Targovishte	Bulgaria	Services/auto	100.0	0.1	0.0	Rebus Trans Auto Ltd.
1994	Auto repair station, Vidin	Bulgaria	Services/auto	100.0	0.1	0.0	Kristi Ltd.
1994	Auto repair station, Drujba	Bulgaria	Services/auto	100.0	0.3	0.0	Employees
1994	Auto repair station IUG	Bulgaria	Services/auto	100.0	0.1	0.0	SP Ivan Ivanov
1994	Autokomplex 90 Ltd.	Bulgaria	Automobile services	100.0	0.1	0.0	A.V.G.-94
1994	Auto repair station, Drianovo	Bulgaria	Services/auto	100.0	0.1	0.0	SP Boriana Saba Christova
1994	Autorepair Station Express Ltd.	Bulgaria	Services/auto	100.0	0.1	0.0	Autorepair-Station Express
1994	Balkanmes SC	Bulgaria	Industry	100.0	0.0	0.0	Balkanmes Ltd.
1994	Besparski Halmove	Bulgaria	Agribusiness	80.0	0.0	0.0	Pig-Pazardjik
1994	Betonintelekt Ltd.	Bulgaria	Construction	100.0	0.1	0.0	Employees
1994	Building	Bulgaria	Real estate	—	0.6	0.0	First Private Bank JSC
1994	Building, Dimitrovgrad	Bulgaria	Real estate	100.0	0.1	0.0	SP Burgelov-Inko Burgelov
1994	Bulgarikum Ltd.	Bulgaria	Industry	100.0	0.8	0.0	Alom Ltd.
1994	Bulgarreklama Ltd.	Bulgaria	Trade	80.0	0.8	0.0	Bulgarreklama 94 JSC
1994	Bulgarzvet-Plovdin Ltd.	Bulgaria	Horticulture	54.0	0.4	0.0	Balkanfrut Ltd.
1994	Chinimport	Bulgaria	Chemicals	59.0	7.0	0.0	
1994	Delta Ltd.	Bulgaria	Industry	80.0	0.4	0.0	SP Avko Group
1994	Dervent Ltd.	Bulgaria	Recycling	100.0	1.9	0.0	Dervent 94 Ltd.
1994	Diampolis Pivo	Bulgaria	Industry	100.0	0.2	0.0	Gloria-SP

(table continues on next page)

127

Table A6.10 Privatization transactions in developing countries, 1994–95 (continued)

(millions of U.S. dollars)

Year	Company	Country	Sector	Equity share Percent	Equity share Amount	Foreign exchange	Purchaser
1994	Dobrudganski Plod Ltd.	Bulgaria	Industry	80.0	0.1	0.0	SP Detelina-90
1994	Ecology and Technology Ltd.	Bulgaria	Industry	100.0	0.1	0.0	VI Vesta Metal JSC
1994	Ekarisage Zagore	Bulgaria	Food	100.0	0.1	0.0	Ekarisage Zagore Ltd.
1994	Elektron Universe Ltd.	Bulgaria	Manufacturing	100.0	1.1	0.0	Electroninvest ltd.
1994	Eskos Dograma Ltd.	Bulgaria	Manufacturing	80.0	0.5	0.5	Gibu ltd.
1994	Expressproekt	Bulgaria	Services	100.0	0.1	0.0	Construction House-Chonkov
1994	Fodder Enterprise Ltd.	Bulgaria	Agribusiness	100.0	0.3	0.0	Bon Marin Ltd.
1994	Galus Ltd.-21 buildings	Bulgaria	Real Estate	—	0.2	0.0	Peev-Starr 90
1994	Gazobeton Ltd.	Bulgaria	Cement	100.0	3.2	3.2	YTONG Holding (Germany)
1994	Godman 91 Ltd.	Bulgaria	Industry	100.0	0.1	0.0	Valdin Export Import
1994	Grand Hotel Varna JSC	Bulgaria	Tourism/hotels	62.0	11.9	0.0	Multigroup Bulgaria JSC Holding; Balkanbank JSC
1994	Harpun 93 Ltd.	Bulgaria	Trade	100.0	0.1	0.0	Employees
1994	Hemus Ltd.	Bulgaria	Industry	100.0	0.3	0.0	SP V. Danchev-MD-Furnace-Building; SP Furnace-Building-Jordan Vasil
1994	Hidroprobivna Technika Ltd.	Bulgaria	Manufacturing	97.0	0.4	0.4	Breakers A/S(Denmark)
1994	Himimport JSC	Bulgaria	Trade	58.7	7.1	0.0	Himimport-Invest
1994	Interrurimpex JSC	Bulgaria	Tourism	100.0	0.2	0.0	Multimex(91%); employees(9%)
1994	Izomatgranit Ltd.	Bulgaria	Manufacturing	—	0.1	0.0	Vesan Keramika Ltd.
1994	Kamengrad Ltd	Bulgaria	Tourism	100.0	0.1	0.0	Asarel-Medet JSC
1994	Kembarow Ltd.	Bulgaria	Livestock breeding	80.0	0.2	0.0	GP MM-5 Krasimir Mihailov & Partners
1994	Klokotnitza Ltd.	Bulgaria	Agribusiness	100.0	0.8	0.0	Santo-Comers Ltd.
1994	Knigorazprostranenie	Bulgaria	Trade	100.0	1.0	0.0	Burt JSC
1994	Komdor Ltd.	Bulgaria	Construction	100.0	0.1	0.0	Employees
1994	Menada Vinprom JSC	Bulgaria	Winery	70.0	1.5	0.0	GP Siarov Brothers
1994	Mesokombinat-Elena Ltd.	Bulgaria	Industry	75.0	0.2	0.0	Management
1994	Mesokombinat Ltd.	Bulgaria	Industry	100.0	0.3	0.0	Management
1994	Metalik Ltd.	Bulgaria	Industry	80.0	1.5	0.0	SP NV-Special Valentin Karamanov; Rapira Ltd
1994	Mlekozavod Ltd.	Bulgaria	Industry	100.0	0.5	0.0	Multex Ltd.
1994	Orbita	Bulgaria	Trade	100.0	0.2	0.0	Kaspi JSC
1994	PAAS Ltd.	Bulgaria	Transportation	100.0	0.1	0.0	Employees
1994	Pig-Breeding Complex-Apriltzi	Bulgaria	Agribusiness	100.0	0.1	0.0	Tera Comers
1994	Pig-Breeding Complex-Stojer	Bulgaria	Agribusiness	100.0	0.1	0.0	SP Kasel
1994	Poap JSC	Bulgaria	Industry	80.0	0.9	0.0	Polichrom-Bulgaria
1994	Popova-Auto Ltd.	Bulgaria	Services/auto	100.0	0.1	0.0	SP Jan-21
1994	Poultry-Breeding Complex-Nova Zagora	Bulgaria	Agribusiness	100.0	0.1	0.0	Kamea-Mentesh
1994	Power Engineering-Jambol JSC	Bulgaria	Power engineering	90.0	0.1	0.0	Employees
1994	Progress Ltd.	Bulgaria	Industry	100.0	0.1	0.0	SP Maia-Marin
1994	Prolet	Bulgaria	Industry	100.0	0.1	0.0	Prolet Ltd.
1994	Provimi Ltd.	Bulgaria	Agribusiness	100.0	0.2	0.0	Employees
1994	Psit SC	Bulgaria	Industry	100.0	0.3	0.0	GEBO-92 JSC
1994	Rakovitza	Bulgaria	Agribusiness	—	0.1	0.0	Sinit JSC
1994	Repair Shop-Agricultural Machinery-Haskovo	Bulgaria	Services/Machinery	100.0	0.2	0.0	Trakia Comers
1994	Rodopaimpex	Bulgaria	Trade	100.0	0.4	0.0	Rodexim Ltd.
1994	Ruen Ltd.	Bulgaria	Trade	80.0	0.1	0.0	Local investors
1994	Salvelinus Ltd.	Bulgaria	Fish breeding	100.0	0.1	0.0	Salvelinus-Sariev
1994	SC Kvarzkomers	Bulgaria	Trade	100.0	0.3	0.0	Employees
1994	SC Pi-Breeding Complex Karapelit	Bulgaria	Agribusiness	100.0	0.1	0.0	Eltex Ltd.; Evrosfin Ltd.
1994	SC Poligraphic Works Dimitar Blagoev	Bulgaria	Printing	100.0	0.6	0.0	168 Hours Ltd
1994	SC Trakia-Auto	Bulgaria	Services/auto	100.0	0.1	0.0	Trakia

Table A6.10 Privatization transactions in developing countries, 1994–95 (continued)

(millions of U.S. dollars)

Year	Company	Country	Sector	Equity share Percent	Amount	Foreign exchange	Purchaser
1994	Semena-Dobrich Ltd.	Bulgaria	Agribusiness	100.0	1.0	0.0	Evroenergi Holding Ltd.
1994	Sevlievo Autotransport Ltd.	Bulgaria	Transportation	80.0	0.5	0.0	Buldeg Ltd.
1994	SH.Z.I.	Bulgaria	Food processing	90.0	2.5	2.3	Nestle S.A. Switzerland (76%); management(14%)
1994	Sikonko JSC	Bulgaria	Industry	100.0	1.4	1.3	Siberia Ltd. (92.5%); employees(7.5%)
1994	Simesto Ltd.	Bulgaria	Industry	100.0	0.1	0.0	Bedson Ltd.
1994	Skarvana Ltd.	Bulgaria	Agribusiness	100.0	0.6	0.0	Furagi-Pravetz JSC & Agrovil
1994	Somat JSC	Bulgaria	Transportation	55.0	55.0	55.0	Internationale Spedition Willi Betz GmbH & CoKG
1994	Sredna Gora JSC	Bulgaria	Industry	80.0	0.7	0.0	Srenda Gora-Invest
1994	Stil Ltd.	Bulgaria	Industry	100.0	0.3	0.0	Local investor
1994	Stopanstvo	Bulgaria	Fish breeding	100.0	0.1	0.0	Starbat Bulgaria Ltd.
1994	Sugen Ltd	Bulgaria	Agribusiness	100.0	0.0	0.0	GP Agropromstroi-BD & Partners
1994	Supermarkets Ltd. No.103	Bulgaria	Retail	100.0	0.1	0.0	Kargoexpress-Nedelchev, Dimitrov
1994	Supermarkets Ltd. No.2	Bulgaria	Retail	100.0	0.2	0.0	Kargoexpress-Nedelchev, Dimitrov
1994	Supermarkets Ltd. No.23	Bulgaria	Retail	100.0	0.1	0.0	SP SIM
1994	Supermarkets Ltd. No.25	Bulgaria	Retail	100.0	0.1	0.0	Deroni Ltd.
1994	Supermarkets Ltd. No.30	Bulgaria	Retail	100.0	0.1	0.0	Kargoexpress-Nedelchev, Dimitrov
1994	Supermarkets Ltd. No.45	Bulgaria	Retail	100.0	0.1	0.0	Kargoexpress-Nedelchev, Dimitrov
1994	Supermarkets Ltd. No.7	Bulgaria	Retail	100.0	0.1	0.0	KEA Ltd
1994	Supermarkets Ltd. No.77	Bulgaria	Retail	100.0	0.1	0.0	Kargoexpress-Nedelchev, Dimitrov
1994	Supermarkets Ltd. No.9	Bulgaria	Retail	100.0	0.3	0.0	Kargoexpress-Nedelchev, Dimitrov
1994	Trakia-Agro	Bulgaria	Agribusiness	100.0	1.1	0.0	Trakia Argo
1994	Turistreklama	Bulgaria	Tourism	100.0	0.1	0.0	Employees
1994	Vamo Detached Parts	Bulgaria	Manufacturing/auto parts	100.0	1.4	1.4	Rover-Bulgaria
1994	Vethok Ltd.	Bulgaria	Services	80.0	0.1	0.0	Vethok A Ltd.
1994	Vitosha Hotel	Bulgaria	Tourism/hotels	80.0	1.2	1.2	Mr. Zografski
1994	Warehouse	Bulgaria	Services	—	0.1	0.0	Tobi Ltd.
1994	Warehouse Base, Pleven	Bulgaria	Services	100.0	0.1	0.0	SP Karabulev
1994	Warehouse Base No. 4, Russe	Bulgaria	Real estate	100.0	0.1	0.0	Sp Ivan Petrov Minev
1994	Workshop No. 7 Katunitza	Bulgaria	Services	—	0.1	0.0	GP Helius-Plovdiv
1994	Workshop No. 9	Bulgaria	Services	—	0.0	0.0	Simak-Industrial
1994	Workshop Varshetz	Bulgaria	Services	100.0	0.0	0.0	SP Iovi-Iovka Goranova
1994	Zagorka JSC	Bulgaria	Brewery	80.0	21.7	21.7	Brewinvest S/A(Greece)
1994	ZMM-PIZ PO MO NA GAPS Ltd.	Bulgaria	Industry	88.9	0.1	0.0	Management
1995	FLEX-FASO	Burkina Faso	Industry	85.4	0.3	0.0	
1995	Cabo Verde Telecom	Cape Verde	Telecommunications	40.0	0.3		
1995	Empremar S.A.	Chile	Maritime transport	100.0	4.3	0.0	Salinas Punta de Lobos, SA (97%); employees (3%)
1995	Minsal S.A.	Chile	Chemicals	18.0	7.1	0.0	Soquimich, S.A.
1995	Radio Nacional, S.A.	Chile	Broadcasting	100.0	1.7	0.0	Santiago Agliati
1994	Colbun	Chile	Power utility	5.0	20.0	0.0	Compania General de Electricidad Industrial
1994	Edelnor	Chile	Power utility	30.0	86.4	0.0	SEI Chile S.A. 59%, minority shareholders 9%
1994	Emperar	Chile	Transportation	99.0	—	—	
1994	Linea Aerea Nacional	Chile	Airlines	23.8	10.7	0.0	Sociedad de Inversiones Costa Verde
1994	Valdivia	Chile	Sanitary services	100.0	10.5	0.0	Consorcio Aguas Decima SA
1994	Foshan Electrical & LightingCo.	China	Manufacturing	—	36.0	36.0	
1995	Guangdong Electric Power	China	Power utility	—	110.0	110.0	
1995	Inner Mongolia Erdos Cashmere Products	China	Textiles	32.7	52.0	52.0	
1995	Jiangling Motors Corp.	China	Motors	25.1	45.0	45.0	
1995	Jilin Chemical Industrial	China	Petrochemicals	18.0	200.2	200.2	ADRS (US$181.67m); H shares ($18.530m)

(table continues on next page)

Table A6.10 Privatization transactions in developing countries, 1994–95 (continued)

(millions of U.S. dollars)

Year	Company	Country	Sector	Equity share Percent	Amount	Foreign exchange	Purchaser
1995	Northeast Electrical Transmission	China	Power transmission	30.0	60.0	60.0	
1995	Shanghai Jintai	China	Manufacturing	43.7	22.0	22.0	
1995	Tibet Pearl Star	China	Hotel	41.0	11.0	0.0	
1995	Weifu Fuel Injection Company	China	Machinery	—	21.5	21.5	Robert Bosch Germany 16.2%)
1995	Yizheng Chemical Fibre Co.	China	Petrochemicals	35.0	127.0	127.0	
1994	Chengdu Telecommunications Cable Co.	China	Telecommunications	40.0	57.9	57.9	Foreign investors
1994	China First Pencil Co.	China	Manufacturing	—	7.6	7.6	Foreign investors
1994	Dongfang Electrical Machinery Co.	China	Manufacturing/electrical	—	62.3	62.3	Foreign investors
1994	Harbin Power Equipment	China	Manufacturing	37.7	156.6	156.6	Foreign investors
1994	Huaneng Power International Inc.	China	Power utility	25.0	625.0	625.0	Foreign investors
1994	Huaxin Cement Co.	China	Cement	—	20.2	20.2	Foreign investors
1994	Luoyand Glass Co.	China	Manufacturing/glass	38.0	117.9	117.9	Foreign investors
1994	Shanghai Automation Instrumentation	China	Manufacturing	—	17.4	17.4	Foreign investors
1994	Shanghai Hai Xing Shipping Co.	China	Shipping	44.0	204.0	204.0	Foreign investors
1994	Shanghai Lujiazui Finance &Trade Zone	China	Services	—	133.6	133.6	Foreign investors
1994	Shanghai Material Trading Centre Co. Ltd.	China	Services	—	12.9	12.9	Foreign investors
1994	Shanghai Posts & Telecommunications Equipment	China	Manufacturing	—	23.8	23.8	Foreign investors
1994	Shanghai Shangling Electric Appliances Co. Ltd.	China	Manufacturing	—	52.5	52.5	Foreign investors
1994	Shanghai Steel Tube Co. Ltd	China	Manufacturing	—	31.8	31.8	Foreign investors
1994	Tainjin Bohai Chemical Industry	China	Chemicals	—	52.8	52.8	Foreign investors
1994	Yizheng Chemical Fibre Co. Ltd.	China	Chemicals	29.4	308.1	308.1	Foreign investors
1994	Zhenhai Refining & Chemicals	China	Chemicals	25.0	185.0	185.0	Foreign investors
1994	Zhenhai Refining & Chemicals Co. Ltd.	China	Chemicals	25.0	156.8	156.8	Foreign investors
1994	Banco Corpavi	Colombia	Banking	23.8	170.0	170.0	
1994	Banco Popular	Colombia	Banking	93.0	—	0.0	Management-employee buyout
1994	C.I. Frigopesca S.A.	Colombia	Agroindustry	47.4	—	—	
1995	Fertilizantes de Centramerica SA	Costa Rica	Fertilizer	85.0	5.3	0.0	local investors
1994	Cements of the Pacific (CEMPASA)	Costa Rica	Cement	100.0	25.1	0.0	30% company employees; other local investor
1995	Bettie	Côte d'Ivoire	Industry	70.0	9.0	9.0	Eurofind (UK)
1995	CAI ANGUENDEDOU	Côte d'Ivoire	Agroindustry	80.0	4.0	0.0	Saphic & GMG Investment
1995	CI-Telecom	Côte d'Ivoire	Telecommunications	55.0			
1995	COFINCI	Côte d'Ivoire	—		16.0	0.0	
1995	Complexe de Sinematiali	Côte d'Ivoire	Services	100.0	0.5	0.0	
1995	ELF-Oil 2	Côte d'Ivoire	services	—	2.5		
1995	Hotel Ivoire	Côte d'Ivoire	Tourism				
1995	PFCI	Côte d'Ivoire	Fishing	18.0	0.4		
1995	SACO	Côte d'Ivoire	Agriculture	—	3.4		
1995	Shell-CI	Côte d'Ivoire	Petroleum	30.0	3.5		
1995	SICO de San Pedro	Côte d'Ivoire	—	—	35.7		
1995	SIFAL	Côte d'Ivoire	Lubricants	20.0	0.6		
1995	SIFIDA	Côte d'Ivoire	—	—	0.2		
1995	SMB	Côte d'Ivoire	Mining	50.0	5.8		
1995	SOCB	Côte d'Ivoire	Industry	60.0	38.3		
1994	Fiultisac	Côte d'Ivoire	Packaging material	22.0	1.6	0.5	Local investors; IFC; AKFED:Proparco
1994	Saph	Côte d'Ivoire	Industry	45.0	9.8	0.0	Local investors
1994	SICOR	Côte d'Ivoire	Agribusiness	51.0	2.1	0.0	Local investors
1995	Brionka	Croatia	Food Processing	100.0	3.0	0.0	Kovecic Invest
1994	Automehanika-Servis Ltd	Croatia	Services/auto	18.8			

Table A6.10 Privatization transactions in developing countries, 1994–95 (continued)

(millions of U.S. dollars)

Year	Company	Country	Sector	Equity share Percent	Equity share Amount	Foreign exchange	Purchaser
1994	Bjelvar's Central Ltd	Croatia	Trading and tourism	28.8			
1994	Bokanjac d.d.	Croatia	Agribusiness	28.6			
1994	Cetra Ltd	Croatia	Financial services	20.5	0.0		
1994	Elektroprojekt d.d.	Croatia	Electrical engineering	31.9			
1994	Gradevno	Croatia	Construction	34.3			
1994	Karbon	Croatia	Manufacturing	29.5			
1994	Podarvka	Croatia	Food processing				
1994	Poljutenhika d.d.	Croatia	Agribusiness	25.6			
1994	Stocar Ltd.	Croatia	Agribusiness/cattle				
1994	Transagent d.d.	Croatia	Shipping	23.8		0.0	
1994	Unijapapir	Croatia	Recycling	18.1			
1994	Vela Luka	Croatia	Trade				
1994	Zagreb Breweries	Croatia	Brewery	23.7	13.0		
1994	Emtel Cuba	Cuba	Telecommunications	49.0	706.0	706.0	Foreign investors
1995	Kabel Plus	Czech Republic	Telecommunications	27.0	19.0	19.0	US West
1995	Podnik mlecne vyzivy Hradec Kralove	Czech Republic	Construction materials	80.0	35.0	35.0	Heinz USA
1995	SPT Telecom	Czech Republic	Telecommunications	27.0	1320.0	1320.0	Telsource (PTT Nederland and Swiss Telecom)
1995	Trinecke Zelezarny	Czech Republic	Steel	50.9	100.0	0.0	Moravia Steel
1995	Unipetrol	Czech Republic	Petroleum	49.0	149.0	149.0	Royal Dutch/Shell;Agip(Ital);Conoco(US)
1995	Vratislavice & Ostravar	Czech Republic	Brewery	—	22.0	22.0	Bass Breweries (UK)
1994	Plzenske Prazdroj	Czech Republic	Brewery				
1994	SCVK	Czech Republic	Banking	20.0	7.0	7.0	
1994	Sklo Union Teplice	Czech Republic					
1994	Skoda	Czech Republic	Manufacturing/Autos				VW allowed to increase its stake to 60% from 31%
1995	Cemento Selva Alegre	Ecuador	Cement	51.0	40.0	40.0	Spanish investor
1995	Ecuatoriana	Ecuador	Airline	50.1	33.0	0.0	Viacao Aerea Sao Paulo (VASP)/Juan Eljuri Anton (Ecuador)
1994	Azucarera Tropical Americana	Ecuador	Sugar	94.4	0.1	0.0	Grupo Isaias (LFinance)
1994	Bolsa de Valores de Guayaquil	Ecuador	Financial services	—	0.3	0.0	
1994	Bolsa de Valores de Quito	Ecuador	Financial services	—	0.3	0.0	
1994	Cementos Selva Alegre	Ecuador	Cement	51.0	40.0	N/A	Finlatam
1994	Fertisa	Ecuador	Fertilizer	100.0	0.9	0.0	Grupo Wong; local investor
1994	Hotel Colon	Ecuador	Tourism/hotel	—	0.0	0.0	
1994	La Cemento Nacional	Ecuador	Cement	100.0	53.8	53.8	Foreign investors
1994	Parque Industrial Cuenca	Ecuador	Industrial domplex	—	0.2	0.0	Grupo Orellana
1995	Alexandria Pharmaceuticals	Egypt	Pharmaceutical	11.0	4.3	—	
1995	Ameriya Cement	Egypt	Cement	2.5	7.9	—	Investment funds
1995	Eastern Tobacco	Egypt	Agriculture	10.0	35.0		
1995	Egyptian Electric Cables Co.	Egypt	Engineering	30.0	23.1		
1995	El-Nil Pharmaceuticals	Egypt	Pharmaceutical	10.0	5.0		
1995	El Nasr Cothing & Textiles Co. (Kabo)	Egypt	Textiles	7.9	2.0		
1995	Extracted Oils and Derivatives Co.	Egypt	Food	10.0	7.0		
1995	Heliopolis for Housing & Dev.	Egypt	Construction	10.0	7.7		
1995	Helwan Portland Cement	Egypt	Cement	10.0	49.0		
1995	North Cairo Flour Mills	Egypt	Food	10.0	7.4		
1995	Torah Portland Cement	Egypt	Mining	8.1	24.3		Second tranche
1994	Ameriya Cement	Egypt	Cement	10.0	16.0	0.0	
1994	Cairo Sheraton Hotel	Egypt	Tourism/hotels	87.0	70.0	70.0	Arab Investment Company for Tourism Development
1994	Egyptian Bottling Co.	Egypt	Food processing	—	46.0	0.0	Investors

(table continues on next page)

Table A6.10 Privatization transactions in developing countries, 1994–95 (continued)

(millions of U.S. dollars)

Year	Company	Country	Sector	Equity share Percent	Equity share Amount	Foreign exchange	Purchaser
1994	El Nasar Boiler	Egypt	Manufacturing	100.0	17.0	0.0	Investors
1994	Torah Portland Cement Company	Egypt	Cement	—	30.0	0.0	
1995	AS Mainor	Estonia	Services/consulting	100.0	0.9	0.0	Maskello
1995	EKE EMV renditud varad	Estonia	Metal	100.0	1.2	0.0	EMV
1995	Elva MEK-I rendinud varad	Estonia	Services	100.0	0.1	0.0	Reo-Kommerts
1995	Kadrina EPT	Estonia	Manufacturing/machinery	—	0.1	0.0	Aumek
1995	Katsemehaanika Tehase TERAS	Estonia	Manufacturing	100.0	0.5	0.0	Valser
1995	Koondis Kaubandustehnika Tallinna osakonna varad	Estonia		100.0	0.3	0.0	Kaubandustehnik
1995	Parnu Olletehase renditud varad	Estonia	Brewery	100.0	0.2	0.0	Parnu Olu
1995	Polumeeri Sportpalliisehh	Estonia	Manufacturing	100.0	1.8	0.0	Elrantus
1995	RAS Ahtme Autobaas	Estonia	Transport	100.0	0.1	0.0	Ahtme Mootor
1995	RAS Balti Manufaktuur	Estonia	Manufacturing/textiles	100.0	2.2	2.2	Asean Interest Ltd
1995	RAS Dvigatel	Estonia	Manufacturing	100.0	1.7	0.0	Diamark
1995	RAS Eesti Elektrimontaaz	Estonia	Manufacturing/electronics	100.0	0.1	0.0	Narva EM
1995	RAS Eesti Energeetikaehitus	Estonia		100.0	0.2	0.0	
1995	RAS Eesti Maaehitusprojekt Parnu jaoskond	Estonia	Engineering	—	0.1	0.0	Talinvest
1995	RAS Eesti Naitused	Estonia	Real estate	51.0	1.7	0.0	Eferelt
1995	RAS Eesti Taara	Estonia	Wholesale	100.0	0.7	0.0	Talboks, IVP, Parnu Empak, Vilpak, Valpak
1995	RAS Elkomt	Estonia	Manufacturing	100.0	0.4	0.0	
1995	RAS Elva Pollumajandustehnika	Estonia	Manufacturing	100.0	0.2	0.0	
1995	RAS Esmeta	Estonia	Metal	76.0	2.0	0.0	Fermetal
1995	RAS Estoplast	Estonia	Manufacturing	100.0	0.6	0.0	Talinvest
1995	RAS Estoplast Rapla osakond	Estonia	Manufacturing	100.0	0.2	0.0	Isopik
1995	RAS Hotell Stroomi	Estonia	Tourism	76.0	0.1	0.0	Suviren
1995	RAS Hotell Tallinn	Estonia	Hotel	100.0	1.3	0.0	Irnese
1995	RAS Jarvakandi Tehased	Estonia	Industry	100.0	0.2	0.0	Glaskek
1995	RAS Kalev	Estonia	Confectionary	55.0	4.9	0.0	Talinvest
1995	RAS Keila TERKO	Estonia	Agribusiness	76.0	2.4	0.0	Prinsiip PM
1995	RAS Kopli Autobaas	Estonia	Transport	100.0	0.2	0.0	Skriiner
1995	RAS Mehis	Estonia	Industry	100.0	0.1	0.0	Jenpak
1995	RAS Metsakaubandus	Estonia	Paper products	100.0	0.5	0.0	MK Investeeringu
1995	RAS Nakro	Estonia	Industry	100.0	0.9	0.0	Viru Gerberei
1995	RAS Narva Autobaas	Estonia	Transportation	100.0	0.7	0.0	Narva Auto
1995	RAS Palmet	Estonia	Manufacturing	100.0	0.5	0.0	Palmetto
1995	RAS Parnu EPT puidutoo	Estonia	Manufacturing	—	0.1	0.0	A.L.A.
1995	RAS Parnu EPT	Estonia	Manufacturing	100.0	0.8	0.0	Torfex
1995	RAS Parnu Metsamajand	Estonia	Timber	100.0	1.0	0.0	
1995	RAS Polva Autobas	Estonia	Transport	100.0	0.2	0.0	Kagustrans
1995	RAS Progress	Estonia	Manufacturing/electronics	—	0.9	0.9	Eesti Elecster (Finland)
1995	RAS Pussii PPK	Estonia	Construction/building material	100.0	1.7	0.0	Repo
1995	RAS Rakvere Lihakombinaat	Estonia	Agribusiness	37.0	6.2	0.0	R-Lihatoostus
1995	RAS Rakvere Lihakombinaat	Estonia	Agribusiness	34.0	4.4	0.0	Nigula Pollumajandusuhi stu
1995	RAS Rapla Metsamajand	Estonia	Manufacturing	100.0	0.1	0.0	Primo
1995	RAS REV	Estonia	Construction	100.0	0.2	0.0	Ammer
1995	RAS Saaremaa Autobaas	Estonia	Services	100.0	0.3	0.0	SAB
1995	RAS Saku AB	Estonia	Transport	76.0	2.1	0.0	A.TV.
1995	RAS Salvo-Suvenir	Estonia		100.0	0.1	0.0	Kespri
1995	RAS Sangla	Estonia	Agribusiness	51.0	0.3	0.0	Turbatooted

Table A6.10 Privatization transactions in developing countries, 1994–95 (continued)
(millions of U.S. dollars)

Year	Company	Country	Sector	Equity share Percent	Equity share Amount	Foreign exchange	Purchaser
1995	RAS Silikaat	Estonia	—	100.0	1.7	0.0	Esraven
1995	RAS Silmet filtrite tsehh	Estonia	Manufacturing/machinery	—	0.2	0.0	Esfil
1995	RAS Tallinna Kulmhoone	Estonia	Services	76.0	0.5	0.0	Jaalil
1995	RAS Tallinna Lihatoostus	Estonia	Food processing	80.0	1.4	0.0	Kroonikuld
1995	RAS Tallinna Meretehas	Estonia	Ship-building	51.0	3.2	0.0	Vavekor
1995	RAS Tallinna Toiduveod	Estonia	Transportation	76.0	0.7	0.0	Ombrello
1995	RAS Tamsalu EPT	Estonia	Manufacturing	76.0	0.3	0.0	Tamsalu EPT
1995	RAS Tartu Kulmhoone	Estonia	Industry	51.0	0.1	0.0	Talinvest
1995	RAS Tartu Maja	Estonia	Manufacturing	—	0.1	0.0	M.S.J. Grupp
1995	RAS Tootsi	Estonia	Industry	51.0	1.3	0.0	LaTo
1995	RAS Uku	Estonia	Manufacturing	100.0	0.9	0.0	Fondiine
1995	RAS Universaal	Estonia	Industry	100.0	0.8	0.0	Universaal-kaubandus
1995	RAS Varteko	Estonia	Wholesale	100.0	0.3	0.0	Raales
1995	RAS Veterinaar-varustus	Estonia	Wholesale	100.0	0.3	0.0	ProMed
1995	RAS Viisnurk	Estonia	Manufacturing	72.7	1.7	0.0	NV Holding
1995	RAS Viljandi AB	Estonia	Services	—	0.1	0.0	Belest
1995	RAS Viljandi AB	Estonia	Services	—	0.2	0.0	Tamm ja Pojad
1995	RAS Viljandi Metsakombinaat	Estonia	Manufacturing/wood products	—	0.2	0.0	Vilbri
1995	RAS Voit	Estonia	Manufacturing/machinery	100.0	0.3	0.0	Livoonia Holding
1995	RAS Voru Agrovarustus	Estonia	Wholesale	100.0	0.1	0.0	Grant
1995	RAS Voru Autobaas	Estonia	Transportation	100.0	0.7	0.0	Maur
1995	RAS Voru Juustutoostus	Estonia	Dairy	100.0	0.2	0.0	IBD
1995	RAS Wermo	Estonia	Manufacturing/furniture	100.0	2.1	0.0	Thompson
1995	RdE-le Santeko rendItud varad	Estonia	Services/plumbing	100.0	0.3	0.0	Tasmo Arigrupi
1995	Rde Kohtla-Jarve Ehitus	Estonia	Construction	100.0	0.3	0.0	Viru Ehitaja
1995	Rde Paekivitoodete Tehas	Estonia	Mining	100.0	0.2	0.0	Paeko
1995	RdE Parnu MEK	Estonia	Construction	100.0	0.3	0.0	Savi
1995	Rde Siegel renditud varad	Estonia	Services	100.0	0.4	0.0	Liitsiegel
1995	Rde Tallinna Ehitustrust	Estonia	Construction	—	0.1	0.0	Suurlinnaehitus
1995	Rde Tallinna Ehitustrust SEV-6	Estonia	Construction	—	0.1	0.0	M.S.J. Grupp
1995	Rde Tallinna Ehitustrusti	Estonia	Construction	100.0	0.5	0.0	Formeri
1995	RdE Tartu Ehitustrusti peahoone	Estonia	Services	100.0	0.6	0.0	Vana-viru Inseneriburoo
1995	RdE Tartu Ehitustrusti Spetsialiseeritud Toode Valitsus	Estonia	Metals	100.0	0.5	0.0	Astra STV
1995	Rde Tin-a Ehitustrusti Tootmise	Estonia	—	100.0	0.5	0.0	Nord DV
1995	Rde Toostusehitustrust	Estonia	Construction	100.0	0.6	0.0	Ehitus-vahendaja
1995	Rde Viljandi MEK	Estonia	Construction	100.0	0.1	0.0	Viljandi MEK
1995	RE Kohila Eksperimentaalne Remondi-ja Mehaanikatehas	Estonia	Manufacturing/Machinery	100.0	0.2	0.0	Corbex Engineering
1995	RE Saaremaa Liha–ja Piimatootmiskoondis	Estonia	Agribusiness	100.0	1.6	0.0	
1995	Saku Olletehase AS	Estonia	Construction/Building Material	10.0	1.7	1.7	Baltic Beverages (Sweden)
1995	Tallinna Ehituskeraamikatehase renditud varad	Estonia	—	—	0.2	0.0	Tekt
1995	Tapa Autobassi renditud varad	Estonia	Transport	100.0	0.1	0.0	Tapa Autobaas
1995	Tapa Haigla	Estonia	Services	100.0	0.1	0.0	Tapa Haigla
1995	Tartu Ehitustrusti Komplekteerimise Valitsus	Estonia	Wholesale	100.0	0.2	0.0	Linnaehitus
1995	Tartu Olletehas	Estonia	Brewery	100.0	2.3	0.0	Magnum Konsuumer
1995	TE Terg Viimsi baas	Estonia	Metal	—	0.3	0.0	Ectarus
1995	TK Marat renditud varad	Estonia	Textiles	100.0	1.5	0.0	KND Marat
1995	TK Uhendus	Estonia	Services	100.0	0.9	0.0	Bensont
1995	U Elvex	Estonia	—	51.0	1.9	1.9	Securit-Saint Gobain Scnadinavia

(table continues on next page)

Table A6.10 Privatization transactions in developing countries, 1994–95 (continued)

(millions of U.S. dollars)

Year	Company	Country	Sector	Equity share Percent	Equity share Amount	Foreign exchange	Purchaser
1995	VE Kebar	Estonia	Transportation	100.0	0.2	0.0	Otrans
1995	Viljandi Leiva-ja Makaronitoostus	Estonia	Agribusiness	100.0	0.2	0.0	Vilma
1994	RE Keila	Estonia	Manufacturing/clothing	—	0.2	0.0	Evilkan
1994	Ajakiri Eesti Naine	Estonia	Media	100.0	0.1	0.0	Paevaleht
1994	Auto Vazteenindus	Estonia	Services/autos	100.0	1.5	0.0	Mega Auto
1994	Eesti Mustakirju Karja Aretuskeskus	Estonia	Agribusiness	100.0	0.1	0.0	Eesti Mustakirju Karja Aretuskeskus
1994	Kaubandusliku Reklaami	Estonia	Media/advertising	100.0	0.1	0.0	Neon
1994	Majapidamistarvete Hulgikaubanduse Baasi	Estonia	Wholesale	100.0	1.4	0.0	Koviro
1994	Narva Mooblikombinaadi	Estonia	Manufacturing/furniture	100.0	1.0	0.0	Narova
1994	Otepaa Autoremonditehase	Estonia	Services/autos	100.0	0.3	0.0	Otepaa Autoremonditehase
1994	Paide Piimakombinaadi Jarva-Jaani	Estonia	Food processing	100.0	0.1	0.0	Jarva-Jaani Piimandusuhistu
1994	Parnu Ehitusmaterjalide Tehase	Estonia	Construction/building material	100.0	0.2	0.0	Reiden
1994	Raasiku Elektriseadmete Tehase RAS	Estonia	Manufacturing/electronics	100.0	0.2	0.0	Raasiku Elekter
1994	Rapla Piimatoostuce	Estonia	Food processing	100.0	0.4	0.0	Uhistu Rapla Piim
1994	RAS ABT	Estonia	Wholesale	100.0	2.1	0.0	KAR
1994	RAS Aegviidu Metsamajand	Estonia	Manufacturing	100.0	0.1	0.0	Trivilander
1994	RAS Alutaguse Metsamajand	Estonia	Manufacturing/furniture	100.0	0.1	0.0	Ware
1994	RAS Autokeskus KAMAZ	Estonia	Services/autos	100.0	0.2	0.0	Vipo
1994	RAS Autoteenindus	Estonia	Services/autos	100.0	1.6	0.0	Jarve Autokeskus
1994	RAS Avinurme Metsatoostus	Estonia	Manufacturing/furniture	100.0	0.1	0.0	Metro Estates
1994	RAS Balti Baas	Estonia	Services/ship repair	51.0	2.3	0.0	Hoisti Kraana
1994	RAS Bark	Estonia	Construction/building material	68.0	0.3	0.0	Estkon
1994	RAS Cibus	Estonia	Food processing	66.6	0.8	0.0	Parnu Leib
1994	RAS Eesti Roivas	Estonia	Manufacturing/clothing	100.0	0.7	0.0	E.V.M.
1994	RAS Eesti Taara Tallinna	Estonia	Wholesale	—	0.8	0.0	Espak
1994	RAS Eesti Taara Tartu Baas	Estonia	Wholesale	—	0.2	0.0	Tartem
1994	RAS Eesti Taara Voru	Estonia	Wholesale	—	0.1	0.0	Voru Empak
1994	RAS Eesti Tekstiil	Estonia	Manufacturing/textiles	80.0	1.0	0.0	ET-Riie
1994	RAS Elamu	Estonia	Construction/building material	100.0	0.5	0.0	M.S.J. Group
1994	RAS Elva Metsamajand	Estonia	Manufacturing/furniture	100.0	0.2	0.0	Alnus
1994	RAS Eriehitustood	Estonia	Construction	100.0	2.0	0.0	Samulin
1994	RAS Estjal	Estonia	Wholesale/retail	100.0	0.4	0.0	Kaveli
1994	RAS Estoplast	Estonia	Manufacturing/plastic	100.0	0.3	0.0	Eswind; Mecro
1994	RAS Galantex	Estonia	Manufacturing/clothing	100.0	0.4	0.0	Fobar
1994	RAS Haapsalu Leivatehas	Estonia	Food processing	65.7	0.1	0.0	Alfred Schledorn
1994	RAS Harju Asfaltbetoonitehas	Estonia	Cement	100.0	0.5	0.0	Harbet
1994	RAS Hotell Viru	Estonia	Hotel	100.0	11.7	0.0	Harmaron
1994	RAS Ilmarine	Estonia	Machinery	—	0.6	0.6	Ilmera-Bergemann(Ger)
1994	RAS Klementi	Estonia	Manufacturing/clothing	80.0	1.2	0.0	Klementi Kaubandus
1994	RAS Kohtla-Jarve Metsamajand	Estonia	Manufacturing/furniture	100.0	0.2	0.0	Eukalupt
1994	RAS Koil	Estonia	Paper products	100.0	0.1	0.0	Kohila Paberivabrik
1994	RAS Kommunaar	Estonia	Manufacturing/footwear	—	1.7	0.0	Hansapank; Sryle Wear; Kingston; Vatu
1994	RAS Kommunaar kauplus	Estonia	Retail	—	0.1	0.0	Jaarlo
1994	RAS Kommunaar Narva	Estonia	Manufacturing/footwear	N/A	0.2	0.2	Schmidt & Ko
1994	RAS Kreenholmi Manufactuur	Estonia	Manufacturing/textiles	N/A	1.0	0.0	Kreenholmi
1994	RAS Kultuurivarustus	Estonia	Wholesale	100.0	0.4	0.0	Abe Rahvusvaheline
1994	RAS Kuressaare Autoteenindus	Estonia	Services/auto	100.0	0.1	0.0	Salome
1994	RAS Kuusalu Remonditehas	Estonia	Services/machinery	100.0	0.2	0.0	G.J.H.

Table A6.10 Privatization transactions in developing countries, 1994–95 (continued)

(millions of U.S. dollars)

Year	Company	Country	Sector	Equity share Percent	Amount	Foreign exchange	Purchaser
1994	RAS Laanemaa Metsamajand	Estonia	Timber	100.0	0.1	0.0	Arkliruba
1994	RAS Loksa Laevaremonditehas	Estonia	Services/ship repair	100.0	1.6	0.0	OSF Portfolio Investment V
1994	RAS Mahtra Metsamajand	Estonia	Manufacturing/furniture	100.0	0.1	0.0	Iris
1994	RAS Mistra	Estonia	Manufacturing/textiles	100.0	0.2	0.0	Erkobest
1994	RAS Mistra-Viva	Estonia	Manufacturing/textiles	100.0	0.5	0.0	Lauser
1994	RAS Mistra pooleliolev ehitus	Estonia	Real estate	—	0.1	0.0	Projekt
1994	RAS MRE	Estonia	Services/repair	100.0	0.6	0.0	Rudig
1994	RAS MRE lopetamata	Estonia	Real estate	—	0.1	0.0	Key OU
1994	RAS Narva Autoteenindus	Estonia	Services/auto	100.0	0.1	0.0	Brothers Ltd
1994	RAS Narva Ehitus	Estonia	Construction	100.0	0.6	0.1	Narvastroi
1994	RAS Narva Leib	Estonia	Food processing	100.0	0.7	0.0	Lenar
1994	RAS Nordek	Estonia	Industry	100.0	0.2	0.0	Estpuud
1994	RAS Paide Piimakombinaat	Estonia	Food processing	51.0	0.6	0.0	Paide Piimatoostus
1994	RAS Parnu Autoteenindus	Estonia	Services/auto	100.0	0.2	0.0	Jarve Autokeskus
1994	RAS Parnu Linakombinaat	Estonia	Manufacturing/textiles	100.0	1.3	1.3	Herdsmans Holding
1994	RAS Poltsamaa Autobaas	Estonia	Transportation	100.0	0.1	0.0	Astra
1994	RAS Polumeer	Estonia	Manufacturing	—	0.5	0.0	Neilmei
1994	RAS Puiteks	Estonia	Manufacturing	100.0	0.1	0.0	Silvest
1994	RAS Rakvere Metsamajand	Estonia	Timber	75.0	0.4	0.0	Viru Puit
1994	RAS Rakvere ATP	Estonia	Transportation	100.0	0.1	0.0	Rakvene Buss
1994	RAS Rakvere Autobaas	Estonia	Transportation	—	0.1	0.0	Rakvere Autobaas
1994	RAS Rakvere Leivakombinaat	Estonia	Food Processing	80.0	0.5	0.0	Viru Pagar
1994	RAS Rakvere Piimatoostus	Estonia	Food Processing	100.0	0.5	0.0	Rakvere Piimauhistu
1994	RAS Rapina Metsamajand	Estonia	Timber	100.0	0.6	0.0	Oskar
1994	RAS Reka	Estonia	Transportation	100.0	0.2	0.0	Rehaku
1994	RAS Repeli	Estonia	Services/auto	100.0	0.1	0.0	Repel
1994	RAS Rongu Tehas	Estonia	Manufacturing	66.6	0.3	0.0	Berry
1994	RAS Saaremaa Metsamajand	Estonia	Manufacturing/furniture	100.0	0.2	0.0	Norman
1994	RAS Salis Tartu	Estonia	Food processing	100.0	0.3	0.0	Salvest
1994	RAS Sangar	Estonia	Manufacturing/clothing	100.0	0.1	0.0	Klementi; Kaubandus
1994	RAS Silbet	Estonia	Construction/building material	100.0	0.3	0.0	Mittetundusuhis tu Silberi Liit
1994	RAS Silla	Estonia	Manufacturing/furniture	100.0	0.7	0.0	Silleks
1994	RAS Silmeti Olletehas	Estonia	Food processing	—	0.3	0.0	Ventra
1994	RAS Spordilaevade Tehas	Estonia	Manufacturing	65.0	0.6	0.0	Vikta, Naviko
1994	RAS Standard	Estonia	Manufacturing/furniture	100.0	1.1	0.0	Eripuu
1994	RAS Standard Madara Mooblivabrik	Estonia	Manufacturing/furniture	—	0.1	0.0	UNIVER International Eesti
1994	RAS Suure-Jaani Metsamajand	Estonia	Manufacturing	100.0	0.9	0.0	Fonseka
1994	RAS Tallinna Ehitusteenindus	Estonia	Construction/building material	100.0	1.5	0.0	Erak
1994	RAS Tallinna Farmaatsiatehas	Estonia	Pharmaceuticals	66.6	2.1	0.0	Magnum Pharma
1994	RAS Tallinna Helikassetitehas	Estonia	Wholesale	100.0	0.5	0.0	Theka
1994	RAS Tallinna Kaubamaja	Estonia	Retail	51.0	4.9	0.0	Hiis
1994	RAS Tallinna Klaverivabrik	Estonia	Manufacturing/piano	100.0	0.5	0.0	H&M
1994	RAS Tamsalu TERKO	Estonia	Agribusiness	65.0	4.0	0.0	Denos; Lindahl; Ramco; Kurmet
1994	RAS Tarbeklaas	Estonia	Manufacturing/glass	100.0	0.8	0.0	FMC
1994	RAS Tarmeko	Estonia	Manufacturing/furniture	66.6	5.2	0.0	Puumel
1994	RAS Tarmel	Estonia	Timber	84.1	0.9	0.0	Estiko
1994	RAS Tarneks	Estonia	Wholesale	100.0	0.6	0.0	Tref
1994	RAS Tartu Asfaltbetoonitehas	Estonia	Cement	100.0	0.2	0.0	

(table continues on next page)

135

Table A6.10 Privatization transactions in developing countries, 1994–95 (continued)

(millions of U.S. dollars)

Year	Company	Country	Sector	Equity share Percent	Amount	Foreign exchange	Purchaser
1994	RAS Tartu Autoteenindus	Estonia	Services/auto	100.0	0.4	0.0	A.B.S.
1994	RAS Tartu Lihakombinaat	Estonia	Food processing	55.0	1.3	0.0	Landrek
1994	RAS Tartu Maja	Estonia	Construction	80.0	1.2	0.0	Erabet
1994	RAS Tartu Parmitoostus	Estonia	Food processing	100.0	0.2	0.0	Ofelia
1994	RAS TarruMetsamajand	Estonia	Timber	100.0	0.2	0.0	Marry
1994	RAS Tekstiil	Estonia	Manufacturing/textiles	100.0	0.3	0.0	Tekshen
1994	RAS Tondi Elektroonika	Estonia	Manufacturing/electronics	100.0	1.5	0.0	Mikrel
1994	RAS Ulemiste Autoteenindus	Estonia	Services/auto	100.0	0.5	0.0	Belesta
1994	RAS Valga Terko	Estonia	Food processing	100.0	0.3	0.0	Valga Teraviljauhistu
1994	RAS Valgamaa Metsamajand	Estonia	Manufacturing/furniture	100.0	0.3	0.0	Alkador
1994	RAS Vasar	Estonia	Metal products	100.0	2.1	0.0	Finmec; Erivasar
1994	RAS Veerenni Autoteenindus	Estonia	Services/auto	100.0	0.2	0.0	Ravor
1994	RAS Vesiehitus	Estonia	Construction	66.6	0.5	0.0	UB Vesiehitus
1994	RAS Viljandi ATP	Estonia	Transportation	51.0	0.2	0.0	Maur
1994	RAS Viljandi Metsakombinaat	Estonia	Manufacturing/furniture	—	0.5	0.0	Dold Holzwerke
1994	RAS Villak	Estonia	Manufacturing/clothing	100.0	0.1	0.0	Klementi; Kaubandus
1994	RAS Virko	Estonia	Manufacturing/furniture	100.0	0.4	0.0	Dalerand
1994	RAS Viru Siirup	Estonia	Food Processing	100.0	0.2	0.0	Asko
1994	RAS Virulane	Estonia	Manufacturing/clothing	100.0	0.3	0.0	Wirulane
1994	RAS Virumaa Eriehitustood	Estonia	Construction	100.0	0.1	0.0	Ventra
1994	RAS Virumaa Metsatoostus	Estonia	Manufacturing	100.0	0.4	0.0	Virmeks
1994	RAS Volta	Estonia	Machinery	—	0.4	0.0	Ravori Investeeringute
1994	RAS Voru EPT	Estonia	Machinery	100.0	0.3	0.0	Lapi Metallitood; Kagu-Eesti Tyrvas
1994	RAS Voru EPT Umbsaare	Estonia	Services/machinery	100.0	0.2	0.0	SWE Balt Wood; Ekso
1994	RAS Voru Metsamajand	Estonia	Manufacturing/furniture	100.0	0.4	0.0	Karu
1994	RdE Kerr	Estonia	Manufacturing	100.0	0.3	0.0	Tarberaud
1994	RdE Merk	Estonia	Construction	100.0	0.2	0.0	Malmrek
1994	RdE Tartu Sideehituse	Estonia	Construction	100.0	0.1	0.0	Tartu Sideehituse
1994	RdE Toostusaparaat varad	Estonia	Machinery	100.0	1.4	0.0	RdE Toostusaparaat
1994	RdE Toostuskomplekt	Estonia	Construction/building material	—	4.8	0.0	Moigu EK; Vikolo
1994	RE Eesti Punasa Karja Aretuskeskus	Estonia	Agribusiness	100.0	0.2	0.0	Aretusuhistu Eesti Puname Kari
1994	RE Juveel	Estonia	Manufacturing/jewellery	100.0	2.4	0.0	Juveliir
1994	RE Keila	Estonia	Manufacturing/clothing	100.0	0.4	0.0	Aldus
1994	RE Kohtla-Jarve	Estonia	Food processing	100.0	0.4	0.0	Uhistu Johvi Piim
1994	RE Kohtla-Jarve Lihatoostus	Estonia	Food processing	100.0	0.1	0.0	Pandivere Lihauhistu
1994	RE Parnu Kalakombinaat	Estonia	Food processing	—	1.5	0.0	Maseko
1994	RE Parnu Lihakombinaat	Estonia	Food processing	100.0	0.4	0.0	Parnu Lihauhistu
1994	RE Pioneer varad, renditud as STS-le	Estonia	Metals	100.0	1.7	1.7	United Autos
1994	RE Polva Piimatoodete	Estonia	Food processing	100.0	0.6	0.0	Polva Piim
1994	RE Rakvere Viljasalv	Estonia	Agribusiness	100.0	0.2	0.0	Rks
1994	RE Sillaehitusrong	Estonia	Construction	100.0	0.3	0.0	Local investors
1994	RE Stamp	Estonia	Machinery	100.0	1.9	0.0	SH Tamp
1994	RE Tallinna Viljasalv	Estonia	Agribusiness	100.0	0.5	0.0	Tulundusuhistu Nisuveski
1994	RE Tartu Piimatoodete Kombinaat	Estonia	Food processing	100.0	0.2	0.0	Keskpiimauhistu "Tarru Pii"
1994	RE Tartu Viljasalv	Estonia	Agribusiness	100.0	0.5	0.0	Tartu Teraviljauhistu
1994	RE Termiso	Estonia	Construction	100.0	0.1	0.0	Isterm, Esman
1994	RE Valga LEMK	Estonia	Machinery	100.0	0.1	0.0	Uhistu
1994	RE Valga Liha-ja Piimatootmiskoondis	Estonia	Food processing	100.0	0.2	0.0	Valgamaa Lihauhistu

136

Table A6.10 Privatization transactions in developing countries, 1994–95 (continued)

(millions of U.S. dollars)

Year	Company	Country	Sector	Equity share Percent	Equity share Amount	Foreign exchange	Purchaser
1994	RE Viljandi EPT LEMK	Estonia	Machinery	100.0	0.1	0.0	Figaro
1994	RE Viljandi Piimakombinaadi	Estonia	Food processing	100.0	0.8	0.0	Viljandi Piimaosauhing
1994	Tallinna Ehituskeraamikatehase	Estonia	Construction/building material	—	0.3	0.0	Saviton
1994	Tallinna Karastusjookide Tehase	Estonia	Food processing	100.0	1.1	0.9	Coca-Cola Joogid; Tallinna Karastusjoogid
1994	Tartu Aparaaditehase	Estonia	Machinery	100.0	0.4	0.0	Tartu Instrument
1994	VE Kommertskeskus Inreko	Estonia	Services	100.0	0.2	0.0	Inreko Laeva
1994	VE Raudval	Estonia	Railroads	100.0	0.3	0.0	Radlik
1994	VE Sidnon	Estonia	Communications	100.0	0.1	0.0	Matiko
1995	Akokerri Oil Palm Plantation	Ghana	Agroindustry	100.0	0.1		
1995	Ashanti Goldfields	Ghana	Mining	—	62.0	62.0	
1995	Ghana National Manganese Corp	Ghana	Industry	90.0	4.0	4.0	Elkem (Norway)
1995	Ghana Oil Palm Development	Ghana	Agroindustry	100.0	6.5		
1995	Ghana Pioneer Aluminum Company	Ghana	Mining		0.6		
1995	Juapong Textile	Ghana	Industry	100.0	0.3		
1995	Kumasi Catering Rest House	Ghana	Services	100.0	0.3		
1995	Pankrono Poultry Farm	Ghana	Agriculture	100.0	0.1		
1995	SAMCO	Ghana	Industry	100.0	0.2		
1995	SFC-8 Fishing Vessels	Ghana	Agroindustry	100.0	2.0		
1994	African Timber and Plywood	Ghana	Lumber	100.0	4.0	0.0	Local investor
1994	Ashanti Goldfields Company(AGC)	Ghana	Mining	27.5	454.0	398.0	Local aand foreign investors
1994	Bakmark part of NIC Estates	Ghana		100.0	0.2	0.0	SSB
1994	Dunkwa Goldfields	Ghana	Mining	50.0	0.4	0.4	Foreign investor
1994	Fafa Auto Parts	Ghana	Manufacturing/autos	65.0	0.1	0.0	
1994	Ghana Textile Printing	Ghana	Manufacturing/textiles	25.0	0.8	0.0	CWA Holdings Ltd.
1994	ICAP/GIHOP Pharmaceutical	Ghana	Pharmaceuticals	60.0	0.4	0.0	
1994	Kentirkrono	Ghana	Agribusiness	100.0	0.1	0.1	Juskubi Enterprises
1994	L'Air Liquide	Ghana	Airline services	35.0	0.6	0.6	Air France
1994	NIC Vehicle Assembly Plant	Ghana	Manufacturing/autos	100.0	0.2	0.2	CARICI of Côte d'Ivoire
1994	Tema Food Complex Corp.	Ghana	Food processing	100.0	15.0	0.0	Local investor
1994	Umarco	Ghana		15.0	0.1	0.0	Local investors
1995	GNTC Botling Co. Ltd	Ghana	Industry	100.0	7.0		
1995	National Investment Bank	Ghana	Financial	55.0			
1994	Heorion Shipyard	Greece	Shipyard	100.0	9.0	9.0	Amber Maritime International(Liberia)
1994	Gravel, Concrete & Emulsion Production Corp	Grenada	Mining	—	—	—	Dipcon Engineering Services of Trinidad
1994	Grenada Electricity Services(Grenlec)	Grenada	Power utility	90.0	6.1	5.6	WRB Enterprises of U.S. 50%; local invenstors 40%
1994	Empressa Guineese Automovels	Guinea-Bissau	Services/Autos	100.0	0.2	0.0	Local investor
1994	Azucarera Cantaranas S.A.	Honduras	Sugar	100.0	5.0	0.0	Romulo Javier Montoa
1994	Bodega De Cerro de Hula/IHMA	Honduras	Grain storage	100.0	0.5	0.0	Edgardo Lezama Castellanos
1994	Bolsas Bijao de Centroamerica SA(BOBICASA)	Honduras	Paper Products	100.0	0.5	0.0	Inversiones Industriales del Norte SA (INVINSA)
1994	Plana Regional de Choluteca/IHMA	Honduras	Grain storage	100.0	0.4	0.0	Molinos Modernos de Honduras
1995	Budapest Bank	Hungary	Banking	60.0	87.0	87.0	GEC & ENRD Consortium
1995	Budapesti Elekiromos Muvek	Hungary	Electricity	46.2	397.4	397.4	RWE-EVS Consortium
1995	Csepeli Eromu Rt.	Hungary	Electricity	95.5	12.7	4.3	Powergen UK
1995	DDGAZ	Hungary	Gas utility	50.0	52.4	52.4	Ruhrgas Germany
1995	DEGAZ	Hungary	Gas utility	50.0	88.2	88.2	Gas de France
1995	Deldunantuli	Hungary	Electricity	47.3	119.9	119.9	Bayemwerk AG
1995	Delmagyarorszagi	Hungary	Electricity	47.9	172.1	172.1	Electricite de France
1995	Dunamenti Power Station	Hungary	Power utility	48.8	156.6	156.6	Powerfin(Belguim)

(table continues on next page)

137

Table A6.10 Privatization transactions in developing countries, 1994–95 (continued)

(millions of U.S. dollars)

Year	Company	Country	Sector	Equity share Percent	Equity share Amount	Foreign exchange	Purchaser
1995	EGAZ	Hungary	Gas utility	50.0	76.8	76.8	Gas de France
1995	Eszakdunantuli	Hungary	Electricity	47.6	218.7	218.7	Electricite de France
1995	Eszakmagyarorszagi	Hungary	Electricity	48.8	182.1	182.1	RWE-EVS Consortium
1995	FOGAZ	Hungary	Gas utility	39.0	52.4	52.4	Ruhrgas Germany
1995	Gedeon Richter	Hungary	Pharmaceutical	18.6	48.6	36.0	Institutional investors
1995	Hajdutej Dairy Ltd.	Hungary	Food processing	—	6.0	4.3	
1995	Hungarian Oil and Gas Company (MOL)	Hungary	Oil and gas	29.5	190.3	165.3	
1995	KOGAZ	Hungary	Gas utility	50.0	67.0	67.0	Bayernwerk (EVN)
1995	Matravideki	Hungary	Power utility	38.1	82.1	82.1	RWE-EVS Consortium
1995	National Savings & Commercial Bank (OTP)	Hungary	Banking	10.0	75.0	53.2	
1995	TIGAZ	Hungary	Gas utility	50.0	170.0	170.0	Italgas-SNAM (Italy)
1995	Tiszantuli	Hungary	Electricity	49.2	146.4	146.4	Isar-Amperwerke AG
1994	Belapatfalva Cement and Lime	Hungary	Cement	—	12.8	0.0	Local investors
1994	Buda Brick	Hungary	Manufacturing	—	9.2	—	Buda Brick Management
1994	Buda Mill	Hungary	Manufacturing	—	9.5	—	GM Industrial
1994	Budapest Kozet	Hungary	Manufacturing	—	12.0	—	Super-Sol
1994	Cerbona Food Industry & Trading	Hungary	Trade	—	10.7	—	Cerbona consortium
1994	Chemical Works Building & Fitting	Hungary	Chemicals	—	10.0	—	Epszer-Unio consortium
1994	Chemical Works of Gedeon Richter	Hungary	Chemicals	33.0	68.5	68.5	Local and foreign investors
1994	Civis Hotel & Gasztronomia	Hungary	Hotel	—	9.3	—	Budapest Bsank, cooperative farm consortium
1994	Csepel	Hungary	Power utility/plant	100.0			PowerGen (UK)
1994	EGIS	Hungary	Chemicals	29.0	46.1	0.0	Local investors
1994	Globus Canning	Hungary	Food processing	—	6.2	—	Investors
1994	Hajdusag Bakeries	Hungary	Food processing	—	8.2	4.0	Civis Food; New York Broker Budapest
1994	Magyar Kulkereskedelmi Bank	Hungary	Banking	42.0	92.0	0.0	
1994	Pannongabona Trading & Processing	Hungary	Trade	—	12.2	—	Investors
1994	Pannonplast Industries	Hungary	Chemicals	28.5	17.8	0.0	Local investors
1994	Sopron Brewery Ltd	Hungary	Brewery	38.4	18.6	0.0	Local investors
1994	Szeged Food Industry	Hungary	Food processing	—	8.2	—	PICK Szeged
1994	Szekszard Agroker	Hungary	agribusiness	—	6.0	—	KSZE Agro Development
1995	Matav	Hungary	Telecommunications	37.0	852.0	852.0	Deutsche Telekom/Ameritech
1994	Baja	Hungary	Food processing	93.6	3.7	3.7	Unilever NV (Dutch)
1994	Danubius Hotel Rt.	Hungary	Hotel	—	27.5	20.0	Foreign consortium
1994	Graboplast	Hungary	—	—	13.3	0.0	Local investors
1994	Hejocsaba Cement and Lime	Hungary	Cement	—	18.1	0.0	Local investors
1995	ACC Babcock	India	Industry	76.0	20.0	20.0	Asea Brown Boveri (ABB)
1995	Container Corp. of India	India	Transportation	3.1	4.4		
1995	Industrial Development Bank of India	India	Financial	25.0	758.0		
1995	Mahanagar Telephone Nigam	India	Telecommunications	1.5	41.9		
1995	Oil & Natural Gas Commission	India	Petroleum/petrochemicals	0.1	1.6		
1995	Steel Authority of India	India	Steel	0.1	4.1		
1994	Bharat Earthmovers	India	Manufacturing	20.0	12.8	—	
1994	Bharat Electronics Ltd.	India	Manufacturing	4.0	15.0	—	
1994	Bharat Heavy Electricals Ltd.	India	Manufacturing	11.0	96.0	—	
1994	Container Corp. of India	India	Transportation	20.0	31.8	—	
1994	Hindustan Organic Chemicals	India	Chemicals	23.0	—	—	
1994	Hindustan Petroleum Corp.	India	Petroleum	7.0	179.3	—	
1994	Indian Oil Corp.	India	Petroleum	10.0	329.2	—	

138

Table A6.10 Privatization transactions in developing countries, 1994–95 (continued)

(millions of U.S. dollars)

Year	Company	Country	Sector	Equity share Percent	Amount	Foreign exchange	Purchaser
1994	Indian petrochemicals Corp.	India	Petroleum/petrochemicals	—	85.0	85.0	Local and foreign investors
1994	Mahanagar Telephone Nigam	India	Telecommunications	12.8	421.1	—	
1994	Oil & Natural Gas Commission	India	Petroleum	2.0	334.9	—	
1995	PT Semen Gresik	Indonesia	Construction	8.0	127.0	127.0	
1995	PT Tambang Timah	Indonesia	Mining	35.0	224.2	160.0	
1995	PT Telekomunikasi Indonesia	Indonesia	Telecommunications	20.0	1680.0	630.0	Foreign and local investors
1994	PT Indonesian Satellite (Indosat)	Indonesia	Telecommunications	32.0	1,161.6	904.0	Deutsche Telekom
1994	Satelit Palapa Indonesia (Satelindo)	Indonesia	Telecommunications	25.0	586.0	586.0	Local investor
1995	Sanayeh Felezi Iran	Iran	Metals	40.0	6.5	0.0	
1995	Transjamaican	Jamaica	Airlines	55.0	1.1	0.0	Air Jamaica Acquisition Group (AJAG)
1994	Air Jamaica	Jamaica	Airlines	70.0	26.0	0.0	ApplianceTradersLtd 30%, Mo-Young 20%, Jamaica Hotel and Tourist 10% etc
1994	Frome, Monyusk, Bernard Lodge	Jamaica	Food processing	100.0	36.0	0.0	Local investors
1994	Long Pond sugar mill	Jamaica	Food processing	100.0	5.0	0.0	
1994	Eastern Banana Estates	Jamaica	Agribusiness	50.0	8.0	4.0	Foreign investors, UK/Ireland, Jamaican Producers Group
1995	Jordan Hotels and Tourism Company	Jordan	Hotel	54.0	14.7	0.0	Zara Investment Company
1995	Karmet Steelworks	Kazakstan	Steel	10.0	0.0	—	Ispat International (UK)
1994	Almaty Tobacco Kombinat	Kazakstan	Tobacco	50.0	314.9	314.9	Philip Morris
1994	Chimkent	Kazakstan	Food processing	100.0	—	—	Nabisco Brands
1995	Booth Manufacturers Ltd	Kenya	Metal fabrication	29.0	0.2	0.0	
1995	East African Fine Spinners	Kenya	Textiles	100.0	3.5	0.0	
1995	Golf Hotel Ltd.	Kenya	Services	80.0	1.4	0.0	
1995	Hola Ginnery Ltd	Kenya	Industry	100.0	0.2	0.0	
1995	Homa Bay Hotel Ltd	Kenya	Services	99.0	0.4	0.0	
1995	Kenya Airways	Kenya	Airline	26.0	26.0	26.0	KLM Royal Dutch Airlines
1995	Kenya Fruit Processors Ltd	Kenya	Agroindustry	35.0	0.2	0.0	
1995	Kenya Furfural Ltd	Kenya	Industry	55.0	1.1	0.0	
1995	Kenya Taitex Mills	Kenya	Industry	81.0	1.6	0.0	
1995	Kerio Valley Ginnery Ltd.	Kenya	Agroindustry	100.0	0.2	0.0	
1995	Mwea Ginnery Ltd	Kenya	Agroindustry	100.0	0.3	0.0	
1995	Pan Vegetable Processors	Kenya	Agribusiness	100.0	1.8	0.0	
1995	Synthetic Fibre (K) Ltd.	Kenya	Industry	100.0	1.0	0.0	
1995	Synthetic Fibre (K) Ltd.	Kenya	Textiles	100.0	1.0	0.0	
1995	Uchumi	Kenya	Retail	18.5			
1995	Wire Products Ltd.	Kenya	Metal fabrication	30.0	0.2	0.2	Foreign joint venture
1995	Wire Products Ltd.	Kenya	Metals	30.0	0.2	0.7	Foreign joint venture
1994	African Marine General Engineering Co. Ltd.	Kenya	Service/engineering	33.0	0.7	—	Foreign joint venture
1994	Arks Ltd.	Kenya	Hotel	6.0	—	0.7	Foreign joint venture
1994	Associated Battery Manufacturers Ltd.	Kenya	Manufacturing/autos	20.0	0.7	—	
1994	Associated Vehicle Assembly Ltd.	Kenya	Manufacturing/autos	51.0	—	—	
1994	C.PC Industrial Products Ltd.	Kenya	Agribusiness	18.0	0.7	0.7	Foreign joint venture
1994	Chloride Exide Ltd.	Kenya	Services	18.0	0.1	0.1	Foreign joint venture
1994	Clarkson Notcutt Ltd.	Kenya	Insurance	50.0	—	—	
1994	Dawa Pharmaceutical Ltd.	Kenya	Pharmaceuticals	40.0	—	—	Foreign joint venture
1994	East Africa Industries Ltd.	Kenya	Manufacturing	45.0	—	—	
1994	Embu Hotel	Kenya	Hotel	29.0	—	—	
1994	Eslon Plastics of Kenya	Kenya	Manufacturing/plastics	30.0	—	—	Foreign joint venture
1994	Everready Batteries	Kenya	Manufacturing/batteries	25.0	—	—	Everready
1994	Firestone (E.A.) Ltd.	Kenya	Manufacturing/rubber	20.0	2.4	2.4	Firestone

(table continues on next page)

Table A6.10 Privatization transactions in developing countries, 1994–95 (continued)
(millions of U.S. dollars)

Year	Company	Country	Sector	Equity share Percent	Equity share Amount	Foreign exchange	Purchaser
1994	Kenya Cashewnuts Co. Ltd.	Kenya	Agribusiness	—	1.9	1.9	Foreign joint venture
1994	Kenya Fishnet Industries	Kenya	Textiles	43.0	0.1	0.1	Foreign joint venture
1994	National Bank of Kenya	Kenya	Banking	20.0	10.0	0.0	Local investors
1995	Agro Machinery and Oxygen	Lao PDR	Machinery	—	0.2	0.0	Local investor
1995	Animal Slaughter	Lao PDR	Agribusiness	—	0.2	0.0	Local investor
1995	Bridge Road Construction #20	Lao PDR	Construction	—	1.4	0.0	Local investor
1995	Lao Freight Forwarder	Lao PDR	Freight forwarding	—	0.2	0.0	Local investor
1995	Road Construction Co. Vientiane	Lao PDR	Construction	—	0.6	0.0	Local investor
1995	Thong Pong Cement Factory	Lao PDR	Cement	—	1.5	1.5	Foreign investor
1995	Veum Kham Agric. Co.	Lao PDR	Agribusiness	—	0.1	0.0	Local investor
1994	Lattelekom	Latvia	Telecommunications	49.0	160.0	160.0	Consortium consisting of UK's Cable and Wireless & Telecom Finland
1995	Akemenes cementas	Lithuania	Industry	39.8	9.9	0.0	Local investor
1995	Baltija	Lithuania	Industry	4.3	1.9	0.0	Local investor
1995	Gamega	Lithuania	Industry	24.5	1.3	0.0	Local investor
1995	Kauno televizijos aparaturos gamykla	Lithuania	Industry	19.7	1.3	0.0	Local investor
1995	Laivite	Lithuania	Industry	52.6	7.6	0.0	Local investor
1995	Lietaga	Lithuania	Construction	13.3	1.4	0.0	Local investor
1995	Limeta	Lithuania	Industry	57.4	0.9	0.0	Local investor
1995	Lithuanian state rivers navigation	Lithuania	Transport	73.0	2.7	0.0	Local investor
1995	Metalas	Lithuania	Industry	86.8	1.2	0.0	Local investor
1995	Petrasiunu Konstrukcijos	Lithuania	Construction	79.7	1.6	0.0	Local investor
1995	Ragutis	Lithuania	Industry	2.9	1.1	0.0	Local investor
1995	Skaiteks	Lithuania	Industry	61.5	7.2	0.0	Local investor
1995	Svyturys	Lithuania	Industry	29.3	1.0	0.0	Local investor
1995	Utenos trikotazas	Lithuania	Industry	6.2	4.4	0.0	Local investor
1994	Alyrus	Lithuania	Agribusiness	100.0	0.0	0.0	Local investor
1994	Azotois	Lithuania	Manufacturing	100.0	7.7	0.0	Local investor
1994	Baltikvairas	Lithuania	Manufacturing	50.0	3.4	0.0	Local investor
1994	Elektra	Lithuania	Manufacturing	100.0	10.0	0.0	Local investor
1994	Gausa	Lithuania	Commerce	100.0	0.5	0.0	Local investor
1994	Klaipeda	Lithuania	Manufacturing	100.0	1.6	0.0	Local investor
1994	Mildeta	Lithuania	Commerce	100.0	0.3	0.0	Local investor
1994	Rutele	Lithuania	Commerce	100.0	0.2	0.0	Local investor
1994	Siaulius	Lithuania	Manufacturing	100.0	3.4	0.0	Locla investor
1994	Tauras	Lithuania	Commerce	100.0	0.3	0.0	Local investors
1994	Vilmaus Sigma	Lithuania	Manufacturing	100.0	9.5	0.0	Local investor
1994	Vilnius	Lithuania	Manufacturing	100.0	3.9	0.0	Local investor
1994	Vygaile	Lithuania	Commerce	100.0	0.1	0.0	Local investor
1994	Zaliakalnis	Lithuania	Retail/food services	100.0	0.6	0.4	Foreign and local investors
1995	AD Beton, Bitola	Macedonia, FYR	Construction	66.9	0.1	0.0	Local investor
1995	AD Beton, Ohrid	Macedonia, FYR	Construction	33.5	0.1	0.0	Local investor
1995	AD Beton, Skopje	Macedonia, FYR	Construction	88.6	0.4	0.0	Local investor
1995	AD Beton, Stip	Macedonia, FYR	Construction	67.9	0.1	0.0	Local investor
1995	AD Blagoj Gorev	Macedonia, FYR	Oil production	3.8	0.7	0.0	Local investor
1995	AD Jugooprema, Skopje	Macedonia, FYR	Trade	48.3	0.1	0.0	Local investor
1995	AD Karaorman, Struga	Macedonia, FYR	Construction materials	92.6	0.1	0.0	Local investor
1995	AD Kiro Cucuk	Macedonia, FYR	Bricks	3.2	0.2	0.0	Local investor
1995	AD Moda	Macedonia, FYR	Garments	22.9	0.1	0.1	XATT Gmbh (Germany)

Table A6.10 Privatization transactions in developing countries, 1994–95 (continued)

(millions of U.S. dollars)

Year	Company	Country	Sector	Equity share Percent	Amount	Foreign exchange	Purchaser
1995	AD Plastika, Skopje	Macedonia, FYR	Plastic packaging materials	5.1	0.1	0.0	Local investor
1995	AD Trgoiug, Skopje	Macedonia, FYR	Trade	43.4	0.1	0.0	Local investor
1995	ADMS Geras Cunev	Macedonia, FYR	Textiles	56.7	0.1	0.0	Local investor
1995	Alkaloid, Berovo	Macedonia, FYR	Textiles	36.9	0.1	0.0	Local investor
1995	Alkaloid, Skopje	Macedonia, FYR	Pharmaceuticals	45.4	1.7	0.0	Local investor
1995	DIK Straso Pindzur	Macedonia, FYR	Construction materials	44.0	0.1	0.0	Local investor
1995	DOO Kale	Macedonia, FYR	Trade	100.0	0.1	0.0	Local investor
1995	DOO Tigar, Kriva Palanka	Macedonia, FYR	Trade	40.7	0.1	0.0	Local investor
1995	DOO Zelop, Sveti Nikole	Macedonia, FYR	Food Processing	100.0	0.0	0.0	Local investor
1995	DOO Zito Struga, Struga	Macedonia, FYR	Bakery products	100.0	0.0	0.0	Local investor
1995	Evropa	Macedonia, FYR	Confectionary	3.7	0.7	0.0	Local investor
1995	Fersped	Macedonia, FYR	Trade/warehousing	44.0	0.6	0.0	Management (51%)
1995	Inteks, Skopje	Macedonia, FYR	Trade	4.2	0.3	0.0	Local investor
1995	Javor, Bitola	Macedonia, FYR	Trade	5.7	0.4	0.0	Local investor
1995	Karaorman, Skopje	Macedonia, FYR	Construction materials	3.3	0.5	0.0	Employees
1995	Komuna, Skopje	Macedonia, FYR	Paper products	43.5	0.4	0.0	Local investor
1995	Makedonija Sport	Macedonia, FYR	Garments	100.0	0.1	0.1	Westfr Trade, Germany (51%)
1995	Makedonija turist	Macedonia, FYR	Tourism	37.2	0.6	0.0	Management buyout
1995	Makosped, Skopje	Macedonia, FYR	Freight forwarding	23.0	0.6	0.0	Local investor
1995	Nov zivot, Tetovo	Macedonia, FYR	Tourism/catering	44.9	0.1	0.0	Local investor
1995	Pivara	Macedonia, FYR	Brewery	30.9	1.0	0.0	Management buyout
1995	POS Izolmont	Macedonia, FYR	Construction materials	100.0	0.0	0.0	Local investor
1995	POS Jugotrans	Macedonia, FYR	Transport/freight	68.3	0.1	0.0	Local investor
1995	POS Maktrans, Skopje	Macedonia, FYR	Transportation	80.7	0.1	0.1	Energy Group Marshal Islands
1995	POS Treska, Osogovo	Macedonia, FYR	Furniture	100.0	0.0	0.0	Local investor
1995	Prilepska Pivarnica, Prilep	Macedonia, FYR	Brewery	42.5	0.3	0.0	Local investor
1995	Treska, Boris Kidric	Macedonia, FYR	Furniture	92.9	0.1	0.0	Foreign investor (51%); local investor (49%)
1995	Usje, Skopje	Macedonia, FYR	Cement	70.4	1.5	0.0	Local investor
1995	Veteks, Titov Veles	Macedonia, FYR	Yarn/cotton fibers	55.0	0.1	0.0	Local investor
1995	Vinka, Vinica	Macedonia, FYR	Textiles	58.1	0.1	0.0	Local investor
1995	Zito Luks, Skopje	Macedonia, FYR	Bakery products	40.8	1.0	0.0	Local investor
1995	Zito Makedonija	Macedonia, FYR	Trade	2.8	0.1	0.0	Local investor
1994	Avtorska Agencija na Makedonija	Macedonia, FYR	Services	100.0	—	0.0	Local investor
1994	Bitola Promet	Macedonia, FYR	Retail/wholesale	100.0	—	0.0	Local investor
1994	Gradinar	Macedonia, FYR	—	100.0	—	0.0	Local investor
1994	Graditel	Macedonia, FYR	Services	100.0	—	0.0	Local investor
1994	Oteks	Macedonia, FYR	Textiles	83.0	24.9	0.0	Local investor
1994	Pelister	Macedonia, FYR	Real estate	100.0	—	0.0	Local investor
1994	PKB	Macedonia, FYR	Retail/wholesale	100.0	—	0.0	Local investor
1994	Solun	Macedonia, FYR	Retail/wholesale	100.0	—	0.0	Local investor
1994	Stopanski Pecat	Macedonia, FYR	Retail/wholesale	100.0	—	0.0	Local investor
1994	Tetovo Gradba	Macedonia, FYR	Real estate	100.0	—	0.0	Local investor
1994	Tutun	Macedonia, FYR	Trade	100.0	—	0.0	Local investor
1994	Zelezar	Macedonia, FYR	Trade	100.0	—	0.0	Local investor
1995	Malawi Book Service	Malawi	Book store	—	1.8	0.0	
1995	Hicom Holdings	Malaysia	Manufacturing	32.0	708.0	0.0	Mega Consolidated
1995	Johor Port	Malaysia	Transport	100.0	48.7	0.0	Seaport Terminal (Johor)
1995	National Paddy and Rice Board	Malaysia	Agriculture	100.0	79.8	0.0	Consortium Budaya Generasi

(table continues on next page)

141

Table A6.10 Privatization transactions in developing countries, 1994–95 (continued)
(millions of U.S. dollars)

Year	Company	Country	Sector	Equity share Percent	Equity share Amount	Foreign exchange	Purchaser
1995	Naval Dockyard	Malaysia	Manufacturing	100.0	120.0	0.0	Penang Shipbuilding & Construction
1995	Petronas Gas	Malaysia	Gas	21.3	1121.1	439.6	Local and foreign investors
1995	Sarawak Electricity Supply Corp	Malaysia	Electricity	50.0	424.1	0.0	Dunlop Estate Berhad
1995	Sindora	Malaysia	Agriculture		17.3	0.0	
1994	Malaysia Airlines	Malaysia	Airlines	32.0	702.0	0.0	
1994	Petronas Dagangan	Malaysia	Petroleum, oil, and gas	75.0	96.0	0.0	
1995	MAUSOV	Mauritania	Fishing	51.0	0.9	0.0	Local investor
1995	SIMAR	Mauritania	Fishing	24.0	0.2	0.0	Local investor
1995	Altamira I	Mexico	Cargo and containers	100.0	5.5	0.0	Local investor
1995	Inmueble en Sn. Andres Tuxtla, Ver.	Mexico	Storage		0.1	0.0	Local investor
1995	Inmueble en Cd. Obregon, Son.	Mexico	Storage		0.2	0.0	Local investor
1995	Lazaro Cardenas I	Mexico	Cargo and containers	100.0	2.9	0.0	Local investor
1995	Lazaro Cardenas II	Mexico	Cargo and containers	100.0	2.5	0.0	Local investor
1995	Manzanillo I	Mexico	Cargo and containers	100.0	49.2	50.0	Operadora Portuaria de Manzanillo, S.A. de C.V.
1995	Manzanillo II	Mexico	Cargo and containers	100.0	2.9	0.0	Local investor
1995	Veracruz	Mexico	Cargo and containers	100.0	103.7	50.0	International de Contenedores Asociados de Veracruz
1994	Aldea Vacacional Cancun	Mexico	Tourism		31.8	0.0	CancunProperty, S. de R.L.; Villa Playa Blanca y Operadora de Aldeas Vacac
1994	Almacenes Nacionales de Deposito,S.A.	Mexico	Services		0.2	0.0	El Estado Libre y Soberano de Zacatecas
1994	Banca Serfin S.A.	Mexico	Banking	11.4	147.9	0.0	
1994	Complejos Turisticos de Huatuclo, S.A. de C.V.	Mexico	Tourism		2.5	0.0	Vacation Properties de Mexico, S.A. de C.V.
1994	Profotur, S.A. de C.V.	Mexico	Tourism		7.4	0.0	Vacation Properties de Mexico, S.A. de C.V.
1994	Puerto Interno Pantaco	Mexico	Warehouse		18.5	0.0	Ferrocarriles Nacionales de Mexico
1994	Telefonos de Mexico, S.A.	Mexico	Telecommunications	1.5	550.0	550.0	Foreign Investors
1994	Villa Arquelogica de Chichen Itza	Mexico	Tourism		1.8	0.0	Villa Playa Blanka, S.A. y Operadora de Aldeas Vacacionales, S.A. de C.V.
1994	Villa Arqueologica de Cholula	Mexico	Tourism		2.5	0.0	Villa Playa Blanca, S.A. y Operadora de Aldeas Vacacionales, S.A. de C.V.
1994	Villa Arqueologica de Coba	Mexico	Tourism		0.9	0.0	Villa Playa Blanca, S.A. y Operadora de Aldeas Vacacionales, S.A. de C.V.
1994	Villa Arqueologica de Teotihuacan	Mexico	Tourism		1.5	0.0	Villa Playa Blanca, S.A. y Operadora de Aldeas Vacacionales, S.A. de C. V.
1994	Villa Arqueologica de Uxmal	Mexico	Tourism		1.3	0.0	Villa Playa Blanca, S.A. y Operadora de Aldeas Vacacionales, S.A. de C.V.
1995	BMCE	Morocco	Banking	43.0	208.6	12.2	Moroccan/Swiss/US/UK
1995	CIOR	Morocco	Cement	1.2	1.2	0.0	Local investors
1995	Credit EQDOM	Morocco	Financial services/banking	19.5	9.0	0.0	Local investors
1995	Hotel Arghour	Morocco	Hotel	100.0	1.7	0.0	Morocon Tourism Company
1995	Hotel de la Tour Hassan	Morocco	Hotel	100.0	5.9	0.0	Local investors
1995	Hotel Doukkala	Morocco	Hotel	100.0	2.6	2.6	Saudi Arabia
1995	Hotel Friouato	Morocco	Hotel	100.0	1.5	0.0	Local investors
1995	Hotel les Merinides	Morocco	Hotel	100.0	3.5	0.0	Local investors
1995	Hotel Oukaimeden	Morocco	Hotel	100.0	0.4	0.0	Local investors
1995	ICOZ	Morocco	Textiles	97.4	1.2	1.2	Local/foreign consortium
1995	SICO-Centre	Morocco	Textiles	30.0	0.2	0.0	Local investors
1995	SIMEF	Morocco	Automobiles	100.0	—	—	Local/Belgian/Tunisian consortium
1995	SOCHEPRESS	Morocco	Newspapers	40.0	2.8	0.0	Local investors
1995	SOFAC/Credit	Morocco	Consumer credit	0.8	0.2	0.0	Local investors
1995	SOTRAMEG	Morocco	Agribusiness	60.0	1.0	0.0	Local investor
1994	Casablanca Hotel	Morocco	Hotel	100.0	20.0	0.0	Interedec
1994	Compagnie Marocaine des Transports-Lignes Nationales	Morocco	Transportation	18.9	5.5	0.0	
1994	Compagnie Marocaine des Hydrocarbures	Morocco	Petroleum, oil, and gas	50.0	10.5	0.0	Hogespar increasing its stake to 68%
1994	Dragon Gas	Morocco	Petroleum, oil, and gas	50.0	0.1	0.1	Dragofina Investment Trust of Italy
1994	General Tire and Rubber Company of Morocco	Morocco	Manufacturing	22.0	—	—	local investors

Table A6.10 Privatization transactions in developing countries, 1994–95 (continued)

(millions of U.S. dollars)

Year	Company	Country	Sector	Equity share Percent	Equity share Amount	Foreign exchange	Purchaser
1994	Hotel des Ilcs	Morocco	Hotel	100.0	2.0	0.0	Expertotel
1994	Hotel Rissani	Morocco	Hotel	100.0	1.0	0.0	SHAT
1994	Hotel Zalagh	Morocco	Hotel	100.0	2.0	0.0	Dar Si Aissa
1994	Malabata Hotel	Morocco	Hotel	100.0	6.0	6.0	Malabata International(Saudi Arabia)
1994	Mobil-Maroc	Morocco	Petroleum, oil, and gas	50.0	12.3	12.3	Mobil Petroleum Corporation (US)
1994	Modulec	Morocco	Manufacturing	85.0	0.0	0.0	Local investor
1994	Societe Nationale d'Investissement	Morocco	Insurance	57.0	226.6	36.3	Local and foreign investors
1994	Sofac-Credit	Morocco	Banking	53.4	14.4	0.0	Local consortium
1994	Total Maroc	Morocco	Petroleum, oil, and gas	50.0	33.5	33.5	Total of France
1994	Toubkal Hotel	Morocco	Hotel	100.0	4.3	0.0	local investors
1994	Transatlantic hotel	Morocco	Hotel	100.0	4.6	0.0	Tikida-Ismailia
1994	Volubilis Hotel	Morocco	Hotel	100.0	3.9	0.0	Fram
1995	Caju de Mocambique, Chamanculo	Mozambique	Agroindustry	95.0	1.2	0.0	Local investors
1995	Caju de Mocambique, Inhambane	Mozambique	Agroindustry	90.0	0.9	0.0	Local investors
1995	Caju de Mocambique, Machava	Mozambique	Agroindustry	85.0	2.6	0.0	Local investors
1995	Caju de Mocambique, Manjacaze	Mozambique	Agroindustry	80.0	0.6	0.0	Local investors
1995	Cervejas de Mozambique	Mozambique	Brewery	70.0	14.0	14.0	Indol a Dutch subsidiery of South Africa Brewery
1995	Companhia Ind. Matola Nacala	Mozambique	Industry	55.0	1.0	0.0	Local investors
1995	Dimac-Dept. Transport	Mozambique	Transport	100.0	0.9	0.0	Local investors
1995	Emplama—Unit 1	Mozambique	Industry	80.0	0.7	0.7	Portugal
1995	Emplama—Unit 2	Mozambique	Industry	80.0	0.4	0.0	Local investors
1995	Emplama—Unit 3	Mozambique	Industry	80.0	0.4	0.0	Local investors
1995	Encatex-Del. Reg. Sul-Maputo	Mozambique	Textiles	80.0	0.2	0.0	Local investors
1995	Encatex-Del. Prov. Inhambane	Mozambique	Textiles	80.0	0.1	0.0	Local investors
1995	Encatex-Head Office	Mozambique	Textiles	80.0	0.2	0.0	Local investors
1995	Encatex-Central region—533	Mozambique	Textiles	80.0	0.0	0.0	Local investors
1995	Encatex-Central region—3223	Mozambique	Textiles	80.0	0.1	0.0	Local investors
1995	Encatex-Creche	Mozambique	Textiles	100.0	0.0	0.0	Local investors
1995	Hidromoc-South	Mozambique	Utilities	100.0	0.1	0.0	Local investors
1995	Hortofruticola	Mozambique	Trade	60.0	0.2	0.0	Employees
1995	Mocargo	Mozambique	Services	60.0	0.3	0.3	Denmark
1995	Soveste	Mozambique	Garments	100.0	0.4	0.0	Local investors
1995	Soveste	Mozambique	Garments	100.0	0.2	0.0	Local investors
1995	Soveste	Mozambique	Garments	80.0	0.7	—	Local/South Africa/UK
1995	Stcia-Warehouse	Mozambique	Garments	100.0	0.1	0.0	Local investors
1995	Sweets and Chocolates	Mozambique	Industry	55.0	0.6	0.6	Portugal
1994	Emopesca	Mozambique	Agribusiness	70.0	0.8	0.0	
1994	Forjadora	Mozambique	Manufacturing	80.0	0.3	0.3	Forein investor
1994	Indico Construcoes	Mozambique	Construction	80.0	0.2	0.2	Foreign investor
1994	Industrias Costas	Mozambique	Manufacturing	100.0	0.1	0.0	
1994	Metalurgica de Chimoio	Mozambique	Mining	100.0	0.1	0.0	
1994	Tipografia Classica Comercial	Mozambique	Printing	100.0	0.1	0.0	
1994	Nepal Bitumen	Nepal	Chemicals	65.0	0.2	0.0	Suresh Vaidya and Associates
1994	Nepal Lube Oil	Nepal	Petroleum, oil, and gas	40.0	0.6	0.0	Chaudhary Group
1995	Los Brasiles, S.A.	Nicaragua	Meat processing	75.0	2.4	0.0	Importadora Cruz, S.A.
1995	NICA	Nicaragua	Services	51.0	1.2	0.0	Local investors/employees
1995	Plywood de Nicaragua	Nicaragua	Forestry	35.0	0.4	0.0	Employees
1994	Companic	Nicaragua	Paper processing	30.0	0.5	0.0	Local investor

(table continues on next page)

143

Table A6.10 Privatization transactions in developing countries, 1994–95 (continued)

(millions of U.S. dollars)

Year	Company	Country	Sector	Equity share Percent	Amount	Foreign exchange	Purchaser
1994	COPA	Nicaragua	Chemicals	58.3	0.6	0.0	COFESA-local investors
1994	Empresa Francisco Meza Rojas	Nicaragua	Mining	100.0	4.0	2.0	Foreign and local investors
1994	Enasal	Nicaragua	Salt processing	100.0	0.1	0.0	Employees
1994	Eniplast	Nicaragua	Plastics	100.0	0.7	0.0	Local investors
1994	Envases	Nicaragua	Metals	100.0	1.4	0.7	Foreign (50%), local (50%)
1994	Induquinisa	Nicaragua	Chemicals	25.8	0.4	0.0	Intrabinquisa; local investors; employees
1994	Industrias Delmor	Nicaragua	Meat processing	100.0	0.5	0.0	Local investors-employees
1994	Ingenio Camilo Ortega	Nicaragua	Sugar	100.0	0.5	0.5	Agroindustrial Kucra Hill-foreign investor
1994	Intercasa	Nicaragua	Metal	100.0	0.7	0.0	Incofisa
1994	Licores Bell, S.A.	Nicaragua	Chemicals	10.6	0.0	0.0	Intrafalibesa
1994	Lukasa	Nicaragua	Chemicals	25.0	0.1	0.0	Local investors
1994	Macen	Nicaragua	Textiles	17.5	0.3	0.0	Contrainpa; local investors
1994	Madsa	Nicaragua	Forestry	13.2	0.0	0.0	J. Gatlin-local investor
1994	Proagro	Nicaragua	Agribusiness	100.0	1.8	0.0	Agrotersa-local investor
1994	Proinco	Nicaragua	Cement	100.0	1.0	0.0	Local investors 60%; employees 40%
1994	Sumagro	Nicaragua	Agribusiness	100.0	0.6	0.0	Employees
1994	Tricotextil	Nicaragua	Textiles	100.0	0.2	0.0	Pimatex-local investor
1994	Valle de Sebaco	Nicaragua	Agribusiness	100.0	3.0	1.5	Fruit World (50%) foreign; local investors (50%)
1994	Electricity Meter Co. of Nigeria /Ltd.	Nigeria	Power generation	7.7	0.5	0.0	Local investors
1994	Federal Palace Hotel	Nigeria	Hotel	100.0	22.4	0.0	
1994	Motor Engineering Services Co.	Nigeria	Services/auto	24.0	0.3	0.0	
1994	Niger Insurance Co.	Nigeria	Insurance	100.0	0.4	0.0	
1994	Nigeria Food Co.	Nigeria	Food processing	100.0	0.1	0.0	Local investors
1994	Nigerian Beverage Production Co. Ltd.	Nigeria	Brewery	100.0	0.2	0.0	
1994	Nigerian Dairies Co. Ltd.	Nigeria	Food processing	100.0	—	—	
1994	Oman cement Company	Oman	Cement	36.0	31.5	0.0	Local investors
1995	Cotton Ginning Factory	Pakistan	Textiles	—	0.1	0.0	Local investors
1995	General Refractories	Pakistan	Manufacturing	90.0	0.9	0.0	Local investors
1995	Ittehad Pesticides & Chemicals	Pakistan	Chemicals	90.0	13.2	0.0	Local investors
1995	Lyallpur Chemicals & Fertilizer	Pakistan	Chemicals	90.0	9.1	0.0	Employees
1995	Makerwall Collieries Mianwali	Pakistan	Manufacturing	90.0	0.1	0.0	Local investors
1995	Mashriq-Peshawar	Pakistan	Manufacturing	90.0	0.6	0.0	Local investors
1995	National Petrocarbon Ltd.	Pakistan	Manufacturing	90.0	2.2	0.0	Local investors
1995	Nowshera Chemicals	Pakistan	Chemicals	90.0	0.6	0.0	Local investors
1995	Pak Hyoils	Pakistan	food processing	90.0	2.2	0.0	Local investors
1995	Ravi Engineering	Pakistan	Construction	90.0	0.5	0.5	Petrosin (Singapore)
1995	Republic Motors	Pakistan	Manufacturing	—	2.0	0.0	Local investors
1995	Shikarpur	Pakistan	Food Products		0.9	0.0	Local investors
1995	Swat Ceramics	Pakistan	Manufacturing	90.0	1.8	0.0	Local investors
1995	Textile Machinery Co.	Pakistan	Manufacturing	90.0	1.1	0.0	Local investors
1994	Associated Cement Rouri	Pakistan	Cement	90.0	16.6	0.0	Local investor
1994	Hazara Phosphate Fertilizers	Pakistan	Chemicals	100.0	5.7	0.0	
1994	Marafco Ghee Mills	Pakistan	Food processing	51.0	1.2	0.0	Employees
1994	Mari Gas	Pakistan	Gas	20.0	3.4	0.0	Foreign and local investors
1994	Newshara Chemicals	Pakistan	Chemicals	100.0	16.9	0.0	Local investors
1994	Pakistan Telecommunications Corp. (PTC)	Pakistan	Telecommunications	12.0	1,000.0	898.0	Foreign and local investors
1994	Sina Engineering	Pakistan	Construction	90.0	14.1	14.1	Franklin Investments (UK)
1994	Spinning Machinery	Pakistan	Manufacturing	90.0	2.5	0.0	Local investors

Table A6.10 Privatization transactions in developing countries, 1994–95 (continued)

(millions of U.S. dollars)

Year	Company	Country	Sector	Equity share Percent	Amount	Foreign exchange	Purchaser
1994	Thatta Cement	Pakistan	Cement	90.0	45.8	0.0	Local investor
1994	Cementos Bayanos S.A.	Panama	Cement	100.0	59.7	57.7	Cementos Mexicanos 95%; employees 5%; Check LF listsCORPACEM
1994	Lineas Aereas Paraguayas S.A. (LAPSA)	Paraguay	Airlines	80.0	22.0	11.0	Cielos de America a joint venture between Paraguayan/Ecuadorian
1995	Andahuaylas Parador	Peru	Tourism	60.0	0.1	0.0	Local investors
1995	Banco Continental	Peru	Banking	60.0	352.3	196.7	Banco Bilbao Vizcaya (Spain)+employees ($4.45m)
1995	Berenguela	Peru	Mining	—	0.8	0.0	Kappes, Cassiday and Associates(Canada)
1995	Cajamarquilla Refinery	Peru	Mining	—	0.7	0.0	Employees
1995	Cemento Norte Pacasmayo	Peru	Cement	—	68.2	56.1	Local and foreign investors
1995	Cemento Sur S.A.	Peru	Industry	100.0	33.3	0.0	
1995	Chiclayo Hotel	Peru	Tourism	100.0	3.3	0.0	Local investors
1995	Complejo Agroindustrial de Chao	Peru	Agribusiness	—	—	0.0	Promotora Merchantil-local investor
1995	Complejo Pesquero de Samanco	Peru	Fisheries	100.0	4.7	0.0	Local investor
1995	EDE Chancay	Peru	Electricity	60.0	10.4	0.0	Inversiones Distrilima, S.A.
1995	Edegel	Peru	Power utility	60.0	524.5	—	Generandes consortium (US, Chile, Peru)
1995	Edelnor	Peru	Electricity		10.8	0.0	Employees
1995	Empresa de Generacion Electrica Cahua	Peru	Electricity	60.0	41.8	0.0	Sindicato Pesquero
1995	Empresa Peruana de Servicios Pesqueros (EPSEP)	Peru	Fishing		5.2	0.0	Local investor
1995	Empresa Regional Pesquera Grau	Peru	Fishing		6.8	0.0	Local investor
1995	Entel Peru	Peru	Telecommunications		19.7	0.0	Employees
1995	Epersur–Tacna fishing frigorific	Peru	Fisheries		0.3	0.0	Local consortium
1995	Epsep	Peru	Fisheries		4.4	0.0	
1995	Epsep-Mercado Mayorista Callao	Peru	Fisheries	90.0	1.2	0.0	Local investor
1995	ERTSA Puno	Peru	Transport	60.0	0.2	0.0	Local investors
1995	Etevensa	Peru	Thermal power	60.0	121.0	121.0	Consortium led by Endesa (Spain)
1995	Hoteles de Turistas (14)	Peru	Tourism		17.5	0.0	Local investors
1995	Huarmey Hotel	Peru	Tourism	100.0	0.1	0.0	Local investors
1995	Huaytara Touristic Parador	Peru	Tourism	60.0	0.1	0.0	Local investors
1995	Machu Picchu Ruins Hotel	Peru	Tourism		2.1	0.0	Peru Hotel, S.A
1995	Planta Pesca Peru Atico	Peru	Fishmeal factory	100.0	7.5	0.0	Local investor
1995	Planta Pesca Peru La Planchada	Peru	Fishmeal factory	100.0	10.3	0.0	Local investor
1995	Planta Pesquera Supe Norte	Peru	Fishmeal factory	100.0	5.6	0.0	
1995	Seminario San Antonio Abad Hotel	Peru	Tourism		4.5	0.0	Peru Hotel, S.A.
1995	Tingo Maria Hotel	Peru	Tourism	60.0	0.3	0.0	Local investors
1995	Tourist hotels (17)	Peru	Tourism		18.7	0.0	Local investors
1994	Cajamarquilla	Peru	Mining	100.0	193.0	192.2	consortium consisting of Comico(CAN) and Marubeni; employees (1.9%)
1994	Canarriaco/Jehuamarca	Peru	Mining	100.0	7.0	7.0	Placer Dome del Peru (Canada)
1994	Cartavio-SPL	Peru	Liquors	100.0	4.4	4.4	Fierro Group (Spain)
1994	Cementos Lima S.A.	Peru	Cement	48.9	103.3	82.2	Local and foreign investors
1994	Cementos Yura	Peru	Cement	100.0	67.0	0.0	Rodriguez Group (LF Gloria SA)
1994	CERPER	Peru	Sanitary products	100.0	1.6	0.0	Drogueria Kahan SA
1994	Chillon-SPL	Peru	Corrugated board	100.0	6.5	0.0	Ribini Group
1994	Cimentos Norte Pacasmayo	Peru	Cement	10	19.658	0.0	Local investors
1994	Colpar/Hualatan/Pallac	Peru	Mining	100.0	1.75	1.8	San Jose Chilean subsidiary of a Canadian firm
1994	Edelnor	Peru	Power utility	60.0	176.49	116.5	Inversiones Distrilima (Spain/Chile/Peru)
1994	Edelsur	Peru	Power utility	100.0	212	212.0	Ontario Quinta AVV (Canada/Chile)
1994	Empresa de la Sal (EMSAL)	Peru	Salt producer	100.0	14.68	0.0	Quimica del Pacifico
1994	Empresa Peruana de Servicios Pesqueros	Peru	Warehouse		1.0	0.0	
1994	Entel/CPT	Peru	Telecommunications	35.0	1,400.0	1,400.0	Consortium led by Telefonica de Espana(Spain)

(table continues on next page)

Table A6.10 Privatization transactions in developing countries, 1994–95 (continued)

(millions of U.S. dollars)

Year	Company	Country	Sector	Equity share Percent	Amount	Foreign exchange	Purchaser
1994	ILO Copper Refinery	Peru	Mining	100.0	67.5	67.5	Southern Peru Copper (US)
1994	Interbanc	Peru	Banking	100.0	51.0	50.0	International consortium
1994	LaGranja	Peru	Mining	100.0	1.0	1.0	Cambior Inc. (Canada)
1994	Lar Carbon	Peru	Mining	100.0	1.3	0.0	Cementos Lima
1994	Las Huaquillas	Peru	Mining		0.0	0.0	AndesCorp and Vegsa
1994	Minor Particip. B. Nacion	Peru	Banking	100.0	0.6	0.0	Investors
1994	Mishki	Peru	Mining		0.7	0.0	Licar SA
1994	Nuevas Inversiones SA	Peru	Insurance	—	2.6	0.0	NISA and Cementos Lima
1994	Planta Pesca Peru Chicama	Peru	Food processing/fishing industry	100.0	8.9	0.0	Local investors
1994	Planta Pesca Peru Chimbote Centro	Peru	Food processing/fishing industry	100.0	5.93	0.0	International Fish Protein
1994	Planta Pesca Peru Mollendo	Peru	Food processing/fishing industry	100.0	5.1	0.0	Sipesa
1994	Refineria de Cajamarquilla	Peru	Mining		193	193.0	Coarinco Marubeni Corp.
1994	San Antonio de Poto	Peru	Mining	100.0	8.6	0.0	AndesCorp and Vegsa
1994	Sindicato de Inversiones y Administracion	Peru	Insurance	—	4.7	0.0	SIA and Cementos Lima
1994	Tierras de Chao	Peru	Agriculture	—	3.8	0.0	Investors
1994	Tintaya Mines	Peru	Mining	100.0	277.0	274.7	Magma Copper (US)
1995	Basay Mining Corp	Philippines	Mining	—	0.7	0.0	Local investors
1995	Delta Motors	Philippines	Manufacturing	—	0.2	0.0	Sitio Fatima Kawayana Parenthood
1995	Fort Bonifacio Devt. Corp.	Philippines	Real estate	55.0	1.5	0.0	Metro Pacific Consortium
1995	Manila Hotel	Philippines	Tourism	51.0	30.0	30.0	ITT Sheraton
1995	Metro Manila Transit Corp.	Philippines	Transport	—	4.3	0.0	Employees
1995	Monarch Estate & Devt. Corp.	Philippines	Real estate	—	0.0	0.0	Local investors
1995	Nasurefco	Philippines	Sugar refinery	—	14.8	0.0	Terener Development Corp/South Pacific Sugar Corp.
1995	National Trucking & Forwarding Corp.	Philippines	Transport	100.0	2.6	0.0	Employees
1995	PCGG-Antipolo Property	Philippines	Real estate	—	1.1	0.0	Rapid City Development Corp.
1995	People's Industrial and Commercial Corp.	Philippines	Trade	—	0.2	0.0	B. Villaneuva
1995	Philippine National Bank	Philippines	Banking	7.2	72.8	0.0	Local and foreign investors
1995	Philippine National Construction Corp.	Philippines	Construction	—	58.9	0.0	—
1995	Philippines Plate Mills	Philippines	Mining	—	20.1	0.0	National Steel Corp.
1995	Prime White Cement Corp.	Philippines	Cement	—	0.2	0.0	Davao Goldland
1995	Sanifods Processing Corp.	Philippines	Food	—	0.0	0.0	Lirobenson Food Prod.
1994	National Shipping Co.	Philippines	Transportation	100.0	19.0	8.0	Madrigal Shipping; Wan Hai Lines (Taiwan)
1994	Oriental Petroleum and Minerals	Philippines	Petroleum, oil, and gas	19.6	—	—	G. Summit Holdings
1994	Paper Industries Corporation (PICOP)	Philippines	Paper manufacturing	72.0	88.0	88.0	Consurium led by Valderamma Lumber Manufacturing
1994	Petron	Philippines	Petroleum, oil, and gas	—	387.0	148.4	Foreign and local investors
1995	Bank Gdanski	Poland	Banking	60.1	112.0	112.0	—
1995	Bank Przemyslowo-Handlowy	Poland	Banking	29.6	102.0	102.0	—
1995	Cement Polski	Poland	Cement	40.0	9.6	9.6	CRH (Ireland)
1995	Cementownia Ozarow SA	Poland	Cement	75.0	58.5	—	Holding Cement Polski
1995	Fabryka Lozysk Tocznych SA Poznan	Poland	Machinery	79.0	6.0	6.0	Aktiebolaget (Sweden)
1995	Huta Otawa SA	Poland	Chemicals	75.0	2.7	—	—
1995	Jelcz	Poland	Transport	51.0	5.0	—	Local investor
1995	KCW Kujawy SA	Poland	Minerals	75.0	46.0	46.0	Lafarge (France)
1995	Kieleckie Zaklady Wyrobow Papierowych SA	Poland	Paper products	75.0	15.0	15.0	David S. Smith (UK)
1995	Korgaz	Poland	Liquid gas bottling	47.0	7.9	7.9	British Petroleum
1995	Krosno Glass	Poland	Manufacturing	11.3	6.4	6.4	Arnold and S. Bleichroeder
1995	Pollena-Uroda SA, Warszawa	Poland	Chemicals	75.0	7.8	7.8	Cussons Group (UK)
1995	Polmo Praszka SA	Poland	Machinery	75.0	3.8	0.0	Local investor

Table A6.10 Privatization transactions in developing countries, 1994–95 (continued)

(millions of U.S. dollars)

Year	Company	Country	Sector	Equity share Percent	Amount	Foreign exchange	Purchaser
1995	Przedsiebiorstwo Wyrobow Tytoniowych w Augustowic	Poland	Tobacco	65.0	88.0	88.0	BATIG (Germany)
1995	Stomil Olsztyn	Poland	Chemicals	16.8	26.7	0.0	
1995	Wywornia Wyrobow Tytoniowych SA Poznan	Poland	Tobacco	65.0	130.0	130.0	Reemtsma Cigarettenfabricken GMBH (Germany)
1995	Zaklady Metali Lekkich	Poland	Minerals	48.2	25.6	0.0	
1995	Zaklady Metali Lekkich	Poland	Metallurgy	16.0	9.5	—	
1995	Zaklady Miesne Jaroslaw SA	Poland	Meat processing	55.0	—	0.0	Local investors
1995	Zaklady Ponlarowo-Badawcze Energetykl "Energopomiar"	Poland	industry	—	1.6	0.0	
1995	Zaklady Przemyslu Tytoniowego w Krakowie	Poland	Tobacco	65.0	227.0	227.0	Philip Morris (Holland)
1995	Zaklady Przemyslu Tytoniowego Radom	Poland	Tobacco	65.0	64.0	64.0	SEITA (France)
1995	ZCW Gorazde	Poland	Cement	26.1	24.5	0.0	
1994	Agros Holding	Poland	Manufacturing	14.0	16.0	0.0	Local investors
1994	Bank BPH-Bank Przemyslowo-Handlowwy	Poland	Banking	—	148.0	0.0	
1994	Browar Szozecin	Poland	Brewery	51.0	0.2	0.0	Jozel Adelson
1994	Byron Clothing	Poland	Textiles	35.0	4.1	0.0	Local investors
1994	Centra	Poland	Electric equipment and batteries	95.0	11.4	8.6	Compagnie Europeenne D'Accumulateurs(France; 75%)
1994	Debica	Poland	Tire manufacturing	49.0	56.0	0.0	Public offer
1994	Elektronomiaz Warszawa	Poland	Construction	75.0	7.0	0.0	Mostostal Export
1994	Elester	Poland	—	95.0	2.0	0.0	Elektrim (75%)
1994	ELWO	Poland	Manufacturing/electric machinery	75.0	0.3	0.0	Rafaco (55%), Polski Bank Rozwoju (20%)
1994	Fabryka Kuchni WRONKI	Poland	Manufacturing	60.0	9.0	0.0	Amica Holding and Bank Handlowy Warszawa
1994	Fabryka Lin I Drutu	Poland	Telecommunications	51.0	23.3	0.0	Poznanska Grupa Kapitalowa
1994	Fabryka Silnlkow Elektrycznych	Poland	Manufacturing/electric machinery	95.0	2.0	0.0	Elekrim (75%)
1994	Fenlks	Poland	—	100.0	0.0	0.0	Altra Group (80%)
1994	Golenlowskie Fabryk	Poland	Manufacturing/furniture	75.0	0.9	0.5	management (25%), Steinhoff (German 55%)
1994	Goplana	Poland	Food processing	47.0	43.0	43.0	Nestle
1994	HSK JUlia	Poland	Glass	100.0	1.0	1.0	Weslon International (US)
1994	Huta Szkla Jaroslaw	Poland	Glass	36.0	3.4	2.2	Consortium led by Owens-Illinois (US) and includes Polish American Enterprise
1994	Huta Szkla Oklennego "Kunice"	Poland	Glass	100.0	2.7	2.2	Sekuff Saint-Gobain Deutschland Belelgungen (Ger 80%); employees(20%)
1994	Hydrobudow	Poland	Construction	100.0	8.0	5.6	Bilfinger and Berger (Ger 70%), Polish Dev. Bank 10%; employees 20%
1994	INDUKTA	Poland	Manufacturing/electric machinery	80.0	0.0	0.0	Elektrim S.A.
1994	Jelfa	Poland	Pharmaceuticals	70.0	22.0	0.0	Local investors
1994	Kutnowskie Zaklady Farmaceutyozna	Poland	Pharmaceuticals	100.0	4.5	0.0	Polish Amer. Enter. Fund, Pol Private Equity Fund,Pol. Private Equity FundII
1994	Nadodrzanskle Zaklady Przemyslu	Poland	Food processing	95.0	18.8	14.8	Schooner Capital Corp (US 55%); employees (20%)
1994	Okcim	Poland	Brewery	25.0	20.0	20.0	Brau und Brunen (Ger)
1994	Polam Myslakowice	Poland	Manufacturing/lights	80.0	1.3	0.0	Elekrim S.A.
1994	Polam Szczecinek S.A.	Poland	Manufacturing/lights	80.0	32.0	32.0	Ahlstrom (Sweden)
1994	Polifarb Wroclaw S.A.	Poland	Manufacturing	80.0	30.0	0.0	
1994	Przedslebiorstwo Opakowan "Pakpol"	Poland	Manufacturing	79.2	4.5	2.3	Local and U.S. investors
1994	Przedsleblorstwo Robot Instalacyjno"PRIM"	Poland	Industry	99.0	0.5	0.3	Powerpipe (Swenden 55%), Polski Bank (20%)
1994	Rafako Industrial Boiler	Poland	Manufacturing	25.0	20.0	0.0	
1994	Rolimpex	Poland	Tobacco	50.0	11.0	0.0	
1994	San Biscuit Company	Poland	Food processing	80.0	27.0	27.0	McVitie's
1994	Sefako S.A.	Poland	Manufacturing	62.0	—	0.0	Aspra-Sefako (20%), Rafako (20%), Polimex (22%)
1994	Slupsk Kobylnica	Poland	Food and beverage manufacturing	—	13.0	13.0	
1994	Slupskle Fabrykl	Poland	Manufacturing/furniture	75.0	1.1	1.1	SFM Belelgungen (Germany)
1994	Stalexport	Poland	Steel	60.0	74.0	0.0	
1994	Telzas Szozecinek	Poland	Telecommunications	80.0	3.1	0.0	Elektrim
1994	Torpo Torun	Poland	Manufacturing/clothing	100.0	3.2	0.0	Tor-Men (51%), Elegant (29%), employees (20%)

(table continues on next page)

Table A6.10 Privatization transactions in developing countries, 1994–95 (continued)

(millions of U.S. dollars)

Year	Company	Country	Sector	Equity share Percent	Amount	Foreign exchange	Purchaser
1994	WARTA S.A.	Poland	Cement	75.0	5.0	5.0	Polen Zement (Germany)
1994	Wojcieszowskle Zaklady Przemyslu	Poland	Cement	95.0	1.4	0.8	Rheinsche Kalksteinwerke (Ger 60%); Polski Bank Rozwoju (15%)
1994	Wytwornia Kozysk Slizgowych	Poland	Manufacturing/auto parts	95.0	2.3	0.0	Invest Bimet (45%), Bank Gdanski (20%), Bank Zachodni (10%)
1994	Zaklady Konlekcjl Technloznej "Lubawa"	Poland	Manufacturing	51.0	1.1	0.0	Local investors
1994	Zaklady Miasne Gdynia	Poland	Food processing	75.0	1.4	0.0	MVN Holdings S.A.
1994	Zaklady Phwowarskle Warka	Poland	Brewery	100.0	2.7	2.2	Ryezard Varisella (80%), employees (20%)
1994	Zaklady Przemyslu Cuklernloozgo	Poland	Food processing	60.0	0.9	0.9	United Biscuits, McVities (UK)
1994	Zaklady Remontowe Energetyk Warszawa	Poland	Manufacturing	75.0	2.4	0.0	Local investors
1995	Dero	Romania	Manufacturing	70.0	20.0	20.0	Unilever
1995	Romtensid	Romania	Manufacturing	70.0	40.0	40.0	Procter & Gamble
1994	Poiana-Produse Zachariase(PIPZ)	Romania	food processing	82.0	4.4	4.4	Kraft Jacobs Suchard of Switzerland a subsidiary od PhMorris, 18% employees
1995	Lukoil	Russia	Oil and gas	5.0	35.0	0.0	Local investors
1995	Lukoil	Russia	Oil and gas	—	320.0	250.0	Arco (US) $250
1995	Mechel	Russia	Metalworks	15.0	13.3	0.0	Rabikom
1995	Mosenergo	Russia	Electricity	—	22.5	22.5	
1995	Murmanskoye Parokhodsrvo	Russia	Shipping	23.5	4.1	0.0	Srateg
1995	Norilsk Nickel	Russia	Mining	40.0	170.0	0.0	Oneximbank
1995	North-west River Lines	Russia	Transportation	38.0	6.1	0.0	International Finance Company
1995	Novolipetsky Metallurgichesky Kombinat	Russia	Steel	14.8	31.0	0.0	International Finance Company
1995	Novorossiisk Sea Shipping Co.	Russia	Shipping	20.0	22.7	0.0	Novorossiisk Sea Shipping Co.
1995	Sidanko	Russia	Oil and gas	51.0	130.0	0.0	International Finance Company
1995	Surgutneftegaz	Russia	Oil and gas	40.1	88.0	0.0	Company's pension fund
1995	Yukos	Russia	Oil and gas	45.0	159.0	0.0	AOZT Laguna
1994	Balashiha Kislarodnyi Zavod	Russia	Petroleum, oil, and gas	35.0	—	—	Aga (Swedish)
1994	Bansk, stavby s.p. Prievidza	Slovak Republic	Construction	100.0	8.3	0.0	Local investors
1994	Bratislavsk cvernova tovaren	Slovak Republic	Textiles	89.0	2.2	2.2	Foreign investor
1994	Bratislavsk tlaciarne	Slovak Republic	Printing	100.0	2.5	0.0	Local investors
1994	CASSOVIA AIR Services	Slovak Republic	Transportation	52.0	0.6	0.0	Local investors
1994	Chemosvit Svit	Slovak Republic	Chemicals	100.0	63.4	0.0	Local investors
1994	COZ s.p. Bratislava	Slovak Republic	Manufacturing	100.0	0.9	0.9	Foreign investor
1994	Demetal Bratislava	Slovak Republic	Construction	100.0	0.1	0.0	Local investors
1994	Domace potreby Banska	Slovak Republic	Trade	100.0	2.0	0.0	Local investors
1994	ESAD Zilina	Slovak Republic	Transportation	100.0	1.9	0.0	Local investors
1994	Gemerske tlaciarne	Slovak Republic	Printing	100.0	0.5	0.0	Local investors
1994	Hotel Nitra v Nitre	Slovak Republic	Hotel	100.0	2.4	0.0	Local investors
1994	Jas s.p. Bardejov	Slovak Republic	Clothing	100.0	16.3	0.0	Local investors
1994	Keramicke zavody Kosice	Slovak Republic	Construction material	100.0	24.9	0.0	Local investors
1994	Kovosrot Bratislava	Slovak Republic	Metal	100.0	0.6	0.0	Local investors
1994	LR Crystal	Slovak Republic	Food processing	100.0	6.2	0.0	Local investors
1994	Makyra	Slovak Republic	Textiles	100.0	25.6	0.0	Local investors
1994	Matador	Slovak Republic	Chemicals	100.0	50.2	0.0	Local investors
1994	Matadorfix	Slovak Republic	Chemicals/rubber	100.0	2.2	0.0	Local investors
1994	Milsy	Slovak Republic	Food processing	91.0	0.8	0.0	Local investors
1994	Mlyn Pohronsky	Slovak Republic	Food processing	100.0	1.2	0.0	Local investors
1994	Nakl. automobil-Michalovce	Slovak Republic	Transportation	100.0	1.1	0.0	Local investors
1994	Nakl. automobil Puchov	Slovak Republic	Transportation	100.0	0.5	0.0	Local investors
1994	Nitrianske	Slovak Republic	Food processing	100.0	2.6	0.0	Local investors
1994	Novofruct	Slovak Republic	Food processing	100.0	0.1	0.0	Local investors

Table A6.10 Privatization transactions in developing countries, 1994–95 (continued)

(millions of U.S. dollars)

Year	Company	Country	Sector	Equity share Percent	Amount	Foreign exchange	Purchaser
1994	Obchod palivami	Slovak Republic	Industry/fuel	100.0	1.1	0.0	Local investors
1994	Orex Odevy	Slovak Republic	Textiles	100.0	0.3	0.0	Local investors
1994	Paliva omarno	Slovak Republic	Industry/fuel	100.0	0.7	0.0	Local investors
1994	Podnik priemysel.automatizacie	Slovak Republic	Manufacturing	100.0	1.4	0.1	Local investors
1994	Podtatranske Konzervarne	Slovak Republic	Food processing	100.0	1.6	0.0	Local investors
1994	Pol'nohosp.stavby Malacky	Slovak Republic	Agriculture	100.0	2.0	0.0	Local investors
1994	Pol'nohosp.stavby Pies'any	Slovak Republic	Agriculture	100.0	3.2	0.0	Local investors
1994	Pol'nohospodarske stavby Presov	Slovak Republic	Agriculture	100.0	1.0	0.0	Local investors
1994	Pol'nonaup Slovpol Trencin	Slovak Republic	Agriculture	100.0	0.1	0.0	Local investors
1994	Pozcm	Slovak Republic	Agriculture	100.0	9.0	0.0	Local investors
1994	Pozemn	Slovak Republic	Construction	100.0	0.1	0.0	Local investors
1994	Senzor Kosice	Slovak Republic	Industry	100.0	0.8	0.0	Local investors
1994	Slovak magnezit. zavody Jelsava	Slovak Republic	Manufacturing/iron	100.0	19.0	0.0	Local investors
1994	Slovak magnezit. zavody Lubenik	Slovak Republic	Manufacturing/iron	100.0	13.9	0.0	Local investors
1994	Slovakofarma	Slovak Republic	Chemicals	100.0	48.8	48.8	Foreign investors
1994	Stavoinvesta Banska Bystrica	Slovak Republic	Construction	100.0	0.2	0.0	Local investors
1994	Stavoinvesta Bratislava	Slovak Republic	Construction	100.0	0.5	0.0	Local investors
1994	Stavoinvesta Kosice	Slovak Republic	Construction	100.0	0.1	0.0	Local investors
1994	Stavotechnika Zilina	Slovak Republic	Construction	100.0	0.1	0.0	Local investors
1994	Stredostav Zilina	Slovak Republic	Construction	100.0	0.5	0.0	Local investors
1994	Tatramat	Slovak Republic	Manufacturing	100.0	0.5	0.0	Local investors
1994	Tesla	Slovak Republic	Agriculture	100.0	7.3	0.0	Local investors
1994	Tesla Prievidza	Slovak Republic	Manufacturing	100.0	1.4	0.0	Local investors
1994	Topvar Topol'cany	Slovak Republic	Food processing	100.0	17.6	0.0	Local investors
1994	Trnava masovy priemysel Trnava	Slovak Republic	Food processing	100.0	1.5	0.0	Local investors
1994	UEOS Bratislava	Slovak Republic	Services	100.0	0.7	0.0	Local investors
1994	Ustav cest.hospod dopravy	Slovak Republic	Transportation	100.0	3.0	0.0	Local investors
1994	VSZ akciova spolocnost Kosice	Slovak Republic	Manufacturing	75.0	10.0	0.0	Local investors
1994	VU sprac.a aplik.plast.latok	Slovak Republic	Industry	100.0	2.9	0.0	Local investors
1994	VUIS Bratislava	Slovak Republic	Industry	100.0	1.1	0.0	Local investors
1994	VUJE Trnava	Slovak Republic	Industry	100.0	7.5	0.0	Local investors
1994	Zapadoslov Chynorany	Slovak Republic	Services	100.0	4.4	0.0	Local investors
1994	Zapadoslov Trnava	Slovak Republic	Services	100.0	6.1	0.0	Local investors
1994	ZDROJ Kosice	Slovak Republic	Construction/material	100.0	4.2	0.0	Local investors
1994	Zipp Bratislava	Slovak Republic	Manufacturing	100.0	6.0	0.0	Local investors
1994	Zlatokov Trencin	Slovak Republic	Manufacturing	100.0	1.9	0.0	Local investors
1994	ZPA Dulka Presov	Slovak Republic	Industry	100.0	17.6	0.0	Local investors
1995	Agrozet Zvolen	Slovak Republic	Agriculture	100.0	3.5	0.0	Local investor
1995	Baliarne OBCHODU a.s. POPRAD	Slovak Republic	Food	200.0	13.1	0.0	Local investor
1995	Benzinol	Slovak Republic	Petroleum	51.0	43.7	0.0	Local investor
1995	Bucna	Slovak Republic	Wood/cellulose materials	100.0	6.7	0.0	Local investor
1995	Bukoza	Slovak Republic	Wood/cellulose materials	100.0	0.9	0.0	Local investor
1995	Cementaren Turna	Slovak Republic	Construction	61.0	8.5	0.0	Local investor
1995	Chemes	Slovak Republic	Chemicals	61.7	22.1	0.0	Local investor
1995	Clara s.p. Utekac	Slovak Republic	Glass	100.0	4.9	0.0	Local investor
1995	Danubius Elektrik Bratislava	Slovak Republic	Engineering	100.0	4.3	0.0	Local investor
1995	Data-Zdroj	Slovak Republic	Food	54.0	2.0	0.0	Local investor
1995	Doprastav	Slovak Republic	Construction	66.0	10.8	0.0	Local investor

(table continues on next page)

Table A6.10 Privatization transactions in developing countries, 1994–95 (continued)

(millions of U.S. dollars)

Year	Company	Country	Sector	Equity share Percent	Amount	Foreign exchange	Purchaser
1995	Dopravnomech	Slovak Republic	Transport	100.0	1.9	0.0	Local investor
1995	Drevovyvoj	Slovak Republic	Wood/cellulose materials	100.0	0.9	0.0	Local investor
1995	Drobny tovar Presov s.p.	Slovak Republic	Trade	100.0	4.2	0.0	Local investor
1995	Drotovna	Slovak Republic	Metal industry	100.0	1.3	0.0	Local investor
1995	Dubravanak	Slovak Republic	Food	88.0	1.3	0.0	Local investor
1995	Duslo	Slovak Republic	Chemicals	70.0	89.7	0.0	Local investor
1995	Elektrovod Zilina	Slovak Republic	Energy utility	54.0	3.9	0.0	Local investor
1995	ELV Produkt	Slovak Republic	Engineering	70.0	3.9	0.0	Local investor
1995	EZ Elektrosystemy Bratislava	Slovak Republic	Electronics	100.0	5.6	0.0	Local investor
1995	Fatra	Slovak Republic	Food	100.0	3.2	0.0	Local investor
1995	Gastropol Presov	Slovak Republic	Food	100.0	3.7	0.0	Local investor
1995	GeLiMa	Slovak Republic	Food	78.4	10.5	10.5	Foreign investor
1995	Hirocem	Slovak Republic	Chemicals	100.0	17.9	14.5	Foreign investor
1995	Hotel Tatra	Slovak Republic	Services	54.0	1.8	0.0	Local investor
1995	Interhotely Tatry, s.p.	Slovak Republic	Services	100.0	4.9	0.0	Local investor
1995	Juhozdroj, a.s. Hurbanovo	Slovak Republic	Food	54.0	3.4	0.0	Local investor
1995	Korasan Rajec	Slovak Republic	Textiles	100.0	7.6	0.0	Local investor
1995	Levicky masovy priemysel	Slovak Republic	Food	67.0	4.5	0.0	Local investor
1995	Levitex	Slovak Republic	Textiles	54.0	3.8	0.0	Local investor
1995	Liptovske liecebne kupele	Slovak Republic	Health service	81.0	4.2	0.0	Local investor
1995	Lute	Slovak Republic	Textiles	54.0	1.8	0.0	Local investor
1995	Lykove textilne zavody Revuca	Slovak Republic	Textiles	100.0	19.5	0.0	Local investor
1995	Malokarpatsky vinarsky podnik	Slovak Republic	Food	100.0	15.4	0.0	Local investor
1995	Maso-Vychod	Slovak Republic	Food	54.0	9.7	0.0	Local investor
1995	Masovy priemysel Lucenec s.p.	Slovak Republic	Food	100.0	14.8	0.0	Local investor
1995	Mineralne vody	Slovak Republic	Food	64.0	7.3	0.0	Local investor
1995	Montaze	Slovak Republic	Construction	70.0	2.5	0.0	Local investor
1995	Nabytok Presov	Slovak Republic	Wood/cellulose materials	70.0	5.4	0.0	Local investor
1995	Obch.-semen.podnik Kosice	Slovak Republic	Agriculture	100.0	7.5	0.0	Local investor
1995	Ocna optika	Slovak Republic	Health service	100.0	1.0	0.0	Local investor
1995	Ozeta, a.s. Trencin	Slovak Republic	Textiles	97.1	1.4	0.0	Local investor
1995	Petrochema, s.p. Dubova	Slovak Republic	Chemicals	100.0	21.9	0.0	Local investor
1995	Pilo Impregna Kosice	Slovak Republic	Engineering	100.0	6.5	0.0	Local investor
1995	Povazska cementaren	Slovak Republic	Construction	61.0	7.6	0.0	Local investor
1995	Prefabrikat Velke Levare s.p.	Slovak Republic	Construction	100.0	15.7	0.0	Local investor
1995	Priemstav s.p. Bratislava	Slovak Republic	Construction	100.0	18.4	0.0	Local investor
1995	Raselinove zavody Bratislava	Slovak Republic	Agriculture	100.0	10.3	0.0	Local investor
1995	Rempex s.p. Bratislava	Slovak Republic	Trade	100.0	5.2	0.0	Local investor
1995	SIRAVAR a.s., Michalovce	Slovak Republic	Food	54.0	2.0	0.0	Local investor
1995	Skloobal a.s. Nemsova	Slovak Republic	Glass	73.3	4.8	0.0	Local investor
1995	Skloplast	Slovak Republic	Glass	70.0	40.0	0.0	Local investor
1995	Slopak Malacky	Slovak Republic	Food	100.0	4.2	0.0	Local investor
1995	Slovak magnezit. zavody Hacava	Slovak Republic	Metal industry	100.0	30.0	0.0	Local investor
1995	Slovak zavody tech. skla	Slovak Republic	Glass	70.0	4.7	0.0	Local investor
1995	Slovenska armaturka Myjava	Slovak Republic	Metal industry	100.0	1.9	0.0	Local investor
1995	Slovenske sladovne Trnava	Slovak Republic	Agriculture	100.0	9.0	0.0	Local investor
1995	Slovnaft	Slovak Republic	Petroleum	20.0	112.7	112.7	EBRD, Slovak and Czech Institutional Investors
1995	Slovnaft	Slovak Republic	Petroleum	38.0	216.2	0.0	Slovintegra (Employees)

Table A6.10 Privatization transactions in developing countries, 1994–95 (continued)

(millions of U.S. dollars)

Year	Company	Country	Sector	Equity share Percent	Amount	Foreign exchange	Purchaser
1995	Slovpanel	Slovak Republic	Construction	70.0	1.0	0.0	Local investor
1995	St. Nicolaus	Slovak Republic	Food	100.0	4.7	0.0	Local investor
1995	Stavohotely Bratislava	Slovak Republic	Construction	100.0	4.8	0.0	Local investor
1995	Stavomontaze	Slovak Republic	Construction	100.0	1.5	0.0	Local investor
1995	Strojarne Malacky	Slovak Republic	Metal industry	70.0	3.3	0.0	Local investor
1995	Strojsmalt	Slovak Republic	Metal industry	54.0	1.5	0.0	Local investor
1995	Tos Trencin	Slovak Republic	Metal industry	97.5	1.1	0.0	Local investor
1995	Trebisovske strojarne	Slovak Republic	Engineering	70.0	1.7	0.0	Local investor
1995	Trenzdroj	Slovak Republic	Food	100.0	1.2	0.0	Local investor
1995	Turcianske drevarske zavody	Slovak Republic	Wood/cellulose materials	100.0	8.6	0.0	Local investor
1995	Vahostav	Slovak Republic	Construction	100.0	1.2	0.0	Local investor
1995	Vinoprodukt	Slovak Republic	Food	100.0	3.5	0.0	Local investor
1995	VSZ akciova spolocnost Kosice	Slovak Republic	Metal	100.0	28.0	0.0	Local investor
1995	Zastrova	Slovak Republic	Engineering	54.0	0.8	0.0	Local investor
1995	Zavody 29.augusta Partizanske	Slovak Republic	Footwear	100.0	15.0	0.0	Local investor
1995	Zdroj Banska Bystrica s.p.	Slovak Republic	Food	100.0	8.7	0.0	Local investor
1995	Zdroj Kosice OZ 11-02 Bardejov	Slovak Republic	Food	100.0	3.0	0.0	Local investor
1995	Zekon Michalovce	Slovak Republic	Textiles	100.0	4.2	0.0	Local investor
1995	ZOS Vrutky	Slovak Republic	Transport	80.0	8.5	0.0	Local investor
1995	ZOS Zvolen	Slovak Republic	Transport	80.0	6.1	0.0	Local investor
1995	Krka	Slovenia	Pharmaceuticals	60.0	81.0		
1995	Mercator	Slovenia		34.0	70.0		
1995	Radenska	Slovenia	Mineral water	75.0	7.1	7.1	Coca-Cola Amatil (Australian)
1994	Coca-Cola Franchise	Sri Lanka	Food processing	51.0	2.6	0.0	Local investor
1995	Agalawatte Plantations Ltd.	Sri Lanka	Agriculture	51.0	2.6	0.0	Local investor
1995	Bogawantalawa Plantations Ltd	Sri Lanka	Agriculture	40.0	6.9	0.0	Local investor
1995	Capital Development and Investment Co.	Sri Lanka	Financial services/banking	51.0	37.0	37.4	Shell Co.
1995	Colombo Gas Co. Ltd	Sri Lanka	Petroleum/petrochemicals	51.0	2.6	0.0	Local investor
1995	Horana Plantations Ltd.	Sri Lanka	Agriculture	51.0	2.6	0.0	Local investor
1995	Kegalle Plantations	Sri Lanka	Agriculture	51.0	2.6	0.0	Local investor
1995	Kelani Valley Plantations Ltd.	Sri Lanka	Agriculture	55.0	0.3	0.0	Local investor
1995	Koragala Plantations Ltd.	Sri Lanka	Agriculture	51.0	5.7	0.0	Local investor
1995	Statcon Rubber Co. Ltd	Sri Lanka	Agriculture	90.0	1.7	0.0	Jayagiri Transporters Ltd.
1995	Watawala Plantations Ltd.	Sri Lanka	Agriculture	90.0	0.6	0.0	Lanka Agencies
1994	Colombo Commercial Company	Sri Lanka	Agribusiness supplies	51.0	10.0	0.0	Caltex Trading Company
1994	Kantale Sugar Industries	Sri Lanka	Manufacturing	60.0	2.9	0.0	Globe Commercial Trading ltd.
1994	Lanka Lubricant Ltd.	Sri Lanka	Manufacturing	60.0	3.1	0.0	Local investors; Hattos National Bank
1994	Lanka Tractors Ltd.	Sri Lanka	Trading	100.0	1.3	0.0	E.H. Cooray and Yoshoda Enterprises ltd
1994	Peoples Merchant Bank Lts.	Sri Lanka	Banking	90.0	0.6	0.0	Yoshoda Enterprise
1994	Plywoods Company Ltd.	Sri Lanka	Plywood manufacturing	55.0	20.0	0.0	
1994	Ruhunu Agro Fertilizer Ltd.	Sri Lanka	Agricultural supplies	51.0	1.5	0.0	John Keells Holding Co; National Development Bank, Central Finance Co.
1994	Steel Corp.	Sri Lanka	Steel	90.0	0.5	0.0	CIC Fertilizer Company Ltd
1994	Tea Small Holders Ltd.	Sri Lanka	Agriculture	51.0	0.0	0.0	
1994	Wyamba Fertilizer Co.	Sri Lanka	Trading	70.0	0.2	0.0	Local investor
1995	Blanket Manufacturers Ltd.	Tanzania	Textiles	60.0	0.7	0.7	Docare Ltd.
1995	Imara Wood Products	Tanzania	Natural resources	—	0.2	0.2	Switzerland/Singapore
1995	Keko Pharmaceuticals	Tanzania	Chemicals				
1995	Kibaha Factory	Tanzania	Agriculture				

(table continues on next page)

151

Table A6.10 Privatization transactions in developing countries, 1994–95 (continued)

(millions of U.S. dollars)

Year	Company	Country	Sector	Equity share Percent	Amount	Foreign exchange	Purchaser
1995	Masasi Factory	Tanzania	Agriculture	—	0.1	0.1	Kenya Assets
1995	Mbaya Ceramics Co.	Tanzania	Manufacturing/ceramics	100.0	0.0	0.0	Kyela Valley
1995	Mbozi Coffee Farms Ltd	Tanzania	Agriculture	100.0	1.4		
1995	Mkata Saw Mills	Tanzania	Natural resources	100.0	0.2		
1995	Mulipurpose Oil Processing Co. Ltd	Tanzania	Agriculture	80.0	3.0	0.0	Local investor
1995	Nachingwea Factory	Tanzania	Agriculture	—	0.1	0.1	Beechomber
1995	National Poultry Co. Ltd	Tanzania	Agriculture	100.0	1.4		
1995	New Savoy Hotel	Tanzania	Tourism	100.0	0.2	0.0	Local investor
1995	Nilarna Factory	Tanzania	Agriculture	—	0.1	0.1	Export Trading
1995	T. Pharmaceutical Ind.	Tanzania	Chemicals	60.0	1.4	1.4	Pharmac. Inv.
1995	Tang Meerschaum Company	Tanzania	Mining	70.0	0.2	0.0	Local investor
1995	Tanga Cement Co. Ltd	Tanzania	industry	51.0	11.5	11.5	Holderbank
1995	Tanzania Cigarette Co.	Tanzania	industry	41.0	55.0	55.0	R.J. Reynolds
1995	Tanzania Shoe Company	Tanzania	Manufacturing	100.0	1.2	0.0	Local investor
1994	Kisarawa Brick Factory	Tanzania	Manufacturing	70.0	1.4	0.0	Universal Electric
1994	Morogoro Canvas	Tanzania	Manufacturing	75.0	2.3	2.3	Carpet Manufacturing
1994	Tanzanian Post Bank	Tanzania	Banking	19.0	—	—	
1994	Williamson Diamonds	Tanzania	Mining	75.0	1.2	1.2	Wilcraft
1994	Bankchak Petroleum Public Co., Ltd.	Thailand	Petroleum/petrochemicals	20.0	41.8	13.0	Investors
1994	Electricity Generating Public Co., Ltd.	Thailand	Power utility	51.0	180.0	50.4	Investors
1994	PTT Exploration & Production Public Co., Ltd.	Thailand	Petroleum/petrochemicals	29.0	20.0	12.0	Investors
1995	Railway Management Co.	Togo	Transport	—	—	—	Foreign company
1995	BWIA	Trinidad & Tobago	Airlines	51.0	26.0	20.0	Local investors (18%), Loeb Investmwnt Corp./The Acker Group
1995	National Fisheries	Trinidad & Tobago	Agribusiness	51.0	2.3	2.3	Kwo Jeng Trading Comp. Ltd.
1994	Airline Caterers Ltd.	Trinidad & Tobago	Services/food	40.0	1.0	1.0	Alpha Flight Services Ltd.
1994	Arawak Cement Comp.	Trinidad & Tob-go	Cement	100.0	1.1	0.0	Local investors
1994	Iron & Steel Comp. of Trinidad & Tobago	Trinidad & Tobago	Steel	100.0	70.5	70.5	Caribbean Ispat Ltd.
1994	National Poultry Company	Trinidad & Tobago	Agribusiness	100.0	1.1	0.0	Local investors
1994	Petroleum company of Trinidad & Tobago	Trinidad & Tobago	Petroleum/petrochemicals	100.0	4.4	4.4	Foreing investors
1994	Point Lisas Industrial Port Development Corp.	Trinidad & Tobago	Transportation	47.5	4.2	0.0	Trinidad & Tobago Stock Exchange
1994	Polymer Ltd.	Trinidad & Tobago	Manufacturing	25.5	0.1	0.0	Local investors
1994	Trinidad & Tobago Electricity	Trinidad & Tobago	Power Utility	49.0	107.5	107.5	Southern Electric International/Amoco Business Dev. Company
1994	Trinidad & Tobago Methanol Comp.	Trinidad & Tobago	Chemicals	31.0	47.0	47.0	Ferrostaal A.G.(26%) ; Helm A.G. (5%)
1994	Trinidad & Tobago Mortgage Finance	Trinidad & Tobago	Financial Services	2.6	0.2	0.0	Local investors
1994	Trinidad Cement Ltd.	Trinidad & Tobago	Cement	20.0	10.8	10.8	Cemento Mexicanos
1995	SEK	Tunisia	Industry	75.1			
1995	Societe Transp. Marchandises de Kairouan	Tunisia	Transport	—	0.5	0.0	Local investors
1995	Societe Transp. Marchandises de Medrini	Tunisia	Transport	—	0.7	0.0	Local investors
1995	Societe. Transp. Marchandises de Kasserine	Tunisia	Transport	—	0.0	0.0	Local investors
1995	SOSTEM	Tunisia	Industry	51.0	9.2	0.0	Local investor
1995	Tunis Air	Tunisia	Airlines	15.0	22.0		
1995	Abana	Turkey	Electrical		0.3		
1995	Adiyaman Cimento	Turkey	Cement	100.0	52.5	0.0	Local investor
1995	Cinkur	Turkey	Mining	—	0.1	0.0	Local investor
1995	Deniz Nakliyati	Turkey	Shipping	—	13.0		Local investor
1995	EBK	Turkey	Agriculture	—	41.3	0.0	Local investors
1995	Fruko Tamek Meyva	Turkey			1.7	0.0	Local investor
1995	Havas	Turkey	Airport services	60.0	36.0	0.0	Local investor

152

Table A6.10 Privatization transactions in developing countries, 1994–95 (continued)

(millions of U.S. dollars)

Year	Company	Country	Sector	Equity share Percent	Amount	Foreign exchange	Purchaser
1995	Konya Seker Fabrikan	Turkey	Food processing	24.0	9.8	0.0	Local investor
1995	Koyteks	Turkey	Industry	—	0.3	0.0	Local investor
1995	Kumas	Turkey	Mining	99.7	108.1	0.0	Local investor
1995	Metas	Turkey	Metallurgy	42.6	57.9	—	
1995	Petkim	Turkey	Petrochemicals		2.0		Local investor
1995	SEK	Turkey	Agribusiness		68.5	0.0	Local investors
1995	Sivas	Turkey	Mining	—	0.2	0.0	Local investor
1995	Sumer Holdings	Turkey	Textiles	—	11.7	0.0	Local investor
1995	Sumerbank	Turkey	Banking	100.0	103.5	0.0	Local investor
1995	Testas	Turkey	Electronics	—	1.2	1.2	Taiwan
1995	Tofas	Turkey	Automobiles	2.0	19.4	0.0	Local investor
1995	Turban	Turkey	Tourism		43.4	0.0	Local investor
1995	Yem Sanayi	Turkey	Agribusiness		0.8	0.0	Local investors
1994	AEG ETI	Turkey	Manufacturing	27.9	5.9	0.0	AEG Aktiengesellschaft
1994	Altec	Turkey	Power utility	30.0	0.6	0.0	Anmak Holding
1994	Canakkale Seramik	Turkey	Manufacturing/ceramics	5.8	0.9	0.0	Canakale Seramik
1994	Cestas	Turkey	Power utility	2.3	0.0	0.0	Cukurova Electrik A.S.
1994	Guneysu	Turkey	Food processing	67.3	0.3	0.0	Ayse Balci
1994	Hascan Gida	Turkey	Food processing	3.4	0.0	0.0	Ali Baysal
1994	Layne Bowler	Turkey	Manufacturing	4.2	0.0	0.0	Konya Seker Fab
1994	Pancar Motor	Turkey	Manufacturing	16.0	0.0	0.0	Seker Sanayi Vakfi
1994	Sivas Yem	Turkey	Agribusiness	3.6	0.0	0.0	Haluk Dincer
1994	TOFAS Otomobil Fabrikalari	Turkey	Auto manufacturing	17.0	346.5	330.0	Local and foreign investors (99%)
1994	Toros Ilac Paz	Turkey	Agribusiness	25.0	0.1	0.0	Teknik Servis
1995	Acholl Inn	Uganda	Tourism/hotel	100.0	0.0	0.0	Laco Ltd
1995	Hilltop Hotel	Uganda	Tourism/hotel	100.0	0.0	0.0	Unvex Ltd.
1995	Kampala Auto Centre	Uganda	Services		0.1	0.0	Management
1995	Lake Victoria Hotel	Uganda	Tourism		3.2	3.2	British investor
1995	Lira Hotel	Uganda	Tourism/hotel	100.0	0.3	0.0	Showa Trade Company
1995	Mt. Elgon Hotel	Uganda	Tourism/hotel	100.0	0.7	0.0	Bugisu Cooperative Union
1995	Mweya Safari Lodge	Uganda	Tourism		1.9	0.0	Local investors
1995	Nile Hotel Complex	Uganda	Tourism/hotel	60.0	28.9	14.4	African Continental Hotels(Uganda/Tunisia)
1995	Republic Motors	Uganda	Services		0.4	0.0	Local investors
1995	Sorol Hotel	Uganda	Tourism/hotel	100.0	0.2	0.0	Speedbird Aviation
1995	Tororo Cement Works	Uganda	Cement		5.9	0.0	Local investors
1995	Uganda Fisheries Enterprises	Uganda	Fisheries	100.0	1.1	1.1	Foreign investor (registered in Uganda)
1995	Uganda Hardwares Ltd.	Uganda	Manufacturing		0.3	0.0	Management
1995	Uganda Hire Purchase Co.	Uganda	Financial services/banking		0.0	0.0	Local investors
1995	Uganda Leather and Tanning Industry	Uganda	Leather products		1.8	—	Local and foreign investors
1995	Uganda Meat Packers Ltd	Uganda	Food processing/meat		0.7	0.0	Local investors
1995	Uganda Motors Ltd.	Uganda	Services	100.0	0.8	0.0	Management
1995	White Rhino Hotel	Uganda	Tourism		0.2		Local investors
1995	Winits (U) Ltd	Uganda	Manufacturing		0.3	0.0	Local investors
1994	Blenders (U) Ltd	Uganda	Manufacturing	49.0	0.5	0.5	Unilever Overseas Holding BVC (UK)
1994	Hotel Margherita	Uganda	Hotel	100.0	0.4	0.0	Reco Industries
1994	Mt. Moroto Hotel	Uganda	Hotel	100.0	0.0	0.0	Kodel International
1994	Rock Hotel	Uganda	Hotel	100.0	0.3	0.0	Local investors
1994	Steel Corp. of East Africa	Uganda	Steel	49.0	—	0.0	Local investor

(table continues on next page)

Table A6.10 Privatization transactions in developing countries, 1994–95 (continued)

(millions of U.S. dollars)

Year	Company	Country	Sector	Equity share Percent	Equity share Amount	Foreign exchange	Purchaser
1994	TUMPECO	Uganda		100.0	1.2	0.0	Local investors
1994	Uganda Cement Company	Uganda	Cement	85.0	20.5	20.5	Rawals Group of Industries
1994	Uganda Tea Corp.	Uganda	Food processing	51.0	—	0.0	Mehia Group
1994	White Horse Inn	Uganda	Hotel	100.0	0.6	0.0	Kabala Development Company
1995	Ukraina Chocolate	Ukraine	Manufacturing	88.4	—	0.0	Kraft Jacobs Suchard
1994	Ukrrechflot	Ukraine	Shipping		—		
1995	General Industry Corporation	United Arab Emirates	Manufacturing		190.0		
1995	Aeropuerto Internacional Laguna del Sauce	Uruguay	Transportation	25.5	—	—	
1994	Administracion Nacional de Puertos	Uruguay	Port utilities	—	—	—	
1994	Compania del Gas de Montevideo	Uruguay	Gas	—	—	—	
1994	Pluna	Uruguay	Airlines	51.0	2.0	1.0	Consortium of Argentine and Uruguaian companies
1994	Uzbek Tobacco	Uzbekistan	Tobacco	51.0	212.0	212.0	BAT industries
1995	Ensal-Sucre	Venezuela	Salt	70.0	24.1	—	International consortium
1995	Industrias Lacteas de Venezuela (Indulac)	Venezuela	Food processing	41.4	14.7	14.7	Parmalat(Italy)
1994	Banco de Fomeno de Coro	Venezuela	Banking	41.6	4.0	0.0	
1994	Central Urena	Venezuela	Sugar	100.0	3.0	0.0	CIAMSA
1994	Hotel Moruco	Venezuela	Hotel	100.0	0.9	0.0	Local investor(UK)
1994	Inchinbrok	Vietnam	Insurance	—	—		Inchape(UK)
1995	Abyan Rest House	Yemen	Hotel	100.0	0.0	0.0	Local investor
1995	Arwa Rest House	Yemen	Hotel	100.0	0.0	0.0	Local investor
1995	Crescent Hotel	Yemen	Hotel	100.0	0.1	0.0	Local investor
1995	Dar El Hajar	Yemen	Hotel	100.0	0.0	0.0	Local investor
1995	Gold Mohr Hotel	Yemen	Hotel	100.0	0.5	0.0	Local investor
1995	Rock Hotel	Yemen	Hotel	100.0	0.1	0.0	Local investor
1995	Chilanga Cement	Zambia	Cement	37.3	9.0	0.0	
1995	Northern Breweries	Zambia	Brewery	51.0	1.9	—	Lonrho Zambia
1995	Refined Oil Products	Zambia	Food processing	70.0	8.3	—	Lever Brothers (Zambia)
1995	Zambia Sugar Company	Zambia	Agribusiness	40.0	50.0	50.0	Tate & Lyle and CDC
1995	Delta Corporation	Zimbabwe	Tourism	—	75.0	14.6	Foreign and local investors
1994	Harley Platinum Project	Zimbabwe	Mining	—	225.0	225.0	BHP & Delta Gold of Australia
1994	Tinto Industries	Zimbabwe	Manufacturing	100.0	6.5	6.5	FSI Holdings (South Africa)

— Not available.

Source: World Bank Privatization Database, International Economics Department.

Regional trends in debt and flows

	1986	1995	1996[a]
Total debt outstanding	1,132.4	2,065.7	2,177.0
World Bank/IDA	91.4	183.4	190.4
Concessional share (%)	17.1	21.1	19.9
Net resource flows	66.3	237.2	284.6
Net transfers	2.4	136.3	175.6
Debt service/exports (%)	23.6	17.0	16.4

a. Preliminary.

Global overview

Aggregate net resource flows to low- and middle-income countries rose to an estimated $285 million in 1996, an increase of 20.0 percent over 1995. Net flows from private sources rose $60 billion, while official development finance fell $12 billion. Official flows were driven largely by the $10.5 billion (excluding the IMF's contribution) rescue package to Mexico in 1995 and by Mexico's $7 billion prepayment in 1996. Excluding these transactions, net official lending increased in 1996.

Private capital flows continued the strong growth achieved in 1995. Net bond flows jumped 62 percent to $46.1 billion. Portfolio equity flows rose 42 percent to $45.7 billion and foreign direct investment rose from the 1995 level of $95.5 billion to $109.5 billion in 1996, mainly led by China's $6.5 billion increase. Other countries with significant increases were India, Vietnam, and several Latin American countries.

The 9 percent rise in export earnings in 1996 outpaced the 5 percent rise in the stock of debt. The ratio of debt to exports declined in all regions except East Asia and the Pacific (owing to a sharp rise in private nonguaranteed debt), and debt service ratios declined in all regions except Latin America (owing to the prepayment of debt from the Mexico rescue package). Further progress was made in debt restructurings, as seven countries reduced their debt to commercial banks by a total of $5.5 billion and fifteen countries reached agreements on rescheduling their debt to Paris Club creditors. The total arrears of low- and middle-income countries fell by $19.9 billion in 1996, mostly due to Russia's debt restructuring agreements. Many poor countries failed to make significant progress toward a sustainable debt burden, however.

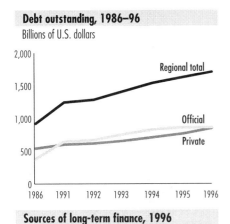

Debt outstanding, 1986–96
Billions of U.S. dollars

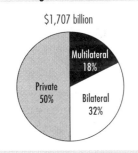

Sources of long-term finance, 1996

$1,707 billion

Multilateral 18%
Bilateral 32%
Private 50%

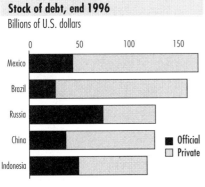

Stock of debt, end 1996
Billions of U.S. dollars

Mexico
Brazil
Russia
China
Indonesia

■ Official
□ Private

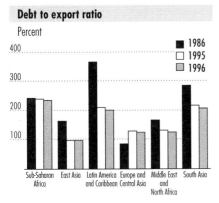

Debt to export ratio
Percent

■ 1986
□ 1995
▨ 1996

Sub-Saharan Africa / East Asia / Latin America and Caribbean / Europe and Central Asia / Middle East and North Africa / South Asia

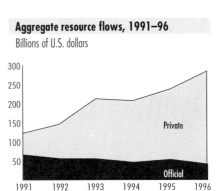

Aggregate resource flows, 1991–96
Billions of U.S. dollars

Private
Official

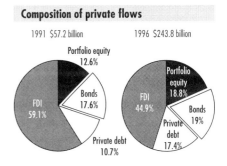

Composition of private flows

1991 $57.2 billion

Portfolio equity 12.6%
Bonds 17.6%
FDI 59.1%
Private debt 10.7%

1996 $243.8 billion

Portfolio equity 18.8%
Bonds 19%
FDI 44.9%
Private debt 17.4%

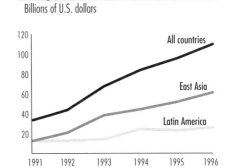

Foreign direct investment, 1991–96
Billions of U.S. dollars

All countries
East Asia
Latin America

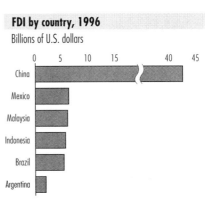

FDI by country, 1996
Billions of U.S. dollars

China
Mexico
Malaysia
Indonesia
Brazil
Argentina

Key indicators
Billions of U.S. dollars

	1986	1995	1996ᵃ
Total debt outstanding	139.7	226.5	235.4
World Bank/IDA	14.8	35.6	37.2
Concessional share (%)	24.6	34.8	34.6
Net resource flows	11.6	23.2	26.1
Net transfers	5.5	15.2	17.6
Debt service/exports (%)	25.1	14.5	12.4

a. Preliminary.

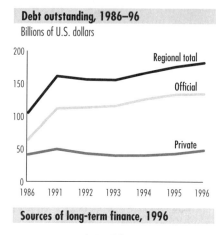

Debt outstanding, 1986–96
Billions of U.S. dollars

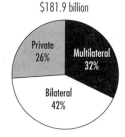

Sources of long-term finance, 1996

$181.9 billion

Private 26%
Multilateral 32%
Bilateral 42%

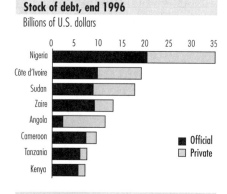

Stock of debt, end 1996
Billions of U.S. dollars

Nigeria, Côte d'Ivoire, Sudan, Zaire, Angola, Cameroon, Tanzania, Kenya

■ Official
□ Private

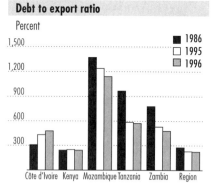

Debt to export ratio
Percent

■ 1986
□ 1995
▨ 1996

Côte d'Ivoire, Kenya, Mozambique, Tanzania, Zambia, Region

Sub-Saharan Africa

Increased export revenues coupled with moderate growth in outstanding debt resulted in a slight decline in the aggregate ratio of debt to exports in Sub-Saharan Africa. Still, many countries continued to face an unsustainable debt burden. Aggregate net transfers rose to an estimated $17.6 billion in 1996, or 5.6 percent of the region's GNP, the highest net transfer as a share of GNP of any region. Almost all official flows came in the form of bilateral grants or highly concessional loans from multilateral creditors; a net $1.1 billion was repaid on nonconcessional loans. Private flows are estimated to have increased strongly in 1996 to $11.7 billion, or 45 percent of total net flows, although the bulk of these flows are provided to only a few of the region's forty-eight countries (notably, Angola, Ghana, Nigeria, and South Africa).

DEBT AND INDICATORS

The total debt of Sub-Saharan African countries rose about 4 percent in 1996, a slower rate of increase than in 1995, when total debt rose 7 percent. Moreover, $7.1 billion of the $8.8 billion increase was incurred by South Africa, and another $0.7 billion was incurred by Ghana; elsewhere in the region countries registered marginal increases in debt or absolute declines. Private debt accounted for almost all of the increase in debt in 1996; public and publicly guaranteed debt increased by only about 0.2 percent.

DEBT IS LARGELY OWED BY AND TO GOVERNMENTS. Despite the strong rise in private nonguaranteed debt in 1996, 93 percent of Sub-Saharan Africa's long-term debt is owed to or guaranteed by debtor governments. Of the region's $182 billion in long-term debt, 74 percent is owed to official creditors (about 42 percent to multilateral agencies and the rest to bilateral creditors).

PRIVATE DEBT IS HIGHLY CONCENTRATED. The bulk of the region's $48.6 billion in private-source, long-term debt is owed by Angola, Cameroon, Côte d'Ivoire, Nigeria, and South Africa. Most private-source debt is in the form of commercial bank loans and export credits (a portion of which is guaranteed by official export credit agencies). At the end of 1996 countries in the region owed less than $4.5 billion in bonds and an estimated $44.8 billion in short-term loans, of which almost half represented interest arrears on long-term debt.

REDUCING AFRICA'S DEBT BURDEN HAS BECOME A MAJOR GOAL OF BILATERAL AND MULTILATERAL AGENCIES. Sub-Saharan Africa has become a major focus of efforts by official agencies to ease debt burdens, through Paris Club concessional reschedulings, commercial bank buybacks funded through IDA's Debt Reduction Facility, debt forgiveness by selected bilateral creditors, payments by bilateral creditors of debt service on multilateral debt, and most recently the initiative to solve the debt problem of heavily indebted poor countries. These efforts have eased short-term liquidity constraints facing many debtors and in some cases have resulted in significant declines in the net present value of the debt outstanding.

STILL, AFRICA'S DEBT BURDEN REMAINS HIGH. The region's aggregate ratio of debt to exports was estimated at 236.9 percent in 1996, down from 241.7 percent in 1995. If South Africa is excluded, the debt to exports ratio was 327.5 percent in 1996, a much higher share than the 146.2 percent average for low- and middle-

External debt and resource flows

income countries. This comparison is somewhat misleading, however, because a much higher portion of the region's debt (35 percent) is concessional than the average for developing countries (20 percent). Debt service paid fell from 14.5 percent of exports in 1995 to an estimated 12.4 percent in 1996, the lowest ratio this decade (and well below the almost 20 percent in the late 1980s), in part reflecting the estimated $4 billion increase in arrears. Of the forty-eight countries in Sub-Saharan Africa, thirty-one are classified as severely indebted low-income countries.

AGGREGATE RESOURCE FLOWS

Aggregate net flows to Sub-Saharan Africa rose 12 percent in 1996 to an estimated $26.1 billion. More than half of this amount came from official creditors. The $2.9 billion increase in net flows in 1996 reflects the rise in South Africa's borrowing from private creditors. Net flows from official sources rose by less than $200 million in 1996.

OFFICIAL DEVELOPMENT ASSISTANCE INCREASES SLIGHTLY BUT REMAINS BELOW HISTORICAL LEVELS. Official development assistance to Sub-Saharan Africa rose to an estimated $15.3 billion in 1996, slightly above 1995 levels but below the $16.1 billion a year provided in 1990-92. The region was the leading recipient of grants, which in 1996 totaled $11.8 billion (representing 38 percent of total grants received by developing countries in 1996). Grants have changed little in nominal terms since the early 1990s, but concessional lending from bilateral agencies has dropped sharply, from an average of $1.5 billion in 1990–92 to just $0.2 billion in 1996. Multilateral agencies provided $3.5 billion in concessional loans, of which IDA contributed $2.6 billion.

NET PRIVATE FLOWS RISE SHARPLY. Private flows have risen from less than $1 billion in the early 1990s to $11.8 billion in 1996 and now account for about 45 percent of net flows to Sub-Saharan Africa. Such flows are concentrated in only a few countries, however. Commercial bank lending to the region increased by an estimated $4 billion in 1996. However, South Africa accounted for $5.6 billion of the $5.8 billion borrowed from commercial banks in 1996, as several countries in the region reduced their exposure to commercial banks. More than half of the $0.8 billion in net bond issues were from South Africa, which tapped the market in three transactions by the government and in one by a public utility. Portfolio equity flows (of which 89 percent go to South Africa) declined by $1.3 billion, reflecting uncertainty about South Africa's prospects following depreciation of the rand. Foreign direct investment rose from $2.2 billion in 1995 to $2.6 billion in 1996, most of which was invested in the oil-exporting countries (Angola, Cameroon, Gabon, and Nigeria).

AFRICA CONTINUES TO BENEFIT FROM PARIS CLUB RESCHEDULINGS. Ten African countries reached rescheduling agreements with Paris Club creditors, most at a present value reduction of 67 percent on eligible debt (Naples terms). Benin, Burkina Faso, and Mali rescheduled their stock of debt outstanding; Chad, Congo, Mozambique, Niger, Sierra Leone, and Zambia rescheduled debt service due over one to two years; and Ghana rescheduled arrears due as of July 1995. In addition, Ethiopia, Mauritania, and Senegal reduced $0.5 billion in commercial bank debt (including interest arrears) through operations funded by IDA's Debt Reduction Facility, which includes funds from bilateral donors.

GNP per capita, 1995: $490

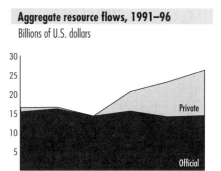

Aggregate resource flows, 1991–96
Billions of U.S. dollars

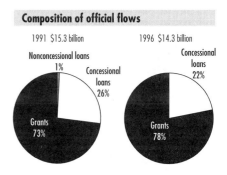

Composition of official flows

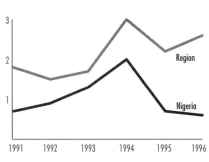

Foreign direct investment, 1991–96
Billions of U.S. dollars

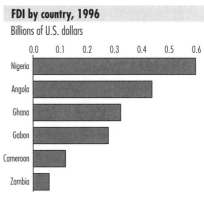

FDI by country, 1996
Billions of U.S. dollars

Key indicators
Billions of U.S. dollars

	1986	1995	1996[a]
Total debt outstanding	146.4	404.5	451.8
World Bank/IDA	15.4	37.6	38.9
Concessional share (%)	20.0	25.5	22.7
Net resource flows	12.7	95.8	116.1
Net transfers	3.3	71.7	88.5
Debt service/exports (%)	22.5	12.8	12.2

a. Preliminary.

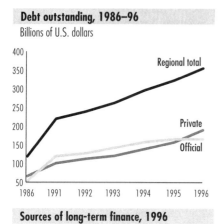

Debt outstanding, 1986–96
Billions of U.S. dollars

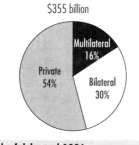

Sources of long-term finance, 1996

$355 billion

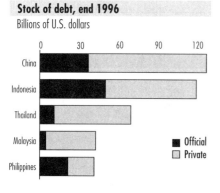

Stock of debt, end 1996
Billions of U.S. dollars

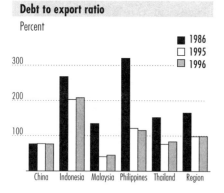

Debt to export ratio
Percent

East Asia and the Pacific

In East Asia and the Pacific an estimated 12 percent increase in debt stocks in 1996 raised the ratio of debt to exports to 99 percent. Debt service as a share of exports fell to just over 12 percent, much lower than the 16 percent average for low- and middle-income countries. The region received about 40 percent of aggregate flows to low- and middle-income countries, a smaller share than in 1995, largely reflecting the recovery in flows to Latin America. Aggregate net transfers rose 23 percent to more than $88 billion, equivalent to 6.0 percent of the combined GNP of the countries in the region.

DEBT AND INDICATORS

DEBT STOCKS INCREASE. The stock of debt in East Asia and the Pacific increased 12 percent to about $452 billion in 1996, following a 12 percent rise in 1995. The region accounted for about 21 percent of the total debt of developing countries, up from about 20 percent in 1995.

PRIVATE NONGUARANTEED DEBT BOOMS. The most significant development in the region's debt profile was the strong jump in disbursements on private nonguaranteed debt, in which a private creditor contracts with a private debtor without any form of guarantee from the debtor's government. Private nonguaranteed debt disbursements are estimated to have almost doubled to about $39 billion in 1996, from $20.8 billion in 1995. As a result, net inflows rose to about $29 billion, and the stock of private nonguaranteed debt in the region rose 50 percent, from $58 bil-

lion in 1995 to $87 billion in 1996, or 19 percent of total external debt. A substantial part of the new private nonguaranteed debt disbursements went to Indonesia, and significant activity was also seen in China, Malaysia, and Thailand.

SHORT-TERM DEBT INCREASES. Net short-term debt inflows increased significantly in 1995 and 1996, and short-term debt now accounts for about 21 percent of the region's total external debt, up from about 16 percent in 1989. The rise occurred in most of the region's major economies, but it has been concentrated in China, Indonesia, and Thailand and has been motivated by, among other things, differentials between domestic and international interest rates. In Thailand short-term debt now accounts for about 33 percent of total debt.

DEBT INDICATORS REMAIN HEALTHY. Although growth in the region's debt stock outpaced growth of exports, the region's debt to export ratio remained moderate at 99 percent in 1996, much lower than the average debt to export ratio of 146 percent for low- and middle-income countries. The region's ratio of debt service to exports fell to about 12 percent, much lower than South Asia's 23 percent and Latin America's 30 percent.

DEBT BURDENS VARY. The debt to export ratio rose in Indonesia, Malaysia, and Thailand but fell in China and the Philippines. Within the region debt to export ratios ranged from 19 percent

External debt and resource flows

(Fiji) to 451 percent (Lao PDR), while debt to GNP ratios ranged from 15 percent (China) to 113 percent (Vietnam). The countries with the heaviest estimated burden of debt service as a percentage of exports are Indonesia (34 percent), the Philippines (19 percent), Papua New Guinea (18 percent), and Myanmar (18 percent).

NO DEBT IS RESCHEDULED IN 1996. There have been no new debt rescheduling agreements in East Asia since Cambodia's Paris Club deal in February 1995. Myanmar, however, is classified as a heavily indebted poor country. The Russian Federation is a major creditor of both countries.

AGGREGATE RESOURCE FLOWS

Aggregate net resource flows into East Asia rose about 21 percent in 1996 to $116 billion. About 66 percent of this total was non-debt-creating flows, and 96 percent was from private sources. The region accounted for about 41 percent of inflows to low- and middle-income countries and about 45 percent of private flows. Net inflows on long-term debt increased by about 50 percent to reach $39 billion, more than compensating for the modest declines in aggregate portfolio equity and grants.

FOREIGN DIRECT INVESTMENT TO CHINA RISES. For the region as a whole foreign direct investment rose by about $9 billion to $61 billion in 1996, largely as a result of an estimated $6 billion rise in investment flows into China. Modest increases in foreign direct investment were observed in Indonesia, Malaysia, the Philippines, Thailand, and Vietnam. Portfolio equity flows fell to $12.9 billion in 1996 from $14.7 billion in 1995. About 60 percent of portfolio equity to the region reflects direct investment in local exchanges; the rest is international equity issues. China continues to account for about 69 percent of foreign direct investment to the region and about 22 percent of portfolio equity.

REGIONAL BOND ISSUES RECOVER. Bond issuance rebounded in 1996, with the net inflow for the year estimated at $11.4 billion, up from about $7.9 billion in 1995 and $9.7 billion in 1994. Increased activity was observed in China, Indonesia, the Philippines, and Thailand; net inflows fell sharply in Malaysia. China and Malaysia issued bonds with 100 year maturities, and Indonesia was successful in diversifying its investor base into Europe.

AID FLOWS DECLINE AGAIN. Official development assistance to East Asia fell for the second consecutive year in 1996, as net concessional flows from multilateral lenders declined to just $1.1 billion, down from an average of $1.3 billion in 1991–95. The decline mainly reflected weaker flows to China and Indonesia. Grants to the region also fell slightly, from $3.1 billion to $2.8 billion. Official development assistance flows to East Asia now account for about 14 percent of all such aid to low- and middle-income countries, down from 15 percent in 1990.

GNP per capita, 1995: $800

Aggregate resource flows, 1991–96
Billions of U.S. dollars

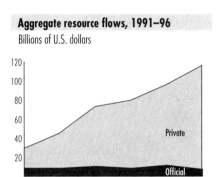

Composition of private flows

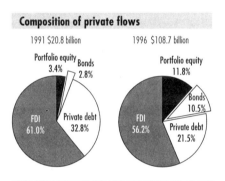

Foreign direct investment, 1991–96
Billions of U.S. dollars

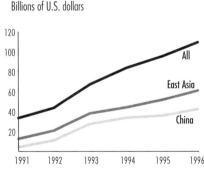

FDI by country, 1996
Billions of U.S. dollars

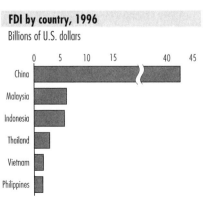

Key indicators

Billions of U.S. dollars

	1986	1995	1996[a]
Total debt outstanding	79.1	156.8	161.0
World Bank/IDA	19.6	42.0	43.1
Concessional share (%)	57.5	57.1	53.3
Net resource flows	9.6	8.4	17.0
Net transfers	7.2	2.3	11.4
Debt service/exports (%)	28.6	24.6	23.1

a. Preliminary.

Debt outstanding, 1986–96

Billions of U.S. dollars

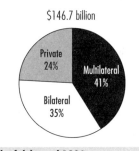

Sources of long-term finance, 1996

$146.7 billion

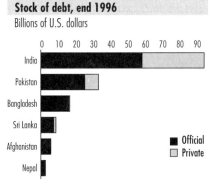

Private 24%
Multilateral 41%
Bilateral 35%

Stock of debt, end 1996

Billions of U.S. dollars

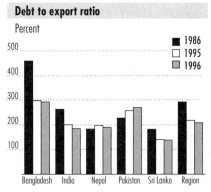

■ Official
□ Private

Debt to export ratio

Percent

■ 1986
□ 1995
▨ 1996

South Asia

Substantially stronger inflows of foreign investment to South Asia helped net aggregate inflows rebound to an estimated $17 billion in 1996, after having fallen to less than $9 billion in 1995 in the aftermath of the Mexican peso crisis. Stronger borrowing in 1996 raised the debt stock, which fell in 1995, but the region's ratio of debt to exports fell to 209 percent. South Asian economies continue to boast an impressive debt servicing record. The region is dominated by India, where reforms have attracted substantial volumes of private capital in recent years. South Asia is estimated to have received about 6 percent of total net aggregate flows to low- and middle-income countries in 1996, up from about 4 percent in 1995. Net transfers to the region increased to $11.4 billion, or about 2 percent of regional GNP in 1996.

DEBT AND DEBT INDICATORS

EXTERNAL DEBT STOCK RISES. An increase in disbursements to India and Pakistan in 1996 helped raise total debt outstanding in the region to an estimated $161 billion, up 2.5 percent over 1995. The region's debt accounted for about 7 percent of the outstanding external debt of low- and middle-income countries. India holds about 59 percent of the region's outstanding debt, Pakistan about 21 percent, and Bangladesh about 10 percent.

TWO-FIFTHS OF LONG-TERM DEBT IS OWED TO MULTILATERALS. About 40 percent of the region's long-term outstanding debt is owed to multilateral institutions, a much higher share than in Sub-Saharan Africa (32 percent) or Latin America (15 percent). The largest multilateral creditor is IDA, which holds about half the multilateral debt stock and 19 percent of total debt.

PRIVATE NONGUARANTEED DEBT IS GROWING. Private debt not guaranteed by the debtor governments increased to 6.1 percent of the region's debt stock in 1996, up from 5.3 percent in 1995 and just 1.9 percent in 1993. About 75 percent of private nonguaranteed debt is owed by India, where the stock is estimated to have increased to $7.4 billion in 1996, up from about $1.8 billion in 1993.

THE REGION'S DEBT SERVICING RECORD REMAINS IMPRESSIVE. South Asia continues to be the one region that has managed to keep arrears low and avoid debt restructuring during the past decade.

DEBT BURDEN INDICATORS ARE HIGH BUT IMPROVING. The rise in the debt stock in 1996 was more than compensated for by stronger regional exports, and the debt to export ratio is estimated to have fallen to about 209 percent in 1996 from about 219 percent in 1995, the fourth straight year of improvement. The ratio of debt to GNP fell to about 28 percent, down from 31 percent in 1995 and 36 percent in 1994, and the ratio of debt service to exports fell from about 25 percent in 1995 to about 23 percent in 1996.

Steady improvement in the region is driven by events in India, where large principal repayments and a stronger dol-

External debt and resource flows

GNP per capita, 1995: $350

lar helped the dollar valuation of the debt stock fall about 8 percent in 1995. Despite an increase in disbursements in 1996, India's debt to export ratio fell to 186 percent, well below the average level of just over 300 percent for the previous seven years. India's ratio of debt service to exports fell from about 28 percent to about 25 percent.

COUNTRY EXPERIENCES IN THE REGION VARY. In Pakistan a deterioration in the current account deficit in 1996 was financed in part by stronger net flows of external borrowing. As a result Pakistan's debt to export ratio rose to 270 percent from 258 percent in 1995, and the debt service ratio rose to 29 percent, the highest in the region. Debt to export ratios in Bangladesh, Nepal, and Sri Lanka all improved slightly in 1996. Within the region debt to export ratios ranged from 72 percent (Bhutan) to 292 percent (Bangladesh), and debt-GNP ratios ranged from 26 percent (India) to 62 percent (Sri Lanka).

AGGREGATE RESOURCES FLOWS

A rebound in portfolio equity inflows, direct investment, and long-term borrowing helped boost aggregate resource inflows to South Asia to nearly $17 billion in 1996, after having fallen to less than $9 billion in 1995. India accounted for about 75 percent of the increase. Portfolio equity flows to India are estimated to have increased substantially in 1996, and the net disbursements of long-term debt to the region as a whole increased by $4.4 billion to about $6.2

billion. Higher borrowing meant that the share of non-debt-creating flows fell to an estimated 62 percent in 1996.

OFFICIAL DEVELOPMENT ASSISTANCE REBOUNDS. Preliminary estimates suggest that net official development assistance to South Asia increased to about $6 billion in 1996, after having fallen to just $3.3 billion in 1995, partly as a result of a large prepayment by India on a concessional loan to a bilateral creditor. Grants (excluding technical assistance) remained constant at an estimated $2.5 billion in 1996, equivalent to about 14 percent of net resource inflows to the region. South Asia received about 8 percent of total grants to developing countries.

NET PRIVATE FLOWS MORE THAN DOUBLED, ACCOUNTING FOR TWO-THIRDS OF AGGREGATE FLOWS. Much stronger portfolio equity flows to India and stronger foreign direct investment and higher borrowing for the region all contributed to a rise in net private flows from about $5.2 billion in 1995 to about $10.7 billion in 1996, or 63 percent of aggregate flows. The continued upward trend in foreign direct investment to India was offset in 1996 by a decrease in foreign direct investment to Pakistan and very small inflows in Sri Lanka and Bangladesh.

LARGE REPAYMENTS LEAD TO NEGATIVE FLOWS ON BONDS IN 1996. Net flows on international bonds were negative in 1996, with nearly $2 billion in repayments falling due. New bonds worth about $0.6 billion were issued in India and Pakistan.

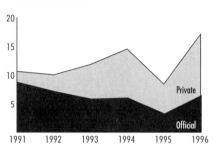

Aggregate resource flows, 1991–96
Billions of U.S. dollars

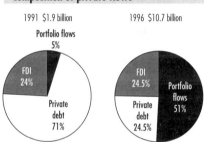

Composition of private flows

Foreign direct investment, 1991–96
Billions of U.S. dollars

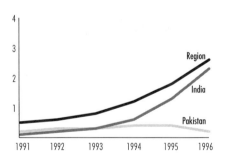

FDI by country, 1996
Billions of U.S. dollars

Key indicators
Billions of U.S. dollars

	1986	1995	1996ᵃ
Total debt outstanding	185.4	425.3	451.4
World Bank/IDA	10.1	16.9	18.9
Concessional share (%)	6.7	11.3	10.3
Net resource flows	6.3	40.6	45.3
Net transfers	-3.1	25.5	29.7
Debt service/exports (%)	14.2	13.8	11.3

a. Preliminary.

Long-term debt outstanding, 1986–96
Billions of U.S. dollars

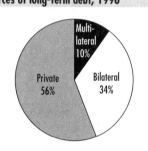

Sources of long-term debt, 1996

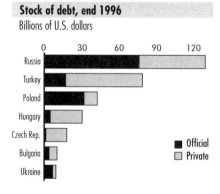

Stock of debt, end 1996
Billions of U.S. dollars

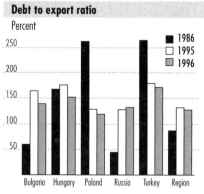

Debt to export ratio
Percent

Europe and Central Asia

Export earnings in Europe and Central Asia rose 9.9 percent (in dollar terms) in 1996, outpacing the rate of increase in debt and leading to a slight reduction in the aggregate debt to export ratio. Aggregate net transfers to the region continued to rise, reaching an estimated $29.7 billion in 1996 (2 percent of GNP), up from $25.5 billion in 1995. The largest net transfers were recorded by the few countries with access to private markets, notably Poland ($5.8 billion), the Russian Federation ($5.7 billion), Greece ($2.9 billion), and Romania ($2.5 billion). Total official development finance to the region increased in 1996, and a number of countries continued to benefit from concessional assistance. However, total official development assistance fell from $10.1 billion in 1995 to an estimated $8.9 billion in 1996, largely as a result of a decline in grants to Poland after their peak level in 1995.

DEBT AND INDICATORS

DEBT STOCKS UP. Total external debt of Europe and Central Asia rose an estimated 6 percent in 1996, following a 7 percent increase in 1995. Most of the $26 billion increase in debt in 1996 was accounted for by only a few countries, including the Russian Federation ($8.5 billion), Greece ($7.9 billion), Turkey ($4.9 billion), Romania ($2.2 billion), and the Czech Republic ($1.3 billion). Total debt outstanding in the region was estimated at $451 billion in 1996, with 35 percent owed by Greece and Turkey.

MORE THAN HALF OF OUTSTANDING DEBT IS OWED TO PRIVATE CREDITORS. Countries in Europe and Central Asia owed an estimated 52 percent of their long-term external debt to private creditors in 1996. Greece and Turkey account-

ed for 40 percent of the region's private-source debt, and the Russian Federation accounted for another 24 percent. Some of the countries that emerged from the breakup of the Soviet Union and Yugoslavia are also beginning to access private markets. Belarus, Slovenia, Turkmenistan, and Ukraine, for example, each owe more than 20 percent of their long-term external debt to private creditors.

DEBT INDICATORS IMPROVE SLIGHTLY. The region's average ratio of debt to exports fell from 130.7 percent in 1995 to an estimated 126.3 percent in 1996. Significant improvements in the debt to export ratios of a few major borrowers (Hungary, Poland, Turkey) were offset by the deterioration in the Russian Federation's ratio, which rose from 127 percent in 1995 to an estimated 131 percent in 1996. Total debt service dropped from 13.8 percent of exports in 1995 to an estimated 11.3 percent in 1996.

AGGREGATE RESOURCE FLOWS

Aggregate resource flows to Europe and Central Asia rose from $40.6 billion in 1995 to an estimated $45.3 billion in 1996. Most of this increase reflected greater private flows to Greece and Turkey. Flows to Eastern Europe and the former Soviet republics rose only marginally, as an estimated $2.2 billion rise in net official lending was almost matched by a decline in private flows. The estimated $5 billion decline in net private flows to Hungary (which returned to historical levels following unusually large inflows in 1995) and a decline in private flows to the Czech Republic more than offset significant increases in private flows to Poland, Romania, and the Russian Federation.

External debt and resource flows

OFFICIAL FLOWS RISE SHARPLY. Total official development finance increased to an estimated $14.1 billion in 1996, up from $10.5 billion in 1995. Grants and concessional loans fell by about $2.6 billion as a result of a decline in grants to Poland. Nonconcessional lending rose sharply, however, from $0.4 billion in 1995 to $5.2 billion in 1996, with German loans to the Russian Federation accounting for a large portion of the increase. Net official development assistance to the region fell by an estimated $1.2 billion in 1996.

NET PRIVATE FLOWS HIT A NEW HIGH. Net private flows reached an estimated $31.2 billion in 1996, up from $30 billion in 1995. Commercial bank lending to the region declined from $4.4 billion in 1995 to an estimated $2.2 billion in 1996, largely as a result of slightly lower net lending to Greece, Hungary, and Turkey. Still, commercial bank lending to Europe and Central Asia remained far above the net repayment of $3.3 billion a year in 1990–92, as a number of countries achieved access to private markets. The decline in commercial bank lending was offset by a $200 million rise in bond issues and a $1.5 billion jump in other private lending.

PRIVATE NONDEBT FLOWS REMAIN HIGH. Foreign direct investment to developing countries in Europe and Central Asia fell from $17.2 billion in 1995 to an estimated $15 billion in 1996 but remained well above the levels of the early 1990s ($4.3 billion a year in 1990–92 and $8.5 billion in 1994). The 1995 figure reflected large-scale privatization in Hungary. By contrast, portfolio equity flows rose sharply in 1996 to an estimated $6.7 billion, up from almost zero in 1990–92 and just $2.8 billion in 1995. Equity issues in sup-

port of privatization programs in the Czech Republic, Greece, Hungary, Poland, and the Russian Federation accounted for the surge.

COMPOSITION OF PRIVATE FLOWS CHANGES SIGNIFICANTLY. From 1991 to 1996 the breakup of the Soviet Union and the transformation of Eastern European economies led to more than a threefold increase in net private flows—to $31.2 billion—as the Czech Republic, Poland, Romania, and the Russian Federation, joined Greece, Hungary, and Turkey in receiving more than $1 billion each in net private flows. Among the smaller countries, Croatia, Estonia, Lithuania, Slovakia, Slovenia, and Turkmenistan benefited from syndicated loans in 1996, while Cyprus, Estonia, Lithuania, and Slovenia tapped the international bond markets. Overall, the share of foreign direct investment has declined, while the share of portfolio equity, private loans, and bonds has risen.

THE RUSSIAN FEDERATION SIGNS MAJOR DEBT RESTRUCTURING AGREEMENTS. The Russian Federation reached an agreement with its Paris Club creditors in April 1996 to restructure $40.2 billion in outstanding debt. This agreement, the largest ever for the Paris Club, reschedules eligible debt service due at market rates and is closely tied to the Russian Federation's compliance with its IMF program. In September 1996 the Russian Federation completed the first phase of its 1995 agreement with London Club creditors, restructuring $20 billion of the $33 billion in debt covered by the agreement. Acting as a creditor, the Russian Federation reached agreement with Nicaragua to reduce that country's outstanding ruble debt by 90 percent and reschedule the remainder.

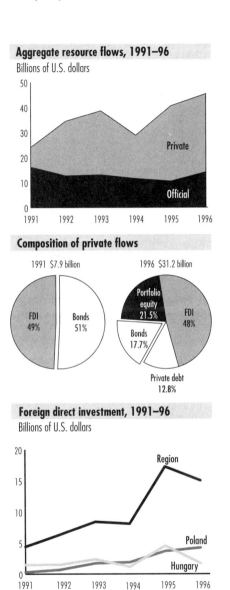

GNP per capita, 1995: $2,220

Aggregate resource flows, 1991–96
Billions of U.S. dollars

Composition of private flows

1991 $7.9 billion

FDI 49%
Bonds 51%

1996 $31.2 billion

Portfolio equity 21.5%
FDI 48%
Bonds 17.7%
Private debt 12.8%

Foreign direct investment, 1991–96
Billions of U.S. dollars

Region
Poland
Hungary

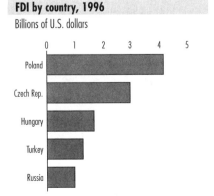

FDI by country, 1996
Billions of U.S. dollars

Poland
Czech Rep.
Hungary
Turkey
Russia

Key indicators
Billions of U.S. dollars

	1986	1995	1996ᵃ
Total debt outstanding	428.5	636.6	656.5
World Bank/IDA	24.2	38.6	39.3
Concessional share (%)	8.4	9.3	9.0
Net resource flows	11.9	66.9	69.2
Net transfers	−18.3	26.8	26.6
Debt service/exports (%)	41.8	26.1	30.0

a. Preliminary.

Debt outstanding, 1986–96
Billions of U.S. dollars

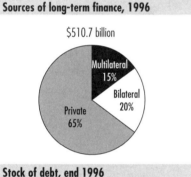

Sources of long-term finance, 1996

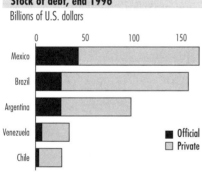

Stock of debt, end 1996
Billions of U.S. dollars

Debt to export ratio

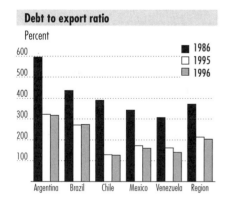

Latin America and the Caribbean

Capital flows to Latin America and the Caribbean continued to recover in 1996. Although the early repayment of $7.5 billion in debt by Mexico in 1996 resulted in only a small rise in net aggregate flows to $69.2 billion, flows continued the strong increase of 1995. Private capital flows rose 37 percent in 1996 to $74 billion. Despite large payments on official debt, strong bond issuing activity meant that net transfers to the region remained at the 1995 level of $26 billion, or 1.6 percent of regional GNP.

DEBT AND INDICATORS

GROWTH OF DEBT STOCK SLOWS. The region's external debt increased about 3 percent in 1996 to reach $656 billion, a slower rate of growth than in 1995, when the international community's support package of loans for Mexico raised the debt stock 9 percent. Higher than average increases in debt occurred in Argentina (12 percent), Chile (8 percent), and Mexico (4 percent); lower than average increases occurred in Brazil (1 percent) and Venezuela (–0.2 percent).

The region's debt represents about 30 percent of all debt of low- and middle-income countries, down from 35 percent in 1988. Within the region, Mexico is estimated to hold 27 percent of outstanding debt, followed by Brazil (25 percent), Argentina (16 percent), and Venezuela (5 percent).

MEXICO PREPAYS OFFICIAL DEBT. An exceptional $7.5 billion debt prepayment by Mexico to its official creditors helped raise debt service as a share of exports to about 30 percent for the region in 1996, up from 26 percent in 1995. The region's debt stock as a share of exports fell, however from 212 percent in 1995 to an estimated 203 percent in 1996 (compared with more than 300 percent in 1988). Country experiences varied widely, with estimated debt to export ratios within the region ranging from 26 percent (Suriname) to 880 percent (Nicaragua).

POOR COUNTRIES ACHIEVE DEBT REDUCTION. In 1996 Honduras and Guyana obtained Naples terms agreements from their Paris Club creditors; similar agreements were concluded with Bolivia, Haiti, and Nicaragua in 1995. In 1996 Nicaragua also reached agreement with the Russian Federation on a debt restructuring deal that provides for 90 percent forgiveness on its ruble debt. This deal followed the buyback of commercial bank debt in 1995, under which Nicaragua extinguished more than $1 billion of principal at a cost of 8 cents on the dollar. Nicaragua's debt is estimated to have been reduced to about $6 billion in 1996, from $11 billion in 1994. Bolivia, Guyana, and Nicaragua, are all classified as heavily indebted poor countries.

AGGREGATE RESOURCE FLOWS

Estimated aggregate resource flows into Latin America in 1996 reflected the

External debt and resource flows

decline in inflows of official support to Mexico, which rose sharply in 1995 following the peso crisis. Aggregate net flows are estimated at $69.2 billion, a slight increase over 1995 flows of $66.9 billion. Within the aggregate figures, however, official nonconcessional loans showed an outflow of $8.9 billion (reflecting Mexico's large prepayment on its aid package) compared with an exceptionally large inflow of $7.6 billion in 1995.

PRIVATE CAPITAL FLOWS REBOUND. Private capital flows into the region increased 37 percent in 1996, following relatively weak performance in 1994 and 1995. Net flows from commercial banks fell from the high levels of 1995 but were more than compensated for by higher inflows from bonds, foreign direct investment, and portfolio equity, as confidence in the region recovered.

NET BOND FLOWS REACH RECORD HIGH. Net flows from bonds rebounded from their low levels in the wake of the Mexican peso crisis, reaching a record $28 billion in 1996. Activity was up in all the major economies of the region, with Mexico and Argentina accounting for two-thirds of the inflow. Confidence started returning to the bond market in the second half of 1995, led by the most creditworthy countries. In January 1996 Mexico successfully issued a $1 billion five-year global bond issue, its first sovereign issue since 1993. The proceeds of a $6 billion sovereign floating rate note were used later in the year to prepay 1995

borrowings from the U.S. Treasury and the IMF.

FOREIGN DIRECT INVESTMENT PICKS UP AGAIN. Foreign direct investment in Latin America and the Caribbean is estimated to have increased by more than 13 percent in 1996, after falling slightly in 1995. The increase was seen in all the major economies of the region. Argentina, Brazil, and Mexico, each accounted for about 20 percent of the total; Colombia and Peru also received significant amounts. The region accounted for about a quarter of foreign direct investment flows into low- and middle-income countries in 1996.

PORTFOLIO EQUITY FLOWS DOUBLE. The recovery of confidence in the region is expected to have attracted more than $16 billion in net portfolio equity inflows in 1996, up from about $7 billion in 1995. Portfolio equity flows nevertheless remain well below the record level of $27 billion reached in 1993. Brazil, Mexico, and Peru account for about 85 percent of portfolio equity inflows. In Argentina the lack of blue-chip stocks outside the oil and gas sector has limited investor diversification. The region's share of portfolio equity flows to low- and middle-income countries increased from about a fifth in 1995 to about a third in 1996.

AID FLOWS FALL. Official development assistance fell from $5 billion in 1995 to an estimated $3.6 billion in 1996, with Bolivia, Haiti, and Nicaragua receiving the largest shares of aid.

GNP per capita, 1995: $3,320

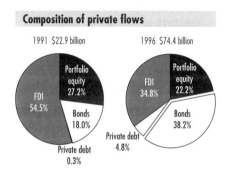

Aggregate resource flows, 1991–96
Billions of U.S. dollars

Composition of private flows

1991 $22.9 billion — Portfolio equity 27.2%, FDI 54.5%, Bonds 18.0%, Private debt 0.3%

1996 $74.4 billion — Portfolio equity 22.2%, FDI 34.8%, Bonds 38.2%, Private debt 4.8%

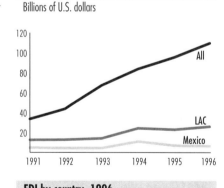

Foreign direct investment, 1991–96
Billions of U.S. dollars

FDI by country, 1996
Billions of U.S. dollars

Key indicators
Billions of U.S. dollars

	1986	1995	1996[a]
Total debt outstanding	153.4	216.0	220.8
World Bank/IDA	7.3	12.7	12.7
Concessional share (%)	23.2	26.0	25.6
Net resource flows	13.8	2.4	10.9
Net transfers	7.4	−5.6	1.9
Debt service/exports (%)	21.0	14.9	12.1

a. Preliminary.

Debt outstanding, 1986–96
Billions of U.S. dollars

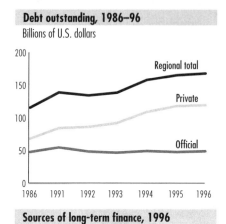

Sources of long-term finance, 1996

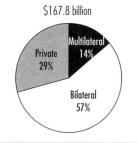

$167.8 billion

Stock of debt, end 1996
Billions of U.S. dollars

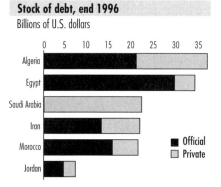

Debt to export ratio
Percent

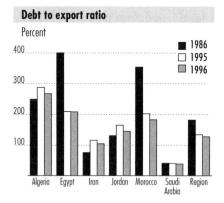

Middle East and North Africa

GNP in the Middle East and North Africa is estimated to have increased by 12 percent in dollar terms in 1996, as oil exporters continued to benefit from higher oil prices and Algeria, Morocco, and Tunisia continued to recover from the droughts of 1994–95. Slow growth in debt and an estimated 8 percent rise in export receipts led to an improvement in debt indicators. Net transfers to the region increased from a net outflow of $5.6 billion in 1995 (reflecting Iran's repayment of arrears) to a net inflow of $1.9 billion in 1996. Inflows nevertheless remained below the $4 billion a year reached in 1990–91. Net transfers represented only 0.3 percent of GNP in 1996, the lowest share among all developing regions and well below the 0.8 percent reached in 1990. The distribution of net transfers was relatively even in the region, although four countries (Iran, Libya, Morocco, and Oman) experienced significant outflows.

DEBT AND INDICATORS

DEBT CONTINUES TO RISE SLOWLY. Total debt in the region reached an estimated $221 billion in 1996, up 2.2 percent over 1995. Most of the rise ($3.7 billion of $4.8 billion) reflected the increase in debt from Algeria. Otherwise, only Bahrain and Saudi Arabia registered increases of $1 billion or more, almost entirely bank lending to the private sector. Some countries in the region experienced significant declines in outstanding debt. The region accounted for 10 percent of the outstanding debt of low- and middle-income countries at the end of 1996. About three-quarters of the region's external debt was owed or guaranteed by debtor governments.

SLOW GROWTH OF DEBT AND HIGHER EXPORTS LEAD TO IMPROVED DEBT INDICATORS. The aggregate ratio of debt to exports in the region fell from 133 percent in 1995 to 127 percent in 1996. However, Saudi Arabia's large weight and low debt to export ratio somewhat distorts the region's debt profile. Excluding Saudi Arabia, the region's debt to export ratio rose to 172 percent in 1996. The region is relatively dependent on official concessional assistance, with a larger share of debt outstanding on concessional terms (25 percent) than the average for low- and middle-income countries (20 percent).

The ratio of debt service to exports fell from 14.9 percent to an estimated 12.1 percent in 1996, well below the 16.4 percent average for low- and middle-income countries. This relatively low debt service ratio in part reflects a buildup of arrears of about $1 billion in 1996, but even full repayment of arrears would not have increased the ratio greatly. Only one country in the region (Republic of Yemen) underwent a formal rescheduling of debt service in 1996. Of the fifteen countries in the region, all but Algeria, Egypt, and Syria had debt to export ratios below 200 percent.

AGGREGATE RESOURCE FLOWS

Net aggregate resource flows to the Middle East and North Africa rose to an

External debt and resource flows

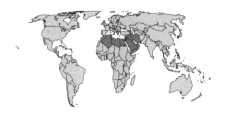

estimated $10.9 billion in 1996, up sharply from their 1995 level of $2.4 billion and their 1990–94 average of $9.4 billion.

OFFICIAL DEVELOPMENT FINANCE RISES BUT REMAINS LOW. Official development finance to the Middle East and North Africa rose to an estimated $3.9 billion in 1996, up dramatically from the $1 billion in 1995 but still well below the $9.6 billion reached in 1990. The decline in official assistance (following the exceptional circumstances of the Gulf war) largely reflects a drop in grants, which fell from $8.2 billion in 1990 to $2.8 billion in 1996; concessional loans from multilateral and bilateral creditors increased slightly during this period. The 1990s have seen particularly sharp declines in assistance from official creditors to Bahrain, Egypt, Jordan, Morocco, and the Republic of Yemen. Official lending to the region is almost entirely in the form of grants and highly concessional loans. Net nonconcessional loans were negative in 1996.

SEVERAL COUNTRIES IMPROVE THEIR ACCESS TO PRIVATE FINANCE. Private loans to the Middle East and North Africa totaled $4 billion in 1996 (compared with net repayments of $1.2 billion a year in 1990–92) as Algeria, Bahrain, Lebanon, and Tunisia greatly increased their borrowing from commercial banks. Bond issues also picked up, with issues from the region reaching $1.1 billion in 1995 and $0.7 billion in 1996, with transactions recorded by Lebanon

and Tunisia in 1996. While the volume of bond issuances by the region remains low, accounting for only about 7 percent of net flows in 1996, issuances in 1995 and 1996 compare favorably with the net repayments of bonds in 1990–94.

FOREIGN DIRECT INVESTMENT RISES BUT FALLS AS A SHARE OF TOTAL PRIVATE FLOWS. Foreign direct investment increased 19 percent to an estimated $2.5 billion in 1996, with 80 percent of the region's net foreign direct investment going to Egypt, Morocco, and Tunisia. Many of the other countries in the region had net inflows of less than $100 million. Jordan and Lebanon are beginning to attract foreign direct investment, albeit at low levels. The rise in private-source debt finance has reduced the share of foreign direct investment in total private flows from 83 percent in 1991 to 35 percent in 1996.

PORTFOLIO EQUITY FLOWS RISE. Portfolio equity flows to the Middle East and North Africa reached an estimated $650 million in 1996, almost entirely a result of Morocco's privatization efforts and investments in Egypt's stock market. Although portfolio equity flows more than tripled over their 1995 level of $203 million, portfolio equity flows continue to account for a small share of the region's external financial resources. There are signs of increased attention to the region, however, including the startup of new investment funds focusing on the Middle East and North Africa.

GNP per capita, 1995: $1,780

Aggregate resource flows, 1991–96
Billions of U.S. dollars

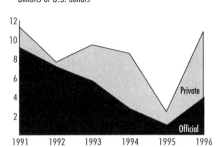

Composition of private flows

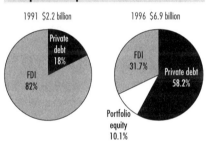

Foreign direct investment, 1991–96
Billions of U.S. dollars

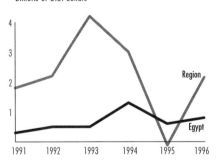

FDI by country, 1996
Billions of U.S. dollars

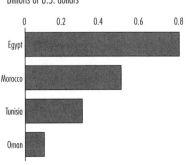

Part III

Summary tables

Methodology

The World Bank is the sole repository for statistics on the external debt of developing countries on a loan-by-loan basis. The Debtor Reporting System (DRS), set up in 1951 to monitor these statistics, is maintained by the staff of the Financial Data Team (FIN), part of the Development Data Group of the International Economics Department (IECDD).

Methodology for aggregating data

Using the DRS data, in combination with information obtained from creditors through the debt data collection systems of other agencies such as the Bank for International Settlements (BIS) and the Organization for Economic Cooperation and Development (OECD), the staff of the IECDD estimate the total external indebtedness of developing countries. The data are also supplemented by estimates made by country economists of the World Bank and desk officers of the International Monetary Fund (IMF).

Converting to a common currency

Since debt data are normally reported to the World Bank in the currency of repayment, they have to be converted into a common currency (usually U.S. dollars) to produce summary tables. Stock figures (such as the amount of debt outstanding) are converted using end-period exchange rates, as published in the IMF's *International Financial Statistics* (line ae). Flow figures are converted at annual average exchange rates (line rf). Projected debt service is converted using end-period exchange rates. Debt repayable in multiple currencies, goods, or services and debt with a provision for maintenance of value of the currency of repayment are shown at book value. Because flow data are converted at annual average exchange

rates and stock data at year-end exchange rates, year-to-year changes in debt outstanding and disbursed are sometimes not equal to net flows (disbursements less principal repayments); similarly, changes in debt outstanding including undisbursed debt differ from commitments less repayments. Discrepancies are particularly significant when exchange rates have moved sharply during the year; cancellations and reschedulings of other liabilities into long-term public debt also contribute to the differences.

Public and publicly guaranteed debt

All data related to public and publicly guaranteed debt are from debtors except for lending by some multilateral agencies, in which case data are taken from the creditors' records. These creditors include the African Development Bank, the Asian Development Bank, the Central Bank for Economic Integration, the IMF, the Inter-American Development Bank, and the International Bank for Reconstruction and Development (IBRD) and International Development Association (IDA). (The IBRD and IDA are components of the World Bank.)

Starting with the 1988–89 edition of *World Debt Tables* (as this book was previously titled), all data pertaining to World Bank loans from 1985 onward are recorded at their current market value. Starting with the 1991–92 edition, all data pertaining to Asian Development Bank loans from 1989 onward are recorded at their current market value as well.

Private nonguaranteed debt

The DRS was expanded in 1970 to incorporate private nonguaranteed long-term debt. Reports, submitted annually, contain aggregate data for disbursed and outstanding debt, disbursements, principal repayments, interest payments, principal and interest rescheduled for the reporting year, and projected payments of principal and interest. Data are usually presented in dollars and currency conversion is not necessary. A few reporting countries choose to provide data on their private nonguaranteed debt in the loan-by-loan format used for reporting public and publicly guaranteed debt. In those cases the currency conversion and projection methodology just described is used.

Although the reporting countries fully recognize the importance of collecting data on private nonguaranteed debt when it constitutes a significant portion of total external debt, detailed data are available only in countries that have registration requirements covering private debt, most commonly in connection with exchange controls. Where formal registration of foreign borrowing is not mandatory, compilers must rely on balance of payments data and financial surveys.

Thirty-one countries report their private nonguaranteed debt to the DRS. Estimates are made for twenty-nine others that do not report but for which this type of debt is known to be significant.

For private nonguaranteed debt that is not reported, the standard estimation approach starts from a calculation of the stock of debt outstanding, using data available from creditors. Figures on guaranteed export credits, obtained from the OECD's Creditor Reporting System (CRS), are supplemented by loan-by-loan information on official lending to private borrowers and by information on noninsured commercial bank lending to the private sector.

Disbursements and debt service payments for private nonguaranteed debt are more difficult to estimate. Amortization is estimated by making an assumption regarding the proportion of debt repaid each year and then applying these ratios to generate a first approximation of annual principal repayments. Disbursements are then estimated as a residual between net flows (equal to the change in the stock of debt) and estimated amortization. Interest payments are estimated by applying an assumed average interest rate to the stock of debt outstanding.

Data on balance of payments flows provide useful guidelines in the process of building a time series

because private nonguaranteed debt can be treated as a residual between total net long-term borrowing and net long-term borrowing recorded in the DRS for public and publicly guaranteed debt.

Short-term debt

The World Bank regards the individual reporting country as the authoritative source of information on its own external liabilities. But for short-term debt, defined as debt with an original maturity of one year or less, accurate information is not widely available from debtors. By its nature, short-term debt is difficult to monitor; loan-by-loan registration is normally impractical, and most reporting arrangements involve periodic returns to a country's central bank from its banking sector. Since 1982 the quality of such reporting has improved, but only a few developing countries have figures available for short-term debt.

Where information from debtors is not available, data from creditors can indicate the magnitude of a country's short-term debt. The most important source is the BIS's semiannual series showing the maturity distribution of commercial banks' claims on developing countries. Those data are reported residually. However, an estimate of short-term liabilities by original maturity can be calculated by deducting from claims due in one year those that had a maturity of between one and two years twelve months earlier.

There are several problems with this method. Valuation adjustments caused by exchange rate movements will affect the calculations, as will prepayment and refinancing of long-term maturities falling due. Moreover, not all countries' commercial banks report in a way that allows the full maturity distribution to be determined, and the BIS data include liabilities only to banks within the reporting area. Nevertheless, combining these estimates with data on officially guaranteed short-term suppliers' credits compiled by the OECD gives what may be thought of as a lower-bound estimate of a country's short-term debt. Even on this basis, however, the results need to be interpreted with caution. Where short-term debt has been rescheduled, the effect of lags in reporting and differences in the treatment of the rescheduled debt by debtors and creditors may result in double counting if short-term debt derived from creditor sources is added to long-term debt reported by the country to obtain total external liabilities.

Some of the short-term debt estimates published are drawn from debtor and creditor sources, but most are from creditor sources. Only for a few countries can the data be regarded as authoritative, but they offer a guide to the size of a country's short-term (and, hence, its total) external debt. The quality of these data is likely to improve.

Use of IMF credit

Data related to the operations of the IMF come from the IMF Treasurer's Department and are converted from special drawing rights (SDRs) into dollars using end-of-period exchange rates for stocks and average over the period exchange rates for converting flows, as described earlier. IMF trust fund loans and operations under the structural adjustment and enhanced structural adjustment facilities are presented together with all of the Fund's special facilities (the buffer stock, compensatory financing, extended fund, and oil facilities).

Treatment of arrears

The DRS collects information on arrears in both principal and interest. Principal in arrears is included and identified in the amount of long-term debt outstanding. Interest in arrears of long-term debt and the use of IMF credit is included and identified in the amount of short-term debt outstanding. If and when interest in arrears is capitalized under a debt reorganization agreement, the amount of interest capitalized will be added to the amount of long-term debt outstanding and the corresponding deduction made from the amount of short-term debt outstanding.

Treatment of debt restructurings

The DRS attempts to capture accurately the effects of the different kinds of restructurings on both debt stocks and debt flows, consistent with the circumstances under which the restructuring takes place. Whether a flow has taken place is sometimes difficult to determine.

In compiling and presenting the debt data, a distinction is made between cash flows and imputed flows. Based on this criterion, rescheduled service payments and the shift in liabilities from one financial instrument to another as a result of rescheduling are considered to be imputed flows.

The imputed flows are recorded separately in the Revised External Debt (RXD) system, but these debt restructuring transactions are not evident in the main body of the debt data—only the resulting effect of these transactions is reflected.

Changes in creditor and debtor status that can result from debt restructuring are also reflected. For example, when insured commercial credits are rescheduled, the creditor classification shifts from private sources to official sources (bilateral). This reflects the assumption of the assets by the official credit insurance agencies of the creditor countries. The debts to the original creditors are reduced by the amounts rescheduled, and a new obligation to the official creditor agencies is created. This shift also applies to private nonguaranteed debt that is reduced by the amounts rescheduled, which in turn are included in the public and publicly guaranteed debt owed to official creditors. On the debtor side, when a government accepts responsibility for the payment of rescheduled debt previously owed by private enterprises, the DRS registers a change in debtor categories in the DRS. Similarly, when short-term debt is included in a restructuring agreement, the rescheduled amount is shifted from short-term to long-term debt.

Methodology for projecting data

An important feature of the RXD system of the DRS is its ability to project future disbursements of unutilized commitments and future debt service payments.

Undisbursed debt

Projections of disbursements help underpin future capital requirements in the implementation of externally financed projects. In addition, they help determine the interest portion of projected debt service. Future interest payments are based on projected debt outstanding that is itself determined by projected disbursements and repayments. The underlying assumptions of these projections are that loan commitments will be fully utilized and that the debtor country will repay all sums due. Future disbursements and debt service refer only to existing debt and do not reflect any assumptions on future borrowing.

Disbursement projections use two methods:

• *Specific schedules.* Debtor countries are requested to submit a calendar of future disbursements, if available, at the time individual loans are first reported. Country authorities are in a better position to provide estimated disbursement schedules when there is a solid public sector investment program in place.

• *Standard schedules.* In the absence of specific schedules, the RXD system projects disbursements by applying a set of profiles to the last actual undisbursed balance of individual loans. The profiles are derived under the assumption that specific sources of funds have some common characteristics that cause them to disburse, in the aggregate, in some observable pattern. Accordingly, some thirty profiles have been derived that roughly correspond to creditor type. Profiles exist for concessional and nonconcessional loans from official creditors. For bilateral lending, profiles have been developed for the Development Assistance Committee, the Organization of Petroleum-Exporting Countries (OPEC), and other creditor groupings. For multilateral lending, specific profiles are available for major international organizations. An estimating equation for each profile is derived by applying regression analysis techniques to a body of data that contains actual disbursement information for more than 100,000 loans. Although these standard profiles are reestimated from time to time, under the best scenario they can only approximate the disbursement pattern of any single loan.

Future debt service payments

Most projections of future debt service payments generated by the RXD system are based on the repayment terms of the loans. Principal repayments (amortization) are based on the amount of loan commitments, and the amortization profile of most loans follows a set pattern. Using the first and final payment dates and the frequency of the payments, the system calculates the stream of principal payments due. If future payments are irregular, the RXD system requires a schedule.

Projected future interest payments are calculated similarly. Interest is based on the amount of debt disbursed and outstanding at the beginning of the period. Again, using the first and final interest payment dates and the frequency of payments, the system calculates the stream of interest payments due. If interest payments are irregular, the RXD system requires a schedule.

The published figures for projected debt service obligations are converted into U.S. dollars using the end-December 1995 exchange rates. Likewise the projection routine for variable interest rate debt, such as commercial bank debt based on the London interbank offer rate (LIBOR), assumes that the rate prevailing at the end of December 1995 will be effective throughout.

Sources and definitions

This edition of *Global Development Finance* presents reported or estimated data on the total external debt of all low- and middle-income countries.

Format

Volume 2 has been expanded to include summary tables along with the standard country tables for the 136 individual countries that report to the World Bank's Debtor Reporting System. Summary tables present selected debt and resource flow statistics for the individual reporting countries and external debt data for regional and income groups. Regional and income group totals in the summary tables include estimates for the fourteen low- and middle-income countries that do not report to the DRS. Because these estimates are not shown separately in the tables, most group totals are larger than the sum of the DRS figures shown. The format of the regional and income group tables in this volume draws on the individual country table format of volume 2 and includes graphic presentations.

For the 136 individual countries that report to the World Bank's Debtor Reporting System (DRS), tables are presented in a four-page layout containing ten sections.

SECTION 1 summarizes the external debt of the country.

Total debt stocks (EDT) consist of public and publicly guaranteed long-term debt, private nonguaranteed long-term debt (whether reported or estimated by the staff of the World Bank), the use of IMF credit, and estimated short-term debt. Interest in arrears on long-term debt and the use of IMF credit are added to the short-term debt estimates and shown as separate lines. Arrears of principal and of interest have been disaggregated to show the arrears owed to official creditors and those owed to private creditors. Export credits and principal in arrears on long-term debt are shown as memorandum items.

Total debt flows are consolidated data on disbursements, principal repayments, and interest payments for total long-term debt and transactions with the IMF.

Net flows on debt are disbursements on long-term debt and IMF purchases minus principal repayments on long-term debt and IMF repurchases up to 1984. Beginning in 1985 this line includes the change in stock of short-term debt (including interest arrears for long-term debt). Thus if the change in stock is positive, a disbursement is assumed to have taken place; if negative, a repayment is assumed to have taken place.

Total debt service (TDS) shows the debt service payments on total long-term debt (public and publicly guaranteed and private nonguaranteed), use of IMF credit, and interest on short-term debt.

SECTION 2 provides data series for aggregate net resource flows and net transfers (long term).

Net resource flows (long term) are the sum of net resource flows on long-term debt (excluding IMF) plus net foreign direct investment, portfolio equity flows, and official grants (excluding technical cooperation). Grants for technical cooperation are shown as a memorandum item.

Net transfers (long term) are equal to net long-term resource flows minus interest payments on long-term loans and foreign direct investment profits.

SECTION 3 provides data series for major economic aggregates. The gross national product (GNP) series uses yearly average exchange rates in converting GNP from local currency into U.S. dollars. The economic aggregates are prepared for the convenience of users; the usual caution should be exercised in using them for economic analysis.

SECTION 4 provides debt indicators: ratios of debt and debt service to some of the economic aggregates.

SECTION 5 provides detailed information on stocks and flows of long-term debt and its various components. Data on bonds issued by private entities without public guarantee, compiled for major borrowers, are included in private nonguaranteed debt. IBRD loans and IDA credits are shown as memorandum items.

SECTION 6 provides information on the currency composition of long-term debt. The six major currencies in which the external debt of low- and middle-income countries is contracted are separately identified, as is debt denominated in special drawing rights and debt repayable in multiple currencies.

SECTION 7 provides information on restructurings of long-term debt starting in 1985. It shows both the stock and flows rescheduled each year. In addition, the amount of debt forgiven (interest forgiven is shown as a memorandum item) and the amount of debt stock reduction (including debt buyback) are also shown separately. (See the Methodology section for a detailed explanation of restructuring data.)

SECTION 8 reconciles the stock and flow data on total external debt for each year, beginning with 1989. This section is designed to illustrate the changes in stock that have taken place due to five factors: the net flow on debt, the net change in interest arrears, the capitalization of interest, the reduction in debt resulting from debt forgiveness or other debt reduction mechanisms, and the cross-currency valuation effects. The residual difference—the change in stock not explained by any of the factors identified above—is also presented. The residual is calculated as the sum of identified accounts minus the change in stock. Where the residual is large it can, in some cases, serve as an illustration of the inconsistencies in the reported data. More often, however, it can be explained by specific borrowing phenomena in individual countries. These are explained in the Country Notes section.

SECTION 9 provides information on the average terms of new commitments on public and publicly guaranteed debt and information on the level of commitments from official and private sources.

SECTION 10 provides anticipated disbursements and contractual obligations on long-term debt contracted up to December 1995.

Sources

The principal sources of information for the tables in these two volumes are reports to the World Bank through the DRS from member countries that have received either IBRD loans or IDA credits. Additional information has been drawn from the files of the World Bank and the IMF.

Reporting countries submit detailed (loan-by-loan) reports through the DRS on the annual status, transactions, and terms of the long-term external debt of public agencies and that of private ones guaranteed by a public agency in the debtor country. This information forms the basis for the tables in these volumes.

Aggregate data on private debt without public guarantee are compiled and published as reliable reported and estimated information becomes available. This edition includes data on private nonguaranteed debt reported by thirty-one developing countries and complete or partial estimates for an additional twenty-nine countries.

The short-term debt data are as reported by the debtor countries or are estimates derived from creditor sources. The principal creditor sources are the semiannual series of commercial banks' claims on developing countries, published by the Bank for International Settlements (BIS), and data on officially guaranteed suppliers' credits compiled by the Organization for Economic Cooperation and Development (OECD). For some countries, estimates were prepared by pooling creditor and debtor information.

Interest in arrears on long-term debt and the use of IMF credit are added to the short-term debt estimates and shown as separate lines in section 1. Arrears of interest and of principal owed to official and to private creditors are identified separately.

Export credits are shown as a memorandum item in section 1. They include official export credits, and suppliers' credits and bank credits officially guaranteed or insured by an export credit agency. Both long-term and short-term export credits are included. The source for this information is the Creditor Reporting System (CRS) of the OECD.

Data on long-term debt reported by member countries are checked against, and supplemented by, data from several other sources. Among these are the statements and reports of several regional development banks and government lending agencies, as well as the reports received by the World Bank under the CRS from the members of the Development Assistance Committee (DAC) of the OECD.

Every effort has been made to ensure the accuracy and completeness of the debt statistics. Nevertheless, quality and coverage vary among debtors and may also vary for the same debtor from year to year. Coverage has been improved through the efforts of the reporting agencies and the work of World Bank missions, which visit member countries to gather data and to provide technical assistance on debt issues.

Definitions

For all regional, income, and individual country tables, data definitions are presented below or footnoted where appropriate. Data definitions for other summary tables are, likewise, consistent with those below.

Summary debt data

TOTAL DEBT STOCKS are defined as the sum of public and publicly guaranteed long-term debt, private nonguaranteed long-term debt, the use of IMF credit, and short-term debt. The relation between total debt stock and its components is illustrated on page xi.

Long-term external debt is defined as debt that has an original or extended maturity of more than one year and that is owed to nonresidents and repayable in foreign currency, goods, or services. Long-term debt has three components:

• *Public debt,* which is an external obligation of a public debtor, including the national government, a political subdivision (or an agency of either), and autonomous public bodies

• *Publicly guaranteed debt,* which is an external obligation of a private debtor that is guaranteed for repayment by a public entity

• *Private nonguaranteed external debt,* which is an external obligation of a private debtor that is not guaranteed for repayment by a public entity.

In the tables, public and publicly guaranteed long-term debt are aggregated.

Short-term external debt is defined as debt that has an original maturity of one year or less.

Available data permit no distinction between public and private nonguaranteed short-term debt.

Interest in arrears on long-term debt is defined as interest payment due but not paid, on a cumulative basis.

Principal in arrears on long-term debt is defined as principal repayment due but not paid, on a cumulative basis.

The memorandum item *export credits* includes official export credits, suppliers' credits, and bank credits officially guaranteed or insured by an export credit agency. Both long-term and short-term credits are included here.

Use of IMF credit denotes repurchase obligations to the IMF with respect to all uses of IMF resources (excluding those resulting from drawings in the reserve tranche) shown for the end of the year specified. Use of IMF credit comprises purchases outstanding under the credit tranches, including enlarged access resources and all special facilities (the buffer stock, compensatory financing, extended fund, and oil facilities), trust fund loans, and operations under the structural adjustment and enhanced structural adjustment facilities. Data are from the Treasurer's Department of the IMF.

• *IMF purchases* are total drawings on the general resources account of the IMF during the year specified, excluding drawings in the reserve tranche.

• *IMF repurchases* are total repayments of outstanding drawings from the general resources account during the year specified, excluding repayments due in the reserve tranche.

To maintain comparability between data on transactions with the IMF and data on long-term debt, use of IMF credit outstanding at year end (stock) is converted to dollars at the SDR exchange rate in effect at the end of the year. Purchases and repurchases (flows) are converted at the average SDR exchange rate for the year in which transactions take place.

Net purchases will usually not reconcile changes in the use of IMF credit from year to year. Valuation effects from the use of different exchange rates frequently explain much of the difference, but not all. Other factors are increases in quotas (which expand a country's reserve tranche and can thereby lower the use of IMF credit as defined here), approved purchases of a country's currency by another member country drawing on the general resources account, and various administrative uses of a country's currency by the IMF.

TOTAL DEBT FLOWS include disbursements, principal repayments, net flows and transfers on debt, and interest payments.

Disbursements are drawings on loan commitments during the year specified.

Principal repayments are the amounts of principal (amortization) paid in foreign currency, goods, or services in the year specified.

Net flows on debts (or net lending or net disbursements) are disbursements minus principal repayments.

Interest payments are the amounts of interest paid in foreign currency, goods, or services in the year specified.

Net transfers on debt are net flows minus interest payments (or disbursements minus total debt service payments).

The concepts of net flows on debt, net transfers on debt, and aggregate net flows and net transfers are illustrated on pages xxi and xxii.

Total debt service paid (TDS) is debt service payments on total long-term debt (public and publicly guaranteed and private nonguaranteed), use of IMF credit, and interest on short-term debt.

Aggregate net resource flows and transfers

NET RESOURCE FLOWS (LONG TERM) are the sum of net resource flows on long-term debt (excluding IMF) plus non-debt-creating flows.

NON-DEBT-CREATING FLOWS are net foreign direct investment, portfolio equity flows, and official grants (excluding technical cooperation). Net foreign direct investment and portfolio equity flows are treated as private source flows. Grants for technical cooperation are shown as a memorandum item.

Foreign direct investment (FDI) is defined as investment that is made to acquire a lasting management interest (usually 10 percent of voting stock) in an enterprise operating in a country other than that of the investor (defined according to residency), the investor's purpose being an effective voice in the management of the enterprise. It is the sum of equity capital, reinvestment of earnings, other long-term capital, and short-term capital as shown in the balance of payments.

Portfolio equity flows are the sum of country funds, depository receipts (American or global), and direct purchases of shares by foreign investors.

Grants are defined as legally binding commitments that obligate a specific value of funds available for disbursement for which there is no repayment requirement.

The memo item *technical cooperation grants* includes free-standing technical cooperation grants, which are intended to finance the transfer of technical and managerial skills or of technology for the purpose of building up general national capacity without reference to any specific investment projects; and investment-related technical cooperation grants, which are provided to strengthen the capacity to execute specific investment projects.

Profit remittances on foreign direct investment are the sum of reinvested earnings on direct investment and other direct investment income and are part of net transfers.

Major economic aggregates

Five economic aggregates are provided for the reporting economies.

Gross national product (GNP) is the measure of the total domestic and foreign output claimed by residents of an economy, less the domestic output claimed by nonresidents. GNP does not include deductions for depreciation. Data on GNP are from the Macroeconomic Indicators Team of the Development Data Group of the World Bank's International Economics Department.

Exports of goods and services (XGS) are the total value of goods and services exported as well as income and worker remittances received.

Imports of goods and services (MGS) are the total value of goods and services imported and income paid.

International reserves (RES) are the sum of a country's monetary authority's holdings of special drawing rights (SDRs), its reserve position in the IMF, its holdings of foreign exchange, and its holdings of gold (valued at year-end London prices).

Current account balance is the sum of the credits less the debits arising from international transactions in goods, services, income, and current transfers. It represents the transactions that add to or subtract from an economy's stock of foreign financial items.

Data on exports and imports (on a balance of payments basis), international reserves, and current account balances are drawn mainly from the files of the IMF, complemented by World Bank staff estimates. Balance of payments data are presented according to the fifth edition of the IMF's *Balance of Payments Manual,* which made several adjustments to its presentation of trade statistics. Coverage of goods was expanded to include in imports the value of goods received for processing and repair (on a gross basis). Their subsequent re-export is recorded in exports (also on a gross basis). This approach will cause a country's imports and exports to increase without affecting the balance of goods. In addition, all capital transfers, which were included with current transfers in the fourth edition of the *Balance of Payments Manual,* are now shown in a separate capital (as opposed to financial) account, and so do not contribute to the current account balance.

Debt indicators

The macroeconomic aggregates and debt data provided in the tables are used to generate ratios that analysts use to assess the external situations of developing countries. Different analysts give different weights to these indicators, but no single indicator or set of indicators can substitute for a thorough analysis of the overall situation of an economy. The advantage of the indicators in *Global Development Finance* is that they are calculated from standardized data series that are compiled on a consistent basis by the World Bank and the IMF. The ratios offer various measures of the cost of, or capacity for, servicing debt in terms of the foreign exchange or output forgone. The following ratios are provided based on total external debt:

EDT/XGS is total external debt to exports of goods and services (including workers' remittances).

EDT/GNP is total external debt to gross national product.

TDS/XGS, also called the debt service ratio, is total debt service to exports of goods and services (including workers' remittances).

INT/XGS, also called the interest service ratio, is total interest payments to exports of goods and services (including workers' remittances).

INT/GNP is total interest payments to gross national product.

RES/EDT is international reserves to total external debt.

RES/MGS is international reserves to imports of goods and services.

Short-term/EDT is short-term debt to total external debt.

Concessional/EDT is concessional debt to total external debt.

Multilateral/EDT is multilateral debt to total external debt.

Long-term debt

Data on long-term debt include eight main elements:

DEBT OUTSTANDING AND DISBURSED is the total outstanding debt at year end.

DISBURSEMENTS are drawings on loan commitments by the borrower during the year.

PRINCIPAL REPAYMENTS are amounts paid by the borrower during the year.

NET FLOWS received by the borrower during the year are disbursements minus principal repayments.

INTEREST PAYMENTS are amounts paid by the borrower during the year.

NET TRANSFERS are net flows minus interest payments during the year; negative transfers show net transfers made by the borrower to the creditor during the year.

DEBT SERVICE (LTDS) is the sum of principal repayments and interest payments actually made.

UNDISBURSED DEBT is total debt undrawn at year end; data for private nonguaranteed debt are not available.

Data from individual reporters are aggregated by type of creditor. *Official creditors* includes multilateral and bilateral debt.

• *Loans from multilateral organizations* are loans and credits from the World Bank, regional development banks, and other multilateral and intergovernmental agencies. Excluded are loans from funds administered by an international organization on behalf of a single donor government; these are classified as loans from governments.

• *Bilateral loans* are loans from governments and their agencies (including central banks), loans from autonomous bodies, and direct loans from official export credit agencies.

Private creditors include bonds, commercial banks, and other private creditors. Commercial banks and other private creditors comprise bank and trade-related lending.

• *Bonds* include publicly issued or privately placed bonds.

• *Commercial banks* are loans from private banks and other private financial institutions.

• *Other private* includes credits from manufacturers, exporters, and other suppliers of goods, and bank credits covered by a guarantee of an export credit agency.

Four characteristics of a country's debt are given as memorandum items for long-term debt outstanding and disbursed (LDOD).

Concessional LDOD conveys information about the borrower's receipt of aid from official lenders at concessional terms as defined by the DAC, that is, loans with an original grant element of 25 percent or more.

Variable interest rate LDOD is long-term debt with interest rates that float with movements in a key market rate such as the London interbank offer rate (LIBOR) or the U.S. prime rate. This item conveys information about the borrower's exposure to changes in international interest rates.

Public sector LDOD and private sector LDOD convey information about the distribution of long-term debt by type of debtor (central government, state and local government, central bank; private bank, private debt).

Currency composition of long-term debt

The six major currencies in which the external debt of low- and middle-income countries is contracted are separately identified, as is debt denominated in special drawing rights and debt repayable in multiple currencies.

Debt restructurings

Debt restructurings include restructurings in the context of the Paris Club, commercial banks, debt-equity swaps, buybacks, and bond exchanges. Debt restructuring data capture the noncash or inferred flows associated with rescheduling and restructuring. These are presented to complement the cash-basis transactions recorded in the main body of the data.

Debt stock rescheduled is the amount of debt outstanding rescheduled in any given year.

Principal rescheduled is the amount of principal due or in arrears that was rescheduled in any given year.

Interest rescheduled is the amount of interest due or in arrears that was rescheduled in any given year.

Debt forgiven is the amount of principal due or in arrears that was written off or forgiven in any given year.

Interest forgiven is the amount of interest due or in arrears that was written off or forgiven in any given year.

Debt stock reduction is the amount that has been netted out of the stock of debt using debt conversion schemes such as buybacks and equity swaps or the discounted value of long-term bonds that were issued in exchange for outstanding debt.

Debt stock–flow reconciliation

Stock and flow data on total external debt are reconciled for each year, beginning with 1989. The data show the changes in stock that have taken place due to the net flow on debt, the net change in interest arrears, the capitalization of interest, the reduction in debt resulting from debt forgiveness or other debt reduction mechanisms, and the cross-currency valuation effects. The residual difference—the change in stock not explained by any of these factors—is also presented, calculated as the sum of identified accounts minus the change in stock.

Average terms of new commitments

The average terms of borrowing on public and publicly guaranteed debt are given for all new loans contracted during the year and separately for loans from official and private creditors. To obtain averages, the interest rates, maturities, and grace periods in each category have been weighted by the amounts of the loans. The grant equivalent of a loan is its commitment (present) value, less the discounted present value of its contractual debt service; conventionally, future service payments are discounted at 10 percent. The grant element of a loan is the grant equivalent expressed as a percentage of the amount committed. It is used as a measure of the overall cost of borrowing. Loans with an original grant element of 25 percent or more are defined as concessional. The average grant element has been weighted by the amounts of the loans.

Commitments cover the total amount of loans for which contracts were signed in the year specified; data for private nonguaranteed debt are not available.

Projections on existing pipeline

Projected *debt service* payments are estimates of payments due on existing debt outstanding, including undisbursed. They do not include service payments that may become due as a result of new loans contracted in subsequent years. Nor do they allow for effects on service payments of changes in repayment patterns owing to prepayment of loans or to rescheduling or refinancing, including repayment of outstanding arrears, that occurred after the last year of reported data.

Projected *disbursements* are estimates of drawings of unutilized balances. The projections do not take into account future borrowing by the debtor country. See Methodology section for a detailed explanation of the methods of projecting undisbursed balances.

Exchange rates

Data received by the World Bank from its members are expressed in the currencies in which the debts are repayable or in which the transactions took place. For aggregation, the Bank converts these amounts to U.S. dollars using the IMF par values or central rates, or the current market rates where appropriate. Service payments, commitments, and disbursements (flows) are converted to U.S. dollars at the average rate for the year. Debt outstanding and disbursed at the end of a given year (a stock) is converted at the rate in effect at the end of that year. Projected debt service, how-

ever, is converted to U.S. dollars at rates in effect at end-December 1995. Debt repayable in multiple currencies, goods, or services and debt with a provision for maintenance of value of the currency of repayment are shown at book value.

Adjustments

Year-to-year changes in debt outstanding and disbursed are sometimes not equal to net flows; similarly, changes in debt outstanding, including undisbursed, differ from commitments less repayments. The reasons for these differences are cancellations, adjustments caused by the use of different exchange rates, and the rescheduling of other liabilities into long-term public debt.

Symbols

The following symbols have been used throughout: 0.0 indicates that a datum exists, but is negligible, or is a true zero.

.. indicates that a datum is not available.

Dollars are current U.S. dollars unless otherwise specified.

The following abbreviations are used in the principal ratios and indicator charts:

EDT — Total external debt, including short-term and use of IMF credit

LDOD — Total long-term debt outstanding and disbursed

INT — Total interest payments on long-term and short-term debt, including IMF charges

TDS — Total debt service on long-term debt and short-term (interest only), including IMF credits

FDI — Foreign direct investment

GNP — Gross national product

XGS — Exports of goods and services

MGS — Imports of goods and services

RES — International reserves

Country groups

Geographic groups

East Asia and the Pacific

Cambodia (P)
China (P)
Fiji (A)
Indonesia (P)
Lao PDR (P)
Malaysia (P)
Mongolia (A)
Myanmar (A)
Papua New Guinea (A)
Philippines (P)
Solomon Islands (A)
Thailand (P)
Tonga (A)
Vanuatu (A)
Vietnam (P)
Western Samoa (A)
Kiribati
Korea, Dem. Rep.

Europe and Central Asia

Albania (A)
Armenia (P)
Azerbaijan (P)
Belarus (A)
Bosnia and Herzegovina[a]
Bulgaria (A)
Croatia (A)
Czech Republic (P)
Estonia (A)
Georgia (A)
Hungary (A)
Kazakstan (A)
Kyrgyz Republic (A)
Latvia (P)
Lithuania (A)
Macedonia, FYR (A)
Malta (A)
Moldova (A)
Poland (A)

Romania (A)
Russian Federation[b] (P)
Slovak Republic (P)
Slovenia (A)
Tajikistan (E)
Turkey (A)
Turkmenistan (A)
Ukraine (A)
Uzbekistan (A)
Yugoslavia, former[a] (E)
Gibraltar
Greece

Latin America and the Caribbean

Argentina (A)
Barbados (A)
Belize (A)
Bolivia (A)
Brazil (P)
Chile (A)
Colombia (A)
Costa Rica (A)
Dominica (A)
Dominican Republic (A)
Ecuador (A)
El Salvador (A)
Grenada (A)
Guatemala (P)
Guyana (A)
Haiti (P)
Honduras (A)
Jamaica (P)
Mexico (A)
Nicaragua (P)
Panama (A)
Paraguay (A)
Peru (A)
St. Kitts and Nevis (A)
St. Lucia (A)
St.Vincent and the Grenadines (A)
Trinidad and Tobago (A)

Uruguay (A)
Venezuela (E)
Antigua and Barbuda
Cuba
Suriname

Middle East and North Africa

Algeria (A)
Egypt, Arab Rep. (A)
Iran, Islamic Rep. (E)
Jordan (A)
Lebanon (A)
Morocco (P)
Oman (A)
Syrian Arab Republic (E)
Tunisia (P)
Yemen, Rep. (A)
Bahrain
Iraq
Libya
Saudi Arabia

South Asia

Bangladesh (A)
Bhutan (A)
India (A)
Maldives (A)
Nepal (A)
Pakistan (A)
Sri Lanka (A)
Afghanistan

Sub-Saharan Africa

Angola (A)
Benin (P)
Botswana (A)
Burkina Faso (A)
Burundi (A)
Cameroon (A)

Cape Verde (A)
Central African Republic (A)
Chad (P)
Comoros (A)
Congo (A)
Côte d'Ivoire (A)
Djibouti (E)
Equatorial Guinea (E)
Ethiopia[c] (A)
Gabon (A)
Gambia, The (E)
Ghana (A)
Guinea (P)
Guinea-Bissau (P)
Kenya (A)
Lesotho (A)
Liberia (E)
Madagascar (A)
Malawi (P)
Mali (P)
Mauritania (P)
Mauritius (A)
Mozambique (A)
Niger (A)
Nigeria (E)
Rwanda (E)
São Tomé and Principe (A)
Senegal (A)
Seychelles (E)
Sierra Leone (A)
Somalia (E)
Sudan (E)
Swaziland (P)
Tanzania (A)
Togo (A)
Uganda (P)
Zaire (E)
Zambia (P)
Zimbabwe (A)
Namibia
South Africa

Note: Countries printed in normal type are reporters to the Debtor Reporting System (DRS); those printed in italics are non-DRS countries. Letters in parenthesis indicate DRS reporters' status: (A) as reported, (P) preliminary, and (E) estimated. The status "as reported" indicates that the country was fully current in its reporting under the (DRS) and that World Bank staff are satisfied that the reported data give an adequate and fair representation of the country's total public debt. "Preliminary" data are based on reported or collected information but, because of incompleteness or other reasons, include an element of staff estimation. "Estimated" data indicate that countries are not current in their reporting and that a significant element of staff estimation has been necessary in producing the data tables.

a. For Bosnia and Herzegovina total debt, excluding IBRD and IMF obligations and short-term debt, is included under Yugoslavia, former.
b. Includes the debt of the former Soviet Union on the assumption that 100 percent of all outstanding external debt as of December 1991 has become a liability of the Russian Federation.
c. Debt data for 1995 include $24.3 million of IDA credit for Eritrea.

Income groups

Low-income countries

Afghanistan	São Tomé and Principe
Albania	Senegal
Angola	Sierra Leone
Armenia	Somalia
Azerbaijan	Sri Lanka
Bangladesh	Sudan
Benin	Tajikistan
Bhutan	Tanzania
Bosnia and Herzegovina	Togo
Burkina Faso	Uganda
Burundi	Vietnam
Cambodia	Yemen, Rep.
Cameroon	Zaire
Central African Republic	Zambia
Chad	Zimbabwe
China	
Comoros	
Congo	
Côte d'Ivoire	
Equatorial Guinea	
Eritrea	
Ethiopia	
Gambia, The	
Georgia	
Ghana	
Guinea	
Guinea-Bissau	
Guyana	
Haiti	
Honduras	
India	
Kenya	
Kyrgyz Republic	
Lao PDR	
Liberia	
Madagascar	
Malawi	
Mali	
Mauritania	
Mongolia	
Mozambique	
Myanmar	
Nepal	
Nicaragua	
Niger	
Nigeria	
Pakistan	
Rwanda	

Middle-income countries

Algeria	Macedonia, FYR
American Samoa	Malaysia
Antigua and Barbuda	Maldives
Argentina	Malta
Bahrain	Marshall Islands
Barbados	Mauritius
Belarus	Mayotte
Belize	Mexico
Bolivia	Micronesia, Fed. Sts.
Botswana	Moldova
Brazil	Morocco
Bulgaria	Namibia
Cape Verde	Oman
Chile	Panama
Colombia	Papua New Guinea
Costa Rica	Paraguay
Croatia	Peru
Cuba	Philippines
Czech Republic	Poland
Djibouti	Puerto Rico
Dominica	Romania
Dominican Republic	Russian Federation
Ecuador	Saudi Arabia
Egypt, Arab Rep.	Seychelles
El Salvador	Slovak Republic
Estonia	Slovenia
Fiji	Solomon Islands
Gabon	South Africa
Gibraltar	St. Kitts and Nevis
Guadeloupe	St. Lucia
Greece	St. Vincent and the Grenadines
Grenada	Suriname
Guatemala	Swaziland
Hungary	Syrian Arab Republic
Indonesia	Thailand
Iran, Islamic Rep.	Tonga
Iraq	Trinidad and Tobago
Isle of Man	Tunisia
Jamaica	Turkey
Jordan	Turkmenistan
Kazakstan	Ukraine
Kiribati	Uruguay
Korea, Dem. Rep.	Uzbekistan
Latvia	Vanuatu
Lebanon	Venezuela
Lesotho	West Bank and Gaza
Libya	Western Samoa
Lithuania	Yugoslavia, Fed. Rep. (Serbia and Montenegro)

Note: Low-income countries are those in which 1995 GNP per capita (calculated using the *World Bank Atlas* method) was no more than $765; middle-income countries are those in which GNP per capita was between $766 and $3,035.

Other analytical groups

Severely indebted low-income countries (SILICS)[a]	*Severely indebted middle-income countries (SIMICS)*[a]	*Moderately indebted low-income countries (MILICS)*[b]	*Moderately indebted middle-income countries (MIMICS)*[b]
Afghanistan	Argentina	Bangladesh	Algeria
Angola	Bolivia	Benin	Chile
Burundi	Brazil	Burkina Faso	Colombia
Cambodia	Bulgaria	Chad	Egypt, Arab Rep.
Cameroon	Cuba	Comoros	Gibralter
Central African Republic	Ecuador	Gambia, The	Greece
Congo	Gabon	Haiti	Hungary
Côte d'Ivoire	Iraq	India	Indonesia
Equatorial Guinea	Jamaica	Lao PDR	Macedonia, FYR
Ethiopia	Jordan	Pakistan	Morocco
Ghana	Mexico	Senegal	Papua New Guinea
Guinea	Panama	Zimbabwe	Philippines
Guinea-Bissau	Peru		Poland
Guyana	Syrian Arab Republic		Russian Federation
Honduras			St. Vincent
Kenya			Trinidad and Tobago
Liberia			Tunisia
Madagascar			Turkey
Malawi			Uruguay
Mali			Venezuela
Mauritania			Western Samoa
Mozambique			
Myanmar			
Nicaragua			
Niger			
Nigeria			
Rwanda			
Sâo Tomé and Principe			
Sierra Leone			
Somalia			
Sudan			
Tanzania			
Togo			
Uganda			
Vietnam			
Yemen, Rep.			
Zaire			
Zambia			

Note: Low-income countries are those in which 1995 GNP per capita was no more than $765; middle-income countries are those in which GNP per capita was more than $765 but less than $9,386.

a. Countries in which either one of the two key ratios for 1993–95 is above a critical level. These ratios and their critical levels are present value of debt service to GNP (80 percent) and present value of debt service to exports of goods and all services (220 percent).

b. Countries in which either one of the two key ratios for 1993–95 falls in the following ranges: present value of debt service to GNP, 48 to 80 percent; present value of debt service to exports of goods and all services, 132 to 220 percent.

Other analytical groups (continued)

Other developing countries

Antigua and Barbuda
Armenia
Azerbaijan
Bahrain
Barbados
Belarus
Belize
Bhutan
Botswana
Burkina Faso
China
Costa Rica
Croatia
Czech Republic
Djibouti
Dominica
El Salvador
Estonia
Fiji
Georgia
Grenada
Guatemala
Iran, Islamic Republic
Kazakstan
Korea, Dem. Rep.
Kiribati
Kyrgyz Republic
Latvia
Lebanon
Lesotho
Libya
Lithuania

Macedonia, FYR
Malaysia
Maldives
Malta
Mauritius
Moldova
Mongolia
Namibia
New Caledonia
Oman
Paraguay
Romania
Saudi Arabia
Seychelles
Slovak Republic
Slovenia
Solomon Islands
South Africa
Sri Lanka
St. Kitts and Nevis
St. Lucia
St. Vincent and the Grenadines
Suriname
Swaziland
Tajikistan
Thailand
Tonga
Trinidad and Tobago
Turkmenistan
Ukraine
Uzbekistan
Vanuatu
Yugoslavia, Fed. Rep.

Special Program of Assistance[a]

Benin
Burkina Faso
Burundi
Cameroon
Central African Republic
Chad
Comoros
Congo
Côte d'Ivoire
Equatorial Guinea
Ethiopia
Gambia, The
Ghana
Guinea
Guinea-Bissau
Kenya
Madagascar
Malawi
Mali
Mauritania
Mozambique
Niger
Rwanda
São Tomé and Principe
Senegal
Sierra Leone
Tanzania
Togo
Uganda
Zambia

a. Active Special Program of Assistance–eligible countries as of December 1995.

Summary tables

ALL DEVELOPING COUNTRIES

(US$ billion, unless otherwise indicated)

	1970	1980	1990	1995	Preliminary 1996
SUMMARY DEBT DATA					
TOTAL DEBT STOCKS (EDT)	..	**615.7**	**1480.2**	**2065.7**	**2177.0**
Long-term debt (LDOD)	**59.2**	**452.3**	**1184.5**	**1626.4**	**1708.4**
Public and publicly guaranteed	44.0	384.0	1123.9	1448.6	1486.0
Private nonguaranteed	15.2	68.3	60.6	177.7	222.4
Use of IMF credit	**0.8**	**11.6**	**34.7**	**61.1**	**60.2**
Short-term debt	..	**151.9**	**261.1**	**378.2**	**408.5**
of which interest arrears on LDOD	..	1.0	52.3	43.6	34.5
Memo:					
IBRD	4.4	20.4	92.3	111.9	113.0
IDA	1.8	11.8	45.0	71.5	77.3
TOTAL DEBT FLOWS					
Disbursements	**12.8**	**114.5**	**134.3**	**229.2**	**242.1**
Long-term debt	12.4	109.1	126.0	201.2	233.7
Public and publicly guaranteed	8.3	88.2	108.7	140.0	159.8
Private nonguaranteed	4.1	20.9	17.3	61.2	74.0
IMF purchases	**0.3**	**5.4**	**8.2**	**27.9**	**8.4**
Memo:					
IBRD	0.7	4.2	13.4	13.1	12.7
IDA	0.2	1.6	4.4	5.5	6.3
Principal repayments	**6.5**	**43.4**	**90.5**	**135.3**	**143.4**
Long-term debt	**5.8**	**41.3**	**82.4**	**124.2**	**135.7**
Public and publicly guaranteed	3.3	29.7	75.1	96.5	106.2
Private nonguaranteed	2.4	11.7	7.3	27.7	29.4
IMF repurchases	**0.7**	**2.1**	**8.2**	**11.1**	**7.8**
Memo:					
IBRD	0.2	1.0	7.9	11.7	11.0
IDA	0.0	0.0	0.2	0.5	0.7
Net flows on debt	**15.0**	**114.4**	**62.4**	**133.0**	**138.0**
of which short-term debt	..	..	18.6	39.2	39.3
Interest payments (INT)	..	**49.1**	**73.1**	**96.0**	**101.2**
Long-term debt	2.3	32.9	56.0	74.5	78.7
Net transfers on debt	..	**65.4**	**-10.7**	**37.1**	**36.8**
Total debt service (TDS)	..	**92.5**	**163.6**	**231.3**	**244.6**
AGGREGATE NET RESOURCE FLOWS AND NET TRANSFERS (LONG-TERM)					
NET RESOURCE FLOWS	**10.9**	**86.1**	**100.6**	**237.2**	**284.6**
Net flow of long-term debt (ex. IMF)	6.6	67.7	43.7	77.0	98.1
Foreign direct investment (net)	2.2	5.1	24.5	95.5	109.5
Portfolio equity flows	0.0	0.0	3.2	32.1	45.7
Grants (excluding technical coop.)	2.1	13.2	29.2	32.6	31.3
NET TRANSFERS	**2.2**	**29.4**	**27.2**	**136.3**	**175.6**
Interest on long-term debt	2.3	32.9	56.0	74.5	78.7
Profit remittances on FDI	6.5	23.7	17.4	26.4	30.3
MAJOR ECONOMIC INDICATORS					
Gross national product (GNP)	796.9	2927.2	4250.5	5221.4	5881.2
Exports of goods & services (XGS)	94.4	712.1	896.5	1364.5	1488.7
of which workers' remittances	2.1	20.6	25.8	39.4	35.8
Imports of goods & services (MGS)	99.1	696.6	946.0	1481.7	1629.4
International reserves (RES)	27.6	232.1	239.3	538.4	..
Current account balance	5.8	26.0	-40.9	-101.0	-123.2
DEBT INDICATORS					
EDT / XGS (%)	..	86.5	165.1	151.4	146.2
EDT / GNP (%)	..	21.0	34.8	39.6	37.0
TDS / XGS (%)	..	13.0	18.3	17.0	16.4
INT / XGS (%)	..	6.9	8.2	7.0	6.8
INT / GNP (%)	..	1.7	1.7	1.8	1.7
RES / MGS (months)	3.3	4.0	3.0	4.4	..
Short-term / EDT (%)	..	24.7	17.6	18.3	18.8
Concessional / EDT (%)	..	17.8	20.8	21.1	19.9
Multilateral / EDT (%)	..	7.6	14.2	14.3	14.2

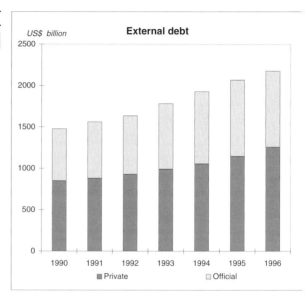

External debt

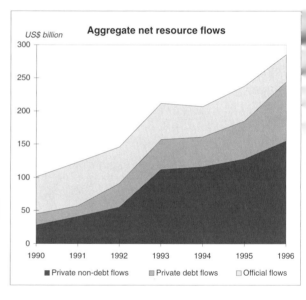

Aggregate net resource flows

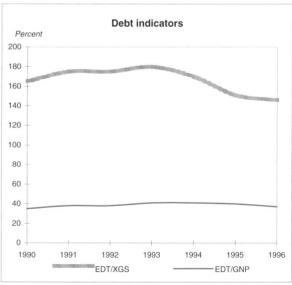

Debt indicators

ALL DEVELOPING COUNTRIES

(US$ billion, unless otherwise indicated)

	1970	1980	1990	1995	Preliminary 1996
LONG-TERM DEBT					
DEBT OUTSTANDING (LDOD)	**59.2**	**452.3**	**1184.5**	**1626.4**	**1708.4**
Public and publicly guaranteed	**44.0**	**384.0**	**1123.9**	**1448.6**	**1486.0**
Official creditors	31.7	171.1	596.2	860.9	860.3
Multilateral	7.3	46.8	209.5	294.9	309.3
Bilateral	24.4	124.3	386.7	566.0	550.9
Private creditors	12.3	212.9	527.6	587.7	625.7
Bonds	1.8	18.8	111.9	267.7	296.5
Private nonguaranteed	**15.2**	**68.3**	**60.6**	**177.7**	**222.4**
Bonds	..	..	0.3	53.2	73.5
DISBURSEMENTS	**12.4**	**109.1**	**126.0**	**201.2**	**233.7**
Public and publicly guaranteed	**8.3**	**88.2**	**108.7**	**140.0**	**159.8**
Official creditors	4.8	28.2	52.1	65.8	56.0
Multilateral	1.2	9.0	27.7	32.4	33.9
Bilateral	3.6	19.1	24.4	33.4	22.1
Private creditors	3.5	60.0	56.6	74.2	103.8
Bonds	0.1	3.1	6.9	29.7	48.7
Private nonguaranteed	**4.1**	**20.9**	**17.3**	**61.2**	**74.0**
Bonds	..	..	0.3	14.6	26.0
PRINCIPAL REPAYMENTS	**5.8**	**41.3**	**82.4**	**124.2**	**135.7**
Public and publicly guaranteed	**3.3**	**29.7**	**75.1**	**96.5**	**106.2**
Official creditors	1.5	7.0	25.0	45.4	46.5
Multilateral	0.4	1.6	12.2	21.3	18.8
Bilateral	1.1	5.4	12.8	24.1	27.7
Private creditors	1.9	22.6	50.1	51.2	59.7
Bonds	0.1	0.5	4.8	11.8	23.4
Private nonguaranteed	**2.4**	**11.7**	**7.3**	**27.7**	**29.4**
Bonds	..	..	0.0	4.0	5.2
NET DEBT FLOWS	**6.6**	**67.7**	**43.7**	**77.0**	**98.1**
Public and publicly guaranteed	**5.0**	**58.5**	**33.6**	**43.5**	**53.5**
Official creditors	3.3	21.1	27.1	20.4	9.5
Multilateral	0.8	7.5	15.5	11.1	15.0
Bilateral	2.5	13.7	11.6	9.4	-5.6
Private creditors	1.7	37.4	6.5	23.1	44.0
Bonds	0.0	2.6	2.0	17.9	25.3
Private nonguaranteed	**1.7**	**9.2**	**10.1**	**33.6**	**44.5**
Bonds	..	..	0.3	10.6	20.8
CURRENCY COMPOSITION OF LONG-TERM DEBT (PERCENT)					
Deutsche mark	8.6	6.4	8.6	7.3	..
French franc	5.3	5.3	5.4	4.5	..
Japanese yen	2.2	5.8	9.9	11.6	..
Pound sterling	11.6	3.3	2.2	1.4	..
U.S. dollars	45.6	47.2	40.3	44.3	..
Multiple currency	12.1	10.3	14.3	14.2	..
All other currencies	14.6	9.6	11.3	9.1	..
DEBT STOCK-FLOW RECONCILIATION					
Total change in debt stocks	..	..	106.0	138.7	111.4
Net flows on debt	..	..	62.4	133.0	138.0
Net change in interest arrears	..	..	15.6	0.8	-9.1
Interest capitalized	..	..	5.9	5.2	..
Debt forgiveness or reduction	..	..	-33.5	-6.0	..
Cross-currency valuation	..	..	51.5	11.6	..
Residual	..	..	4.1	-5.8	..
AVERAGE TERMS OF NEW COMMITMENTS					
ALL CREDITORS					
Interest (%)	5.0	9.1	7.0	6.3	..
Maturity (years)	21.2	15.7	18.1	13.5	..
Grant element (%)	34.7	10.0	20.1	20.2	..
Official creditors					..
Interest (%)	3.6	5.4	5.6	6.0	..
Maturity (years)	28.5	24.0	22.2	18.8	..
Grant element (%)	49.2	34.9	32.7	27.3	..
Private creditors					..
Interest (%)	7.2	11.9	8.5	6.6	..
Maturity (years)	9.5	9.6	13.7	7.5	..
Grant element (%)	11.7	-8.5	6.7	12.3	..
Memo:					
Commitments	11.2	93.7	120.4	132.1	..
Official creditors	6.9	39.9	62.1	69.9	..
Private creditors	4.3	53.7	58.3	62.2	..

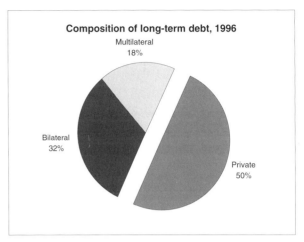

Composition of long-term debt, 1996

Multilateral 18%
Bilateral 32%
Private 50%

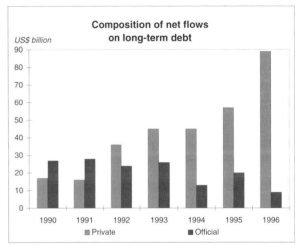

Composition of net flows on long-term debt

US$ billion

■ Private   ■ Official

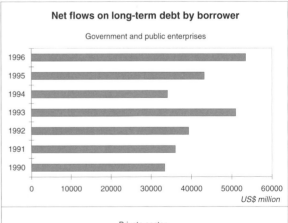

Net flows on long-term debt by borrower

Government and public enterprises

US$ million

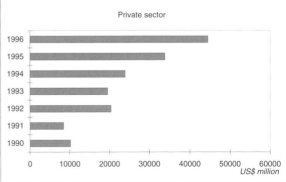

Private sector

US$ million

EAST ASIA AND PACIFIC

(US$ billion, unless otherwise indicated)

	1970	1980	1990	1995	Preliminary 1996
SUMMARY DEBT DATA					
TOTAL DEBT STOCKS (EDT)	..	64.6	239.1	404.5	451.8
Long-term debt (LDOD)	6.0	48.4	199.1	322.6	355.1
Public and publicly guaranteed	4.0	39.7	177.4	264.5	268.1
Private nonguaranteed	2.0	8.8	21.6	58.0	87.0
Use of IMF credit	0.2	1.6	2.1	1.3	1.3
Short-term debt	..	14.6	38.0	80.6	95.5
of which interest arrears on LDOD	..	0.0	1.5	2.8	3.0
Memo:					
IBRD	0.4	3.2	20.2	27.9	28.2
IDA	0.0	0.8	5.1	9.7	10.7
TOTAL DEBT FLOWS					
Disbursements	1.6	12.8	30.0	59.0	73.1
Long-term debt	1.5	12.3	30.0	58.8	72.8
Public and publicly guaranteed	0.8	9.4	20.1	38.0	33.6
Private nonguaranteed	0.8	2.9	9.8	20.8	39.2
IMF purchases	0.1	0.5	0.1	0.2	0.3
Memo:					
IBRD	0.1	0.8	2.5	3.2	2.7
IDA	0.0	0.1	0.6	0.9	1.1
Principal repayments	0.6	4.3	18.0	32.9	33.8
Long-term debt	0.6	4.1	16.8	32.6	33.5
Public and publicly guaranteed	0.2	2.2	14.2	22.2	23.2
Private nonguaranteed	0.4	1.9	2.6	10.4	10.2
IMF repurchases	0.0	0.2	1.3	0.4	0.3
Memo:					
IBRD	0.0	0.1	1.5	2.2	2.4
IDA	0.0	0.0	0.0	0.1	0.1
Net flows on debt	2.2	11.9	20.0	41.4	54.0
of which short-term debt	..	..	8.0	15.4	14.7
Interest payments (INT)	..	4.8	12.7	19.6	21.8
Long-term debt	0.2	3.0	10.3	15.2	16.9
Net transfers on debt	..	7.1	7.4	21.8	32.2
Total debt service (TDS)	..	9.1	30.7	52.5	55.6
AGGREGATE NET RESOURCE FLOWS AND NET TRANSFERS (LONG-TERM)					
NET RESOURCE FLOWS	1.8	10.7	27.3	95.8	116.1
Net flow of long-term debt (ex. IMF)	0.9	8.2	13.2	26.2	39.3
Foreign direct investment (net)	0.2	1.3	10.2	51.8	61.1
Portfolio equity flows	0.0	0.0	1.7	14.7	12.9
Grants (excluding technical coop.)	0.7	1.1	2.1	3.1	2.8
NET TRANSFERS	1.3	2.8	12.1	71.7	88.5
Interest on long-term debt	0.2	3.0	10.3	15.2	16.9
Profit remittances on FDI	0.3	4.9	4.8	8.9	10.6
MAJOR ECONOMIC INDICATORS					
Gross national product (GNP)	127.1	372.5	644.2	1228.1	1465.4
Exports of goods & services (XGS)	9.6	78.9	175.7	411.6	456.8
of which workers' remittances	0.0	0.9	0.6	1.6	1.6
Imports of goods & services (MGS)	11.7	86.6	181.1	447.3	516.8
International reserves (RES)	2.2	30.8	71.4	166.5	..
Current account balance	-1.9	-6.4	-3.6	-25.4	-43.3
DEBT INDICATORS					
EDT / XGS (%)	..	81.8	136.1	98.3	98.9
EDT / GNP (%)	..	17.3	37.1	32.9	30.8
TDS / XGS (%)	..	11.5	17.5	12.8	12.2
INT / XGS (%)	..	6.1	7.2	4.8	4.8
INT / GNP (%)	..	1.3	2.0	1.6	1.5
RES / MGS (months)	2.3	4.3	4.7	4.5	..
Short-term / EDT (%)	..	22.6	15.9	19.9	21.1
Concessional / EDT (%)	..	23.1	30.6	25.5	22.7
Multilateral / EDT (%)	..	8.4	14.6	13.3	12.5

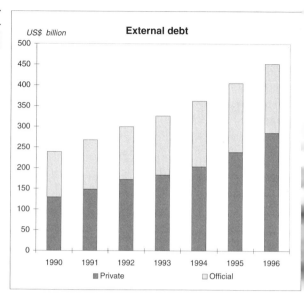

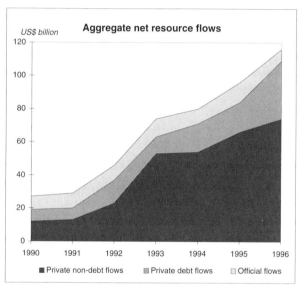

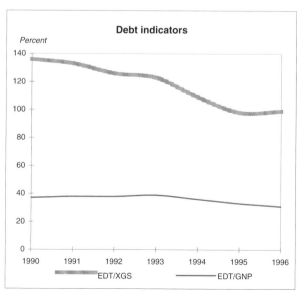

EAST ASIA AND PACIFIC

(US$ billion, unless otherwise indicated)

	1970	1980	1990	1995	*Preliminary* 1996
LONG-TERM DEBT					
DEBT OUTSTANDING (LDOD)	**6.0**	**48.4**	**199.1**	**322.6**	**355.1**
Public and publicly guaranteed	**4.0**	**39.7**	**177.4**	**264.5**	**268.1**
Official creditors	3.1	21.0	107.8	165.5	165.3
Multilateral	0.5	5.5	35.0	53.6	56.3
Bilateral	2.7	15.6	72.8	111.8	109.0
Private creditors	0.9	18.7	69.6	99.1	102.8
Bonds	0.1	1.7	12.7	23.5	24.3
Private nonguaranteed	**2.0**	**8.8**	**21.6**	**58.0**	**87.0**
Bonds	..	..	0.2	16.5	26.0
DISBURSEMENTS	**1.5**	**12.3**	**30.0**	**58.8**	**72.8**
Public and publicly guaranteed	**0.8**	**9.4**	**20.1**	**38.0**	**33.6**
Official creditors	0.5	3.0	10.3	16.8	12.5
Multilateral	0.1	1.2	4.7	6.1	6.1
Bilateral	0.5	1.8	5.6	10.7	6.4
Private creditors	0.2	6.3	9.8	21.2	21.1
Bonds	0.0	0.2	1.1	4.0	5.6
Private nonguaranteed	**0.8**	**2.9**	**9.8**	**20.8**	**39.2**
Bonds	..	..	0.1	6.1	9.9
PRINCIPAL REPAYMENTS	**0.6**	**4.1**	**16.8**	**32.6**	**33.5**
Public and publicly guaranteed	**0.2**	**2.2**	**14.2**	**22.2**	**23.2**
Official creditors	0.1	0.7	4.5	8.2	7.9
Multilateral	0.0	0.2	2.0	3.1	3.3
Bilateral	0.1	0.5	2.4	5.1	4.5
Private creditors	0.1	1.5	9.7	13.9	15.4
Bonds	0.0	0.0	1.1	2.1	3.7
Private nonguaranteed	**0.4**	**1.9**	**2.6**	**10.4**	**10.2**
Bonds	..	..	0.0	0.1	0.3
NET FLOWS ON DEBT	**0.9**	**8.2**	**13.2**	**26.2**	**39.3**
Public and publicly guaranteed	**0.5**	**7.2**	**5.9**	**15.8**	**10.4**
Official creditors	0.5	2.4	5.8	8.6	4.6
Multilateral	0.0	1.1	2.7	3.0	2.8
Bilateral	0.4	1.3	3.1	5.5	1.8
Private creditors	0.1	4.8	0.1	7.2	5.8
Bonds	0.0	0.2	0.0	1.9	1.9
Private nonguaranteed	**0.4**	**1.0**	**7.3**	**10.4**	**28.9**
Bonds	..	..	0.1	6.0	9.5
CURRENCY COMPOSITION OF LONG-TERM DEBT (PERCENT)					
Deutsche mark	7.0	5.5	4.0	2.7	..
French franc	2.9	3.6	1.7	1.4	..
Japanese yen	8.3	18.6	28.4	27.1	..
Pound sterling	6.2	1.0	0.9	0.4	..
U.S. dollars	36.0	35.8	23.0	35.4	..
Multiple currency	11.1	18.1	22.5	18.9	..
All other currencies	28.5	9.0	17.2	11.7	..
DEBT STOCK-FLOW RECONCILIATION					
Total change in debt stocks	..	..	31.9	42.1	..
Net flows on debt	..	..	20.0	41.4	..
Net change in interest arrears	..	..	0.6	0.1	..
Interest capitalized	..	..	0.2	0.1	..
Debt forgiveness or reduction	..	..	-1.1	0.0	..
Cross-currency valuation	..	..	8.4	-1.1	..
Residual	..	..	3.7	1.6	..
AVERAGE TERMS OF NEW COMMITMENTS					
ALL CREDITORS					
Interest (%)	4.5	9.1	6.6	5.9	..
Maturity (years)	25.5	16.4	19.3	15.0	..
Grant element (%)	40.5	10.7	23.7	22.5	..
Official creditors					..
Interest (%)	4.0	5.5	5.0	5.5	..
Maturity (years)	28.7	22.9	24.4	21.1	..
Grant element (%)	46.4	33.0	38.0	30.6	..
Private creditors					..
Interest (%)	6.9	12.7	8.4	6.3	..
Maturity (years)	10.6	9.7	13.6	9.7	..
Grant element (%)	12.6	-12.1	7.6	15.4	..
Memo:					
Commitments	1.0	14.8	23.5	43.4	..
Official creditors	0.9	7.5	12.5	20.2	..
Private creditors	0.2	7.3	11.0	23.2	..

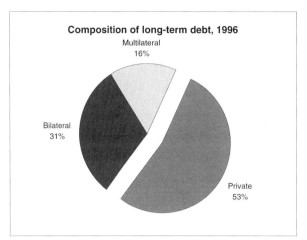

Composition of long-term debt, 1996

Multilateral 16%

Bilateral 31%

Private 53%

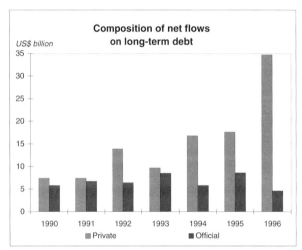

Composition of net flows on long-term debt

US$ billion

■ Private ■ Official

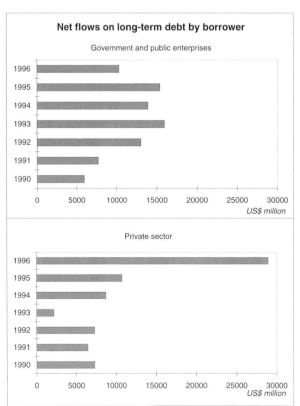

Net flows on long-term debt by borrower

Government and public enterprises

US$ million

Private sector

US$ million

194

EUROPE AND CENTRAL ASIA

(US$ billion, unless otherwise indicated)

	1970	1980	1990	1995	*Preliminary* 1996

SUMMARY DEBT DATA

	1970	1980	1990	1995	1996
TOTAL DEBT STOCKS (EDT)	..	**87.9**	**262.3**	**425.3**	**451.4**
Long-term debt (LDOD)	**4.0**	**63.3**	**199.4**	**330.2**	**346.1**
Public and publicly guaranteed	3.1	51.8	194.5	309.7	323.9
Private nonguaranteed	0.9	11.5	4.9	20.5	22.2
Use of IMF credit	**0.1**	**2.1**	**1.3**	**16.9**	**20.1**
Short-term debt	..	**22.5**	**61.6**	**78.1**	**85.3**
of which interest arrears on LDOD	..	0.3	13.0	8.7	4.9
Memo:					
IBRD	0.3	3.3	10.3	16.2	17.9
IDA	0.1	0.2	0.2	0.7	1.1
TOTAL DEBT FLOWS					
Disbursements	**1.1**	**22.7**	**32.2**	**43.4**	**40.6**
Long-term debt	**1.0**	**21.5**	**31.5**	**35.3**	**35.6**
Public and publicly guaranteed	0.5	18.2	29.7	27.5	31.0
Private nonguaranteed	0.5	3.3	1.8	7.8	4.6
IMF purchases	**0.1**	**1.2**	**0.7**	**8.2**	**5.0**
Memo:					
IBRD	0.1	0.8	1.2	2.7	3.2
IDA	0.0	0.0	0.0	0.4	0.4
Principal repayments	**0.6**	**7.5**	**21.2**	**26.9**	**21.8**
Long-term debt	**0.5**	**7.2**	**20.5**	**23.8**	**20.5**
Public and publicly guaranteed	0.3	5.2	19.0	20.6	17.5
Private nonguaranteed	0.2	2.0	1.5	3.2	3.0
IMF repurchases	**0.1**	**0.3**	**0.7**	**3.1**	**1.3**
Memo:					
IBRD	0.0	0.1	1.1	1.2	1.1
IDA	0.0	0.0	0.0	0.0	0.0
Net flows on debt	**1.5**	**24.5**	**7.1**	**27.2**	**29.7**
of which short-term debt	..	..	-3.9	10.6	10.8
Interest payments (INT)	..	**6.3**	**15.4**	**18.0**	**18.8**
Long-term debt	0.2	4.0	11.3	14.0	14.2
Net transfers on debt	..	**18.2**	**-8.2**	**9.2**	**10.9**
Total debt service (TDS)	..	13.8	36.5	44.8	40.5

AGGREGATE NET RESOURCE FLOWS AND NET TRANSFERS (LONG-TERM)

	1970	1980	1990	1995	1996
NET RESOURCE FLOWS	**0.7**	**15.3**	**15.1**	**40.6**	**45.3**
Net flow of long-term debt (ex. IMF)	0.5	14.3	11.0	11.5	15.2
Foreign direct investment (net)	0.1	0.7	2.1	17.2	15.0
Portfolio equity flows	0.0	0.0	0.2	2.8	6.7
Grants (excluding technical coop.)	0.1	0.3	1.7	9.1	8.5
NET TRANSFERS	**0.5**	**11.2**	**3.5**	**25.5**	**29.7**
Interest on long-term debt	0.2	4.0	11.3	14.0	14.2
Profit remittances on FDI	0.0	0.1	0.3	1.1	1.4

MAJOR ECONOMIC INDICATORS

	1970	1980	1990	1995	1996
Gross national product (GNP)	329.5	889.0	1452.5	1066.8	1301.5
Exports of goods & services (XGS)	34.8	186.6	255.0	325.4	357.6
of which workers' remittances	0.7	3.2	5.1	6.8	6.5
Imports of goods & services (MGS)	31.8	180.2	280.3	346.3	387.7
International reserves (RES)	10.9	23.3	35.2	110.0	..
Current account balance	11.2	7.5	-18.5	-10.6	-23.3

DEBT INDICATORS

	1970	1980	1990	1995	1996
EDT / XGS (%)	..	47.1	102.9	130.7	126.3
EDT / GNP (%)	..	9.9	18.1	39.9	34.7
TDS / XGS (%)	..	7.4	14.3	13.8	11.3
INT / XGS (%)	..	3.4	6.0	5.5	5.2
INT / GNP (%)	..	0.7	1.1	1.7	1.4
RES / MGS (months)	4.1	1.5	1.5	3.8	..
Short-term / EDT (%)	..	25.6	23.5	18.4	18.9
Concessional / EDT (%)	..	8.9	5.4	11.3	10.3
Multilateral / EDT (%)	..	5.4	8.4	7.9	7.9

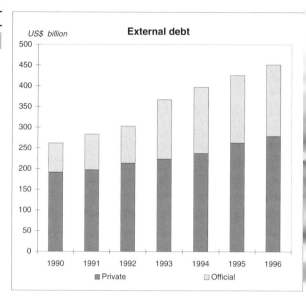

External debt (US$ billion) — Private / Official, 1990–1996

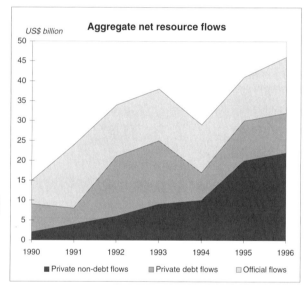

Aggregate net resource flows (US$ billion) — Private non-debt flows / Private debt flows / Official flows, 1990–1996

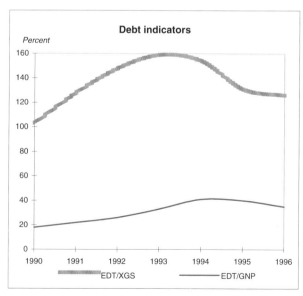

Debt indicators (Percent) — EDT/XGS / EDT/GNP, 1990–1996

EUROPE AND CENTRAL ASIA

(US$ billion, unless otherwise indicated)

	1970	1980	1990	1995	Preliminary 1996
LONG-TERM DEBT					
DEBT OUTSTANDING (LDOD)	**4.0**	**63.3**	**199.4**	**330.2**	**346.1**
Public and publicly guaranteed	**3.1**	**51.8**	**194.5**	**309.7**	**323.9**
Official creditors	2.7	19.1	70.1	145.8	152.5
Multilateral	0.6	4.7	22.1	33.6	35.6
Bilateral	2.0	14.4	48.0	112.2	116.8
Private creditors	0.4	32.7	124.3	163.9	171.4
Bonds	0.0	0.3	16.2	63.0	66.0
Private nonguaranteed	**0.9**	**11.5**	**4.9**	**20.5**	**22.2**
Bonds	..	..	0.0	0.2	0.9
DISBURSEMENTS	**1.0**	**21.5**	**31.5**	**35.3**	**35.6**
Public and publicly guaranteed	**0.5**	**18.2**	**29.7**	**27.5**	**31.0**
Official creditors	0.5	4.9	7.4	7.2	10.3
Multilateral	0.2	1.1	2.6	4.8	5.2
Bilateral	0.3	3.8	4.8	2.4	5.1
Private creditors	0.1	13.3	22.3	20.3	20.7
Bonds	0.0	0.0	3.4	9.6	10.0
Private nonguaranteed	**0.5**	**3.3**	**1.8**	**7.8**	**4.6**
Bonds	..	..	0.0	0.0	0.8
PRINCIPAL REPAYMENTS	**0.5**	**7.2**	**20.5**	**23.8**	**20.5**
Public and publicly guaranteed	**0.3**	**5.2**	**19.0**	**20.6**	**17.5**
Official creditors	0.2	1.7	3.5	5.8	4.7
Multilateral	0.1	0.2	1.7	3.5	2.5
Bilateral	0.1	1.5	1.8	2.2	2.2
Private creditors	0.1	3.4	15.4	14.8	12.8
Bonds	0.0	0.0	0.4	4.4	5.3
Private nonguaranteed	**0.2**	**2.0**	**1.5**	**3.2**	**3.0**
Bonds	..	..	0.0	0.0	0.0
NET FLOWS ON DEBT	**0.5**	**14.3**	**11.0**	**11.5**	**15.2**
Public and publicly guaranteed	**0.2**	**13.0**	**10.8**	**6.9**	**13.5**
Official creditors	0.3	3.1	3.9	1.4	5.6
Multilateral	0.1	0.9	0.9	1.3	2.7
Bilateral	0.2	2.3	3.0	0.1	2.9
Private creditors	-0.1	9.9	6.9	5.5	7.9
Bonds	0.0	0.0	3.1	5.3	4.8
Private nonguaranteed	**0.3**	**1.3**	**0.3**	**4.6**	**1.7**
Bonds	..	..	0.0	0.0	0.8
CURRENCY COMPOSITION OF LONG-TERM DEBT (PERCENT)					
Deutsche mark	15.9	9.6	22.3	15.9	..
French franc	2.7	8.0	4.4	2.8	..
Japanese yen	0.1	2.1	6.7	8.4	..
Pound sterling	5.5	2.3	1.6	0.9	..
U.S. dollars	44.3	36.2	28.5	39.9	..
Multiple currency	15.2	18.7	9.4	10.0	..
All other currencies	16.3	9.5	15.8	9.8	..
DEBT STOCK-FLOW RECONCILIATION					
Total change in debt stocks	..	..	26.1	28.8	..
Net flows on debt	..	..	7.1	27.2	..
Net change in interest arrears	..	..	5.2	1.4	..
Interest capitalized	..	..	2.2	1.4	..
Debt forgiveness or reduction	..	..	-1.1	-0.1	..
Cross-currency valuation	..	..	13.5	6.4	..
Residual	..	..	-0.8	-7.3	..
AVERAGE TERMS OF NEW COMMITMENTS					
ALL CREDITORS					
Interest (%)	4.2	10.3	8.4	6.4	..
Maturity (years)	19.3	12.4	16.7	11.0	..
Grant element (%)	37.0	1.7	8.0	17.0	..
Official creditors					..
Interest (%)	3.9	7.6	8.0	5.8	..
Maturity (years)	20.2	16.7	13.6	16.6	..
Grant element (%)	39.9	18.7	11.2	25.3	..
Private creditors					..
Interest (%)	6.3	11.2	8.6	6.7	..
Maturity (years)	13.4	10.9	18.0	8.2	..
Grant element (%)	18.2	-4.4	6.6	12.9	..
Memo:					
Commitments	0.8	12.6	30.3	21.9	..
Official creditors	0.7	3.3	9.3	7.3	..
Private creditors	0.1	9.3	21.0	14.6	..

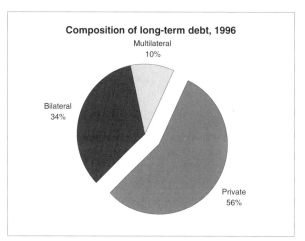

Composition of long-term debt, 1996

Multilateral 10%

Bilateral 34%

Private 56%

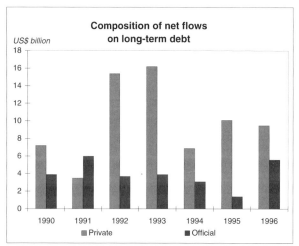

Composition of net flows on long-term debt

US$ billion

■ Private ■ Official

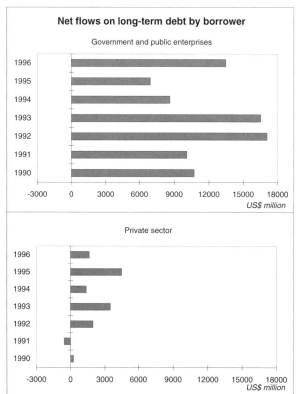

Net flows on long-term debt by borrower

Government and public enterprises

US$ million

Private sector

US$ million

LATIN AMERICA AND THE CARIBBEAN

(US$ billion, unless otherwise indicated)

	1970	1980	1990	1995	Preliminary 1996
SUMMARY DEBT DATA					
TOTAL DEBT STOCKS (EDT)	..	**257.3**	**474.9**	**636.6**	**656.5**
Long-term debt (LDOD)	**27.6**	**187.3**	**379.2**	**490.3**	**510.7**
Public and publicly guaranteed	15.8	144.8	354.1	409.8	424.7
Private nonguaranteed	11.9	42.5	25.1	80.5	86.0
Use of IMF credit	**0.1**	**1.4**	**18.3**	**26.7**	**23.8**
Short-term debt	..	**68.6**	**77.4**	**119.5**	**122.0**
of which interest arrears on LDOD	..	0.1	25.6	9.1	2.5
Memo:					
IBRD	2.1	7.7	34.8	36.4	36.8
IDA	0.1	0.4	1.1	2.2	2.5
TOTAL DEBT FLOWS					
Disbursements	**6.5**	**44.8**	**34.0**	**87.7**	**80.6**
Long-term debt	**6.4**	**44.4**	**29.1**	**71.9**	**79.4**
Public and publicly guaranteed	3.6	31.4	24.4	44.2	59.3
Private nonguaranteed	2.8	13.0	4.7	27.7	20.1
IMF purchases	**0.1**	**0.4**	**4.8**	**15.8**	**1.2**
Memo:					
IBRD	0.4	1.6	6.1	4.6	4.5
IDA	0.0	0.1	0.1	0.3	0.4
Principal repayments	**3.7**	**21.7**	**22.8**	**41.3**	**59.1**
Long-term debt	**3.4**	**21.2**	**19.1**	**38.4**	**55.6**
Public and publicly guaranteed	1.7	14.3	16.9	25.2	40.9
Private nonguaranteed	1.8	7.0	2.2	13.1	14.7
IMF repurchases	**0.3**	**0.5**	**3.7**	**2.9**	**3.5**
Memo:					
IBRD	0.1	0.4	3.3	5.0	4.1
IDA	0.0	0.0	0.0	0.0	0.0
Net flows on debt	**7.5**	**46.1**	**20.3**	**51.4**	**30.6**
of which short-term debt	..	..	9.1	5.0	9.1
Interest payments (INT)	..	**24.6**	**22.6**	**37.2**	**38.2**
Long-term debt	1.4	17.6	18.6	29.5	30.2
Net transfers on debt	..	**21.5**	**-2.3**	**14.1**	**-7.6**
Total debt service (TDS)	..	**46.3**	**45.4**	**78.5**	**97.3**
AGGREGATE NET RESOURCE FLOWS AND NET TRANSFERS (LONG-TERM)					
NET RESOURCE FLOWS	**4.2**	**29.9**	**21.6**	**66.9**	**69.2**
Net flow of long-term debt (ex. IMF)	2.9	23.2	10.0	33.5	23.8
Foreign direct investment (net)	1.1	6.1	8.1	22.9	25.9
Portfolio equity flows	0.0	0.0	1.1	7.2	16.5
Grants (excluding technical coop.)	0.2	0.6	2.4	3.3	2.9
NET TRANSFERS	**0.8**	**7.5**	**-3.3**	**26.8**	**26.6**
Interest on long-term debt	1.4	17.6	18.6	29.5	30.2
Profit remittances on FDI	2.0	4.9	6.4	10.6	12.4
MAJOR ECONOMIC INDICATORS					
Gross national product (GNP)	154.8	714.5	1020.9	1553.8	1587.7
Exports of goods & services (XGS)	19.2	127.5	185.6	300.2	323.7
of which workers' remittances	0.1	1.2	4.8	9.9	9.6
Imports of goods & services (MGS)	22.7	158.9	193.4	337.3	354.8
International reserves (RES)	5.5	57.4	58.3	139.0	..
Current account balance	1.3	-30.5	-2.8	-33.3	-27.8
DEBT INDICATORS					
EDT / XGS (%)	..	201.8	255.9	212.0	202.8
EDT / GNP (%)	..	36.0	46.5	41.0	41.4
TDS / XGS (%)	..	36.3	24.4	26.1	30.0
INT / XGS (%)	..	19.3	12.2	12.4	11.8
INT / GNP (%)	..	3.4	2.2	2.4	2.4
RES / MGS (months)	2.9	4.3	3.6	4.9	..
Short-term / EDT (%)	..	26.7	16.3	18.8	18.6
Concessional / EDT (%)	..	9.6	10.3	9.3	9.0
Multilateral / EDT (%)	..	5.5	12.6	11.4	11.5

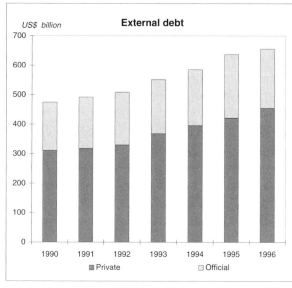

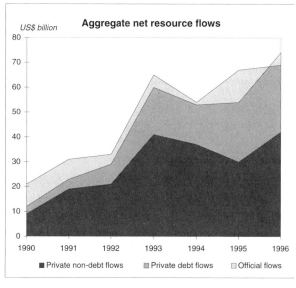

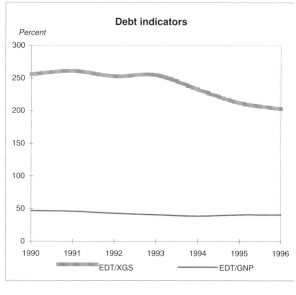

LATIN AMERICA AND THE CARIBBEAN

(US$ billion, unless otherwise indicated)

	1970	1980	1990	1995	Preliminary 1996
LONG-TERM DEBT					
DEBT OUTSTANDING (LDOD)	**27.6**	**187.3**	**379.2**	**490.3**	**510.7**
Public and publicly guaranteed	**15.8**	**144.8**	**354.1**	**409.8**	**424.7**
Official creditors	8.1	45.0	146.5	189.2	177.4
Multilateral	3.0	14.1	60.0	72.7	75.2
Bilateral	5.2	30.9	86.5	116.5	102.2
Private creditors	7.6	99.8	207.6	220.7	247.3
Bonds	1.2	9.6	76.0	171.7	197.2
Private nonguaranteed	**11.9**	**42.5**	**25.1**	**80.5**	**86.0**
Bonds	..	..	0.2	34.9	44.3
DISBURSEMENTS	**6.4**	**44.4**	**29.1**	**71.9**	**79.4**
Public and publicly guaranteed	**3.6**	**31.4**	**24.4**	**44.2**	**59.3**
Official creditors	1.3	6.8	13.7	24.1	12.7
Multilateral	0.6	3.0	9.0	9.9	9.2
Bilateral	0.8	3.9	4.8	14.1	3.5
Private creditors	2.3	24.6	10.7	20.1	46.6
Bonds	0.1	1.2	1.9	14.0	31.5
Private nonguaranteed	**2.8**	**13.0**	**4.7**	**27.7**	**20.1**
Bonds	..	..	0.2	7.4	14.2
PRINCIPAL REPAYMENTS	**3.4**	**21.2**	**19.1**	**38.4**	**55.6**
Public and publicly guaranteed	**1.7**	**14.3**	**16.9**	**25.2**	**40.9**
Official creditors	0.5	2.1	7.0	14.7	20.9
Multilateral	0.2	0.7	4.7	8.3	6.7
Bilateral	0.3	1.4	2.2	6.4	14.2
Private creditors	1.2	12.1	9.9	10.5	20.0
Bonds	0.1	0.4	2.0	4.4	12.4
Private nonguaranteed	**1.8**	**7.0**	**2.2**	**13.1**	**14.7**
Bonds	..	..	0.0	3.9	4.9
NET FLOWS ON DEBT	**2.9**	**23.2**	**10.0**	**33.5**	**23.8**
Public and publicly guaranteed	**1.9**	**17.2**	**7.5**	**19.0**	**18.4**
Official creditors	0.8	4.7	6.7	9.3	-8.2
Multilateral	0.4	2.3	4.2	1.6	2.5
Bilateral	0.4	2.5	2.5	7.7	-10.7
Private creditors	1.1	12.4	0.8	9.6	26.6
Bonds	0.1	0.8	-0.1	9.6	19.1
Private nonguaranteed	**1.0**	**6.0**	**2.5**	**14.5**	**5.4**
Bonds	..	..	0.2	3.5	9.4
CURRENCY COMPOSITION OF LONG-TERM DEBT (PERCENT)					
Deutsche mark	7.8	5.5	5.9	4.9	..
French franc	2.3	1.8	3.6	2.5	..
Japanese yen	0.1	4.4	5.7	6.7	..
Pound sterling	4.5	1.4	1.4	0.7	..
U.S. dollars	63.0	63.1	55.0	58.2	..
Multiple currency	16.9	9.4	17.4	16.6	..
All other currencies	5.5	4.6	3.4	2.6	..
DEBT STOCK-FLOW RECONCILIATION					
Total change in debt stocks	..	..	22.1	50.9	..
Net flows on debt	..	..	20.3	51.4	..
Net change in interest arrears	..	..	9.1	-3.2	..
Interest capitalized	..	..	1.5	2.4	..
Debt forgiveness or reduction	..	..	-18.7	-4.1	..
Cross-currency valuation	..	..	11.3	2.9	..
Residual	..	..	-1.3	1.5	..
AVERAGE TERMS OF NEW COMMITMENTS					
ALL CREDITORS					
Interest (%)	7.0	11.5	7.9	7.4	..
Maturity (years)	14.4	11.2	14.8	10.1	..
Grant element (%)	16.6	-5.7	11.9	12.1	..
Official creditors					..
Interest (%)	6.0	7.8	7.1	7.6	..
Maturity (years)	23.4	16.8	18.0	14.1	..
Grant element (%)	27.4	14.5	18.2	15.4	..
Private creditors					..
Interest (%)	7.7	13.0	9.0	7.1	..
Maturity (years)	8.9	8.9	10.6	4.5	..
Grant element (%)	10.0	-14.1	3.9	7.4	..
Memo:					
Commitments	4.4	33.3	26.2	46.6	..
Official creditors	1.6	9.8	14.7	27.6	..
Private creditors	2.7	23.5	11.5	19.0	..

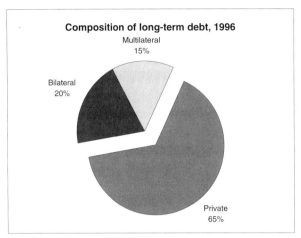

Composition of long-term debt, 1996

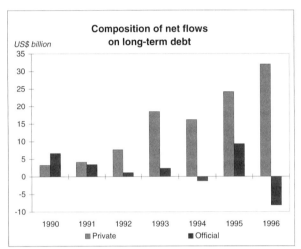

Composition of net flows on long-term debt

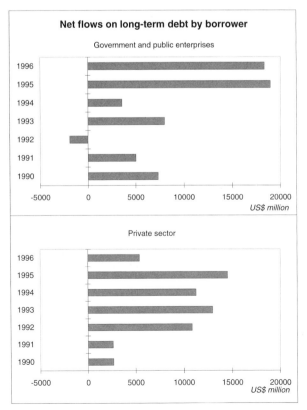

Net flows on long-term debt by borrower

MIDDLE EAST AND NORTH AFRICA

(US$ billion, unless otherwise indicated)

	1970	1980	1990	1995	Preliminary 1996
SUMMARY DEBT DATA					
TOTAL DEBT STOCKS (EDT)	..	**83.8**	**182.5**	**216.0**	**220.8**
Long-term debt (LDOD)	**4.2**	**61.7**	**137.0**	**165.1**	**167.8**
Public and publicly guaranteed	4.2	61.1	135.0	161.8	163.2
Private nonguaranteed	0.0	0.6	2.0	3.3	4.6
Use of IMF credit	**0.1**	**0.9**	**1.8**	**2.2**	**2.6**
Short-term debt	..	**21.1**	**43.8**	**48.8**	**50.4**
of which interest arrears on LDOD	..	0.4	2.8	2.2	2.4
Memo:					
IBRD	0.1	2.4	8.3	10.7	10.5
IDA	0.0	0.7	1.7	2.1	2.2
TOTAL DEBT FLOWS					
Disbursements	**0.9**	**12.3**	**14.6**	**14.0**	**16.1**
Long-term debt	0.9	12.0	14.5	13.5	15.3
Public and publicly guaranteed	0.8	11.7	14.4	12.3	13.9
Private nonguaranteed	0.0	0.3	0.1	1.2	1.4
IMF purchases	**0.0**	**0.4**	**0.1**	**0.6**	**0.8**
Memo:					
IBRD	0.0	0.4	1.2	1.5	1.0
IDA	0.0	0.1	0.0	0.1	0.1
Principal repayments	**0.4**	**5.1**	**15.7**	**14.5**	**10.4**
Long-term debt	0.4	4.8	15.3	14.1	10.1
Public and publicly guaranteed	0.4	4.7	15.1	13.9	9.9
Private nonguaranteed	0.0	0.1	0.2	0.2	0.2
IMF repurchases	0.0	0.2	0.4	0.4	0.3
Memo:					
IBRD	0.0	0.1	0.8	1.1	1.2
IDA	0.0	0.0	0.0	0.0	0.0
Net flows on debt	**1.0**	**8.7**	**0.5**	**2.9**	**7.1**
of which short-term debt	..	..	1.7	3.3	1.4
Interest payments (INT)	..	**6.5**	**8.6**	**9.7**	**10.6**
Long-term debt	0.1	3.9	5.2	6.8	7.6
Net transfers on debt	..	**2.2**	**-8.1**	**-6.9**	**-3.5**
Total debt service (TDS)	..	11.5	24.3	24.2	21.0
AGGREGATE NET RESOURCE FLOWS AND NET TRANSFERS (LONG-TERM)					
NET RESOURCE FLOWS	**1.2**	**8.5**	**10.2**	**2.4**	**10.9**
Net flow of long-term debt (ex. IMF)	0.5	7.1	-0.8	-0.6	5.2
Foreign direct investment (net)	0.3	-3.3	2.8	-0.3	2.2
Portfolio equity flows	0.0	0.0	0.0	0.2	0.7
Grants (excluding technical coop.)	0.4	4.7	8.2	3.2	2.8
NET TRANSFERS	**-1.9**	**-5.3**	**3.7**	**-5.6**	**1.9**
Interest on long-term debt	0.1	3.9	5.2	6.8	7.6
Profit remittances on FDI	2.9	9.9	1.3	1.3	1.4
MAJOR ECONOMIC INDICATORS					
Gross national product (GNP)	45.0	457.2	473.5	579.8	649.2
Exports of goods & services (XGS)	12.9	203.7	154.7	162.0	174.2
of which workers' remittances	1.0	9.7	9.2	11.1	9.8
Imports of goods & services (MGS)	11.3	148.7	142.5	156.6	164.1
International reserves (RES)	4.5	82.3	49.9	70.5	..
Current account balance	-1.3	58.8	-1.8	-10.6	-6.1
DEBT INDICATORS					
EDT / XGS (%)	..	41.1	118.0	133.4	126.8
EDT / GNP (%)	..	18.3	38.6	37.3	34.0
TDS / XGS (%)	..	5.7	15.7	14.9	12.1
INT / XGS (%)	..	3.2	5.6	6.0	6.1
INT / GNP (%)	..	1.4	1.8	1.7	1.6
RES / MGS (months)	4.7	6.6	4.2	5.4	..
Short-term / EDT (%)	..	25.2	24.0	22.6	22.8
Concessional / EDT (%)	..	21.6	23.7	26.0	25.6
Multilateral / EDT (%)	..	6.7	8.6	10.6	11.0

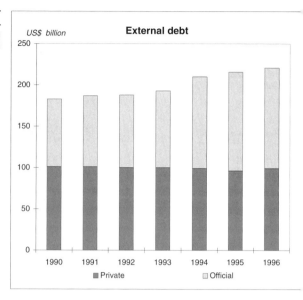

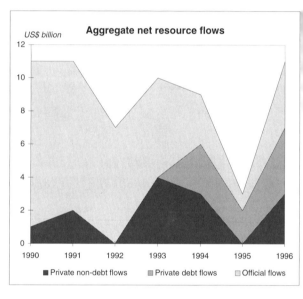

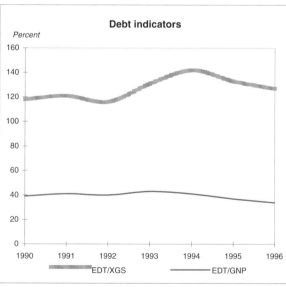

MIDDLE EAST AND NORTH AFRICA

(US$ billion, unless otherwise indicated)

	1970	1980	1990	1995	Preliminary 1996
LONG-TERM DEBT					
DEBT OUTSTANDING (LDOD)	**4.2**	**61.7**	**137.0**	**165.1**	**167.8**
Public and publicly guaranteed	**4.2**	**61.1**	**135.0**	**161.8**	**163.2**
Official creditors	3.0	31.5	80.2	117.7	119.2
Multilateral	0.2	5.6	15.8	22.9	24.3
Bilateral	2.9	25.9	64.4	94.9	95.0
Private creditors	1.1	29.7	54.8	44.1	44.0
Bonds	0.0	0.7	2.2	2.0	2.5
Private nonguaranteed	**0.0**	**0.6**	**2.0**	**3.3**	**4.6**
Bonds	..	..	0.0	0.1	0.3
DISBURSEMENTS	**0.9**	**12.0**	**14.5**	**13.5**	**15.3**
Public and publicly guaranteed	**0.8**	**11.7**	**14.4**	**12.3**	**13.9**
Official creditors	0.4	5.8	6.4	5.6	6.1
Multilateral	0.0	0.7	2.4	3.2	3.5
Bilateral	0.4	5.1	4.0	2.4	2.5
Private creditors	0.4	5.9	8.0	6.6	7.8
Bonds	0.0	0.1	0.0	1.3	0.5
Private nonguaranteed	**0.0**	**0.3**	**0.1**	**1.2**	**1.4**
Bonds	..	..	0.0	0.1	0.2
PRINCIPAL REPAYMENTS	**0.4**	**4.8**	**15.3**	**14.1**	**10.1**
Public and publicly guaranteed	**0.4**	**4.7**	**15.1**	**13.9**	**9.9**
Official creditors	0.2	0.9	5.1	7.8	4.9
Multilateral	0.0	0.2	1.3	2.1	2.1
Bilateral	0.2	0.7	3.7	5.7	2.8
Private creditors	0.2	3.8	10.1	6.1	5.0
Bonds	0.0	0.0	0.1	0.3	0.0
Private nonguaranteed	**0.0**	**0.1**	**0.2**	**0.2**	**0.2**
Bonds	..	..	0.0	0.0	0.0
NET FLOWS ON DEBT	**0.5**	**7.1**	**-0.8**	**-0.6**	**5.2**
Public and publicly guaranteed	**0.5**	**7.0**	**-0.8**	**-1.6**	**4.0**
Official creditors	0.2	4.9	1.4	-2.2	1.2
Multilateral	0.0	0.5	1.1	1.1	1.5
Bilateral	0.2	4.4	0.3	-3.3	-0.3
Private creditors	0.3	2.1	-2.1	0.6	2.8
Bonds	0.0	0.0	-0.1	1.0	0.5
Private nonguaranteed	**0.0**	**0.1**	**0.0**	**1.0**	**1.2**
Bonds	..	..	0.0	0.1	0.2
CURRENCY COMPOSITION OF LONG-TERM DEBT (PERCENT)					
Deutsche mark	7.7	6.4	6.7	7.2	..
French franc	18.5	9.3	10.7	11.1	..
Japanese yen	0.0	5.7	6.3	8.5	..
Pound sterling	4.1	1.3	1.5	1.1	..
U.S. dollars	33.0	46.3	38.3	38.4	..
Multiple currency	3.1	4.7	7.6	8.9	..
All other currencies	33.6	13.8	13.6	12.8	..
DEBT STOCK-FLOW RECONCILIATION					
Total change in debt stocks	..	..	-6.5	5.9	..
Net flows on debt	..	..	0.5	2.9	..
Net change in interest arrears	..	..	-1.5	0.3	..
Interest capitalized	..	..	0.2	0.5	..
Debt forgiveness or reduction	..	..	-10.6	-0.4	..
Cross-currency valuation	..	..	6.1	2.6	..
Residual	..	..	-1.2	0.0	..
AVERAGE TERMS OF NEW COMMITMENTS					
ALL CREDITORS					
Interest (%)	4.7	6.5	7.5	5.9	..
Maturity (years)	17.1	17.8	13.4	14.6	..
Grant element (%)	32.3	23.5	15.4	21.3	..
Official creditors					..
Interest (%)	3.7	4.8	5.6	5.1	..
Maturity (years)	21.6	24.0	21.2	18.4	..
Grant element (%)	42.5	38.1	31.3	27.4	..
Private creditors					..
Interest (%)	6.3	8.6	8.9	7.4	..
Maturity (years)	9.4	10.1	7.4	7.6	..
Grant element (%)	14.7	5.4	3.3	10.1	..
Memo:					
Commitments	1.2	11.4	15.2	7.9	..
Official creditors	0.7	6.3	6.6	5.1	..
Private creditors	0.4	5.1	8.6	2.8	..

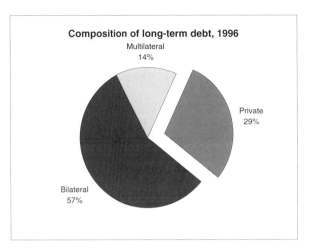

Composition of long-term debt, 1996

Multilateral 14%
Private 29%
Bilateral 57%

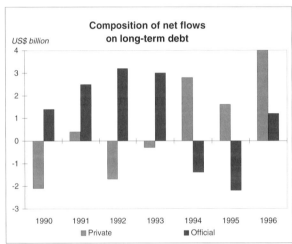

Composition of net flows on long-term debt

US$ billion

■ Private ■ Official

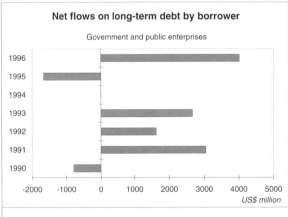

Net flows on long-term debt by borrower

Government and public enterprises

US$ million

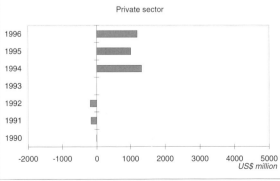

Private sector

US$ million

SOUTH ASIA

(US$ billion, unless otherwise indicated)   *Preliminary*

	1970	1980	1990	1995	1996
SUMMARY DEBT DATA					
TOTAL DEBT STOCKS (EDT)	..	**38.0**	**130.0**	**156.8**	**161.0**
Long-term debt (LDOD)	**11.3**	**33.1**	**113.1**	**142.4**	**146.8**
Public and publicly guaranteed	11.2	32.7	111.4	134.1	137.0
Private nonguaranteed	0.1	0.4	1.7	8.3	9.8
Use of IMF credit	**0.1**	**2.5**	**4.5**	**5.3**	**3.7**
Short-term debt	..	**2.5**	**12.4**	**9.1**	**10.5**
of which interest arrears on LDOD	..	0.0	0.0	0.1	0.1
Memo:					
IBRD	0.9	1.2	9.6	13.0	12.8
IDA	1.3	7.1	21.1	29.0	30.4
TOTAL DEBT FLOWS					
Disbursements	**1.5**	**6.4**	**12.3**	**11.3**	**16.6**
Long-term debt	1.5	4.7	10.4	11.1	16.3
Public and publicly guaranteed	1.4	4.4	10.1	9.1	14.1
Private nonguaranteed	0.0	0.3	0.3	1.9	2.2
IMF purchases	**0.0**	**1.6**	**1.9**	**0.2**	**0.4**
Memo:					
IBRD	0.1	0.2	1.6	0.9	0.9
IDA	0.1	0.9	1.6	1.4	1.6
Principal repayments	**0.7**	**1.6**	**5.3**	**11.3**	**11.5**
Long-term debt	0.5	1.2	4.2	9.3	9.8
Public and publicly guaranteed	0.4	1.1	3.8	8.8	9.1
Private nonguaranteed	0.0	0.1	0.4	0.5	0.7
IMF repurchases	**0.3**	**0.3**	**1.2**	**2.0**	**1.8**
Memo:					
IBRD	0.1	0.1	0.6	1.2	1.1
IDA	0.0	0.0	0.2	0.3	0.4
Net flows on debt	**1.2**	**5.8**	**8.5**	**2.0**	**6.5**
of which short-term debt	..	..	1.6	2.1	1.4
Interest payments (INT)	..	**1.2**	**6.2**	**6.3**	**6.3**
Long-term debt	0.3	0.9	4.7	5.4	5.5
Net transfers on debt	..	**4.6**	**2.3**	**-4.3**	**0.2**
Total debt service (TDS)	..	**2.8**	**11.5**	**17.6**	**17.8**
AGGREGATE NET RESOURCE FLOWS AND NET TRANSFERS (LONG-TERM)					
NET RESOURCE FLOWS	**1.4**	**6.5**	**9.2**	**8.4**	**17.0**
Net flow of long-term debt (ex. IMF)	1.0	3.5	6.2	1.8	6.5
Foreign direct investment (net)	0.1	0.2	0.5	1.8	2.6
Portfolio equity flows	0.0	0.0	0.1	2.3	5.4
Grants (excluding technical coop.)	0.3	2.8	2.4	2.5	2.5
NET TRANSFERS	**1.1**	**5.6**	**4.4**	**2.8**	**11.4**
Interest on long-term debt	0.3	0.9	4.7	5.4	5.5
Profit remittances on FDI	0.0	0.0	0.1	0.2	0.2
MAJOR ECONOMIC INDICATORS					
Gross national product (GNP)	79.0	218.9	390.6	514.2	568.5
Exports of goods & services (XGS)	4.3	23.7	41.0	71.7	77.1
of which workers' remittances	0.2	4.9	5.1	8.3	6.8
Imports of goods & services (MGS)	5.9	30.5	56.3	83.8	89.6
International reserves (RES)	1.4	15.4	8.9	31.1	..
Current account balance	-1.5	-5.6	-13.6	-9.7	-11.1
DEBT INDICATORS					
EDT / XGS (%)	..	160.5	317.0	218.7	208.8
EDT / GNP (%)	..	17.4	33.3	30.5	28.3
TDS / XGS (%)	..	11.7	28.1	24.6	23.1
INT / XGS (%)	..	5.1	15.1	8.8	8.2
INT / GNP (%)	..	0.6	1.6	1.2	1.1
RES / MGS (months)	2.8	6.1	1.9	4.5	..
Short-term / EDT (%)	..	6.5	9.5	5.8	6.5
Concessional / EDT (%)	..	75.3	56.5	57.1	53.3
Multilateral / EDT (%)	..	24.6	29.4	36.4	37.3

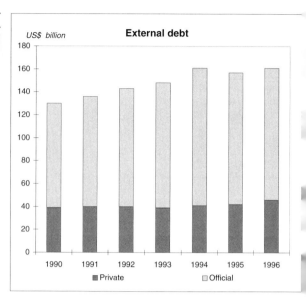

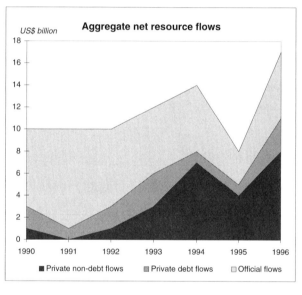

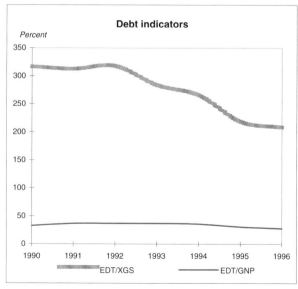

SOUTH ASIA

(US$ billion, unless otherwise indicated)

	1970	1980	1990	1995	Preliminary 1996
LONG-TERM DEBT					
DEBT OUTSTANDING (LDOD)	**11.3**	**33.1**	**113.1**	**142.4**	**146.8**
Public and publicly guaranteed	**11.2**	**32.7**	**111.4**	**134.1**	**137.0**
Official creditors	10.5	30.3	86.8	109.6	111.6
Multilateral	2.2	9.3	38.3	57.1	60.0
Bilateral	8.3	20.9	48.5	52.5	51.6
Private creditors	0.7	2.4	24.6	24.6	25.4
Bonds	0.0	0.0	2.7	3.4	1.9
Private nonguaranteed	**0.1**	**0.4**	**1.7**	**8.3**	**9.8**
Bonds	..	..	0.0	1.1	1.7
DISBURSEMENTS	**1.5**	**4.7**	**10.4**	**11.1**	**16.3**
Public and publicly guaranteed	**1.4**	**4.4**	**10.1**	**9.1**	**14.1**
Official creditors	1.3	3.4	7.0	6.4	8.3
Multilateral	0.2	1.4	4.4	3.9	4.7
Bilateral	1.1	2.0	2.6	2.5	3.5
Private creditors	0.1	1.0	3.1	2.8	5.8
Bonds	0.0	0.0	0.4	0.0	0.6
Private nonguaranteed	**0.0**	**0.3**	**0.3**	**1.9**	**2.2**
Bonds	..	..	0.0	0.5	0.6
PRINCIPAL REPAYMENTS	**0.5**	**1.2**	**4.2**	**9.3**	**9.8**
Public and publicly guaranteed	**0.4**	**1.1**	**3.8**	**8.8**	**9.1**
Official creditors	0.3	0.9	2.4	5.7	4.4
Multilateral	0.1	0.1	1.0	2.2	2.0
Bilateral	0.3	0.8	1.4	3.5	2.4
Private creditors	0.1	0.2	1.4	3.1	4.6
Bonds	0.0	0.0	0.3	0.3	2.0
Private nonguaranteed	**0.0**	**0.1**	**0.4**	**0.5**	**0.7**
Bonds	..	..	0.0	0.0	0.0
NET FLOWS ON DEBT	**1.0**	**3.5**	**6.2**	**1.8**	**6.5**
Public and publicly guaranteed	**1.0**	**3.3**	**6.3**	**0.3**	**5.0**
Official creditors	1.0	2.4	4.6	0.7	3.9
Multilateral	0.1	1.3	3.4	1.7	2.8
Bilateral	0.9	1.1	1.2	-1.0	1.1
Private creditors	0.0	0.9	1.7	-0.4	1.2
Bonds	0.0	0.0	0.1	-0.3	-1.4
Private nonguaranteed	**0.0**	**0.2**	**-0.1**	**1.4**	**1.5**
Bonds	..	..	0.0	0.5	0.6
CURRENCY COMPOSITION OF LONG-TERM DEBT (PERCENT)					
Deutsche mark	9.7	8.3	5.9	5.7	..
French franc	1.5	2.3	1.7	2.0	..
Japanese yen	5.5	8.8	11.9	15.4	..
Pound sterling	22.5	17.7	4.9	3.5	..
U.S. dollars	42.0	41.9	51.6	44.9	..
Multiple currency	8.5	7.3	13.6	19.2	..
All other currencies	10.4	9.9	6.0	5.1	..
DEBT STOCK-FLOW RECONCILIATION					
Total change in debt stocks	..	..	13.3	-4.3	..
Net flows on debt	..	..	8.5	2.0	..
Net change in interest arrears	..	..	0.0	0.0	..
Interest capitalized	..	..	0.0	0.0	..
Debt forgiveness or reduction	..	..	0.0	0.0	..
Cross-currency valuation	..	..	2.6	-3.6	..
Residual	..	..	2.2	-2.7	..
AVERAGE TERMS OF NEW COMMITMENTS					
ALL CREDITORS					
Interest (%)	2.6	4.7	4.6	3.8	..
Maturity (years)	32.6	32.5	24.6	22.4	..
Grant element (%)	59.5	48.0	41.7	43.2	..
Official creditors					..
Interest (%)	2.3	2.2	3.6	3.9	..
Maturity (years)	34.9	39.3	28.9	26.1	..
Grant element (%)	64.2	66.4	51.6	46.1	..
Private creditors					..
Interest (%)	5.9	12.8	6.7	3.3	..
Maturity (years)	11.6	10.9	14.9	8.0	..
Grant element (%)	17.9	-10.7	19.4	31.7	..
Memo:					
Commitments	2.0	8.2	13.7	6.7	..
Official creditors	1.8	6.2	9.5	5.4	..
Private creditors	0.2	2.0	4.2	1.4	..

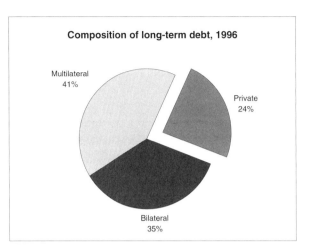

Composition of long-term debt, 1996

Multilateral 41%
Private 24%
Bilateral 35%

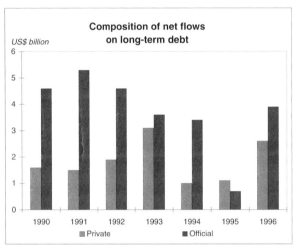

Composition of net flows on long-term debt

US$ billion

■ Private   ■ Official

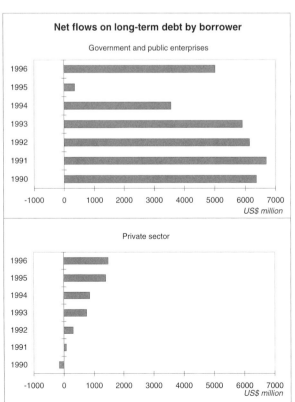

Net flows on long-term debt by borrower

Government and public enterprises

US$ million

Private sector

US$ million

SUB-SAHARAN AFRICA

(US$ billion, unless otherwise indicated)

	1970	1980	1990	1995	*Preliminary* 1996
SUMMARY DEBT DATA					
TOTAL DEBT STOCKS (EDT)	..	**84.1**	**191.3**	**226.5**	**235.4**
Long-term debt (LDOD)	**6.1**	**58.5**	**156.7**	**175.7**	**182.0**
Public and publicly guaranteed	5.7	53.9	151.5	168.6	169.1
Private nonguaranteed	0.3	4.6	5.3	7.1	12.9
Use of IMF credit	**0.1**	**3.0**	**6.6**	**8.7**	**8.7**
Short-term debt	..	**22.6**	**27.9**	**42.1**	**44.8**
of which interest arrears on LDOD	..	0.3	9.3	20.8	21.7
Memo:					
IBRD	0.6	2.5	9.2	7.6	6.8
IDA	0.2	2.6	15.8	27.9	30.5
TOTAL DEBT FLOWS					
Disbursements	**1.2**	**15.5**	**11.2**	**13.8**	**15.1**
Long-term debt	1.2	14.3	10.5	10.8	14.3
Public and publicly guaranteed	1.1	13.1	9.9	8.9	7.9
Private nonguaranteed	0.1	1.2	0.6	1.8	6.4
IMF purchases	**0.0**	**1.2**	**0.7**	**3.0**	**0.8**
Memo:					
IBRD	0.1	0.4	0.8	0.3	0.2
IDA	0.1	0.4	2.0	2.4	2.8
Principal repayments	**0.5**	**3.3**	**7.5**	**8.5**	**6.8**
Long-term debt	**0.4**	**2.8**	**6.5**	**6.1**	**6.3**
Public and publicly guaranteed	0.3	2.2	6.0	5.8	5.7
Private nonguaranteed	0.1	0.6	0.5	0.3	0.6
IMF repurchases	**0.1**	**0.5**	**1.0**	**2.4**	**0.6**
Memo:					
IBRD	0.0	0.1	0.7	1.1	1.1
IDA	0.0	0.0	0.1	0.1	0.2
Net flows on debt	**1.5**	**17.5**	**5.9**	**8.2**	**10.1**
of which short-term debt	..	..	2.2	2.9	1.8
Interest payments (INT)	..	**5.7**	**7.7**	**5.2**	**5.5**
Long-term debt	0.2	3.6	5.9	3.6	4.3
Net transfers on debt	..	**11.8**	**-1.8**	**3.0**	**4.6**
Total debt service (TDS)	..	**9.0**	**15.2**	**13.6**	**12.3**
AGGREGATE NET RESOURCE FLOWS AND NET TRANSFERS (LONG-TERM)					
NET RESOURCE FLOWS	**1.7**	**15.2**	**17.2**	**23.2**	**26.1**
Net flow of long-term debt (ex. IMF)	0.8	11.5	4.0	4.7	8.1
Foreign direct investment (net)	0.4	0.0	0.9	2.2	2.6
Portfolio equity flows	0.0	0.0	0.0	4.9	3.6
Grants (excluding technical coop.)	0.4	3.7	12.3	11.4	11.8
NET TRANSFERS	**0.4**	**7.6**	**6.8**	**15.1**	**17.6**
Interest on long-term debt	0.2	3.6	5.9	3.6	4.3
Profit remittances on FDI	1.1	4.0	4.5	4.4	4.2
MAJOR ECONOMIC INDICATORS					
Gross national product (GNP)	61.4	275.1	269.0	278.6	308.9
Exports of goods & services (XGS)	13.6	91.7	84.4	93.7	99.4
of which workers' remittances	0.1	0.8	1.0	1.6	1.6
Imports of goods & services (MGS)	15.6	91.7	92.2	110.5	116.3
International reserves (RES)	3.1	23.0	15.6	21.2	..
Current account balance	-1.9	2.2	-0.6	-11.4	-11.5
DEBT INDICATORS					
EDT / XGS (%)	..	91.7	226.6	241.7	236.9
EDT / GNP (%)	..	30.6	71.1	81.3	76.2
TDS / XGS (%)	..	9.8	18.0	14.5	12.4
INT / XGS (%)	..	6.2	9.1	5.5	5.6
INT / GNP (%)	..	2.1	2.9	1.9	1.8
RES / MGS (months)	2.4	3.0	2.0	2.3	..
Short-term / EDT (%)	..	26.8	14.6	18.6	19.0
Concessional / EDT (%)	..	18.3	28.9	34.8	34.6
Multilateral / EDT (%)	..	9.0	20.0	24.3	24.6

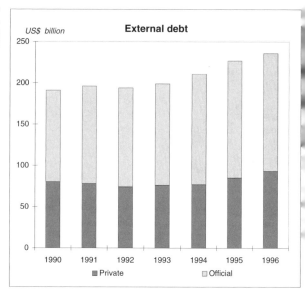

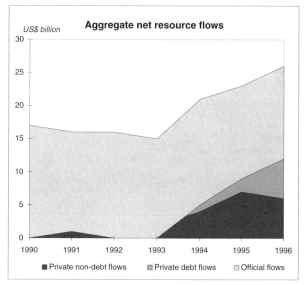

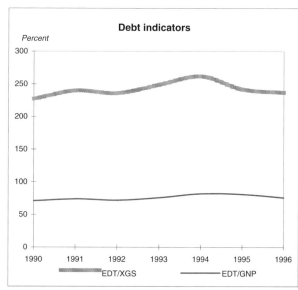

SUB-SAHARAN AFRICA

(US$ billion, unless otherwise indicated)

	1970	1980	1990	1995	Preliminary 1996
LONG-TERM DEBT					
DEBT OUTSTANDING (LDOD)	**6.1**	**58.5**	**156.7**	**175.7**	**182.0**
Public and publicly guaranteed	**5.7**	**53.9**	**151.5**	**168.6**	**169.1**
Official creditors	4.2	24.3	104.7	133.2	134.2
Multilateral	0.9	7.6	38.3	55.1	57.9
Bilateral	3.3	16.7	66.4	78.1	76.4
Private creditors	1.6	29.7	46.7	35.4	34.8
Bonds	0.4	6.5	2.1	4.1	4.5
Private nonguaranteed	**0.3**	**4.6**	**5.3**	**7.1**	**12.9**
Bonds	..	..	0.0	0.5	0.3
DISBURSEMENTS	**1.2**	**14.3**	**10.5**	**10.8**	**14.3**
Public and publicly guaranteed	**1.1**	**13.1**	**9.9**	**8.9**	**7.9**
Official creditors	0.7	4.3	7.2	5.7	6.2
Multilateral	0.2	1.7	4.5	4.4	5.1
Bilateral	0.5	2.6	2.7	1.4	1.1
Private creditors	0.5	8.8	2.7	3.2	1.8
Bonds	0.0	1.6	0.0	0.8	0.5
Private nonguaranteed	**0.1**	**1.2**	**0.6**	**1.8**	**6.4**
Bonds	..	..	0.0	0.5	0.3
PRINCIPAL REPAYMENTS	**0.4**	**2.8**	**6.5**	**6.1**	**6.3**
Public and publicly guaranteed	**0.3**	**2.2**	**6.0**	**5.8**	**5.7**
Official creditors	0.2	0.7	2.5	3.1	3.7
Multilateral	0.0	0.2	1.4	2.0	2.2
Bilateral	0.1	0.5	1.2	1.1	1.5
Private creditors	0.2	1.5	3.5	2.7	2.0
Bonds	0.0	0.0	0.9	0.3	0.0
Private nonguaranteed	**0.1**	**0.6**	**0.5**	**0.3**	**0.6**
Bonds	..	..	0.0	0.0	0.0
NET FLOWS ON DEBT	**0.8**	**11.5**	**4.0**	**4.7**	**8.1**
Public and publicly guaranteed	**0.8**	**10.9**	**3.8**	**3.1**	**2.3**
Official creditors	0.5	3.6	4.7	2.6	2.5
Multilateral	0.1	1.5	3.2	2.3	2.8
Bilateral	0.4	2.1	1.5	0.3	-0.4
Private creditors	0.3	7.3	-0.8	0.5	-0.2
Bonds	0.0	1.5	-0.9	0.5	0.4
Private nonguaranteed	**0.0**	**0.6**	**0.2**	**1.6**	**5.8**
Bonds	..	..	0.0	0.5	0.3
CURRENCY COMPOSITION OF LONG-TERM DEBT (PERCENT)					
Deutsche mark	6.6	5.4	6.1	5.6	..
French franc	14.5	10.8	13.4	13.4	..
Japanese yen	0.1	1.6	3.7	5.2	..
Pound sterling	22.6	4.5	5.2	3.7	..
U.S. dollars	21.5	27.6	34.7	37.8	..
Multiple currency	11.2	6.9	9.9	10.1	..
All other currencies	23.5	18.4	19.2	19.2	..
DEBT STOCK-FLOW RECONCILIATION					
Total change in debt stocks	..	..	19.1	15.3	..
Net flows on debt	..	..	5.9	8.2	..
Net change in interest arrears	..	..	2.2	2.2	..
Interest capitalized	..	..	1.8	0.8	..
Debt forgiveness or reduction	..	..	-1.9	-1.4	..
Cross-currency valuation	..	..	9.6	4.4	..
Residual	..	..	1.5	1.1	..
AVERAGE TERMS OF NEW COMMITMENTS					
ALL CREDITORS					
Interest (%)	3.7	7.0	4.3	3.0	..
Maturity (years)	25.7	17.2	25.1	27.4	..
Grant element (%)	47.7	21.8	43.5	54.1	..
Official creditors					..
Interest (%)	2.0	4.1	3.5	1.7	..
Maturity (years)	34.8	24.8	28.0	33.4	..
Grant element (%)	67.7	42.6	51.1	67.6	..
Private creditors					..
Interest (%)	6.6	10.0	8.1	7.1	..
Maturity (years)	10.2	9.4	11.6	7.5	..
Grant element (%)	13.3	0.1	7.7	9.2	..
Memo:					
Commitments	1.9	13.3	11.5	5.5	..
Official creditors	1.2	6.8	9.5	4.3	..
Private creditors	0.7	6.5	2.0	1.3	..

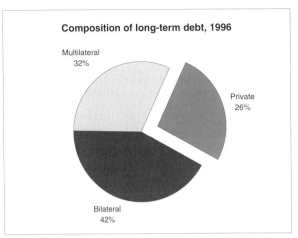

Composition of long-term debt, 1996

Multilateral 32%

Private 26%

Bilateral 42%

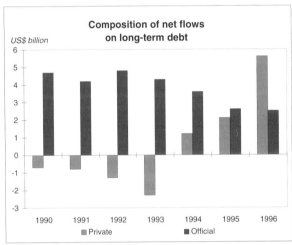

Composition of net flows on long-term debt

US$ billion

■ Private ■ Official

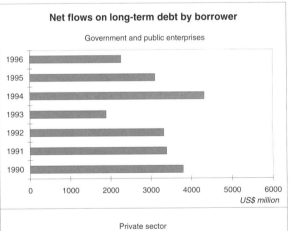

Net flows on long-term debt by borrower

Government and public enterprises

US$ million

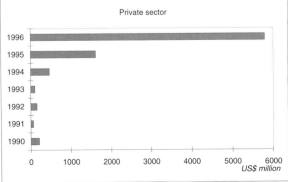

Private sector

US$ million

SEVERELY INDEBTED LOW-INCOME COUNTRIES

(US$ billion, unless otherwise indicated)

	1970	1980	1990	1995	Preliminary 1996
SUMMARY DEBT DATA					
TOTAL DEBT STOCKS (EDT)	..	60.8	212.3	245.2	243.4
Long-term debt (LDOD)	**5.9**	**47.8**	**181.4**	**202.2**	**199.4**
Public and publicly guaranteed	5.6	43.1	176.5	197.7	194.5
Private nonguaranteed	0.3	4.7	5.0	4.5	4.8
Use of IMF credit	**0.1**	**3.0**	**6.3**	**7.4**	**7.6**
Short-term debt	..	**10.0**	**24.6**	**35.6**	**36.4**
of which interest arrears on LDOD	..	0.3	12.6	25.3	25.4
Memo:					
IBRD	0.6	2.6	9.1	7.6	6.3
IDA	0.2	2.6	15.5	27.3	29.9
TOTAL DEBT FLOWS					
Disbursements	**1.3**	**12.4**	**10.5**	**9.6**	**9.1**
Long-term debt	**1.3**	**11.3**	**9.8**	**6.7**	**8.1**
Public and publicly guaranteed	1.2	10.0	9.4	6.5	7.3
Private nonguaranteed	0.1	1.3	0.4	0.2	0.8
IMF purchases	**0.0**	**1.2**	**0.7**	**2.9**	**1.0**
Memo:					
IBRD	0.1	0.4	0.8	0.2	0.2
IDA	0.1	0.5	1.9	2.3	2.9
Principal repayments	**0.5**	**2.9**	**5.4**	**7.0**	**7.1**
Long-term debt	**0.4**	**2.5**	**4.4**	**4.7**	**6.5**
Public and publicly guaranteed	0.3	1.9	4.0	4.5	6.1
Private nonguaranteed	0.1	0.6	0.4	0.1	0.5
IMF repurchases	**0.1**	**0.4**	**1.0**	**2.4**	**0.5**
Memo:					
IBRD	0.0	0.1	0.7	1.0	1.0
IDA	0.0	0.0	0.1	0.1	0.2
Net flows on debt	**1.6**	**11.5**	**7.3**	**3.5**	**2.9**
of which short-term debt	..	..	2.2	0.9	0.8
Interest payments (INT)	..	**3.4**	**5.3**	**3.8**	**4.1**
Long-term debt	0.2	2.4	4.4	2.9	3.5
Net transfers on debt	..	**8.1**	**2.0**	**-0.3**	**-1.2**
Total debt service (TDS)	..	**6.4**	**10.7**	**10.8**	**11.1**
AGGREGATE NET RESOURCE FLOWS AND NET TRANSFERS (LONG-TERM)					
NET RESOURCE FLOWS	**1.6**	**12.5**	**17.2**	**17.2**	**18.0**
Net flow of long-term debt (ex. IMF)	0.9	8.7	5.4	2.0	1.6
Foreign direct investment (net)	0.1	-0.1	0.5	3.6	4.1
Portfolio equity flows	0.0	0.0	0.0	0.4	0.8
Grants (excluding technical coop.)	0.6	3.8	11.3	11.2	11.5
NET TRANSFERS	**0.7**	**7.6**	**11.8**	**13.3**	**13.3**
Interest on long-term debt	0.2	2.4	4.4	2.9	3.5
Profit remittances on FDI	0.8	2.5	1.0	1.1	1.2
MAJOR ECONOMIC INDICATORS					
Gross national product (GNP)	44.1	191.0	157.0	219.6	252.3
Exports of goods & services (XGS)	10.0	59.8	49.1	58.2	61.7
of which workers' remittances	0.1	3.6	2.1	2.5	2.4
Imports of goods & services (MGS)	11.4	62.8	59.4	75.7	80.4
International reserves (RES)	2.1	15.3	9.0	10.4	..
Current account balance	-1.8	-2.9	-3.9	-10.1	-11.7
DEBT INDICATORS					
EDT / XGS (%)	..	101.6	432.8	421.2	394.6
EDT / GNP (%)	..	31.8	135.2	111.7	96.5
TDS / XGS (%)	..	10.7	21.8	18.6	18.0
INT / XGS (%)	..	5.8	10.8	6.5	6.6
INT / GNP (%)	..	1.8	3.4	1.7	1.6
RES / MGS (months)	2.2	2.9	1.8	1.7	..
Short-term / EDT (%)	..	16.4	11.6	14.5	15.0
Concessional / EDT (%)	..	30.3	41.0	45.7	44.9
Multilateral / EDT (%)	..	13.6	18.1	22.1	23.1

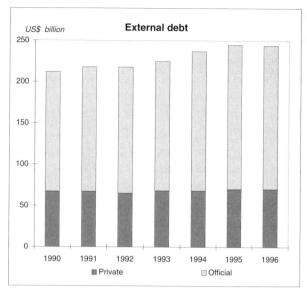

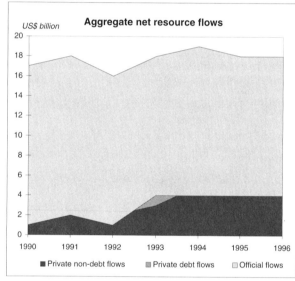

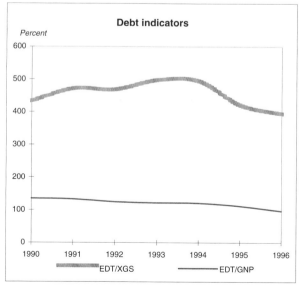

SEVERELY INDEBTED LOW-INCOME COUNTRIES

(US$ billion, unless otherwise indicated)

	1970	1980	1990	1995	Preliminary 1996
LONG-TERM DEBT					
DEBT OUTSTANDING (LDOD)	**5.9**	**47.8**	**181.4**	**202.2**	**199.4**
Public and publicly guaranteed	**5.6**	**43.1**	**176.5**	**197.7**	**194.5**
Official creditors	4.1	27.4	138.6	167.9	166.1
Multilateral	0.9	8.3	38.5	54.2	56.2
Bilateral	3.3	19.1	100.1	113.6	110.0
Private creditors	1.4	15.7	37.9	29.8	28.4
Bonds	0.2	0.1	0.0	2.7	2.7
Private nonguaranteed	**0.3**	**4.7**	**5.0**	**4.5**	**4.8**
Bonds	..	..	0.0	0.0	0.3
DISBURSEMENTS	**1.3**	**11.3**	**9.8**	**6.7**	**8.1**
Public and publicly guaranteed	**1.2**	**10.0**	**9.4**	**6.5**	**7.3**
Official creditors	0.7	5.0	7.5	5.7	6.3
Multilateral	0.2	1.8	4.4	4.1	4.7
Bilateral	0.5	3.2	3.1	1.6	1.6
Private creditors	0.5	5.0	1.9	0.8	1.0
Bonds	0.0	0.0	0.0	0.0	0.0
Private nonguaranteed	**0.1**	**1.3**	**0.4**	**0.2**	**0.8**
Bonds	..	..	0.0	0.0	0.3
PRINCIPAL REPAYMENTS	**0.4**	**2.5**	**4.4**	**4.7**	**6.5**
Public and publicly guaranteed	**0.3**	**1.9**	**4.0**	**4.5**	**6.1**
Official creditors	0.2	0.7	2.6	3.2	4.0
Multilateral	0.0	0.2	1.3	1.9	2.2
Bilateral	0.1	0.5	1.2	1.3	1.8
Private creditors	0.2	1.2	1.4	1.3	2.1
Bonds	0.0	0.0	0.0	0.0	0.0
Private nonguaranteed	**0.1**	**0.6**	**0.4**	**0.1**	**0.5**
Bonds	..	..	0.0	0.0	0.0
NET FLOWS ON DEBT	**0.9**	**8.7**	**5.4**	**2.0**	**1.6**
Public and publicly guaranteed	**0.8**	**8.1**	**5.4**	**2.0**	**1.2**
Official creditors	0.5	4.3	4.9	2.5	2.3
Multilateral	0.1	1.6	3.1	2.2	2.5
Bilateral	0.4	2.7	1.8	0.3	-0.2
Private creditors	0.3	3.8	0.5	-0.5	-1.1
Bonds	0.0	0.0	0.0	0.0	0.0
Private nonguaranteed	**0.1**	**0.6**	**0.0**	**0.0**	**0.4**
Bonds	..	..	0.0	0.0	0.3
CURRENCY COMPOSITION OF LONG-TERM DEBT (PERCENT)					
Deutsche mark	6.6	6.9	5.5	5.2	..
French franc	13.2	10.9	9.9	10.2	..
Japanese yen	0.1	3.4	4.8	6.8	..
Pound sterling	20.6	5.1	4.3	3.1	..
U.S. dollars	25.7	38.2	34.9	35.9	..
Multiple currency	11.5	8.7	9.1	8.9	..
All other currencies	22.8	24.1	28.5	27.1	..
DEBT STOCK-FLOW RECONCILIATION					
Total change in debt stocks	..	..	23.2	8.0	..
Net flows on debt	..	..	7.3	3.5	..
Net change in interest arrears	..	..	3.0	1.9	..
Interest capitalized	..	..	1.9	0.8	..
Debt forgiveness or reduction	..	..	-1.8	-2.8	..
Cross-currency valuation	..	..	9.5	3.5	..
Residual	..	..	3.3	1.1	..
AVERAGE TERMS OF NEW COMMITMENTS					
ALL CREDITORS					
Interest (%)	3.7	6.5	4.3	2.8	..
Maturity (years)	25.2	18.6	24.8	29.3	..
Grant element (%)	47.4	25.5	43.0	56.7	..
Official creditors					..
Interest (%)	2.1	3.8	3.5	1.9	..
Maturity (years)	33.4	25.8	27.7	33.7	..
Grant element (%)	66.0	45.1	50.6	66.7	..
Private creditors					..
Interest (%)	6.6	9.9	8.1	7.0	..
Maturity (years)	10.0	9.5	11.5	8.3	..
Grant element (%)	13.1	1.0	7.9	8.5	..
Memo:					
Commitments	2.0	14.0	11.4	5.9	..
Official creditors	1.3	7.8	9.4	4.9	..
Private creditors	0.7	6.2	2.0	1.0	..

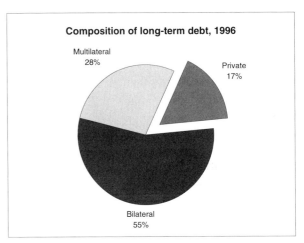

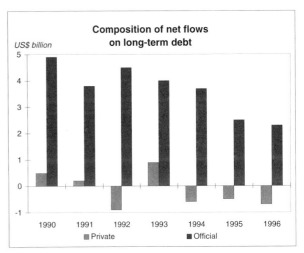

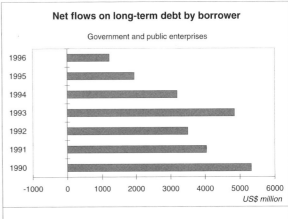

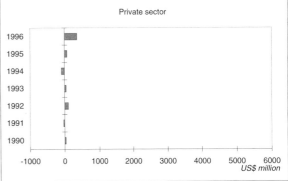

SEVERELY INDEBTED MIDDLE-INCOME COUNTRIES

(US$ billion, unless otherwise indicated)

	1970	1980	1990	1995	Preliminary 1996
SUMMARY DEBT DATA					
TOTAL DEBT STOCKS (EDT)	..	205.0	427.2	578.6	597.2
Long-term debt (LDOD)	21.2	156.6	336.0	439.3	458.1
Public and publicly guaranteed	10.7	124.2	321.0	375.5	389.5
Private nonguaranteed	10.4	32.4	15.0	63.8	68.6
Use of IMF credit	**0.0**	**0.9**	**13.6**	**24.9**	**21.9**
Short-term debt	..	**47.5**	**77.7**	**114.4**	**117.1**
of which interest arrears on LDOD	..	0.0	23.7	9.1	3.7
Memo:					
IBRD	1.2	5.7	26.5	30.2	31.0
IDA	0.0	0.2	0.5	0.9	1.0
TOTAL DEBT FLOWS					
Disbursements	**4.9**	**34.7**	**25.3**	**78.7**	**69.9**
Long-term debt	**4.9**	**34.5**	**22.5**	**62.8**	**69.3**
Public and publicly guaranteed	2.6	26.5	19.5	40.5	52.3
Private nonguaranteed	2.3	7.9	3.0	22.3	16.9
IMF purchases	**0.0**	**0.2**	**2.7**	**15.9**	**0.6**
Memo:					
IBRD	0.2	1.2	4.7	4.3	4.2
IDA	0.0	0.0	0.0	0.1	0.1
Principal repayments	**3.0**	**16.5**	**20.0**	**31.9**	**51.5**
Long-term debt	**2.9**	**16.1**	**16.9**	**29.7**	**48.4**
Public and publicly guaranteed	1.3	11.4	15.6	18.5	36.3
Private nonguaranteed	1.6	4.8	1.3	11.2	12.2
IMF repurchases	**0.1**	**0.3**	**3.1**	**2.2**	**3.0**
Memo:					
IBRD	0.1	0.3	2.5	3.5	3.4
IDA	0.0	0.0	0.0	0.0	0.0
Net flows on debt	**5.2**	**36.2**	**16.7**	**51.0**	**26.5**
of which short-term debt	..	..	11.5	4.2	8.1
Interest payments (INT)	..	**19.4**	**16.3**	**32.1**	**32.7**
Long-term debt	1.1	14.5	12.8	24.8	25.2
Net transfers on debt	..	**16.9**	**0.4**	**18.9**	**-6.2**
Total debt service (TDS)	..	**35.8**	**36.3**	**63.9**	**84.2**
AGGREGATE NET RESOURCE FLOWS AND NET TRANSFERS (LONG-TERM)					
NET RESOURCE FLOWS	**3.1**	**26.7**	**14.8**	**58.7**	**56.6**
Net flow of long-term debt (ex. IMF)	2.0	18.3	5.6	33.1	20.8
Foreign direct investment (net)	0.9	4.9	6.0	16.2	18.1
Portfolio equity flows	0.0	0.0	0.6	7.2	15.2
Grants (excluding technical coop.)	0.2	3.5	2.6	2.1	2.4
NET TRANSFERS	**0.5**	**8.5**	**-2.3**	**26.9**	**23.1**
Interest on long-term debt	1.1	14.5	12.8	24.8	25.2
Profit remittances on FDI	1.5	3.8	4.3	7.0	8.3
MAJOR ECONOMIC INDICATORS					
Gross national product (GNP)	129.1	622.0	941.4	1435.9	1511.0
Exports of goods & services (XGS)	14.1	95.2	143.5	232.6	252.2
of which workers' remittances	0.0	2.3	4.1	9.0	8.7
Imports of goods & services (MGS)	16.5	126.0	157.0	261.6	277.3
International reserves (RES)	4.0	33.9	39.5	108.6	..
Current account balance	-2.0	-15.0	-11.2	-25.4	-23.3
DEBT INDICATORS					
EDT / XGS (%)	..	215.4	297.8	248.8	236.8
EDT / GNP (%)	..	33.0	45.4	40.3	39.5
TDS / XGS (%)	..	37.7	25.3	27.5	33.4
INT / XGS (%)	..	20.3	11.4	13.8	13.0
INT / GNP (%)	..	3.1	1.7	2.2	2.2
RES / MGS (months)	2.9	3.2	3.0	5.0	..
Short-term / EDT (%)	..	23.2	18.2	19.8	19.6
Concessional / EDT (%)	..	11.1	12.2	11.0	10.6
Multilateral / EDT (%)	..	4.8	9.7	9.2	9.4

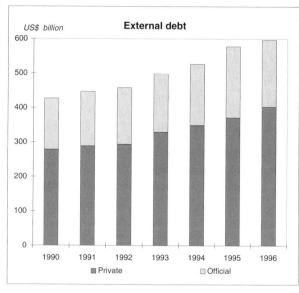

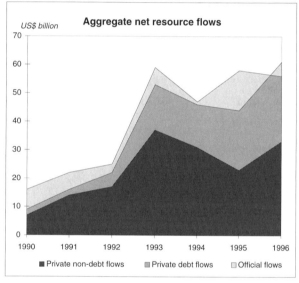

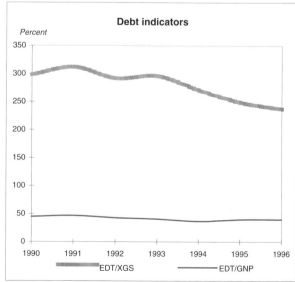

SEVERELY INDEBTED MIDDLE-INCOME COUNTRIES

(US$ billion, unless otherwise indicated)

	1970	1980	1990	1995	Preliminary 1996
LONG-TERM DEBT					
DEBT OUTSTANDING (LDOD)	**21.2**	**156.6**	**336.0**	**439.3**	**458.1**
Public and publicly guaranteed	**10.7**	**124.2**	**321.0**	**375.5**	**389.5**
Official creditors	4.7	40.7	135.3	182.3	172.4
Multilateral	1.7	9.9	41.6	53.3	55.9
Bilateral	3.0	30.9	93.7	129.0	116.5
Private creditors	6.0	83.4	185.7	193.2	217.1
Bonds	1.0	7.7	54.8	151.6	175.0
Private nonguaranteed	**10.4**	**32.4**	**15.0**	**63.8**	**68.6**
Bonds	..	..	0.2	33.1	40.3
DISBURSEMENTS	**4.9**	**34.5**	**22.5**	**62.8**	**69.3**
Public and publicly guaranteed	**2.6**	**26.5**	**19.5**	**40.5**	**52.3**
Official creditors	0.8	6.2	10.4	22.2	10.4
Multilateral	0.4	2.1	6.2	8.4	7.6
Bilateral	0.5	4.1	4.2	13.8	2.9
Private creditors	1.7	20.4	9.1	18.3	41.9
Bonds	0.1	0.8	1.2	12.9	28.5
Private nonguaranteed	**2.3**	**7.9**	**3.0**	**22.3**	**16.9**
Bonds	..	..	0.2	6.3	12.0
PRINCIPAL REPAYMENTS	**2.9**	**16.1**	**16.9**	**29.7**	**48.4**
Public and publicly guaranteed	**1.3**	**11.4**	**15.6**	**18.5**	**36.3**
Official creditors	0.3	1.7	6.5	10.3	18.0
Multilateral	0.1	0.5	3.6	5.1	4.9
Bilateral	0.2	1.2	3.0	5.3	13.1
Private creditors	0.9	9.7	9.0	8.2	18.2
Bonds	0.0	0.4	1.4	3.3	11.6
Private nonguaranteed	**1.6**	**4.8**	**1.3**	**11.2**	**12.2**
Bonds	..	..	0.0	3.9	4.8
NET FLOWS ON DEBT	**2.0**	**18.3**	**5.6**	**33.1**	**20.8**
Public and publicly guaranteed	**1.3**	**15.2**	**3.9**	**22.0**	**16.0**
Official creditors	0.5	4.5	3.9	11.9	-7.6
Multilateral	0.3	1.6	2.7	3.3	2.6
Bilateral	0.2	2.9	1.2	8.5	-10.3
Private creditors	0.8	10.7	0.0	10.1	23.7
Bonds	0.1	0.4	-0.2	9.5	16.9
Private nonguaranteed	**0.8**	**3.1**	**1.7**	**11.1**	**4.8**
Bonds	..	..	0.2	2.3	7.2
CURRENCY COMPOSITION OF LONG-TERM DEBT (PERCENT)					
Deutsche mark	9.8	5.5	6.6	4.5	..
French franc	3.3	2.0	4.1	3.0	..
Japanese yen	0.2	4.5	5.7	6.9	..
Pound sterling	4.4	1.5	1.4	0.7	..
U.S. dollars	59.0	59.2	51.5	56.6	..
Multiple currency	15.5	8.1	13.7	13.5	..
All other currencies	7.7	5.3	4.3	3.4	..
DEBT STOCK-FLOW RECONCILIATION					
Total change in debt stocks	..	..	20.5	51.7	..
Net flows on debt	..	..	16.7	51.0	..
Net change in interest arrears	..	..	9.4	-2.5	..
Interest capitalized	..	..	1.2	2.6	..
Debt forgiveness or reduction	..	..	-14.8	-2.8	..
Cross-currency valuation	..	..	10.1	3.0	..
Residual	..	..	-2.1	0.5	..
AVERAGE TERMS OF NEW COMMITMENTS					
ALL CREDITORS					
Interest (%)	7.2	11.2	8.0	7.5	..
Maturity (years)	13.5	11.2	13.6	9.4	..
Grant element (%)	15.2	-4.4	11.2	10.9	..
Official creditors					..
Interest (%)	6.1	7.5	7.1	7.8	..
Maturity (years)	21.8	16.4	17.2	12.9	..
Grant element (%)	24.8	16.1	18.3	13.4	..
Private creditors					..
Interest (%)	7.8	12.8	9.1	7.1	..
Maturity (years)	8.9	9.0	9.7	4.2	..
Grant element (%)	9.9	-13.0	3.3	7.1	..
Memo:					
Commitments	3.2	27.6	19.7	42.2	..
Official creditors	1.2	8.2	10.4	25.2	..
Private creditors	2.1	19.4	9.3	17.0	..

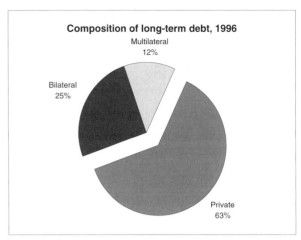

Composition of long-term debt, 1996

Multilateral 12%
Bilateral 25%
Private 63%

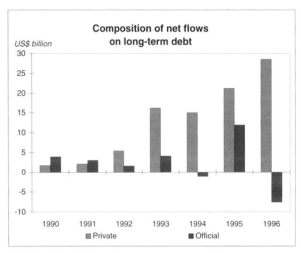

Composition of net flows on long-term debt

US$ billion

■ Private   ■ Official

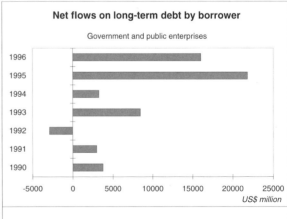

Net flows on long-term debt by borrower

Government and public enterprises

US$ million

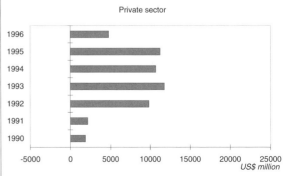

Private sector

US$ million

MODERATELY INDEBTED LOW-INCOME COUNTRIES

(US$ billion, unless otherwise indicated)

	1970	1980	1990	1995	Preliminary 1996
SUMMARY DEBT DATA					
TOTAL DEBT STOCKS (EDT)	..	**38.9**	**130.1**	**156.4**	**160.5**
Long-term debt (LDOD)	**11.5**	**33.8**	**112.3**	**141.1**	**145.2**
Public and publicly guaranteed	11.4	33.5	110.5	132.4	135.2
Private nonguaranteed	0.1	0.4	1.9	8.6	10.0
Use of IMF credit	**0.1**	**2.3**	**4.5**	**5.7**	**4.3**
Short-term debt	..	**2.7**	**13.2**	**9.6**	**11.0**
of which interest arrears on LDOD	..	0.0	0.1	0.1	0.1
Memo:					
IBRD	0.9	1.3	10.0	13.6	13.3
IDA	1.4	7.2	21.7	30.3	31.9
TOTAL DEBT FLOWS					
Disbursements	**1.4**	**6.7**	**12.7**	**11.9**	**16.9**
Long-term debt	**1.4**	**5.0**	**10.8**	**11.5**	**16.4**
Public and publicly guaranteed	1.4	4.7	10.4	9.3	14.2
Private nonguaranteed	0.0	0.3	0.4	2.2	2.2
IMF purchases	**0.0**	**1.7**	**1.9**	**0.5**	**0.5**
Memo:					
IBRD	0.1	0.2	1.6	0.9	1.0
IDA	0.1	0.9	1.7	1.6	1.8
Principal repayments	**0.7**	**1.7**	**5.6**	**11.8**	**11.8**
Long-term debt	**0.5**	**1.4**	**4.4**	**9.7**	**10.1**
Public and publicly guaranteed	0.4	1.3	4.0	9.1	9.2
Private nonguaranteed	0.0	0.1	0.4	0.6	0.8
IMF repurchases	**0.2**	**0.3**	**1.2**	**2.1**	**1.8**
Memo:					
IBRD	0.1	0.1	0.6	1.2	1.2
IDA	0.0	0.0	0.2	0.3	0.4
Net flows on debt	**1.1**	**6.0**	**9.0**	**2.5**	**6.4**
of which short-term debt	..	..	1.9	2.3	1.3
Interest payments (INT)	..	**1.3**	**6.3**	**6.4**	**6.4**
Long-term debt	0.3	0.9	4.8	5.5	5.5
Net transfers on debt	..	**4.7**	**2.7**	**-3.9**	**0.0**
Total debt service (TDS)	..	**3.0**	**11.9**	**18.2**	**18.2**
AGGREGATE NET RESOURCE FLOWS AND NET TRANSFERS (LONG-TERM)					
NET RESOURCE FLOWS	**1.4**	**6.8**	**10.5**	**10.1**	**18.8**
Net flow of long-term debt (ex. IMF)	1.0	3.6	6.4	1.8	6.3
Foreign direct investment (net)	0.1	0.2	0.5	1.9	2.7
Portfolio equity flows	0.0	0.0	0.1	2.3	5.3
Grants (excluding technical coop.)	0.4	3.1	3.5	4.2	4.4
NET TRANSFERS	**1.1**	**5.8**	**5.6**	**4.4**	**13.0**
Interest on long-term debt	0.3	0.9	4.8	5.5	5.5
Profit remittances on FDI	0.0	0.1	0.2	0.2	0.3
MAJOR ECONOMIC INDICATORS					
Gross national product (GNP)	81.5	224.3	387.9	442.6	482.4
Exports of goods & services (XGS)	4.5	25.0	42.9	70.5	75.8
of which workers' remittances	0.2	5.2	5.1	7.9	6.5
Imports of goods & services (MGS)	6.3	31.9	58.4	83.0	88.5
International reserves (RES)	1.4	14.5	8.3	30.0	..
Current account balance	-1.6	-5.8	-13.4	-10.2	-11.2
DEBT INDICATORS					
EDT / XGS (%)	..	155.6	303.5	222.0	211.7
EDT / GNP (%)	..	17.3	33.5	35.3	33.3
TDS / XGS (%)	..	11.9	27.8	25.8	24.0
INT / XGS (%)	..	5.0	14.7	9.1	8.4
INT / GNP (%)	..	0.6	1.6	1.4	1.3
RES / MGS (months)	2.6	5.5	1.7	4.3	..
Short-term / EDT (%)	..	6.9	10.1	6.2	6.8
Concessional / EDT (%)	..	71.6	54.1	54.7	54.5
Multilateral / EDT (%)	..	24.9	30.5	38.1	39.2

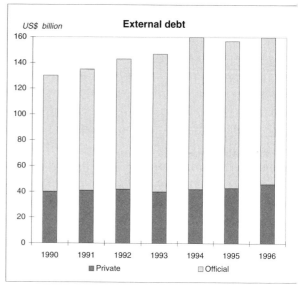

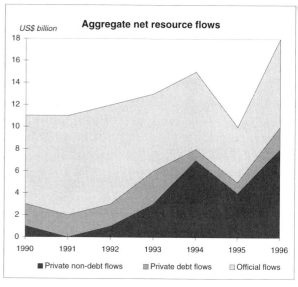

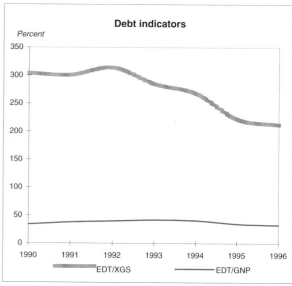

MODERATELY INDEBTED LOW-INCOME COUNTRIES

(US$ billion, unless otherwise indicated)

	1970	1980	1990	1995	Preliminary 1996
LONG-TERM DEBT					
DEBT OUTSTANDING (LDOD)	**11.5**	**33.8**	**112.3**	**141.1**	**145.2**
Public and publicly guaranteed	**11.4**	**33.5**	**110.5**	**132.4**	**135.2**
Official creditors	10.6	29.9	85.4	107.8	109.9
Multilateral	2.2	9.7	39.7	59.6	63.0
Bilateral	8.4	20.2	45.7	48.2	47.0
Private creditors	0.8	3.6	25.1	24.6	25.3
Bonds	0.2	0.6	3.0	3.5	2.0
Private nonguaranteed	**0.1**	**0.4**	**1.9**	**8.6**	**10.0**
Bonds	..	..	0.0	1.1	1.7
DISBURSEMENTS	**1.4**	**5.0**	**10.8**	**11.5**	**16.4**
Public and publicly guaranteed	**1.4**	**4.7**	**10.4**	**9.3**	**14.2**
Official creditors	1.3	3.5	7.3	6.6	8.5
Multilateral	0.2	1.5	4.6	4.3	5.3
Bilateral	1.1	2.0	2.7	2.3	3.2
Private creditors	0.1	1.2	3.1	2.7	5.7
Bonds	0.0	0.1	0.4	0.0	0.6
Private nonguaranteed	**0.0**	**0.3**	**0.4**	**2.2**	**2.2**
Bonds	..	..	0.0	0.5	0.6
PRINCIPAL REPAYMENTS	**0.5**	**1.4**	**4.4**	**9.7**	**10.1**
Public and publicly guaranteed	**0.4**	**1.3**	**4.0**	**9.1**	**9.2**
Official creditors	0.3	0.9	2.5	5.9	4.6
Multilateral	0.1	0.1	1.1	2.4	2.2
Bilateral	0.3	0.8	1.4	3.4	2.4
Private creditors	0.1	0.4	1.5	3.2	4.6
Bonds	0.0	0.0	0.3	0.3	2.0
Private nonguaranteed	**0.0**	**0.1**	**0.4**	**0.6**	**0.8**
Bonds	..	..	0.0	0.0	0.0
NET FLOWS ON DEBT	**1.0**	**3.6**	**6.4**	**1.8**	**6.3**
Public and publicly guaranteed	**1.0**	**3.4**	**6.4**	**0.2**	**4.9**
Official creditors	1.0	2.6	4.8	0.7	3.9
Multilateral	0.1	1.4	3.5	1.9	3.1
Bilateral	0.8	1.2	1.3	-1.2	0.8
Private creditors	0.0	0.8	1.7	-0.5	1.1
Bonds	0.0	0.0	0.1	-0.3	-1.4
Private nonguaranteed	**0.0**	**0.2**	**0.0**	**1.6**	**1.4**
Bonds	..	..	0.0	0.5	0.6
CURRENCY COMPOSITION OF LONG-TERM DEBT (PERCENT)					
Deutsche mark	9.5	8.1	5.7	5.7	..
French franc	1.9	4.2	2.9	2.7	..
Japanese yen	5.2	8.1	11.0	14.1	..
Pound sterling	22.9	18.1	5.1	3.6	..
U.S. dollars	41.2	41.4	52.9	46.6	..
Multiple currency	8.4	8.5	13.8	19.7	..
All other currencies	10.8	11.5	8.5	7.6	..
DEBT STOCK-FLOW RECONCILIATION					
Total change in debt stocks	..	..	13.9	-3.7	..
Net flows on debt	..	..	9.0	2.5	..
Net change in interest arrears	..	..	0.0	-0.1	..
Interest capitalized	..	..	0.0	0.1	..
Debt forgiveness or reduction	..	..	-0.2	-0.2	..
Cross-currency valuation	..	..	3.0	-3.4	..
Residual	..	..	2.1	-2.6	..
AVERAGE TERMS OF NEW COMMITMENTS					
ALL CREDITORS					
Interest (%)	2.6	5.1	4.7	3.6	..
Maturity (years)	32.6	30.2	24.2	23.5	..
Grant element (%)	59.6	44.3	40.5	45.8	..
Official creditors					..
Interest (%)	2.2	2.6	3.8	3.6	..
Maturity (years)	35.3	36.9	28.1	27.2	..
Grant element (%)	64.9	62.5	49.5	49.1	..
Private creditors					..
Interest (%)	5.9	12.5	6.7	3.3	..
Maturity (years)	11.3	10.4	15.0	8.1	..
Grant element (%)	17.5	-9.3	19.5	31.9	..
Memo:					
Commitments	2.0	8.8	14.0	7.2	..
Official creditors	1.7	6.5	9.8	5.8	..
Private creditors	0.2	2.2	4.2	1.4	..

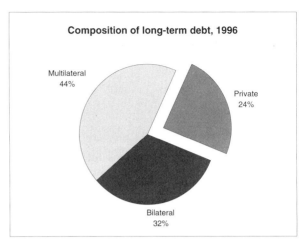

Composition of long-term debt, 1996

Multilateral 44%
Private 24%
Bilateral 32%

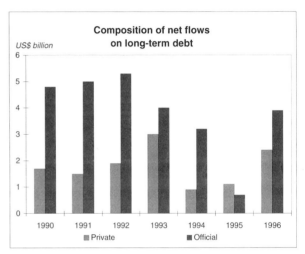

Composition of net flows on long-term debt

US$ billion

■ Private ■ Official

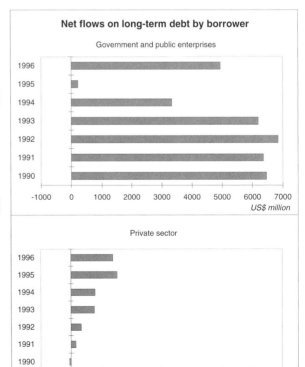

Net flows on long-term debt by borrower

Government and public enterprises

US$ million

Private sector

US$ million

MODERATELY INDEBTED MIDDLE-INCOME COUNTRIES

(US$ billion, unless otherwise indicated)

	1970	1980	1990	1995	Preliminary 1996
SUMMARY DEBT DATA					
TOTAL DEBT STOCKS (EDT)	..	**196.0**	**495.4**	**679.8**	**721.3**
Long-term debt (LDOD)	**15.8**	**140.8**	**401.3**	**550.8**	**575.9**
Public and publicly guaranteed	13.2	125.3	376.6	497.0	510.1
Private nonguaranteed	2.7	15.5	24.7	53.8	65.8
Use of IMF credit	**0.4**	**3.1**	**8.6**	**15.8**	**18.6**
Short-term debt	..	**52.1**	**85.4**	**113.3**	**126.9**
of which interest arrears on LDOD	..	0.7	14.5	6.8	2.5
Memo:					
IBRD	1.0	6.1	35.8	43.8	43.9
IDA	0.1	1.3	2.3	2.5	2.5
TOTAL DEBT FLOWS					
Disbursements	**3.8**	**39.2**	**61.8**	**62.7**	**79.1**
Long-term debt	**3.6**	**37.8**	**59.1**	**56.4**	**74.2**
Public and publicly guaranteed	2.7	31.6	51.1	38.0	51.0
Private nonguaranteed	0.9	6.2	8.0	18.4	23.1
IMF purchases	**0.2**	**1.4**	**2.7**	**6.4**	**5.0**
Memo:					
IBRD	0.2	1.4	4.9	4.7	4.5
IDA	0.0	0.1	0.0	0.1	0.1
Principal repayments	**1.6**	**15.5**	**40.9**	**50.9**	**47.0**
Long-term debt	**1.4**	**15.0**	**39.3**	**47.1**	**45.3**
Public and publicly guaranteed	1.0	11.9	36.5	37.9	34.1
Private nonguaranteed	0.4	3.1	2.8	9.2	11.2
IMF repurchases	**0.2**	**0.6**	**1.6**	**3.8**	**1.7**
Memo:					
IBRD	0.1	0.3	2.8	4.9	4.4
IDA	0.0	0.0	0.0	0.0	0.0
Net flows on debt	**6.0**	**34.4**	**18.9**	**25.4**	**49.9**
of which short-term debt	..	..	-2.1	13.5	17.8
Interest payments (INT)	..	**15.4**	**30.2**	**34.2**	**35.5**
Long-term debt	0.5	9.9	24.3	27.9	28.5
Net transfers on debt	..	**19.1**	**-11.4**	**-8.8**	**14.4**
Total debt service (TDS)	..	**30.9**	**71.1**	**85.0**	**82.5**
AGGREGATE NET RESOURCE FLOWS AND NET TRANSFERS (LONG-TERM)					
NET RESOURCE FLOWS	**3.3**	**27.1**	**35.7**	**53.9**	**75.4**
Net flow of long-term debt (ex. IMF)	2.2	22.8	19.8	9.3	28.8
Foreign direct investment (net)	0.3	3.0	6.2	25.1	25.2
Portfolio equity flows	0.0	0.0	0.8	10.1	14.2
Grants (excluding technical coop.)	0.8	1.3	8.8	9.5	7.1
NET TRANSFERS	**1.6**	**11.5**	**6.4**	**17.7**	**37.3**
Interest on long-term debt	0.5	9.9	24.3	27.9	28.5
Profit remittances on FDI	1.2	5.6	4.9	8.4	9.6
MAJOR ECONOMIC INDICATORS					
Gross national product (GNP)	265.5	885.3	1298.3	1372.2	1551.8
Exports of goods & services (XGS)	30.9	206.4	291.3	409.4	441.7
of which workers' remittances	1.1	7.9	12.6	15.8	14.4
Imports of goods & services (MGS)	28.6	198.2	299.3	437.6	477.1
International reserves (RES)	12.1	67.0	70.6	161.2	..
Current account balance	12.6	12.8	2.3	-19.2	-25.9
DEBT INDICATORS					
EDT / XGS (%)	..	95.0	170.0	166.1	163.3
EDT / GNP (%)	..	22.1	38.2	49.5	46.5
TDS / XGS (%)	..	15.0	24.4	20.8	18.7
INT / XGS (%)	..	7.4	10.4	8.3	8.0
INT / GNP (%)	..	1.7	2.3	2.5	2.3
RES / MGS (months)	5.1	4.1	2.8	4.4	..
Short-term / EDT (%)	..	26.6	17.2	16.7	17.6
Concessional / EDT (%)	..	15.6	12.9	17.4	16.0
Multilateral / EDT (%)	..	6.2	13.1	12.3	11.8

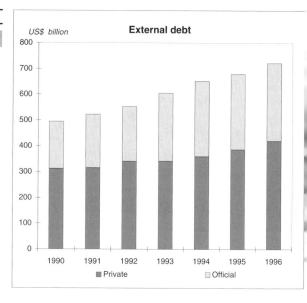

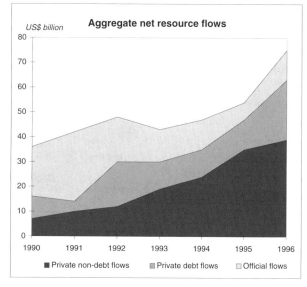

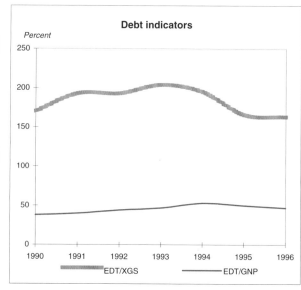

MODERATELY INDEBTED MIDDLE-INCOME COUNTRIES

(US$ billion, unless otherwise indicated)

	1970	1980	1990	1995	Preliminary 1996
LONG-TERM DEBT					
DEBT OUTSTANDING (LDOD)	**15.8**	**140.8**	**401.3**	**550.8**	**575.9**
Public and publicly guaranteed	**13.2**	**125.3**	**376.6**	**497.0**	**510.1**
Official creditors	9.9	51.9	175.6	278.0	283.0
Multilateral	1.6	12.1	64.7	83.6	85.2
Bilateral	8.3	39.8	110.8	194.4	197.8
Private creditors	3.3	73.4	201.1	219.0	227.0
Bonds	0.3	3.9	39.7	85.0	89.6
Private nonguaranteed	**2.7**	**15.5**	**24.7**	**53.8**	**65.8**
Bonds	..	..	0.1	7.3	14.6
DISBURSEMENTS	**3.6**	**37.8**	**59.1**	**56.4**	**74.2**
Public and publicly guaranteed	**2.7**	**31.6**	**51.1**	**38.0**	**51.0**
Official creditors	1.6	9.3	20.2	14.4	18.8
Multilateral	0.3	2.2	9.5	8.2	9.2
Bilateral	1.2	7.1	10.7	6.2	9.6
Private creditors	1.1	22.2	30.9	23.5	32.2
Bonds	0.0	0.6	4.7	12.1	14.2
Private nonguaranteed	**0.9**	**6.2**	**8.0**	**18.4**	**23.1**
Bonds	..	..	0.1	3.8	7.7
PRINCIPAL REPAYMENTS	**1.4**	**15.0**	**39.3**	**47.1**	**45.3**
Public and publicly guaranteed	**1.0**	**11.9**	**36.5**	**37.9**	**34.1**
Official creditors	0.5	2.6	9.1	16.8	13.7
Multilateral	0.1	0.4	4.3	9.4	7.4
Bilateral	0.4	2.1	4.8	7.4	6.3
Private creditors	0.4	9.3	27.4	21.1	20.4
Bonds	0.0	0.1	1.2	5.8	7.5
Private nonguaranteed	**0.4**	**3.1**	**2.8**	**9.2**	**11.2**
Bonds	..	..	0.0	0.1	0.4
NET FLOWS ON DEBT	**2.2**	**22.8**	**19.8**	**9.3**	**28.8**
Public and publicly guaranteed	**1.7**	**19.7**	**14.6**	**0.0**	**16.9**
Official creditors	1.1	6.8	11.1	-2.4	5.1
Multilateral	0.2	1.7	5.2	-1.2	1.8
Bilateral	0.9	5.0	5.9	-1.2	3.3
Private creditors	0.7	12.9	3.5	2.4	11.8
Bonds	0.0	0.5	3.5	6.3	6.8
Private nonguaranteed	**0.5**	**3.2**	**5.2**	**9.2**	**12.0**
Bonds	..	..	0.1	3.7	7.3
CURRENCY COMPOSITION OF LONG-TERM DEBT (PERCENT)					
Deutsche mark	7.4	7.8	13.6	12.2	..
French franc	7.3	8.5	6.7	5.6	..
Japanese yen	2.3	7.4	12.2	14.3	..
Pound sterling	3.7	1.6	1.6	1.0	..
U.S. dollars	48.9	47.4	34.6	37.9	..
Multiple currency	9.5	11.1	13.6	13.0	..
All other currencies	20.8	10.7	11.9	8.4	..
DEBT STOCK-FLOW RECONCILIATION					
Total change in debt stocks	..	..	31.8	29.7	..
Net flows on debt	..	..	18.9	25.4	..
Net change in interest arrears	..	..	3.2	0.9	..
Interest capitalized	..	..	2.6	1.6	..
Debt forgiveness or reduction	..	..	-15.1	-0.2	..
Cross-currency valuation	..	..	22.7	9.0	..
Residual	..	..	-0.5	-7.0	..
AVERAGE TERMS OF NEW COMMITMENTS					
ALL CREDITORS					
Interest (%)	5.1	8.9	7.8	5.9	..
Maturity (years)	19.1	15.2	16.9	14.0	..
Grant element (%)	30.9	8.9	13.2	22.7	..
Official creditors					..
Interest (%)	4.0	6.0	6.8	5.2	..
Maturity (years)	24.8	22.4	18.7	20.0	..
Grant element (%)	41.7	29.6	22.0	30.8	..
Private creditors					..
Interest (%)	6.9	10.8	8.6	6.5	..
Maturity (years)	9.6	10.6	15.5	8.4	..
Grant element (%)	12.8	-4.4	6.1	15.2	..
Memo:					
Commitments	3.3	29.5	56.4	36.0	..
Official creditors	2.1	11.6	25.1	17.4	..
Private creditors	1.2	17.9	31.4	18.6	..

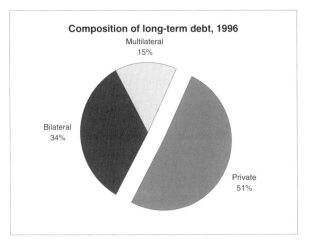

Composition of long-term debt, 1996

Multilateral 15%

Bilateral 34%

Private 51%

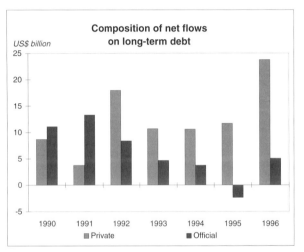

Composition of net flows on long-term debt

US$ billion

■ Private   ■ Official

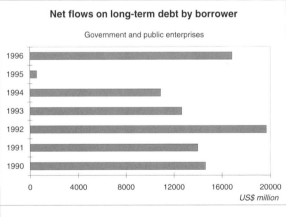

Net flows on long-term debt by borrower

Government and public enterprises

US$ million

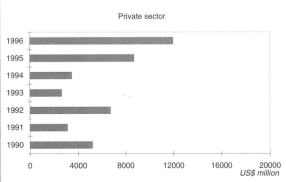

Private sector

US$ million

OTHER DEVELOPING COUNTRIES

(US$ billion, unless otherwise indicated)

	1970	1980	1990	1995	*Preliminary* 1996
SUMMARY DEBT DATA					
TOTAL DEBT STOCKS (EDT)	..	**115.0**	**215.2**	**405.6**	**454.6**
Long-term debt (LDOD)	**4.8**	**73.3**	**153.4**	**293.1**	**329.8**
Public and publicly guaranteed	3.1	58.0	139.3	246.1	256.7
Private nonguaranteed	1.7	15.3	14.0	47.0	73.1
Use of IMF credit	**0.1**	**2.1**	**1.6**	**7.3**	**7.7**
Short-term debt	..	**39.6**	**60.2**	**105.3**	**117.1**
of which interest arrears on LDOD	..	0.0	1.4	2.4	2.9
Memo:					
IBRD	0.7	4.7	10.9	16.7	18.5
IDA	0.0	0.4	5.0	10.6	11.9
TOTAL DEBT FLOWS					
Disbursements	**1.2**	**21.4**	**24.0**	**66.2**	**67.1**
Long-term debt	**1.2**	**20.6**	**23.8**	**63.9**	**65.8**
Public and publicly guaranteed	0.5	15.4	18.3	45.7	35.0
Private nonguaranteed	0.7	5.2	5.5	18.2	30.8
IMF purchases	**0.0**	**0.8**	**0.2**	**2.3**	**1.3**
Memo:					
IBRD	0.1	0.9	1.4	3.0	2.9
IDA	0.0	0.1	0.7	1.4	1.4
Principal repayments	**0.8**	**6.7**	**18.7**	**33.8**	**26.1**
Long-term debt	**0.7**	**6.3**	**17.4**	**33.0**	**25.3**
Public and publicly guaranteed	0.3	3.2	15.0	26.5	20.5
Private nonguaranteed	0.4	3.1	2.3	6.5	4.8
IMF repurchases	**0.1**	**0.4**	**1.3**	**0.7**	**0.7**
Memo:					
IBRD	0.0	0.2	1.3	1.1	1.1
IDA	0.0	0.0	0.0	0.0	0.0
Net flows on debt	**1.1**	**26.3**	**10.4**	**50.7**	**52.4**
of which short-term debt	..	..	5.1	18.3	11.3
Interest payments (INT)	..	**9.7**	**14.9**	**19.5**	**22.5**
Long-term debt	0.2	5.3	9.8	13.4	15.9
Net transfers on debt	..	**16.7**	**-4.5**	**31.2**	**29.9**
Total debt service (TDS)	..	**16.4**	**33.6**	**53.3**	**48.6**
AGGREGATE NET RESOURCE FLOWS AND NET TRANSFERS (LONG-TERM)					
NET RESOURCE FLOWS	**1.5**	**13.0**	**21.4**	**97.2**	**115.8**
Net flow of long-term debt (ex. IMF)	0.5	14.3	6.5	30.9	40.5
Foreign direct investment (net)	0.8	-2.9	11.4	48.7	59.3
Portfolio equity flows	0.0	0.0	0.7	12.1	10.1
Grants (excluding technical coop.)	0.2	1.6	2.9	5.6	5.8
NET TRANSFERS	**-1.6**	**-4.0**	**4.7**	**74.1**	**88.9**
Interest on long-term debt	0.2	5.3	9.8	13.4	15.9
Profit remittances on FDI	2.9	11.7	6.9	9.7	10.9
MAJOR ECONOMIC INDICATORS					
Gross national product (GNP)	276.6	1004.7	1465.9	1751.0	2083.6
Exports of goods & services (XGS)	34.9	325.8	369.8	594.0	657.4
of which workers' remittances	0.6	1.6	1.9	4.1	3.9
Imports of goods & services (MGS)	36.3	277.6	371.9	623.9	706.0
International reserves (RES)	7.9	101.4	112.0	228.2	..
Current account balance	-1.3	36.8	-14.7	-36.1	-51.1
DEBT INDICATORS					
EDT / XGS (%)	..	35.3	58.2	68.3	69.2
EDT / GNP (%)	..	11.4	14.7	23.2	21.8
TDS / XGS (%)	..	5.0	9.1	9.0	7.4
INT / XGS (%)	..	3.0	4.0	3.3	3.4
INT / GNP (%)	..	1.0	1.0	1.1	1.1
RES / MGS (months)	2.6	4.4	3.6	4.4	..
Short-term / EDT (%)	..	34.4	28.0	26.0	25.8
Concessional / EDT (%)	..	8.8	16.0	13.7	12.5
Multilateral / EDT (%)	..	6.0	11.6	10.9	10.8

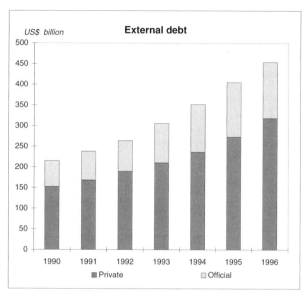

US$ billion — **External debt**

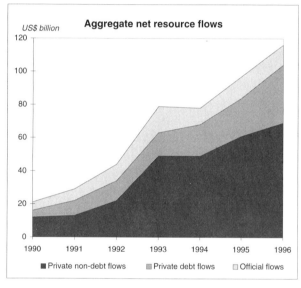

US$ billion — **Aggregate net resource flows**

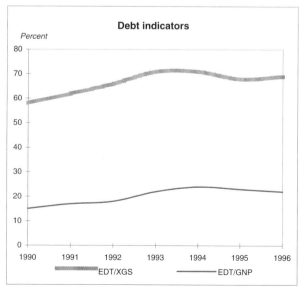

Percent — **Debt indicators**

212

OTHER DEVELOPING COUNTRIES

(US$ billion, unless otherwise indicated)

	1970	1980	1990	1995	*Preliminary* 1996
LONG-TERM DEBT					
DEBT OUTSTANDING (LDOD)	**4.8**	**73.3**	**153.4**	**293.1**	**329.8**
Public and publicly guaranteed	**3.1**	**58.0**	**139.3**	**246.1**	**256.7**
Official creditors	2.3	21.2	61.5	125.0	128.8
Multilateral	0.8	7.0	25.0	44.1	49.1
Bilateral	1.5	14.3	36.5	80.9	79.7
Private creditors	0.8	36.8	77.8	121.1	127.9
Bonds	0.2	6.6	14.4	24.8	27.1
Private nonguaranteed	**1.7**	**15.3**	**14.0**	**47.0**	**73.1**
Bonds	..	..	0.0	11.8	16.6
DISBURSEMENTS	**1.2**	**20.6**	**23.8**	**63.9**	**65.8**
Public and publicly guaranteed	**0.5**	**15.4**	**18.3**	**45.7**	**35.0**
Official creditors	0.4	4.1	6.7	16.9	12.0
Multilateral	0.1	1.5	2.9	7.3	7.1
Bilateral	0.3	2.7	3.8	9.6	4.9
Private creditors	0.1	11.2	11.6	28.8	23.0
Bonds	0.0	1.7	0.5	4.8	5.4
Private nonguaranteed	**0.7**	**5.2**	**5.5**	**18.2**	**30.8**
Bonds	..	..	0.0	4.0	5.4
PRINCIPAL REPAYMENTS	**0.7**	**6.3**	**17.4**	**33.0**	**25.3**
Public and publicly guaranteed	**0.3**	**3.2**	**15.0**	**26.5**	**20.5**
Official creditors	0.2	1.1	4.3	9.2	6.2
Multilateral	0.0	0.3	1.9	2.5	2.1
Bilateral	0.1	0.8	2.4	6.7	4.1
Private creditors	0.2	2.0	10.7	17.3	14.3
Bonds	0.0	0.0	1.9	2.3	2.3
Private nonguaranteed	**0.4**	**3.1**	**2.3**	**6.5**	**4.8**
Bonds	..	..	0.0	0.0	0.0
NET FLOWS ON DEBT	**0.5**	**14.3**	**6.5**	**30.9**	**40.5**
Public and publicly guaranteed	**0.2**	**12.2**	**3.3**	**19.2**	**14.5**
Official creditors	0.2	3.0	2.4	7.7	5.8
Multilateral	0.1	1.2	1.1	4.9	5.0
Bilateral	0.1	1.8	1.4	2.9	0.8
Private creditors	-0.1	9.2	0.8	11.5	8.6
Bonds	0.0	1.7	-1.4	2.5	3.0
Private nonguaranteed	**0.3**	**2.1**	**3.2**	**11.6**	**26.0**
Bonds	..	..	0.0	4.0	5.4
CURRENCY COMPOSITION OF LONG-TERM DEBT (PERCENT)					
Deutsche mark	10.0	4.2	5.5	4.0	..
French franc	1.7	2.1	1.6	1.1	..
Japanese yen	1.7	5.2	18.8	15.9	..
Pound sterling	12.8	0.9	1.0	0.5	..
U.S. dollars	37.4	31.0	26.4	44.1	..
Multiple currency	25.5	15.3	24.0	19.1	..
All other currencies	11.0	4.4	6.6	5.5	..
DEBT STOCK-FLOW RECONCILIATION					
Total change in debt stocks	..	..	16.6	53.0	..
Net flows on debt	..	..	10.4	50.7	..
Net change in interest arrears	..	..	0.1	0.5	..
Interest capitalized	..	..	0.2	0.2	..
Debt forgiveness or reduction	..	..	-1.7	-0.1	..
Cross-currency valuation	..	..	6.3	-0.6	..
Residual	..	..	1.3	2.3	..
AVERAGE TERMS OF NEW COMMITMENTS					
ALL CREDITORS					
Interest (%)	4.9	10.4	6.8	6.4	..
Maturity (years)	22.8	13.6	17.4	13.2	..
Grant element (%)	37.0	3.9	21.0	17.9	..
Official creditors					..
Interest (%)	4.5	6.3	4.4	6.0	..
Maturity (years)	24.8	20.7	25.8	19.0	..
Grant element (%)	41.3	27.8	43.5	25.4	..
Private creditors					..
Interest (%)	7.1	13.3	8.4	6.6	..
Maturity (years)	11.7	8.5	11.9	9.2	..
Grant element (%)	13.1	-13.4	6.4	12.9	..
Memo:					
Commitments	0.8	13.9	18.9	40.8	..
Official creditors	0.7	5.8	7.4	16.6	..
Private creditors	0.1	8.0	11.4	24.3	..

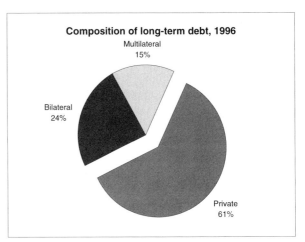

Composition of long-term debt, 1996

Multilateral 15%

Bilateral 24%

Private 61%

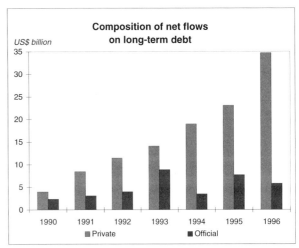

Composition of net flows on long-term debt

US$ billion

■ Private   ■ Official

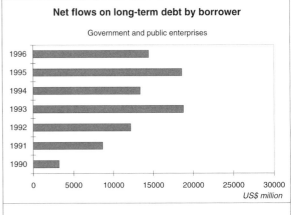

Net flows on long-term debt by borrower

Government and public enterprises

US$ million

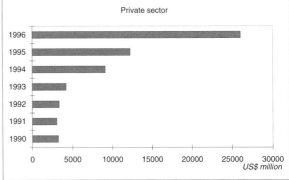

Private sector

US$ million

LOW-INCOME COUNTRIES

(US$ billion, unless otherwise indicated)

	1970	1980	1990	1995	*Preliminary* 1996
SUMMARY DEBT DATA					
TOTAL DEBT STOCKS (EDT)	..	**106.2**	**405.6**	**534.8**	**548.3**
Long-term debt (LDOD)	**17.7**	**87.5**	**346.0**	**452.1**	**461.3**
Public and publicly guaranteed	17.3	82.4	339.1	437.8	441.7
Private nonguaranteed	0.4	5.1	6.9	14.3	19.6
Use of IMF credit	**0.3**	**5.8**	**11.8**	**14.3**	**13.2**
Short-term debt	..	**12.9**	**47.8**	**68.4**	**73.8**
of which interest arrears on LDOD	..	0.3	12.7	25.6	25.7
Memo:					
IBRD	1.5	3.9	22.1	28.5	27.8
IDA	1.6	10.1	41.7	67.6	73.1
TOTAL DEBT FLOWS					
Disbursements	**2.8**	**22.1**	**33.7**	**45.1**	**46.7**
Long-term debt	**2.8**	**19.1**	**31.0**	**41.5**	**45.1**
Public and publicly guaranteed	2.6	17.6	30.2	38.6	38.4
Private nonguaranteed	0.1	1.6	0.8	2.9	6.6
IMF purchases	**0.0**	**3.0**	**2.7**	**3.7**	**1.7**
Memo:					
IBRD	0.2	0.6	3.0	2.6	2.4
IDA	0.1	1.5	4.3	5.2	6.0
Principal repayments	**1.2**	**5.4**	**15.1**	**28.3**	**29.7**
Long-term debt	**0.9**	**4.6**	**12.4**	**23.8**	**27.3**
Public and publicly guaranteed	0.8	3.9	11.5	23.1	26.0
Private nonguaranteed	0.1	0.7	0.8	0.7	1.3
IMF repurchases	**0.3**	**0.8**	**2.7**	**4.5**	**2.4**
Memo:					
IBRD	0.1	0.2	1.6	2.6	2.6
IDA	0.0	0.0	0.2	0.5	0.6
Net flows on debt	**2.8**	**19.8**	**25.4**	**24.2**	**22.4**
of which short-term debt	..	..	6.8	7.4	5.3
Interest payments (INT)	..	**5.1**	**15.0**	**16.5**	**17.5**
Long-term debt	0.5	3.6	11.8	13.3	14.6
Net transfers on debt	..	**14.7**	**10.3**	**7.8**	**4.9**
Total debt service (TDS)	..	**10.5**	**30.1**	**44.8**	**47.2**
AGGREGATE NET RESOURCE FLOWS AND NET TRANSFERS (LONG-TERM)					
NET RESOURCE FLOWS	**3.1**	**21.8**	**38.9**	**81.8**	**93.9**
Net flow of long-term debt (ex. IMF)	1.9	14.5	18.7	17.7	17.7
Foreign direct investment (net)	0.2	0.1	4.5	41.6	49.5
Portfolio equity flows	0.0	0.0	0.1	5.6	9.1
Grants (excluding technical coop.)	1.0	7.2	15.6	16.9	17.6
NET TRANSFERS	**1.8**	**15.6**	**25.8**	**66.4**	**76.3**
Interest on long-term debt	0.5	3.6	11.8	13.3	14.6
Profit remittances on FDI	0.8	2.6	1.3	2.1	3.0
MAJOR ECONOMIC INDICATORS					
Gross national product (GNP)	233.8	650.5	957.3	1381.5	1652.0
Exports of goods & services (XGS)	18.1	109.7	159.5	290.9	315.2
of which workers' remittances	0.3	9.5	7.8	12.1	10.3
Imports of goods & services (MGS)	21.8	124.5	176.4	321.4	361.3
International reserves (RES)	3.6	40.5	52.8	124.4	..
Current account balance	-3.9	-13.3	-7.9	-19.5	-33.9
DEBT INDICATORS					
EDT / XGS (%)	..	96.8	254.2	183.9	173.9
EDT / GNP (%)	..	16.3	42.4	38.7	33.2
TDS / XGS (%)	..	9.6	18.9	15.4	15.0
INT / XGS (%)	..	4.7	9.4	5.7	5.5
INT / GNP (%)	..	0.8	1.6	1.2	1.1
RES / MGS (months)	2.0	3.9	3.6	4.6	..
Short-term / EDT (%)	..	12.1	11.8	12.8	13.5
Concessional / EDT (%)	..	44.7	42.6	42.0	41.1
Multilateral / EDT (%)	..	17.2	21.5	25.5	26.3

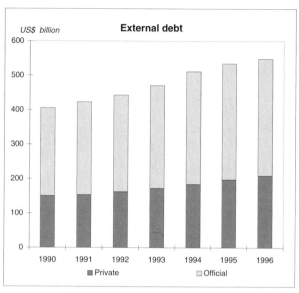

External debt (US$ billion)

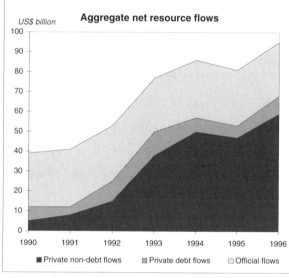

Aggregate net resource flows (US$ billion)

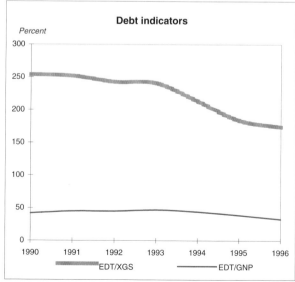

Debt indicators (Percent)

LOW-INCOME COUNTRIES

(US$ billion, unless otherwise indicated)

	1970	1980	1990	1995	Preliminary 1996
LONG-TERM DEBT					
DEBT OUTSTANDING (LDOD)	**17.7**	**87.5**	**346.0**	**452.1**	**461.3**
Public and publicly guaranteed	**17.3**	**82.4**	**339.1**	**437.8**	**441.7**
Official creditors	15.0	59.0	244.3	323.9	326.3
Multilateral	3.1	18.3	87.2	136.1	144.1
Bilateral	11.8	40.7	157.1	187.8	182.2
Private creditors	2.3	23.5	94.8	113.9	115.4
Bonds	0.4	0.7	8.4	17.2	16.0
Private nonguaranteed	**0.4**	**5.1**	**6.9**	**14.3**	**19.6**
Bonds	..	..	0.0	2.2	3.3
DISBURSEMENTS	**2.8**	**19.1**	**31.0**	**41.5**	**45.1**
Public and publicly guaranteed	**2.6**	**17.6**	**30.2**	**38.6**	**38.4**
Official creditors	2.0	9.0	17.9	21.9	19.5
Multilateral	0.4	3.4	10.5	12.1	13.3
Bilateral	1.7	5.6	7.4	9.8	6.2
Private creditors	0.6	8.6	12.3	16.7	18.9
Bonds	0.0	0.1	0.7	1.2	3.1
Private nonguaranteed	**0.1**	**1.6**	**0.8**	**2.9**	**6.6**
Bonds	..	..	0.0	1.1	1.2
PRINCIPAL REPAYMENTS	**0.9**	**4.6**	**12.4**	**23.8**	**27.3**
Public and publicly guaranteed	**0.8**	**3.9**	**11.5**	**23.1**	**26.0**
Official creditors	0.5	1.7	6.1	10.5	10.3
Multilateral	0.1	0.4	2.7	4.9	4.9
Bilateral	0.4	1.4	3.3	5.6	5.4
Private creditors	0.3	2.1	5.5	12.6	15.7
Bonds	0.0	0.0	0.6	1.8	3.7
Private nonguaranteed	**0.1**	**0.7**	**0.8**	**0.7**	**1.3**
Bonds	..	..	0.0	0.0	0.0
NET FLOWS ON DEBT	**1.9**	**14.5**	**18.7**	**17.7**	**17.7**
Public and publicly guaranteed	**1.8**	**13.7**	**18.7**	**15.5**	**12.4**
Official creditors	1.5	7.3	11.9	11.4	9.2
Multilateral	0.3	3.0	7.8	7.2	8.3
Bilateral	1.3	4.2	4.0	4.2	0.8
Private creditors	0.3	6.4	6.8	4.1	3.2
Bonds	0.0	0.1	0.1	-0.6	-0.6
Private nonguaranteed	**0.1**	**0.8**	**0.0**	**2.1**	**5.3**
Bonds	..	..	0.0	1.1	1.2
CURRENCY COMPOSITION OF LONG-TERM DEBT (PERCENT)					
Deutsche mark	8.6	7.5	5.4	4.6	..
French franc	5.5	7.5	6.2	5.5	..
Japanese yen	3.6	6.0	10.5	12.4	..
Pound sterling	22.3	10.0	4.0	2.5	..
U.S. dollars	35.8	38.3	40.1	44.2	..
Multiple currency	9.5	11.3	13.8	14.2	..
All other currencies	14.7	18.0	18.5	15.3	..
DEBT STOCK-FLOW RECONCILIATION					
Total change in debt stocks	..	..	48.7	22.6	..
Net flows on debt	..	..	25.4	24.2	..
Net change in interest arrears	..	..	3.0	2.0	..
Interest capitalized	..	..	1.9	0.9	..
Debt forgiveness or reduction	..	..	-2.0	-3.1	..
Cross-currency valuation	..	..	14.2	-0.1	..
Residual	..	..	6.3	-1.3	..
AVERAGE TERMS OF NEW COMMITMENTS					
ALL CREDITORS					
Interest (%)	3.2	6.5	5.2	5.2	..
Maturity (years)	28.9	21.7	22.6	17.5	..
Grant element (%)	53.4	29.4	35.3	29.6	..
Official creditors					..
Interest (%)	2.2	3.3	3.6	4.5	..
Maturity (years)	34.3	30.5	28.3	25.3	..
Grant element (%)	64.9	52.7	51.1	41.5	..
Private creditors					..
Interest (%)	6.5	11.0	8.0	6.1	..
Maturity (years)	10.3	9.4	13.5	7.5	..
Grant element (%)	14.1	-3.0	10.1	14.3	..
Memo:					
Commitments	4.0	27.4	36.5	36.3	..
Official creditors	3.1	15.9	22.5	20.4	..
Private creditors	0.9	11.4	14.1	15.9	..

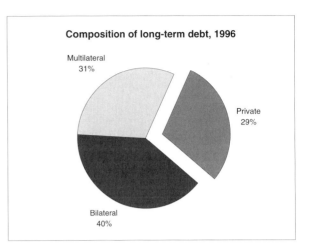

Composition of long-term debt, 1996

Multilateral 31%
Private 29%
Bilateral 40%

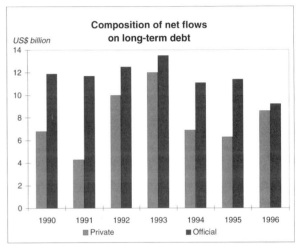

Composition of net flows on long-term debt

US$ billion

■ Private ■ Official

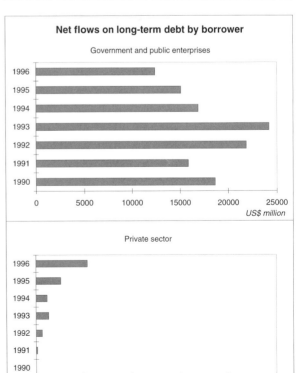

Net flows on long-term debt by borrower

Government and public enterprises

US$ million

Private sector

US$ million

216

MIDDLE-INCOME COUNTRIES

(US$ billion, unless otherwise indicated)

	1970	1980	1990	1995	Preliminary 1996
SUMMARY DEBT DATA					
TOTAL DEBT STOCKS (EDT)	..	**509.5**	**1074.5**	**1530.9**	**1628.8**
Long-term debt (LDOD)	**41.5**	**364.8**	**838.4**	**1174.3**	**1247.1**
Public and publicly guaranteed	26.7	301.6	784.7	1010.8	1044.3
Private nonguaranteed	14.8	63.2	53.7	163.4	202.8
Use of IMF credit	**0.5**	**5.8**	**22.9**	**46.8**	**47.0**
Short-term debt	..	**139.0**	**213.3**	**309.8**	**334.7**
of which interest arrears on LDOD	..	0.7	39.6	18.1	8.9
Memo:					
IBRD	2.9	16.5	70.2	83.4	85.2
IDA	0.2	1.7	3.3	3.9	4.2
TOTAL DEBT FLOWS					
Disbursements	**9.9**	**92.4**	**100.6**	**184.0**	**195.4**
Long-term debt	9.6	90.0	95.0	159.8	188.7
Public and publicly guaranteed	5.7	70.6	78.5	101.4	121.3
Private nonguaranteed	4.0	19.3	16.5	58.4	67.3
IMF purchases	**0.3**	**2.4**	**5.6**	**24.2**	**6.7**
Memo:					
IBRD	0.5	3.6	10.4	10.6	10.3
IDA	0.0	0.1	0.1	0.3	0.4
Principal repayments	**5.3**	**38.0**	**75.5**	**107.1**	**113.7**
Long-term debt	4.9	36.7	70.0	100.4	108.4
Public and publicly guaranteed	2.5	25.8	63.6	73.5	80.2
Private nonguaranteed	2.4	11.0	6.4	26.9	28.1
IMF repurchases	**0.4**	**1.3**	**5.5**	**6.6**	**5.4**
Memo:					
IBRD	0.2	0.8	6.4	9.1	8.4
IDA	0.0	0.0	0.0	0.1	0.1
Net flows on debt	**12.2**	**94.6**	**37.0**	**108.8**	**115.7**
of which short-term debt	..	..	11.9	31.8	34.0
Interest payments (INT)	..	**44.0**	**58.1**	**79.5**	**83.7**
Long-term debt	1.8	29.3	44.2	61.2	64.1
Net transfers on debt	..	**50.7**	**-21.1**	**29.3**	**31.9**
Total debt service (TDS)	..	**82.0**	**133.5**	**186.5**	**197.5**
AGGREGATE NET RESOURCE FLOWS AND NET TRANSFERS (LONG-TERM)					
NET RESOURCE FLOWS	**7.8**	**64.2**	**60.8**	**155.4**	**190.7**
Net flow of long-term debt (ex. IMF)	4.7	53.2	25.0	59.3	80.3
Foreign direct investment (net)	2.0	5.0	20.0	53.9	60.0
Portfolio equity flows	0.0	0.0	2.1	26.5	36.6
Grants (excluding technical coop.)	1.1	6.0	13.6	15.7	13.7
NET TRANSFERS	**0.4**	**13.8**	**0.5**	**69.9**	**99.3**
Interest on long-term debt	1.8	29.3	44.2	61.2	64.1
Profit remittances on FDI	5.7	21.1	16.1	24.3	27.3
MAJOR ECONOMIC INDICATORS					
Gross national product (GNP)	563.1	2276.8	3293.3	3839.8	4229.2
Exports of goods & services (XGS)	76.3	602.5	736.9	1073.7	1173.5
of which workers' remittances	1.7	11.1	18.1	27.3	25.5
Imports of goods & services (MGS)	77.3	572.1	769.6	1160.3	1268.1
International reserves (RES)	23.9	191.6	186.5	414.0	..
Current account balance	9.7	39.3	-33.0	-81.5	-89.3
DEBT INDICATORS					
EDT / XGS (%)	..	84.6	145.8	142.6	138.8
EDT / GNP (%)	..	22.4	32.6	39.9	38.5
TDS / XGS (%)	..	13.6	18.1	17.4	16.8
INT / XGS (%)	..	7.3	7.9	7.4	7.1
INT / GNP (%)	..	1.9	1.8	2.1	2.0
RES / MGS (months)	3.7	4.0	2.9	4.3	..
Short-term / EDT (%)	..	27.3	19.8	20.2	20.5
Concessional / EDT (%)	..	12.2	12.6	13.7	12.7
Multilateral / EDT (%)	..	5.6	11.4	10.4	10.1

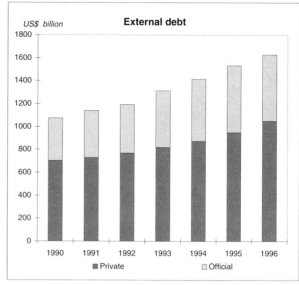

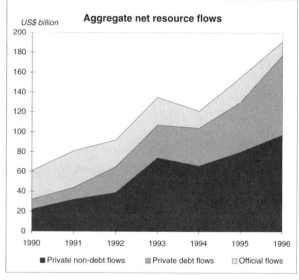

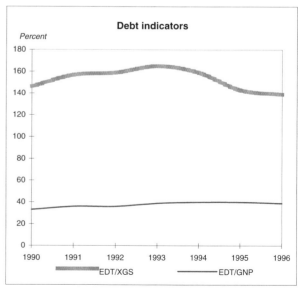

MIDDLE-INCOME COUNTRIES

US$ billion, unless otherwise indicated)

	1970	1980	1990	1995	*Preliminary* 1996
LONG-TERM DEBT					
DEBT OUTSTANDING (LDOD)	**41.5**	**364.8**	**838.4**	**1174.3**	**1247.1**
Public and publicly guaranteed	**26.7**	**301.6**	**784.7**	**1010.8**	**1044.3**
Official creditors	16.7	112.2	351.9	537.0	533.9
Multilateral	4.1	28.5	122.3	158.8	165.2
Bilateral	12.6	83.6	229.6	378.3	368.7
Private creditors	10.0	189.4	432.8	473.8	510.4
Bonds	1.4	18.1	103.5	250.5	280.5
Private nonguaranteed	**14.8**	**63.2**	**53.7**	**163.4**	**202.8**
Bonds	..	..	0.3	51.1	70.2
DISBURSEMENTS	**9.6**	**90.0**	**95.0**	**159.8**	**188.7**
Public and publicly guaranteed	**5.7**	**70.6**	**78.5**	**101.4**	**121.3**
Official creditors	2.7	19.2	34.2	43.9	36.5
Multilateral	0.8	5.6	17.2	20.2	20.6
Bilateral	1.9	13.5	17.0	23.6	15.9
Private creditors	2.9	51.4	44.3	57.5	84.8
Bonds	0.1	3.0	6.2	28.5	45.6
Private nonguaranteed	**4.0**	**19.3**	**16.5**	**58.4**	**67.3**
Bonds	..	..	0.3	13.5	24.8
PRINCIPAL REPAYMENTS	**4.9**	**36.7**	**70.0**	**100.4**	**108.4**
Public and publicly guaranteed	**2.5**	**25.8**	**63.6**	**73.5**	**80.2**
Official creditors	1.0	5.3	18.9	34.9	36.2
Multilateral	0.3	1.2	9.5	16.4	13.9
Bilateral	0.7	4.1	9.5	18.5	22.3
Private creditors	1.6	20.5	44.6	38.6	44.0
Bonds	0.1	0.5	4.2	10.0	19.7
Private nonguaranteed	**2.4**	**11.0**	**6.4**	**26.9**	**28.1**
Bonds	..	..	0.0	4.0	5.2
NET FLOWS ON DEBT	**4.7**	**53.2**	**25.0**	**59.3**	**80.3**
Public and publicly guaranteed	**3.1**	**44.8**	**15.0**	**27.9**	**41.1**
Official creditors	1.7	13.9	15.2	9.0	0.3
Multilateral	0.5	4.4	7.7	3.8	6.7
Bilateral	1.2	9.4	7.6	5.2	-6.4
Private creditors	1.4	31.0	-0.3	18.9	40.8
Bonds	0.0	2.5	2.0	18.5	25.9
Private nonguaranteed	**1.6**	**8.4**	**10.1**	**31.4**	**39.2**
Bonds	..	..	0.3	9.5	19.6
CURRENCY COMPOSITION OF LONG-TERM DEBT (PERCENT)					
Deutsche mark	8.6	6.1	9.9	8.4	..
French franc	5.1	4.7	5.1	4.1	..
Japanese yen	1.3	5.7	9.6	11.3	..
Pound sterling	4.8	1.4	1.5	0.8	..
U.S. dollars	52.0	49.6	40.4	44.4	..
Multiple currency	13.7	10.0	14.4	14.2	..
All other currencies	14.5	7.2	8.3	6.4	..
DEBT STOCK-FLOW RECONCILIATION					
Total change in debt stocks	..	..	57.2	116.1	..
Net flows on debt	..	..	37.0	108.8	..
Net change in interest arrears	..	..	12.6	-1.2	..
Interest capitalized	..	..	4.0	4.3	..
Debt forgiveness or reduction	..	..	-31.5	-3.0	..
Cross-currency valuation	..	..	37.3	11.7	..
Residual	..	..	-2.2	-4.5	..
AVERAGE TERMS OF NEW COMMITMENTS					
ALL CREDITORS					
Interest (%)	6.0	10.2	7.8	6.7	..
Maturity (years)	16.9	13.2	16.1	12.0	..
Grant element (%)	24.3	2.0	13.5	16.7	..
Official creditors					..
Interest (%)	4.8	6.8	6.7	6.6	..
Maturity (years)	23.8	19.6	18.7	16.1	..
Grant element (%)	36.3	23.1	22.2	21.4	..
Private creditors					..
Interest (%)	7.4	12.1	8.7	6.8	..
Maturity (years)	9.2	9.6	13.8	7.6	..
Grant element (%)	11.1	-10.0	5.7	11.7	..
Memo:					
Commitments	7.2	66.3	83.8	95.8	..
Official creditors	3.8	24.0	39.6	49.4	..
Private creditors	3.4	42.3	44.3	46.3	..

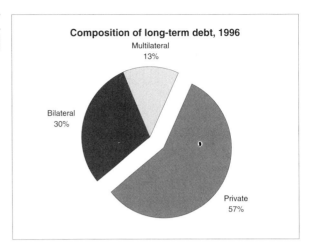

Composition of long-term debt, 1996

Multilateral 13%

Bilateral 30%

Private 57%

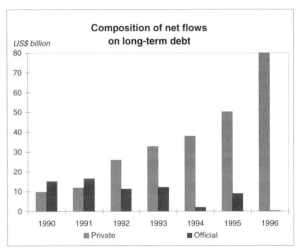

Composition of net flows on long-term debt

US$ billion

■ Private ■ Official

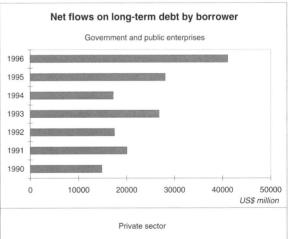

Net flows on long-term debt by borrower

Government and public enterprises

US$ million

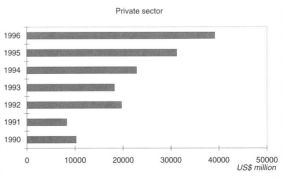

Private sector

US$ million

SPECIAL PROGRAM OF ASSISTANCE

(US$ billion, unless otherwise indicated)

	1970	1980	1990	1995	Preliminary 1996
SUMMARY DEBT DATA					
TOTAL DEBT STOCKS (EDT)	..	**34.2**	**91.4**	**108.8**	**110.3**
Long-term debt (LDOD)	**4.2**	**27.6**	**75.6**	**92.2**	**93.3**
Public and publicly guaranteed	4.0	24.5	71.5	88.6	89.4
Private nonguaranteed	0.2	3.1	4.1	3.6	3.9
Use of IMF credit	**0.1**	**2.0**	**4.5**	**5.2**	**5.3**
Short-term debt	..	**4.7**	**11.4**	**11.3**	**11.7**
of which interest arrears on LDOD	..	0.2	3.4	4.7	4.7
Memo:					
IBRD	0.2	1.7	4.9	3.2	2.7
IDA	0.2	2.0	12.8	23.9	26.2
TOTAL DEBT FLOWS					
Disbursements	**1.0**	**7.7**	**7.1**	**7.7**	**6.3**
Long-term debt	**1.0**	**6.9**	**6.5**	**4.8**	**5.7**
Public and publicly guaranteed	0.9	6.3	6.1	4.7	4.9
Private nonguaranteed	0.1	0.6	0.4	0.1	0.7
IMF purchases	**0.0**	**0.8**	**0.6**	**2.9**	**0.7**
Memo:					
IBRD	0.0	0.3	0.3	0.0	0.0
IDA	0.1	0.3	1.8	2.2	2.6
Principal repayments	**0.3**	**2.1**	**3.4**	**5.1**	**4.0**
Long-term debt	**0.2**	**1.9**	**2.7**	**2.7**	**3.5**
Public and publicly guaranteed	0.2	1.5	2.3	2.6	3.1
Private nonguaranteed	0.0	0.4	0.4	0.1	0.4
IMF repurchases	**0.0**	**0.2**	**0.7**	**2.3**	**0.5**
Memo:					
IBRD	0.0	0.1	0.4	0.6	0.5
IDA	0.0	0.0	0.0	0.1	0.2
Net flows on debt	**1.1**	**6.1**	**5.3**	**3.5**	**2.9**
of which short-term debt	..	..	1.6	0.9	0.5
Interest payments (INT)	..	**1.9**	**2.4**	**2.3**	**2.2**
Long-term debt	0.1	1.4	1.7	1.6	1.9
Net transfers on debt	..	**4.2**	**3.0**	**1.3**	**0.7**
Total debt service (TDS)	..	**4.0**	**5.8**	**7.3**	**6.1**
AGGREGATE NET RESOURCE FLOWS AND NET TRANSFERS (LONG-TERM)					
NET RESOURCE FLOWS	**0.8**	**7.5**	**12.1**	**10.1**	**11.2**
Net flow of long-term debt (ex. IMF)	0.8	5.0	3.8	2.1	2.2
Foreign direct investment (net)	-0.1	0.6	0.4	0.8	1.0
Portfolio equity flows	0.0	0.0	0.0	0.3	0.4
Grants (excluding technical coop.)	0.2	1.9	7.9	7.0	7.6
NET TRANSFERS	**0.5**	**5.4**	**9.8**	**8.2**	**8.9**
Interest on long-term debt	0.1	1.4	1.7	1.6	1.9
Profit remittances on FDI	0.3	0.7	0.5	0.4	0.4
MAJOR ECONOMIC INDICATORS					
Gross national product (GNP)	21.0	69.2	89.2	79.2	87.5
Exports of goods & services (XGS)	5.2	18.8	21.7	25.6	25.6
of which workers' remittances	0.0	0.4	0.7	0.8	0.7
Imports of goods & services (MGS)	5.7	27.3	32.9	35.0	35.5
International reserves (RES)	1.5	2.7	3.4	6.9	..
Current account balance	-0.3	-7.4	-6.9	-5.7	-6.6
DEBT INDICATORS					
EDT / XGS (%)	..	182.6	422.0	424.6	431.5
EDT / GNP (%)	..	49.5	102.6	137.4	126.0
TDS / XGS (%)	..	21.5	26.7	28.6	24.0
INT / XGS (%)	..	10.1	10.9	8.9	8.4
INT / GNP (%)	..	2.7	2.6	2.9	2.5
RES / MGS (months)	3.1	1.2	1.2	2.4	..
Short-term / EDT (%)	..	13.7	12.5	10.4	10.6
Concessional / EDT (%)	..	32.1	44.7	55.8	57.3
Multilateral / EDT (%)	..	15.9	30.0	37.0	38.6

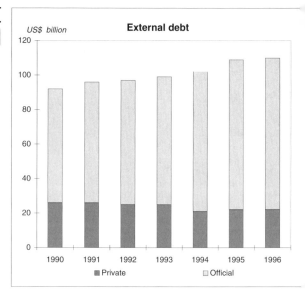

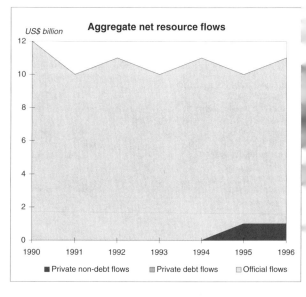

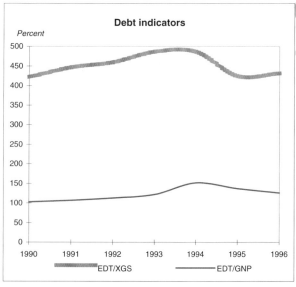

SPECIAL PROGRAM OF ASSISTANCE

(US$ billion, unless otherwise indicated)

	1970	1980	1990	1995	*Preliminary* 1996
LONG-TERM DEBT					
DEBT OUTSTANDING (LDOD)	**4.2**	**27.6**	**75.6**	**92.2**	**93.3**
Public and publicly guaranteed	**4.0**	**24.5**	**71.5**	**88.6**	**89.4**
Official creditors	2.9	15.4	61.3	81.5	82.8
Multilateral	0.5	5.4	27.4	40.2	42.6
Bilateral	2.5	10.0	33.9	41.3	40.1
Private creditors	1.1	9.0	10.2	7.1	6.6
Bonds	0.2	0.0	0.0	0.0	0.0
Private nonguaranteed	**0.2**	**3.1**	**4.1**	**3.6**	**3.9**
Bonds	..	..	0.0	0.0	0.3
DISBURSEMENTS	**1.0**	**6.9**	**6.5**	**4.8**	**5.7**
Public and publicly guaranteed	**0.9**	**6.3**	**6.1**	**4.7**	**4.9**
Official creditors	0.5	3.0	5.3	4.4	4.6
Multilateral	0.1	1.2	3.3	3.4	3.8
Bilateral	0.4	1.8	2.0	1.1	0.8
Private creditors	0.4	3.3	0.7	0.2	0.3
Bonds	0.0	0.0	0.0	0.0	0.0
Private nonguaranteed	**0.1**	**0.6**	**0.4**	**0.1**	**0.7**
Bonds	..	..	0.0	0.0	0.3
PRINCIPAL REPAYMENTS	**0.2**	**1.9**	**2.7**	**2.7**	**3.5**
Public and publicly guaranteed	**0.2**	**1.5**	**2.3**	**2.6**	**3.1**
Official creditors	0.1	0.4	1.4	2.0	2.5
Multilateral	0.0	0.1	0.9	1.3	1.3
Bilateral	0.1	0.3	0.5	0.8	1.2
Private creditors	0.1	1.1	0.9	0.6	0.6
Bonds	0.0	0.0	0.0	0.0	0.0
Private nonguaranteed	**0.0**	**0.4**	**0.4**	**0.1**	**0.4**
Bonds	..	..	0.0	0.0	0.0
NET FLOWS ON DEBT	**0.8**	**5.0**	**3.8**	**2.1**	**2.2**
Public and publicly guaranteed	**0.7**	**4.8**	**3.8**	**2.1**	**1.9**
Official creditors	0.4	2.6	3.9	2.4	2.1
Multilateral	0.1	1.1	2.4	2.1	2.5
Bilateral	0.3	1.5	1.5	0.3	-0.4
Private creditors	0.3	2.2	-0.2	-0.4	-0.2
Bonds	0.0	0.0	0.0	0.0	0.0
Private nonguaranteed	**0.0**	**0.2**	**0.0**	**0.0**	**0.3**
Bonds	..	..	0.0	0.0	0.3
CURRENCY COMPOSITION OF LONG-TERM DEBT (PERCENT)					
Deutsche mark	6.8	6.3	4.4	4.1	..
French franc	19.3	18.8	18.4	16.4	..
Japanese yen	0.0	2.4	3.2	4.7	..
Pound sterling	21.6	5.8	4.1	2.8	..
U.S. dollars	21.4	30.1	32.5	39.9	..
Multiple currency	6.0	9.3	13.4	12.0	..
All other currencies	24.8	27.3	24.1	20.2	..
DEBT STOCK-FLOW RECONCILIATION					
Total change in debt stocks	..	..	10.9	6.2	..
Net flows on debt	..	..	5.3	3.5	..
Net change in interest arrears	..	..	0.3	0.3	..
Interest capitalized	..	..	1.4	0.6	..
Debt forgiveness or reduction	..	..	-1.6	-1.4	..
Cross-currency valuation	..	..	5.0	2.4	..
Residual	..	..	0.5	0.8	..
AVERAGE TERMS OF NEW COMMITMENTS					
ALL CREDITORS					
Interest (%)	3.3	6.5	3.3	1.9	..
Maturity (years)	29.6	18.3	28.3	32.2	..
Grant element (%)	53.4	25.0	52.7	65.7	..
Official creditors					..
Interest (%)	1.8	3.7	2.7	1.3	..
Maturity (years)	38.2	26.5	30.4	35.0	..
Grant element (%)	71.4	46.6	58.5	72.2	..
Private creditors					..
Interest (%)	6.5	9.5	8.5	6.8	..
Maturity (years)	10.3	9.6	11.9	7.5	..
Grant element (%)	13.0	2.1	5.0	8.6	..
Memo:					
Commitments	1.3	8.9	7.7	4.2	..
Official creditors	0.9	4.6	6.9	3.8	..
Private creditors	0.4	4.4	0.8	0.4	..

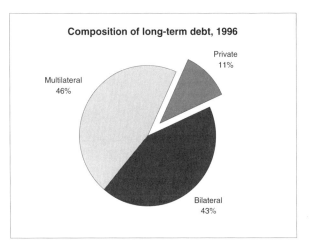

Composition of long-term debt, 1996

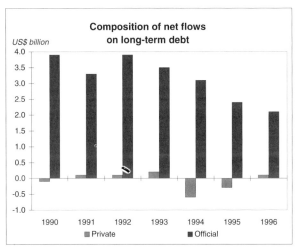

Composition of net flows on long-term debt

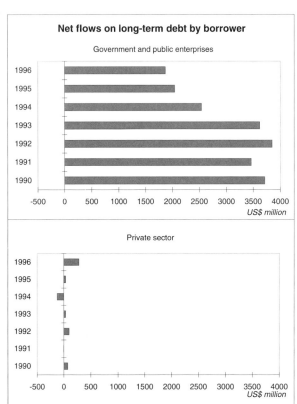

Net flows on long-term debt by borrower

The best in development statistics just got better!

World Development Indicators 1997

The World Bank introduces its most comprehensive, statistics-packed product to date—*World Development Indicators 1997*. Formerly the statistical appendix to the *World Development Report*, these comprehensive data are now available in their own volume and have been enlarged to include more than 80 tables with some 400 indicators. This major new publication provides an expanded view of the world economy for more than 130 countries—with chapters focusing on people, economy, environment, states and markets, and global links. Concise, insightful commentary tells the story of how people live and work, and how countries are expanding and changing.

April 1997 350 Pages Stock no. 13701 (ISBN 0-8213-3701-7) $60.00

new publication!

World Development Indicators on CD-ROM

This comprehensive database, which replaces *World Data*, contains most of the underlying time-series data for the *World Development Indicators* and *World Bank Atlas*. We've added powerful new features—now you can generate maps and charts, and download your results to other software programs. Requires Windows 3.1.™
April 1997   Individual Version: Stock no. 13703 (ISBN 0-8213-3703-3) $275.00
Network Version: Stock no. 13702 (ISBN 0-8213-3702-5) $550.00

more features!

World Bank Atlas 1997

One of the Bank's most popular offerings, the *Atlas* has been redesigned as a companion to the *World Development Indicators*. Tables, charts, and 21 colorful maps address the development themes of people, economy, environment, and states and markets. This easy-to-use, inexpensive book is an international standard in statistical compilations and an ideal reference for office or classroom. Text, maps, and references appear in English, French, and Spanish.

April 1997 48 Pages Stock no. 13576 (ISBN 0-8213-3 576-6) $15.00

expanded data!

World Bank Publications

In the USA, contact The World Bank, P.O. Box 7247-8619, Philadelphia, PA 19170-8619 or Phone: (703) 661-1580, Fax: (703) 661-1501. Shipping and handling: US$5.00. For airmail delivery outside the USA, US$13.00 for one item plus US$6.00 for each additional item. Payment by US$ check to the World Bank or by VISA, MasterCard, or American Express. Customers outside the USA, please contact your World Bank distributor.

Order Form

CUSTOMERS IN THE UNITED STATES

Complete this coupon and return to:

    The World Bank
    P.O. Box 7247-8619
    Philadelphia, PA 19170-8619
    USA.

Or to have your order shipped faster, charge by credit card by calling (703) 661-1580 or send this competed order coupon by facsimile to (703) 661-1501.

CUSTOMERS OUTSIDE THE UNITED STATES

Contact your local Bank publications distributor for information on prices in local currency and payment terms. If no distributor is listed for your country, use this order form and return it to the U.S. address. Orders sent to the U.S. address from countries with distributors will be returned to the customer.

Quantity	Title	Stock #	Price	Total Price
_____	_____	_____	_____	_____
_____	_____	_____	_____	_____
_____	_____	_____	_____	_____
_____	_____	_____	_____	_____

* SHIPPING AND HANDLING charges are US$5.00 per order. If a purchase order is used, actual shipping will be charged. For air mail delivery outside the USA, US$13.00 for one item plus US$6.00 for each additional item.

Subtotal cost   US$ _____

Shipping and handling*   US$ _____

Total   US$ _____

CHECK METHOD OF PAYMENT

❏ Enclosed is my check payable to the World Bank.

❏ Charge my ❏ VISA ❏ MasterCard ❏ American Express

_____
credit card account number

_____
Expiration Date   Signature (required to validate all orders)

❏ Bill me. (Institutional customers only. Purchase order must be included.)

PLEASE PRINT CLEARLY

Name_____

Address _____

_____

City _____ State _____ Postal Code _____

Country _____ Telephone _____

Distributors of World Bank Publications

Prices and credit terms vary from country to country. Consult your local distributor before placing an order.

ARGENTINA
Oficina del Libro Internacional
Av. Cordoba 1877
1120 Buenos Aires
Tel: (54 1) 815-8354
Fax: (54 1) 815-8156

AUSTRALIA, FIJI, PAPUA NEW GUINEA, SOLOMON ISLANDS, VANUATU, AND WESTERN SAMOA
D.A. Information Services
648 Whitehorse Road
Mitcham 3132
Victoria
Tel: (61) 3 9210 7777
Fax: (61) 3 9210 7788
E-mail: service@dadirect.com.au
URL: http://www.dadirect.com.au

AUSTRIA
Gerold and Co.
Weihburggasse 26
A-1011 Wien
Tel: (43 1) 512-47-31-0
Fax: (43 1) 512-47-31-29
URL: http://www.gerold.co/at.online

BANGLADESH
Micro Industries Development
Assistance Society (MIDAS)
House 5, Road 16
Dhanmondi R/Area
Dhaka 1209
Tel: (880 2) 326427
Fax: (880 2) 811188

BELGIUM
Jean De Lannoy
Av. du Roi 202
1060 Brussels
Tel: (32 2) 538-5169
Fax: (32 2) 538-0841

BRAZIL
Publicações Tecnicas Internacionais Ltda.
Rua Peixoto Gomide, 209
01409 Sao Paulo, SP.
Tel: (55 11) 259-6644
Fax: (55 11) 258-6990
E-mail: postmaster@pti.uol.br
URL: http://www.uol.br

CANADA
Renouf Publishing Co. Ltd.
5369 Canotek Road
Ottawa, Ontario K1J 9J3
Tel: (613) 745-2665
Fax: (613) 745-7660
E-mail: renouf@fox.nstn.ca
URL: http://www.fox.nstn.ca/~renouf

CHINA
China Financial & Economic
Publishing House
8, Da Fo Si Dong Jie
Beijing
Tel: (86 10) 6333-8257
Fax: (86 10) 6401-7365

COLOMBIA
Infoenlace Ltda.
Carrera 6 No. 51-21
Apartado Aereo 34270
Santafé de Bogotá, D.C.
Tel: (57 1) 285-2798
Fax: (57 1) 285-2798

CYPRUS
Center for Applied Research
Cyprus College
6, Diogenes Street, Engomi
P.O. Box 2006
Nicosia
Tel: (357 2) 44-1730
Fax: (357 2) 46-2051

CZECH REPUBLIC
National Information Center
prodejna, Konviktska 5
CS – 113 57 Prague 1
Tel: (42 2) 2422-9433
Fax: (42 2) 2422-1484
URL: http://www.nis.cz/

DENMARK
SamfundsLitteratur
Rosenoerns Allé 11
DK-1970 Frederiksberg C
Tel: (45 31) 351942
Fax: (45 31) 357822

EGYPT, ARAB REPUBLIC OF
Al Ahram Distribution Agency
Al Galaa Street
Cairo
Tel: (20 2) 578-6083
Fax: (20 2) 578-6833

The Middle East Observer
41, Sherif Street
Cairo
Tel: (20 2) 393-9732
Fax: (20 2) 393-9732

FINLAND
Akateeminen Kirjakauppa
P.O. Box 128
FIN-00101 Helsinki
Tel: (358 0) 12141
Fax: (358 0) 121-4441
URL: http://booknet.cultnet.fi/aka/

FRANCE
World Bank Publications
66, avenue d'Iéna
75116 Paris
Tel: (33 1) 40-69-30-56/57
Fax: (33 1) 40-69-30-68

GERMANY
UNO-Verlag
Poppelsdorfer Allee 55
53115 Bonn
Tel: (49 228) 212940
Fax: (49 228) 217492

GREECE
Papasotiriou S.A.
35, Stoumara Str.
106 82 Athens
Tel: (30 1) 364-1826
Fax: (30 1) 364-8254

HAITI
Culture Diffusion
5, Rue Capois
C.P. 257
Port-au-Prince
Tel: (509 1) 3 9260

HONG KONG, MACAO
Asia 2000 Ltd.
Sales & Circulation Department
Seabird House, unit 1101-02
22-28 Wyndham Street, Central
Hong Kong
Tel: (852) 2530-1409
Fax: (852) 2526-1107
E-mail: sales@asia2000.com.hk
URL: http://www.asia2000.com.hk

INDIA
Allied Publishers Ltd.
751 Mount Road
Madras - 600 002
Tel: (91 44) 852-3938
Fax: (91 44) 852-0649

INDONESIA
Pt. Indira Limited
Jalan Borobudur 20
P.O. Box 181
Jakarta 10320
Tel: (62 21) 390-4290
Fax: (62 21) 421-4289

IRAN
Ketab Sara Co. Publishers
Khaled Eslamboli Ave.,
6th Street
Kusheh Delafrooz No. 8
P.O. Box 15745-733
Tehran
Tel: (98 21) 8717819; 8716104
Fax: (98 21) 8712479
E-mail: ketab-sara@neda.net.ir

Kowkab Publishers
P.O. Box 19575-511
Tehran
Tel: (98 21) 258-3723
Fax: (98 21) 258-3723

IRELAND
Government Supplies Agency
Oifig an tSoláthair
4-5 Harcourt Road
Dublin 2
Tel: (353 1) 661-3111
Fax: (353 1) 475-2670

ISRAEL
Yozmot Literature Ltd.
P.O. Box 56055
3 Yohanan Hasandlar Street
Tel Aviv 61560
Tel: (972 3) 5285-397
Fax: (972 3) 5285-397

R.O.Y. International
PO Box 13056
Tel Aviv 61130
Tel: (972 3) 5461423
Fax: (972 3) 5461442
E-mail: royil@netvision.net.il

Palestinian Authority/Middle East
Index Information Services
P.O.B. 19502, Jerusalem
Tel: (972 2) 6271219
Fax: (972 2) 6271634

ITALY
Licosa Commissionaria Sansoni SPA
Via Duca Di Calabria, 1/1
Casella Postale 552
50125 Firenze
Tel: (55) 645-415
Fax: (55) 641-257
E-mail: licosa@ftbcc.it
Url: http://www.ftbcc.it/licosa

JAMAICA
Ian Randle Publishers Ltd.
206 Old Hope Road
Kingston 6
Tel: 809-927-2085
Fax: 809-977-0243
E-mail: irpl@colis.com

JAPAN
Eastern Book Service
3-13 Hongo 3-chome, Bunkyo-ku
Tokyo 113
Tel: (81 3) 3818-0861
Fax: (81 3) 3818-0864
E-mail: svt-ebs@ppp.bekkoame.or.jp
URL: http://www.bekkoame.or.jp/~svt-ebs

KENYA
Africa Book Service (E.A.) Ltd.
Quaran House, Mfangano Street
P.O. Box 45245
Nairobi
Tel: (254 2) 223 641
Fax: (254 2) 330 272

KOREA, REPUBLIC OF
Daejon Trading Co. Ltd.
P.O. Box 34, Youida
706 Seoun Bldg
44-6 Youido-Dong, Yeongchengo-Ku
Seoul
Tel: (82 2) 785-1631/4
Fax: (82 2) 784-0315

MALAYSIA
University of Malaya Cooperative
Bookshop, Limited
P.O. Box 1127
Jalan Pantai Baru
59700 Kuala Lumpur
Tel: (60 3) 756-5000
Fax: (60 3) 755-4424

MEXICO
INFOTEC
Av. San Fernando No. 37
Col. Toriello Guerra
14050 Mexico, D.F.
Tel: (52 5) 624-2800
Fax: (52 5) 624-2822
E-mail: infotec@rtn.net.mx
URL: http://rtn.net.mx

NEPAL
Everest Media International
Services (P) Ltd.
GPO Box 5443
Kathmandu
Tel: (977 1) 472 152
Fax: (977 1) 224 431

NETHERLANDS
De Lindeboom/InOr-Publikaties
P.O. Box 202
7480 AE Haaksbergen
Tel: (31 53) 574-0004
Fax: (31 53) 572-9296
E-mail: lindeboo@worldonline.nl
URL: http://www.worldonline.nl-lindeboo

NEW ZEALAND
EBSCO NZ Ltd.
Private Mail Bag 99914
New Market
Auckland
Tel: (64 9) 524-8119
Fax: (64 9) 524-8067

NIGERIA
University Press Limited
Three Crowns Building Jericho
Private Mail Bag 5095
Ibadan
Tel: (234 22) 41-1356
Fax: (234 22) 41-2056

NORWAY
NIC Info A/S
Book Department
P.O. Box 6125 Ette-stad
N-0602 Oslo 6
Tel: (47 22) 57-3300
Fax: (47 22) 68-1901

PAKISTAN
Mirza Book Agency
65, Shahrah-e-Quaid-e-Azam
Lahore 54000
Tel: (92 42) 735 3601
Fax: (92 42) 758 5283

Oxford University Press
5 Bangalore Town
Sharae Faisal
PO Box 13033
Karachi-75350
Tel: (92 21) 446307
Fax: (92 21) 4547640
E-mail: oup@oup.khi.erum.com.pk

Pak Book Corporation
Aziz Chambers 21
Queen's Road
Lahore
Tel: (92 42) 636 3222; 636 0885
Fax: (92 42) 636 2328
E-mail: pbc@brain.net.pk

PERU
Editorial Desarrollo SA
Apartado 3824
Lima 1
Tel: (51 14) 285360
Fax: (51 14) 286628

PHILIPPINES
International Booksource Center Inc.
1127-A Antipolo St.
Barangay, Venezuela
Makati City
Tel: (63 2) 896 6501; 6505; 6507
Fax: (63 2) 896 1741

POLAND
International Publishing Service
Ul. Piekna 31/37
00-677 Warzawa
Tel: (48 2) 628-6089
Fax: (48 2) 621-7255
E-mail: books%ips@ikp.atm.com.pl
URL: http://www.ipscg.waw.pl/ips/export/

PORTUGAL
Livraria Portugal
Apartado 2681
Rua Do Carmo 70-74
1200 Lisbon
Tel: (1) 347-4982
Fax: (1) 347-0264

ROMANIA
Compani De Librarii Bucuresti S.A.
Str. Lipscani no. 26, sector 3
Bucharest
Tel: (40 1) 613 9645
Fax: (40 1) 312 4000

RUSSIAN FEDERATION
Isdatelstvo <Ves Mir>
9a, Lolpachniy Pereulok
Moscow 101831
Tel: (7 095) 917 87 49
Fax: (7 095) 917 92 59

SINGAPORE, TAIWAN, MYANMAR, BRUNEI
Asahgale Publishing Asia Pacific Pte. Ltd.
41 Kallang Pudding Road #04-03
Golden Wheel Building
Singapore 349316
Tel: (65) 741-5166
Fax: (65) 742-9356
E-mail: ashgate@asianconnect.com

SLOVENIA
Gospodarski Vestnik Publishing Group
Dunajska cesta 5
1000 Ljubljana
Tel: (386 61) 133 83 47; 132 12 30
Fax: (386 61) 133 80 30
E-mail: belicd@gvestnik.si

SOUTH AFRICA, BOTSWANA
For single titles:
Oxford University Press
Southern Africa
P.O. Box 1141
Cape Town 8000
Tel: (27 21) 45-7266
Fax: (27 21) 45-7265

For subscription orders:
International Subscription Service
P.O. Box 41095
Craighall
Johannesburg 2024
Tel: (27 11) 880-1448
Fax: (27 11) 880-6248
E-mail: iss@is.co.za

SPAIN
Mundi-Prensa Libros, S.A.
Castello 37
28001 Madrid
Tel: (34 1) 431-3399
Fax: (34 1) 575-3998
E-mail: libreria@mundiprensa.es
URL: http://www.mundiprensa.es/

Mundi-Prensa Barcelona
Consell de Cent, 391
08009 Barcelona
Tel: (34 3) 488-3492
Fax: (34 3) 487-7659

SRI LANKA, THE MALDIVES
Lake House Bookshop
100, Sir Chittampalam Gardiner Mawatha
Colombo 2
Tel: (94 1) 32105
Fax: (94 1) 432104

SWEDEN
Wennergren-Williams AB
P.O. Box 1305
S-171 25 Solna
Tel: (46 8) 705-97-50
Fax: (46 8) 27-00-71
E-mail: mail@wwi.se

SWITZERLAND
Librairie Payot
Service Institutionnel
Côtes-de-Montbenon 30
1002 Lausanne
Tel: (41 21) 341-3229
Fax: (41 21) 341-3235

TANZANIA
Oxford University Press
Maktaba Street
PO Box 5299
Dar es Salaam
Tel: (255 51) 29209
Fax: (255 51) 46822

THAILAND
Central Books Distribution
306 Silom Road
Bangkok 10500
Tel: (66 2) 235-5400
Fax: (66 2) 237-8321

TRINIDAD & TOBAGO, AND THE CARRIBBEAN
Systematics Studies Unit
9 Watts Street
Curepa
Trinidad, West Indies
Tel: (809) 662-5654
Fax: (809) 662-5654
E-mail: tobe@trinidad.net

UGANDA
Gustro Ltd.
PO Box 9997
Madhvani Building
Plot 16/4 Jinja Rd.
Kampala
Tel: (256 41) 254 763
Fax: (256 41) 251 468

UNITED KINGDOM
Microinfo Ltd.
P.O. Box 3
Alton, Hampshire GU34 2PG
England
Tel: (44 1420) 86848
Fax: (44 1420) 89889
E-mail: wbank@ukminfo.demon.co.uk
URL: http://www.microinfo.co.uk

VENEZUELA
Tecni-Ciencia Libros, S.A.
Centro Cuidad Comercial Tamanco
Nivel C2
Caracas
Tel: (58 2) 959 5547; 5035; 0016
Fax: (58 2) 959 5636

ZAMBIA
University Bookshop
University of Zambia
Great East Road Campus
P.O. Box 32379
Lusaka
Tel: (260 1) 252 576
Fax: (260 1) 253 952

ZIMBABWE
Longman Zimbabwe (Pte.)Ltd.
Tourle Road, Ardbennie
P.O. Box ST125
Southerton
Harare
Tel: (263 4) 6216617
Fax: (263 4) 621670

ADECO Van Diermen Editions Techniques
Ch. de Lacuez 41
CH1807 Blonay
Tel: (41 21) 943 2673
Fax: (41 21) 943 3605